# A SPIRIT CHRISTOLOGY
*Recovering the Biblical Paradigm of Christian Faith*

Paul W. Newman

UNIVERSITY
PRESS OF
AMERICA

Lanham • New York • London

Copyright © 1987 by

University Press of America,® Inc.

4720 Boston Way
Lanham, MD 20706

3 Henrietta Street
London WC2E 8LU England

All rights reserved

Printed in the United States of America

British Cataloging in Publication Information Available

**Library of Congress Cataloging-in-Publication Data**

Newman, Paul W., 1934-
  A Spirit Christology.

  Bibliography: p.
  Includes indexes.
  1. Jesus Christ—Person and offices.  I. Title.
BT202.N48  1987      232       87-10390
ISBN 0-8191-6375-9 (alk. paper)
ISBN 0-8191-6376-7 (pbk. : alk. paper)

All University Press of America books are produced on acid-free
paper which exceeds the minimum standards set by the National
Historical Publication and Records Commission.

To

*Gordon and Nellie Newman and Hugh and Lucy Thompson, parents by nature and by law, who lived in the Spirit and sought first the Reigning of God.*

# Acknowledgements

Permission from the publishers to quote portions of the following publications is hereby gratefully acknowledged.

Boff, Leonardo. *Jesus Christ Liberator*. Maryknoll, NY: Orbis Books, 1978.
Driver, Tom F. *Christ in a Changing World*. New York: Crossroad, 1981.
Dunn, James D.G. *Jesus And The Spirit*. London: SCM Press, and Philadelphia: The Westminster Press, 1975.
Goulder, Michael. (ed) *Incarnation and Myth*. London: SCM Press, and Grand Rapids, MI: Wm Eerdmans Publishing Co., 1979.
Frye, Northrop. *The Great Code*. New York: Harcourt Brace Jovanovich, 1981.
Hick, John. (ed) *The Myth Of God Incarnate*. London: SCM Press, and Philadelphia: The Westminster Press, 1977.
Kasper, Walter. *Jesus the Christ*. Tunbridge Wells, England: Search Press, 1976.
Lampe, G.W.H. *God As Spirit*. Oxford: Oxford University Press, 1977.
McFague, Sallie, *Metaphorical Theology*. Philadelphia: Fortress Press, 1982.
Moltmann, Jurgen. *The Trinity and the Kingdom of God*. London: SCM Press, and New York: Harper and Row, 1981.
Rahner, Karl and Thüsing, Wilhelm. *A New Christology*. New York: Crossroad, 1980.
Robinson, H. Wheeler. *The Christian Experience of the Holy Spirit* London: Fontana, 1962.
Robinson, J.A.T. *The Human Face of God*. London: SCM Press, and Philadelphia: The Westminster Press, 1973.
Rosato, Philip J. *The Spirit As Lord*. Edinburgh: T & T Clark Ltd., 1981.
Schillebeeckx, Edward. *Jesus*. New York: Crossroad, 1979.
Schoonenberg, Piet. *The Christ*. New York: Crossroad, 1971.
Sobrino, Jon. *Christology At The Crossroads*. Maryknoll, NY: Orbis Books, 1978.
Taylor, John V. *The Go-Between God*. New York: Oxford University Press, 1972.
Tillich, Paul. *Systematic Theology*. (3 Vol.). Chicago: University of Chicago Press, 1963.
Tracy, David. *The Analogical Imagination*. New York: Crossroad, 1981.

# Table of Contents

Introduction .............................................. xi

**Chapter I**
AN IDEA WHOSE TIME HAS COME ..................... 1
The traditional christological-trinitarian paradigm faces a mounting crisis. The knowledge explosion and the pluralistic world have changed some basic understandings which conflict with the implications of the existing Christian paradigm. The points of crisis can be classed as biblical, theological and cultural. Spirit christology can be seen to provide a promising alternative. The promise can also be seen in terms of its biblical, theological and cultural aspects.

**Chapter II**
METHOD IN CHRISTOLOGY ............................ 35
The method proposed for this Spirit christology corresponds approximately to the four elements that David Tracy discerned in the interpretation of any classic text: analysis of relevant preunderstanding; the realized experience which occurs through recollection or retrieval of Jesus in the classic text; development of a reflective model as an appropriate response to the experience of Jesus as the Christ; and extension of the model in ecclesiology and social ethics.

**Chapter III**
TOWARDS A BIBLICAL AND CONTEMPORARY
THEOLOGY OF SPIRIT ................................. 69
Christological preunderstanding includes:
(1) a biblical and contemporary understanding of Spirit which focuses on seven basic terms: energy, information, imagination, discernment, attitude-virtues, vocation and ethos.
(2) a cosmology in which systems and field theory are related to the biblical view of principalities and powers. This provides the categories for understanding both created pluralism and the demonic against which the saving initiatives of God in Christ are directed.
(3) a brief comparison of four types of monotheism à la Tillich.

**Chapter IV**

THE SPIRIT IN JESUS' LIFE, DEATH AND
RESURRECTION ........................................... 103

The recollection of Jesus is structured according to the basic terms in the theology of Spirit as developed in Chapter Three.

**Chapter V**

THE LOGIC OF SALVATION ............................... 139

Soteriology brings together the preunderstanding of systemic evil and the recollection of Jesus' gospel of the Reigning of God as Spirit. The way of God's Reigning, the way of life in the Spirit, is seen to be the way of the cross which is an active, subversive, non-violent strategy of realizing the Reigning of God in trust and love. Jesus is seen as catalytic agent of processive salvation rather than causative agent of universal "transactional" salvation.

**Chapter VI**

SPIRIT CHRISTOLOGY: AN INTERPERSONAL MODEL .... 171

The reflective construction compares and contrasts two possible models: the traditional "intrapersonal" model and "interpersonal" Spirit christology. The resultant christology affirms a relational unity between the man Jesus and God the Spirit, similar to the most common New Testament christologies and much ante-Nicene christology. Theocentricity, similar to the New Testament, is stressed. Exclusive monotheism, again similar to biblical theology, is proposed in place of the christocentric-trinitarian paradigm. Christ is considered to be an historical figure not a cosmic mythological figure, and his finality is seen to be proleptic rather than absolute.

**Chapter VII**

WHAT IS NEW AND WHAT IS OLD ....................... 211

The historical precedents for "relational" or "functional" christology, as opposed to "ontological" christology, are briefly considered. The Arian-Alexandrian controversy is revisited in light of recent scholarship. The main proposals of the book are summed up.

Works Consulted ............................................ 223

Index of Scripture Passages .................................. 233

Index of Authors ............................................ 236

Index of Subjects ............................................ 238

## *Preface*

I am much indebted to those who have read the manuscript and given criticisms and encouragement. Dr. Rosemary Radford Ruether is foremost among these. I am very grateful for her frank comments and helpful suggestions. My brother, Robert Newman, has also read the manuscript and given a much appreciated response. Students in my classes in christology in Saskatoon over the past twelve years have helped to bring this Spirit christology to birth. To them I wish to express special appreciation.

St. Andrew's College in Saskatoon granted me a sabbatical leave to do the work, and Garrett-Evangelical Theological Seminary in Evanston, Illinois, graciously appointed me Scholar-in-residence for the year. The United Church of Canada provided a "continuing education" grant. Without these institutional supports the book could not have been written.

Moral support in the time of writing came from family and friends. My wife, Edith, gave immeasurable support and assistance in typing the manuscript and by being willing to discuss the contents at all hours of the day and night. This has been a joint effort. The process of working together has given much enjoyment, as well as benefit.

*The Sign of God is that we will be led where we did not plan to go.*

# Introduction

Piet Schoonenberg (1971) asked the question that virtually every Christian theologian is asking in our time:

> What does a real, creative loyalty to our faith in Jesus as the Christ demand? How can this faith be professed today without foreshortening and distortion, but also without holding onto patterns of thought which no longer express what was formerly intended? (p.50).

Many theologians have offered reformulations of the faith but most are determined, at the same time, to hold onto the traditional patterns of thought. Specifically, the deity of Jesus and the trinitarian nature of God which follows from Jesus' deity have continued to be affirmed despite the almost universal consensus that Jesus was a human being in every sense of the word.

In our time, loyalty to Jesus requires the recognition that he was fully human. It also requires that a growing amount of information about the Bible and the ancient world not be suppressed or ignored, even though it is not easily reconciled with some of the claims of the Christian tradition.

Again and again the intention is stated: "Today we must try to do something like what the early Church councils did for their time" (Kasper, 1976, p.181). It is becoming increasingly clear that this cannot be done without giving up some of the patterns of thought from the church councils. Reasons why some of the traditional patterns of thought need to be given up are emerging with increasing urgency. Not least in importance is a growing awareness of the cultural and theological distance between the faith to be found by scholarly study of the scriptures and the faith formulated by the councils of the church.

The traditional christocentric-trinitarian paradigm in Christianity faces a mounting crisis. The explosion of knowledge in the twentieth century includes an explosion in biblical and historical knowledge, and some of this new knowledge is not consistent with the theological interpretations of Jesus held to be orthodox since the ecumenical councils in the fourth, fifth and sixth centuries.

For example, the traditional interpretations of the protological passages in the New Testament, those suggesting pre-existence of the Christ before the time of Jesus, are now seen to be mistaken. According to a growing number of New Testament scholars it is not accurate to interpret the so-called cosmic Christ passages in John I, Colossians I, and Hebrews I as intending to mean the pre-existence of the person of Christ prior to the time of Jesus. If this re-interpretation of the New Testament is correct the biblical basis for the idea of a cosmic Christ is drastically reduced.

Another significant discovery is the consistently theocentric perspective in the New Testament. Even the risen Jesus is thoroughly theocentric. This raises the question as to whether or not the thoroughly christocentric perspective of traditional Christianity is unbiblical. The decision of the Councils that there is no subordination between the Christ and God is clearly not well founded in scripture. Is the principle of "no subordination" then tenable? Should Christianity recover the biblical perspective and be theocentric as Jesus and the New Testament authors were?

Of course, the traditional doctrine of the Trinity would be affected if subordination of Jesus to God were acknowledged. Biblical scholarship is discovering that the doctrine of the Trinity is not well founded in scripture. The Hebrew scriptures suggest a wide range of distinctions in God, including the female Sophia, and provide no valid reason for positing a triune God, while the New Testament is, if anything, more binitarian than trinitarian and can be most accurately understood as maintaining the same view of God that is found in the Hebrew scriptures.

The deity of Jesus which has been claimed as absolutely essential to Christian faith since the fourth century is also not well founded in the New Testament. There are only a very few passages that even suggest that Jesus was God, and exegetes are now saying that it is not accurate to interpret them this way.

At the same time, the christological debates in the early centuries of Christian history are being reassessed and some of the "heretics" or losers in the debates are being seen in a different light. Arius, for example, who lost the crucial debate with Athanasius and the Alexandrians, is now seen to be much better aligned with scripture and with the prevailing faith of the church of his times than has usually been granted. Athanasius is now seen to be a defender of an understanding of salvation consistent more with Hellenistic thinking than biblical thinking. His insistence on "irreversible grace" seems less true to the Bible than Arius' view of salvation occurring in an advancing covenantal process of struggle.

The soteriological factors in the decisions of the Councils are being reassessed and there is a growing awareness that the Latin doctrine of substitutionary atonement which was decisive in the christological debates is not well founded in scripture. The way in which Christianity has traditionally understood the biblical passages about Jesus' death as a sacrifice is now being questioned. Scholars are acknowledging that in the Hellenistic milieu of developing Christianity the biblical understanding of sacrifice for the forgiveness of sins was lost and distorted. If the biblical understanding is recovered it will have immense implications for the interpretation of Jesus' saving significance and for the explanation of his person. The traditional logic that Jesus had to be fully divine in order to make the adequate sacrifice for the sins of the world is no longer compelling because the biblical view of atonement does not entail a logic of retributive justice or *lex talionis*.

Not only the soteriological but also the political factors in the decisions of the Councils are being re-examined. The interpretation of Jesus and his salvation that the Councils chose to affirm proved to be of great material benefit to the clergy and to the church as a powerful institution. The clergy and the church in effect "cornered the market" of salvation and were assured immense power and wealth by becoming the only authorized dispensers of the saving grace of Christ's sacrifice. If Jesus' death were no longer thought to be the source of transferable merit which the church alone dispenses the absolutely essential role of the clergy in dispensing this grace would be reduced. The power and status which clergy and church enjoyed because of the traditional logic of salvation is now seen to be one of the main bulwarks of patriarchal male privilege in the church.

There are cultural as well as theological and biblical reasons for reconsidering the prevailing christocentric-trinitarian paradigm in Christian faith. The cultural and historical relativity of all human knowledge is now incontestable, and the pluralistic nature of the world is an inescapable fact. In a "global village" gross ethnocentrism becomes transparently offensive and destructive. The traditional Christian pretensions of having absolute doctrine and an exclusive access to God are suspect, especially when they cannot be grounded solidly in our own scriptures. Delusions of grandeur, if that is what Christian exclusiveness was, can be seen to be no harmless mistake but the basis for a long and tragic record of anti-Semitism and imperialistic policies towards people of other religious traditions.

The love of God and love of neighbour that Jesus advocated call in our time for a revision of the basic paradigm or framework of thought in Christian theology.

The explosion of knowledge fortunately provides some direction for discovering a more authentic and appropriate paradigm on which to establish Christian faith and practice. The New Testament pictures of Jesus show a human being whose singularity is a result of his particular relationship with God, rather than his being a deity himself. A relational christology is thoroughly biblical whereas a christology of ontological unity with God is not. Relational christology was also the "mainline" thinking of early Christianity before the time of the ecumenical Councils. If contemporary Christian theology develops relational christology it will move closer to both its biblical and historical origins.

Relational christology changes the traditional paradigm of Christianity in very significant ways. Jesus can be acknowledged to be a human being whose relationship with God is not different in kind from the relationship with God that other people can have. His uniqueness, like that of others, consists of his God-given vocation. His particular vocation as the Messiah is not shared by others, but the substance of the Messiah's work and message concerning the Reigning of God is not restricted to Jesus and is shared by any human beings who participate in the life of the Spirit of God who reigns throughout the entire creation.

Because the Bible speaks so much about God present in creation as Spirit it is appropriate to describe the relation of Jesus and God in terms of an interpersonal Spirit christology. In fact, there is significant consensus among New Testament scholars that the most basic New Testament understanding of Jesus was as a man full of the Holy Spirit.

Jesus, so understood, becomes the pioneer of the way of salvation that the Synoptic gospels called the Kingdom of God, the Gospel of John called eternal life, and St. Paul called the life of the Spirit. Jesus can be seen to be the "eschatological prophet" who reveals the ultimate character of God's saving processes. God's Spirit, God's "reigning" or saving presence, is not restricted to the Christian church, and Christian clergy do not have any exclusive role in dispensing the grace of salvation. Jesus is held up to view as the historical, rather than cosmic Christ, and his way of salvation is followed in the belief and hope that it will accomplish peace with justice in the world. The question of Jesus' finality has to remain open even as Christians affirm it proleptically and provisionally.

When Jesus' identity is interpreted in terms of the presence of God's Spirit in him, the theology of God's Spirit becomes a major component in christology. Such a theology of Spirit can and should appropriately be grounded in the scriptures where there is much material to shape and test it. Any such theology has also to be contemporary and contextual if it is to be resonant with the thinking of contemporary people. Thus a *biblical and contemporary* theology of Spirit has to be developed in order to provide terms and concepts for expounding the logic of Jesus as the Christ. This is a major undertaking which I have had to present here in outline rather than completely.

Since a biblical and contemporary theology of Spirit can derive much of its substance from the accounts of God's Spirit active in Jesus himself, it is not the case that Spirit christology imposes an arbitrary and foreign system of thought onto the interpretation of Jesus' person and work.

The development of a new paradigm in Christian thought is a many-faceted undertaking. Like the cutting of a diamond there are numerous sides of the matter to be worked on before the main shape of the proposal becomes apparent. In the several chapters that follow I attempt to work through one aspect after another. Chapters IV, V and VI contain the main substance of the christology. It is in these chapters that the new paradigm is explored.

The development of a christology is larger than one book can possibly accomplish because christology consists partly in its extension in ecclesiology and social ethics. Such extension of this Spirit christology largely awaits further treatment. Furthermore, New Testament studies are in such a state of dynamic ferment at the present time that it is impossible to give anything like a complete account of the state of knowledge in this closely related area. In addition to these unavoidable limitations, experts in the several fields of study related to christology will no doubt see places where the questions under discussion could benefit from much more extensive treatment.

To be a listener and learner in the recent scholarly discussions of christological issues has been a constant pleasure for me in the writing of this book. I have referred to many of the participants in the text. The footnotes are mainly intended to share more of the discussion with the interested reader.

Theological writing in recent years is gradually reducing use of obviously sexist language. I have sometimes furthered this objective in quoted material by replacing gender specific terms with generic terms enclosed in square brackets. I hope that this practice will meet with the approval of many of the authors who, like myself, have only relatively recently been awakened to the offense caused by unnecessarily sexist language.

The point of changing the expressions and formulations of faith in our time is not to change for the sake of change. It is to be loyal to the revelation of God in Jesus Christ. It is to try, in our profession of faith, to love God with all our mind and to love our neighbours as ourselves.

## Chapter One
# AN IDEA WHOSE TIME HAS COME

The time has come for a paradigm shift in Christian theology. Evidence of the need for some basic changes in our tradition has been growing along with the knowledge explosion that characterizes the twentieth century.[1] The explosion of knowledge has ignited the imaginations and curiosity of Christian scholars to look with fresh eyes at every aspect of Christian tradition and thought. The result is that countless new insights have emerged, some with profound implications for the very framework in which Christian faith is understood. While there has been a lot of joy in the creative liberty of discovering new aspects of our tradition there has also been tension in realizing the unresolved conflicts between the new discoveries and what the church has held for many centuries to be orthodox theology.

Nowhere has the tension between creative liberty and orthodox tradition been more poignant than in christological studies. A multitude of books in recent decades have proposed new ways of understanding Jesus and his saving significance for humanity. Besides the systematic christologies, even more books have been written about the biblical and other ancient materials that relate to christological studies. Out of all this scholarly ferment have come many new ideas and much new knowledge that begs to be related to the church's traditional confessions of faith in Jesus Christ. Roman Catholic scholars in particular try very hard to show that their new ideas about Christ or new understandings of the Bible are not basically at variance with the confessed traditions of the church. Their success has been challenged by the Vatican in some well known cases such as Hans Küng, Edward Schillebeeckx or the liberation theologians of Latin America, Leonardo Boff and Jon Sobrino. The official challenges illustrate the increasing tensions surrounding the traditional paradigm of Christian theology that are felt around the whole world.

Most Protestant scholars are equally hesitant about departing from tradition and try to show that even if their new ideas are not directly compatible with tradition their intention is to try to accomplish in the contemporary cultural setting the same purposes that the ancient writers had in expressing the Christian faith in their respective cultural contexts.[2]

---

[1] Tillich (1963) spoke of his apolegetic theology being an attempt "to speak understandably" about the Christian symbols "which have become increasingly problematic within the cultural context of our time"(p.4).

[2] Cf., for example, Cobb (1975): "Clearly, in the present view Jesus is not 'consubstantial' with the Father, for the notion of any two entities being of the 'same substance' is rejected. However, the doctrine chiefly intended at this point, where Nicaea is echoed, is fully affirmed" (p.170).

John A.T. Robinson described his theological efforts as aiming at consonance with tradition and resonance with the contemporary understanding of reality (1973, p.18). As the furor over *Honest to God* illustrated, however, it is certainly not easy to speak about God or Christ in ways that "vibrate" in harmony with modern understanding of reality and at the same time make "sounds" that are similar to the voice of tradition. Since *Honest to God* in 1963 the furor about theologies perceived not to be consonant with tradition has continued unabated through the "Death of God" theology, secular theology, feminist and liberation theologies as well as *The Myth of God Incarnate* debate in Britain and other books that pose radical questions for the ways Christian faith has been understood.[3] The roots of the matter for Christianity are primarily what is confessed about Jesus as the Christ, but there are other radically important questions such as: how do we understand the authority of the Bible *vis a vis* modern knowledge and in the light of literary criticism?; do people of other religious traditions have any contribution to make towards enriching Christians' understanding of God?; and in what ways should the Christian religion adjust to the claims of women, racial groups, economically and politically oppressed people and others who feel that the Christian tradition has created and reinforced prejudice against them?

The need for a paradigm shift in Christian theology has to do with what has emerged in modern biblical studies, especially the studies of the New Testament, but including also the studies of the Hebrew scriptures and apocryphal ancient writings. It has to do with new understanding of the structures and functions of language and, especially, the structures of the stories and parables, allegories, symbols, myths, models, metaphors, legends and concepts in which christological faith has traditionally been expressed. A paradigm shift is needed because of the increasing understanding of pluralism and the awareness of historical relativity that have dawned on the world since orthodox Christian faith was formulated. It has to do with an immense amount of new knowledge about the conflicting systems and ideologies in the world that shapes any adequate view of the evil from which God in Christ may conceivably save the world. Soteriology, the logic of salvation, was a determining factor in the early confessions of faith in Jesus as the Christ. Our contemporary understanding of what is wrong with the world similarly presses to influence what we would wish to confess about God and Christ now.[4]

---

[3] Hick and the other authors of *The Myth of God Incarnate* (1977) have called for a change in christology for some of the same reasons which have led to the writing of this book on Spirit christology. Hick writes: "The writers of this book are convinced that another major theological development is called for in this last part of the twentieth century. The need arises from growing knowledge of Christian origins, and involves a recognition that Jesus was (as he is presented in Acts 2:21) 'a man approved by God' for a special role within the divine purpose, and that the later conception of him as God incarnate, the Second Person of The Holy Trinity living a human life, is a mythological or poetic way of expressing his significance for us. This recognition is called for in the interests of truth; but it also has increasingly important practical implications for our relationship to peoples of the other great world religions" (p.ix).

[4] Pannenberg observes that "almost all Christological conceptions have had soteriological motifs. Changes in the soteriological interest, in man's understanding of salvation, explain, at least in part, the different forms Christology has taken at different times" (1968, p.39). Cf. also Tillich (1957): "Christology is a function of soteriology. The problem of soteriology creates the christological question and gives direction to the christological answer" (p.150).

The traditional paradigm of Christian theology is under pressure from many quarters.

The points of unresolved tension have been getting more and more visible. Scholars are challenging the traditional paradigm in one aspect or another and are having increasing difficulty in reconciling what they feel duty bound to confess on the basis of the best available knowledge with what the church in the past felt duty bound to confess on the basis of its best available knowledge. The anomalies between what is known today and what the church traditionally believed have increased to the point where the possibility of a paradigm shift can no longer be repressed.

In this introductory chapter I will first specify what I mean by a paradigm shift, look briefly at the traditional paradigm of the Christian faith and how it emerged itself as a shift from an earlier paradigm, and then look in more detail at some of the reasons already mentioned why a paradigm shift is needed again. The thesis of this book is that a Spirit christology, developed out of a biblical and contemporary theology of Spirit, can provide a shift in paradigm that will resolve many of the anomalies and tensions arising from the encounter of modern knowledge with what is both presupposed and explicitly acknowledged in the traditional paradigm of Christian theology. In the last part of this chapter I will point briefly to what a new paradigm might look like with the model of Spirit christology replacing the model of hypostatic union of the divine and human in Jesus.

*Definition of Paradigm*

What is a paradigm as the term is used here? The term has been used in a variety of ways by contemporary authors and as yet there does not appear to be a firm consensus on how the term should be used. The dictionary defines paradigm simply as "example, pattern" (*Concise Oxford Dictionary*) but there has been much elaboration on the meaning of the word as it might apply in academic disciplines.

Thomas Kuhn, in his much discussed book *The Structure of Scientific Revolutions* and in subsequent refinements of his thought, proposed that paradigm means the broadest conceptual and methodological framework in which science functions in any particular historical period. A paradigm is "the disciplinary matrix" of a scientific community which includes the accepted theories, laws, traditions and "rules of the game," so to speak, as well as the metaphysical assumptions and the common values and group commitments that make scientists into a community of common interest and endeavour. A paradigm in this sense is a complex, many-faceted reality in which certain elements tend to determine the identity of the paradigm more than other elements.

There is room for difference and on-going debate about the less central features of the paradigm, but on the whole the scientific community has a consensus about the basic and indisputable factors in their *modus operandi*. From time to time new theories will emerge which challenge the basic and indisputable elements of the current paradigm causing a crisis in the community. Eventually, if the new theories are strong enough a "revolution" will occur out of which emerges a new paradigm for the scientific community. The new paradigm will be a new framework of thought in which scientists carry on their work. There will be new concepts and new terminology, new theories, new assumptions, new values, and new data as well as the continuation of some of the old concepts, terms, theories, assumptions, values and data that were not made totally obsolete by the new ways of thinking.

Paradigms in Kuhn's sense are represented typically by standard examples — hence the term paradigm. Examples entail and represent the elements that make up the basic paradigm or pattern of any scientific era. For example, $E = MC^2$ is one of the standard examples in the paradigm currently in effect among scientists. In the history of western science the paradigms of science have shifted from Aristotelian science to Newtonian science to Einsteinian science. All the paradigms belong to the scientific tradition. In the ongoing tradition and community of human scientists the significance of the changing paradigms can hardly be overestimated.

Ian G. Barbour, a physicist who is also a professor of Religious Studies, has written several books comparing scientific method and theological method. In *Myths, Models and Paradigms* (1974) he reviews the history of Thomas Kuhn's use of the term paradigm and proposes a definition of his own which he believes is more adequate, especially for use in theological studies. Barbour defines paradigm as *"a tradition transmitted through historical exemplars."* (p.9) He appears to agree with most of Kuhn's concept of paradigm but wishes to stress the sociological and historical aspects of paradigm rather than the conceptual and methodological. Barbour regards each religion as a paradigm, a tradition transmitted through historical exemplars.

Barbour does not appear to allow for the possibility of paradigm shifts occurring within a religious tradition, although he recognized that a tradition can include much diversity and novelty as successive generations interpret the main exemplars of the tradition in new contexts. The diversity and novelty, however, are limited to changing metaphors and models. In Barbour's view, to change a paradigm would be to leave the particular religion and either join another religion or start a new religion with its own distinctive paradigm. "There can be complementary models within a paradigm, but paradigms are evidently not complementary: a person can fully share the outlook of only one tradition at a time." ( p.147.) True, but can a tradition not have more than one paradigm in the course of time? Is it not a confusion of categories to identify paradigm with tradition?

It seems to me that Kuhn's definition of paradigm as "disciplinary matrix" is more adequate than Barbour's identification of paradigm with religious tradition in itself. Barbour rightly identifies tradition with the ongoing religious community but apparently fails to see that a religious community can survive paradigm shifts as well as changing models and metaphors. A religious community can have different paradigms within its tradition similar to what has happened in the scientific tradition. The fact is that Christianity experienced a paradigm shift in its early tradition.

## *The Original Shift in the Christian Paradigm*

The shift in paradigm in the early centuries of Christian tradition was a shift from theocentricity to christocentricity. Jesus was very theocentric in his life and teachings. He proclaimed the Kingdom of God as a possibility for human existence. In his life and death he was radically trusting of God and invited his disciples to adopt a similar way of living. They understood his specialness at first in terms of the presence of the Spirit of God in him. As we shall show later, he may well have understood his own distinctive identity and vocation in the same terms. In any case, the earliest Christian disciples were theocentric because they understood who Jesus was in terms of what God had done in Jesus and what God might yet do through Jesus returning to inaugurate the Kingdom.

> Except for the prologue of John's Gospel and the beginning of his first Letter, the prevailing New Testament paradigm of Jesus' being is the Spirit-bearer; Jesus is the Christ, the one annointed fully with the Holy Spirit; for this reason He is Messiah and Lord... . With time, however, this paradigm gave way to that of the incarnate Word ( Rosato 1981, p.173).

When Jesus did not return and the world continued on its way, the church changed its basic paradigm from one which was very much theocentric and future oriented to one in which Christ's already having come was the determining factor. Christ became the centre of the Christian religion. The Kingdom of God which he lived and taught so much about devolved to the periphery of concern and attention. Christ became the centre and source not only of the church but of creation, the centre of history and, after Constantine, the centre of society.[5] This christocentric commitment led to the development of trinitarian theology which is perhaps the most adequate term to describe the orthodox Christian paradigm that has continued dominant up to the present time.

It is the christocentric-trinitarian paradigm that is in crisis at the present time. The reasons for the crisis may be gathered into three categories: biblical, theological and cultural. I will look briefly at each group now before going on to introduce the possibilities of a new paradigm that might address the anomalies in the christocentric-trinitarian paradigm. The issues introduced at this time will be taken up in more detail later on in the book as Spirit christology is developed and compared to classical christology.

## *Biblical Reasons for a Paradigm Shift*

Modern biblical studies have revealed a very great deal about the entire Bible and its cultural and historical contexts. This knowledge cannot in good conscience be ignored if it conflicts with some of the traditional rationale for the Christian paradigm.

*a) Heilsgeschichte Questioned*

First, there has been a challenge to the traditional belief in

---
[5] See Driver (1981, pp.48-52).

*heilsgeschichte.* The main idea in *heilsgeschichte* or "salvation history" is that Jesus Christ is the centre of human history and the culmination of a process of progressive revelation in which the Hebrew scriptures are merely a preliminary stage. This idea served to justify the traditional Christian practice of reading Christ back into the Hebrew scriptures as if they were written with a supernatural ability to predict meanings and events related to Jesus of Nazareth. Studies of the Hebrew scriptures show beyond any doubt an authenticity and meaning for the Hebrew scriptures independent from later Christian meanings or interpretations. The traditional Christian way of regarding the Hebrew scriptures as the "Old" Testament which is authenticated and completed by the Christian scriptures is difficult to justify. In a recent study of the role of *heilsgeschichte* in Christian religious education Mary C. Boys observes that:

> Recent developments in biblical studies, particularly in the area of intertestamental studies and in exegetical practice, have manifested the inadequacy of the assumption that the OT is "fulfilled" in the NT. Such a view, in the opinion of numerous contemporary scholars, devalues the OT, denigrates Judaism, and reflects the dogmatic bias of Christianity (1980, p. 249).

Equally certain is that Jesus and most of the writers of the New Testament were Jews, deeply oriented in the Hebrew scriptures. The extent to which they were influenced by their scriptures is becoming increasingly well known with the result that what they said and did and wrote in the New Testament is understood more in the light of their Jewish background and less in light of the future theological dogmas of orthodox Christian tradition. One of the key issues is monotheism and theocentricity.

*b) Theocentricity of the Scriptures*

Wilhelm Thüsing, a Roman Catholic biblical scholar, asks the questions, "Can New Testament faith in Christ be reconciled with Old Testament monotheism? ... Does New Testament Christocentricity lead to a complication and therefore also to a weakening and a reduction of the Old Testament faith in Yahweh, the one God?" (1980, p. 86-87). His answer is that the New Testament authors were consistently and thoroughly monotheistic and theocentric, as was Jesus himself. He further shows that "this theocentricity of Jesus is maintained in a whole series of important New Testament writings referring to the risen and exalted Lord." (p.75.) Thüsing claims that this new biblical understanding of the theocentric risen Christ is *"the most important contribution that the New Testament can make to this attempt to find new approaches to an orthodox Christology"* (p.75). Don Cupitt, after describing at length the theocentric character of Jesus in whom "God is all in all" concludes:

> To say all this is to propose a context of Jewish piety and religious values within which both Jesus and the early Christians' response to Jesus can be interpreted. It is, I believe, the only historically plausible way of understanding Jesus and the rise of Christianity. But what does it leave us saying about

the vexed question of the divinity of Jesus (Cupitt in Goulder (ed.) 1979, p.40)?

The theocentricity of the New Testament and of Jesus is not easily reconciled with the views of Jesus that were developed in classical christology. This is, in fact, one of the most acute crises confronting the traditional Christian paradigm.

*c) Incarnation Christology Is Unbiblical*

Scholars from the whole spectrum of the Christian community ranging from conservative Protestant to conservative Roman Catholic have had to acknowledge that the christology of Incarnation, as defined in the Council of Chalcedon, is not well founded in the New Testament. Walter Kasper, a Roman Catholic theologian of impeccable credentials who is determined to reconcile any new attempts in christology with the classical formulations, has to admit that: "It would be historically mistaken ... to seek the fully-developed two-natures doctrine in the Johannine writings. John is not yet concerned with two natures in a single subject" (1976, p.233). Frances Young makes a broader claim:

> We are bound to admit (i) that the New Testament ... does not provide directly revealed information about [Jesus'] divinity; and (ii) the notion of God being incarnate in the traditionally accepted sense is read into, not out of, the Pauline epistles, and I suggest that ... the same could be argued for the other New Testament documents (Young in Hick (ed.) 1977, p.22).

Anyone familiar with Frances Young's work will know that she is not reckless in making such a claim.

James D. G. Dunn, a very cautious and able Protestant New Testament scholar, in *Christology In The Making* (1980) looks through the whole New Testament for the origins of the doctrine of the Incarnation. The crux of the matter is whether or not the New Testament contains the idea of a personal divine being who was pre-existent to Jesus, who in the Incarnation is identified as Jesus and who is subsequently post-existent as the risen Christ. After looking exhaustively at the evidence he concludes that "Here [in John 1:14] we have an explicit statement of incarnation, the first, and indeed only such statement in the NT" (p.241). In fact, he concludes that "It is only in v. 14 (fourth stanza) that we go beyond anything pre-Christian" (p.242) and "it is only with v. 14 that we can begin to speak of the personal Logos" (p.243). Dunn appears willing to accept the "revolutionary significance" (p.243) of verse 14 in the prologue to John's gospel as justification for the traditional paradigm of classical christology but the question occurs with mounting force: if this is the scriptural basis for the christology of Incarnation, is it not possible that the New Testament could and should be found to provide the basis for other christological models and even other basic paradigms for the Christian tradition?

Schillebeeckx voices a similar concern:

> From the Council of Nicaea onwards one particular Christological model — the Johannine — has been developed as a norm within very narrow limits and one direction; and

in fact only this tradition has made history in the Christian churches. For that reason the course of history has never done justice to the possibilities inherent in the synoptic model; its peculiar dynamic was checked and halted and the model relegated to the 'forgotten truths' of Christianity (1979, p.570).

The intention of this book is to develop a christology akin to that of the Synoptics and other parts of the New Testament in which the dynamic was clearly the Spirit of God.

*d) Scriptural Priority in Safeguarding Beliefs*

The argument is often heard that the classical formulations of christology and trinitarian theology serve the important purpose of safeguarding the Christian faith from heresy and damaging variations or "reductions." It seems to be a commonly accepted tradition to regard any variations from classical orthodoxy as "reductions" although, in fact, they may include meanings and emphases which are missing or reduced in emphasis in the classical formulations themselves. The "reductions" may thus represent an enrichment of the tradition. The use of the term "reduction" serves to emphasize the function of classical dogmas in safeguarding the faith. However, as biblical studies have progressed and the distance in meaning and culture between the Bible and the classical formulations becomes more apparent, the question has arisen "where should the safeguards for Christian faith be sought, in classical dogma or in the Bible itself?".

Thüsing, again, has something to say on this matter which is of particular concern for Roman Catholics who are expected to acknowledge the pre-eminent authority of classical dogmas.

"We cannot nowadays safeguard faith in Jesus from the periphery consisting of later, historically conditioned dogmatic definitions. This safeguarding process has to begin at the centre ... in the New Testament" (p.209). There is a growing consensus that this is the case, and it will constitute a major crisis for the classical Christian paradigm if it turns out that the Bible can better support an alternative paradigm.

*e) Influence of Linguistic Studies*

Another biblical crisis for the classical paradigm of Christianity arises out of the increased knowledge in our time of the structures and functions of language. This understanding can suggest quite different meanings in many of the stories of Jesus, as well as other biblical stories, than the meanings which supported the classical interpretation of Jesus. In particular, the understanding of parables and metaphorical language as literary forms has cast much new light on what Jesus' message and mission were about.

John Dominic Crossan has contributed a great deal to the new understanding of the parables and other sayings of Jesus. He maintains that Jesus' personal experience of God, typical of the Jewish experience of God, was of God "as the one who challenges world and shatters its complacency repeatedly" (1973 p.26). The main point and function of Jesus' parable stories was to introduce people to this experience of God, to reveal the eschatological Kingdom of God which permanently challenges the *status quo*. Jesus criticized the *status quo* of his times in the name of the God who is not identical to anything created in the heavens or the earth. He relativized all the contemporary historical projects by reminding people of "the sovereign freedom of God's advent" (p.35) against "the idolatry of time" conceived in terms of "plans, projects, and programs" for the future. Hence Jesus "was ... crucified ... for ways of acting which resulted from the experience of God presented in parables" (p.32).

Crossan sees Jesus' proclamation of God's Reign as a kind of "comic eschatology" (Crossan 1976, p.45) which laughs appropriately at what Robbie Burns called "the best laid schemes of mice and men" which "gang aft agley." The purpose of such laughter is not in ridicule for its own sake but to liberate creativity and let people freely play as children of God in the making of God's world. Jesus' paradoxicality, so evident in the gospels, is "the almost inevitable result of his Jewish tradition turning its aniconic faith onto language itself and thus onto law and prophecy, wisdom and apocalypse" (Crossan 1980, p.21).

Sallie McFague says that "what the parables stand for is opposition to *all* forms of idolatry and absolutism, even the new orientation to reality brought about through the parables' redescription of reality" (1982, p. 47). Hence, "Christian politics, art, morals, economics, philosophy, and so forth, are all questionable ventures, unless undertaken with appreciation for the relativity and partiality of all such 'systems'" (p.47). McFague's main object in her book is to advocate that theology too become relative and partial as "metaphorical theology" rather than absolutist. Such theology would see Jesus as a parable of God rather than identical to God.

*f) Jesus as Iconoclast*

Along a similar line of thought, Don Cupitt sees Jesus primarily as "The Ironist" (1971, p.14). Cupitt finds irony to be a key to Jesus' message and mission, irony understood as the awareness that "all frameworks of understanding are human constructions and none is objectively secured against collapse" (p.85). This gives "an advance in self-knowledge" which may be painful at first but which opens the possibility of a way of life of radical trust like Jesus' own life of trusting in God. Jesus knew the Reign of God in both its radical judgment on the established systems of the world and in its promise of a new reality yet to come. The human situation that Jesus knew and proclaimed was "a sort of permanent eschatological crisis" (p.89) that is both promising and iconoclastic in light of the reality of God.

The irony and iconoclasm of Jesus were lost and missing in the classical christology which identified Jesus with God. Cupitt asks the question that challenges the classical paradigm of Christianity: "how could [people] iconize an iconoclast without being aware of the absurd irony of their own mistake?" (1976, p.131). Part of the present crisis of the classical Christian paradigm is that its view of Jesus as absolute and, indeed, as deity clashes drastically with the main outlook that Jesus apparently had and which is reflected in nearly everything he said and did.

*g) Salvation Reduced to a Single Event*

Maurice F. Wiles in an essay entitled "Does Christology Rest On A

Mistake?" (1976, pp. 122-131) notes that for the Christian doctrine of creation and the doctrine of the fall, "it was for a very long time felt that a certain specific action in history was essential to the possiblity of affirming the doctrine, essential to its survival as a meaningful doctrine at all" (p.123). Wiles wonders if something similar might apply to the doctrine of redemption. In the case of the doctrine of creation it has come to be accepted by very many Christians that "this kind of approach, which looks for some specific creative act of God ... [is] a mistaken one" (p.124). Evolutionary theories may have their own difficulties but some kind of evolutionary process is difficult to deny. In any case, the old idea of creation as a kind of intervention by God is "a method of reasoning with which we do not and cannot identify ourselves" (p. 124) because *"occasional intervention implies as its correlation a theory of ordinary absence" (p. 124).* Our thinking about God's creating relationship with the universe has changed so that the pre-Darwinian view of creation is no longer tenable.

Similarly with the doctrine of the fall, it is no longer thought by many to refer to "some datable aboriginal calamity in the historic past of humanity but to a dimension of human experience which is always present" (quoted by Wiles on p. 125 from J. S. Whale, *Christian Doctrine*, 1941, p.49). Wiles observes that

> The doctrine of the Incarnation arose in the closest conjunction with these two doctrines both of which had this kind of mistake built into them. It does not therefore seem unreasonable to ask whether it also, in its traditional form, grew up with the same kind of mistake built into it (p. 126).

Wiles goes on to wonder "Is it perhaps possible that the truth of that doctrine [of redemption] would even stand out more clearly if it were not tied to one particular act or life differing in kind from the rest of the series of human acts and human lives?" (p. 126-127).[6]

The classical paradigm of Christianity with its orthodox version of once-for-all incarnation would not allow such an interpretation of redemption. The Christian paradigm will have to be changed if the redemptive work of God is to be seen in a universal context, as God's creative work and the human fall have come to be seen. One of the aims of the Spirit christology in this book is to allow the redemptive work of God anywhere in the world to be seen in relation to God's redeeming work in Jesus.

## *Theological Reasons for a Paradigm Shift*

The awareness of God working redemptively outside the Christian community is a theological matter as well as a matter of biblical

---

[6]Lampe (1977) asks a similar question: "Was there an act of salvation which God performed once and for all at a particular moment in history? Was this a divine irruption into a fallen world to rescue it from the powers of evil, save man from sin and from the consequential wrath of God, and restore him to the divine likeness in which he was created? Or is salvation a process rather than an act, continuous with, and indeed, but one aspect of, the process of creation itself?" (p.14-15). Lampe correctly suggests that "upon the answer to this question the form of our Christology is likely to depend" (p.14).

interpretation. It has to do with the nature of God, the character of evil, the meaning of salvation and the purpose of the church, as well as the significance of Jesus Christ for human fulfillment. These questions will be addressed at length in various parts of this book. In this introduction I will try only to indicate briefly what are some of the theological crises confronting the traditional paradigm in Christian theology.

*a) The Bible Not Basically Trinitarian*

The doctrine of the Incarnation is, of course, the reason why the church developed a trinitarian concept of God. Without the idea of the deity of Jesus Christ there would not likely have arisen the idea of three persons in one God. Jews before the time of Christ and since then have had ideas about diversity in the nature of God, speaking of God in terms of Spirit, Wisdom, Word and in other terms without developing anything comparable to the doctrine of the Trinity. As Frances Young observes "within Judaism, the 'hypostatization' of Wisdom or Torah did not seem to undermine monotheism, since ultimately it was a kind of periphrasis used to circumvent the implication of direct contact between the transcendent God and the creation; ... a faith so theocentric could never allow it really to challenge God's 'monarchy', [God's] ultimate originality and sovereignty" (Hick (ed.) 1977, p. 23).

When the concrete individual person of Jesus Christ was judged to be "of one substance" with God the first step was made towards the ontological doctrine of God as Three-Persons-in-One. It might be argued that much earlier than the Council of Nicaea (325 CE) the early church used the triadic formula of "Father, Son and Holy Spirit" as a kind of comprehensive summary of the various elements by which the agency of God was operative in the Christian experience of salvation, but this "economic" triad was not yet understood ontologically to be the definition and exhaustive description of God's essential being.

There is, in fact very little doubt that the "economic" idea of Trinity preceded the doctrine of the ontological or essential Trinity in Christian history. The question can be asked, however, if it is necessary or valuable for that particular development to take place. Moltmann and many others have insisted that logic requires it. They say that God could only act in a triadic way or be revealed in a trinitarian way if God were in fact triune in God's very essence. "A Trinity of revelation is only possible if the very being of the Godhead which is thus revealed, is itself a Trinity" (J.F. Bethune-Baker cited by Wiles 1976, p.1). This logic, however, completely ignores the wide variety of ways in which God was actively revealed in the Hebrew scriptures. If such logic were applied to those revelations and activities of God, there would surely be many persons in the Godhead. The female Wisdom would have a strong claim to personhood like that of the Spirit and the Son. The ontological Trinity would have to become at least a quaternity and doubtless even more numerically complex.

There is not, in fact, any compelling logic that requires affirmation of an ontological Trinity from the Christian historical experience of God's triadic activity as *Abba,* Spirit and Christ. D. M. Edwards expresses this thought: "the modern mind ... cannot see any necessity of thought for fixing on the number three neither less nor more .... No convincing reason can be given why, in view of the rich manifoldness of divine functions and activities, the number of the hypostases may not be increased indefinitely" (Cited by M. Wiles 1976, p.17).

Increasing the number of hypostases might serve some useful purposes such as guaranteeing the presence of femininity in the Godhead, if Wisdom were included, but the disadvantages would surely outweigh the advantages. The multiplicity of persons or hypostases would look increasingly like polytheism. Would it not be better to remove the idea of more than one person in the Godhead and return to the monotheism of the Jews, which Jesus undoubtedly shared, and regard the various activities or functions of God not as hypostases at all but as different revelations of the one God?

Moltmann complains that this has been the tendency in Western Christianity which has stressed the one substance of divinity in the three persons. In answer to the question "Why are most Christians in the West ... really only 'monotheists'?" he explains: "The representation of the trinitarian Persons in a homogeneous divine substance ... leads unintentionally but inescapably to the disintegration of the doctrine of the Trinity in abstract monotheism" (1981, p.117). For Moltmann monotheism is undesirable. We will look at some of his reasons later on but for the moment merely state the conviction that monotheism is a very important and beneficial idea in a pluralistic world. Not only is it less abstract and mystifying than trinitarian thought, but it constitutes a positive basis for the unity of the world and its peoples.

If Moltmann is correct in discerning a monotheistic bent in Western Christianity it may be because the logic of God pulls heavily in that direction. To any ordinary kind of thinking three divine persons sounds like three different gods, especially if the three are commonly depicted pictorially or iconically in three different images and are addressed separately in worship. There is a real problem in making the idea of Three-Persons-in-One intelligible or coherent. It has elicited some magnificently creative explanations, such as those of Augustine, but the explanations tend to oscillate between modalism and tritheism, neither of which is acceptable in orthodox theology, or else the explanations treat the persons more like principles than persons, making them into dialectical moments in a threefold process or something equally abstract and far removed from any direct relationship with Jesus of Nazareth. Little wonder that the church has made frequent use of the term "the mystery of the Holy Trinity."

*b) Vested Interests and Anti-Semitism*

No believing person, of course, would deny that God is mysterious, but when the mystery is represented dogmatically by an impenetrable enigma of three persons in one identity it is not farfetched to suspect that mystery has become mystification. Mystification usually serves some vested interest. In Dostoevski's *The Brothers Karamazov* the Grand Inquisitor quite frankly acknowledges that promulgating mysteries helps to keep the religious hierarchy in a position of power over ordinary people. There have recently been scholarly suggestions that vested political and ecclesiatical interests had not a little to do with the formulation and continuance of the christocentric-trinitarian paradigm. Tom Driver puts it succinctly: "As long as Christ is center, bishops and Holy Sees are automatically authenticated" (1981, p.52).

The other side of upholding vested interests is undermining the ones who are subjected to the hierarchies. Driver explains:

> I wish to remind my readers of persons and beings who have been rendered weak, invisible or ashamed by the church's affirmation of Jesus Christ as center of all things: ... those who are not male ... those who are neither white nor Semitic ... those who are born without inheritance ... those who feel strongly their sexuality ... those who have never known and do not wish to know Abraham as their father, who have other fathers and mothers to honor ... those who have no community to surround them ... those who have never learned language whose hopes are as mute as buds on a tree ... those who are Jews and have never consented to believe that Jesus is the Christ, the center of all things and have incurred the hatred of many who worshipped the center" (p.44).

Rosemary Ruether has explained and documented the biblical, theological and historical roots of anti-Semitism in *Faith and Fratricide* (1979). After considering all the factors that issue in anti-Semitism Ruether concludes: "At the most fundamental level, the problem is the presuppositions which are still affirmed by Christian theologians as basic to Christian theology" (p. 228). The presuppositions are the prevailing paradigm of christocentric-trinitarianism.

*c) Ethnocentrism*

The God of the Hebrew scriptures who was the God of Jesus of Nazareth was a genuinely monotheistic God who acts in various forms and ways. The development in Christian tradition from this kind of God to a triune God in effect gave Christians, from their point of view, at least, a monopoly on anything approaching a true or accurate idea of God. It left other believers in God in a distinctly inferior position because they did not know the most basic and comprehensive thing about God, namely, that God was actually three persons rather than one. In any dialogue with people of other religious traditions Christians by this account are in a uniquely favoured position because the founder of the Christian religion, unlike that of any other religion was, in fact, one of the three persons of the Godhead.

Instead of entering dialogue with the common assumption that God is potentially, if not necessarily, equally active and present to the various participants in the dialogue so that they each might have some authentic experience of God to share with the other participants, Christians enter dialogue with the claim that their tradition is uniquely in principle more authentic than anyone else's tradition. Christians hold that God Incarnate established our tradition, thereby revealing the Trinity of God which no other peoples have known, nor can they know it without becoming Christians. When a group like the Mormons make such a claim for themselves, insisting that only Mormons have true knowledge of God, it is rightly recognized to be ethnocentrism of a very undesirable and divisive kind. Yet there are equally ethnocentric implications in the traditional christocentric-trinitarian paradigm.

Increasing numbers of Christian theologians are recognizing this difficulty in our tradition. Here is a tiny sample. Sallie McFague says that to exclude other religions from significant revelation is "to limit God to a 'tribal' status and ultimately to make an idol of Christianity" (1982, p.51.). John Hick says that "to claim that [the Christ event] is the only point at which God has been or is acting creatively on earth would be the supreme expression of Christian triumphalism." (Goulder (ed.) 1979, p.80). Frances Young sees that "It is spiritual arrogance to be convinced that we have the truth and everyone else is misguided" (Hick (ed.) 1977, p.39). Rosemary Ruether holds that "to encapsulate Jesus himself as God's 'last word' and 'once-for-all' disclosure of God ... is to repudiate the spirit of Jesus and to recapitulate the position against which he himself protests" (1983, p.122). In the same vein Tom Driver says, "I feel driven to say that in order to be faithful to Jesus one must refuse him as ... central norm. He himself seems not to have needed a center of history" (1981, p.54). Accordingly, Driver concludes that "some kind of repudiation is necessary in order to break the power not of Christ but of the christocentric paradigm we have inherited" (p. 45.).

The Roman Catholic Church in Vatican II repudiated the traditional claim that "outside the church there is no salvation" but there is no indication of changing the paradigm underlying the logic of that claim. Similarly, the World Council of Churches has a very active department for dialogue with the people of living faiths and ideologies that acknowledges their theological significance, but the W.C.C. continues to hold assemblies with highly exclusive christocentric themes such as "Christ The Life of the World." (Vancouver, 1983) or "Christ the Light of the World" (Nairobi, 1976). As John Hick observes

> there is a reluctance to see that this new and more positive attitude towards other religions has christological implications. The "no salvation outside Christianity" attitude depended upon two main factors. one negative and the other positive — the negative factor being a lack of knowledge among most Western church members concerning the other great world faiths, and the positive factor being the conviction that Jesus Christ was uniquely divine. ... The negative factor is now disappearing (Goulder (ed.) 1979, p.193).

The "positive" factor remains very much in force as the prevailing paradigm of Christianity. It will not disappear unless an alternative paradigm replaces it, that is, unless there is a paradigm shift in the ongoing Christian tradition. I believe that a monotheistic Spirit christology is the most promising alternative in view.

*d) Docetism*

Apart from the question of ethnocentrism arising from the trinitarian paradigm there has been an increasing number of questions raised about the problems of incoherence and docetism in the idea of Incarnation, as understood in the two-natures-in-one-person doctrine of the Council of Chalcedon. The two-nature model will be looked at in some detail in Chapter VI. From almost the time of its inception it has been recognized that the anhypostatic Chalcedonian doctrine of Christ has a serious deficiency in it. The divine nature of Christ is grounded in the divine person of the Logos whereas the human nature of Christ is not grounded in human personhood. The one person of Christ is the divine person of the Logos with divine nature to which in some mysterious way human nature is joined. Various solutions to this apparently docetic tendency have been tried over the centuries but none has commended itself to universal acceptance in the church. The official doctrine remains as it was at its formulation at Chalcedon and the Second Council of Constantinople. Christ's humanity is viewed as an addition to the divinity which is his essential and eternal being.

In the 20th Century there has been a sharp increase in the amount of dissatisfaction with the christology of Chalcedon. The explosion of knowledge in the human sciences as well as historical work has strengthened the conviction that Jesus was a human being in every sense of the word. As Schillebeeckx says "there are no ghosts or gods in disguise wandering around in human history; only people" (1979, p.33). One of the main characteristics of modern christology has been that of affirming the humanness of Jesus as the starting point of christology.[7]

Gerald O'Collins S.J. concludes that "Almost all contemporary thinking about Jesus Christ ... takes as its starting point (a) man, (b) the created cosmos, (c) history, or (d) some combination of all three elements" (1977, p.13). At the same time most modern christology tries in the end to claim that it is not really departing from the classical christology but only developing nuances and emphases that are logically consistent with the traditional paradigm. Tom Driver is an exception who explicitly renounces the christocentric paradigm, but he does so in some fear and trembling, asking "will not the churches either ignore me or tear me to pieces, both the liberal ones ... and the conservative ones? (1981, p.44).

By its very nature a religious paradigm is either implicit or explicit in virtually every expression of the religion, including the songs and liturgy. To change the paradigm will require a long period of time and a growing consensus among religious leaders that is increasingly reflected in the rituals and songs of the Christian community. The pressure is mounting for the change to come, but so far no widespread consensus appears to have emerged, except possibly that Jesus was a real human being.

*e) Incoherence*

How he could be a real human being and still be the Second Person

---

[7]Aldwinckle (1976) entitled his book on christology *More Than Man* in order to address the current situation in which "any suggestion that [Jesus] was 'more than man' or even unique in the sense affirmed by most traditional expressions of the Christian faith is often strongly, if not violently, repudiated" (p.5). This is an insupportable view, if it is taken to apply to contemporary books on christology, but it does indicate that "Jesus the man ... is at the center of the modern interest" (p.5).

of the Holy Trinity raises the problem of incoherence. The British authors of *The Myth of God Incarnate* and its sequels have addressed this question with particular intensity. They have asked if the idea of a real human being who is also really God is not in the same class of incoherent ideas as square-circles. They have suggested that the idea of incarnation is valuable as a metaphor for the way in which God is present but insist that the idea of Incarnation, with a capital "I" meaning God become the human being Jesus, is incoherent because "speaking of God being a part of his own creation or a part of that creation being God ... does seem ... to involve a logical self-contradiction (Wiles 1979, p.6). Cupitt uses stronger language: "There is abundant evidence all around us that traditional theological realism is now an intellectual and psychological mess" (1982, p. xvii).

*f) Traditional Theology is Patriarchal*

The "psychological mess" of the traditional paradigm is well known by feminist theologians who have discovered the extent to which patriarchalization is strengthened by it.[8] Rosemary Radford Ruether in *Sexism and God-Talk* explains how christology became patriarchalized. It was largely a political process culminating in the fourth century when the secular and religious hierarchies combined forces to formulate a christology that upholds and affirms the principle of hierarchy.

> The Christological doctrine of Christ as Logos or ground of the created world is identified with the foundation of the existing social system. ... All is integrated into one vast hierarchy of being ... . Christ has become the Pantocrator (All-Ruler) of a new world order. Christology becomes the apex of a system of control ... (1983, p.125).

The control over women by the hierarchy is aided and abetted by the christology which defines Christ "as founder and cosmic governor of the existing social hierarchy and as the male disclosure of a male God whose normative representative can only be male" (p.125). Sallie McFague agrees that "The classic models of the Christian tradition have been and still are hierarchical authoritarian ones which have been absolutized ... [and which] the 'outsiders' to the mainline Christian tradition — women, blacks, third world people — are questioning" (1982, p.29).

Both Ruether and McFague propose basic changes in the traditional christological paradigm. We will hear more of their thinking later on. One more quotation from McFague will illustrate the present point about the psychological problems in Incarnation christology: "To deny [Jesus'] identity with God is important for peoples whose experience has been excluded due to the particularity of Jesus' person and history, for instance, women who feel excluded by Jesus' maleness" (1982, p.52). A new paradigm is needed which will not cause feelings of exclusion or provide a basis for any kind of hierarchical control over disadvantaged groups in society. Spirit christology may be that alternative paradigm.

---

[8] Cf., for example, Daly (1973). The result of coming to understand the patriarchal character of traditional Christian theology is that "radical feminist insight is experienced as stronger than the sanctions of orthodoxy" (p.78).

*g) Soteriological Crisis*

There is a soteriological crisis in Christianity arising from the traditional logic of forgiveness. The so-called "Latin" doctrine of the Atonement holds that Jesus' death was a "full perfect and sufficient sacrifice, oblation and satisfaction for the sins of the whole world," as so many eucharistic liturgies have expressed it. In this view, forgiveness of sins by God takes place as a result of the substitutionary sacrifice or punishment of Jesus on the cross. The transaction of God being atoned by Jesus' death is thought to apply objectively to the sins of the whole world, but forgiveness in this logic is operative for people only if the atoning significance of Jesus' death is appropriated subjectively by people in faith. It follows that only Christians who are "washed in the blood of Jesus" can be truly said to be forgiven.

This logic may have made sense to Hellenistic and medieval thinking but it does not make sense now. It has been criticized by many theologians but it continues to hold a central place in many liturgies and countless hymns.[9] Recent studies by Robert J. Daly, S.J. (1978) and Frances M. Young (1975) have shown that the logic of forgiveness by satisfaction or substitutionary punishment are a departure from Hebrew thinking about expiation and salvation. The metaphor of satisfaction from feudal civil law and the metaphor of punitive justice from criminal law have an entirely different logic from the logic of forgiveness implicit in the Hebrew laws of cultic sacrifice. It would be blasphemous to Jewish thinking to claim that God could be impelled to forgive people by the blood of their sacrifices. Jesus' own logic of forgiveness was the central one from the Hebrew scriptures, namely, forgiveness by "return" *(Tshuvah)* as can be seen, among other places, in his calling people to "repent and believe in the gospel" (Mk 1:15) and in his parable of the Prodigal Son. The word repent *(metanoia)* in the New Testament is the word used to translate the Hebrew word *Tshuvah,* "return". On the Day of Atonement, Yom Kippur, the Jews still read from the book of Jonah which is a paradigmatic case of forgiveness by "return."

Walter Kaufmann in the Prologue to Buber's *I and Thou* (2nd. Edition) claims that Christianity is founded on the implicit denial of the Hebrew idea of *Tshuvah*.[10] To a considerable extent Kaufmann is right because the deity of Christ and, hence, the doctrine of the Trinity are founded to no small degree on the logic of forgiveness by substitutionary atonement. It is generally agreed by theologians and historians of Christian thought that soteriological reasons played a determining role

---

[9] Barry (1968), Dillistone (1968) and Aulen (1969) are among the best known works in recent years that criticize the "Latin" doctrine of atonement. Tillich (1957) offers a psychological explanation of why the Anselmian view of atonement has continued to be so prominent, at least in Western Christianity: "The discovery of an often deeply hidden guilt feeling has given us a new key for an explanation of the tremendous effect of the Anselmian theory on personal piety, hymns, liturgies, and much of Christian teaching and preaching" (p.173).

[10] "This conception of return has been and is at the very heart of Judaism ... . But the theology of Paul in the New Testament is founded on the implicit denial of this doctrine, and so are the Roman Catholic and the Greek Orthodox churches, Lutheranism and Calvinism" (Kaufmann in Buber 1970, p.37). Recent studies of Pauline theology have shown that Kaufmann is incorrect in his interpretation of Paul, but what he says about the other mainline Christian denominations still has considerable validity.

in the outcome of the christological debates in the early church. The writings of the Patristic period make this plain. The claim for Jesus' divinity or deity was based on the logic that if he were not fully divine he could not have accomplished the work of salvation as it was conceived to have taken place. This included the idea that a fully divine person was needed to make a sacrifice of sufficient merit to make amends (expiate) for the sins of the whole world. Cyril, for example, said "It was no ordinary man ... that God the Father delivered over on our behalf ... but it was He Who transcends all creation ... so that He might be seen to be amply equivalent for the life of all" (Kelly 1978, p. 399). Basil is perfectly clear on the point: "It is only the Godman Who can offer to God adequate expiation for us all" (Kelly 1978, p.385). The examples could be multiplied many times.

Kaufmann is right that the denial of the logic of forgiveness by return in favour of the logic of forgiveness by the atoning blood of Jesus is part of the foundation of traditional Christianity. It had a decisive influence on the development of the christocentric-trinitarian paradigm. This logic of forgiveness has severed a major connection with Judaism and made it logically necessary for Jews and other peoples to become Christians in order to have access to God's forgiveness. Jesus became a "bottle-neck" of God's forgiveness — an idea which is more destructively legalistic than anything that could ever be charged against the Pharisees, for example. It is also, as we now see, an ethnocentrism that is totally unacceptable.

If the logical necessity for a fully divine sacrifice to be made in order to expiate sin were relinquished, the christological debate about the deity of Christ might lead to a different conclusion.

*h) Individualism*

There are other current issues of great concern in the modern world which create a crisis for the traditional christological model. There are social polarities such as rich and poor, and individualist and collectivist political movements which the traditional paradigm of Christianity does not effectively address or else lends its support to one side of the polarity at the expense of the other. For example, because of the traditional view of Christ and his significance for salvation there has been a strong tendency in Christianity to support individualism in social order rather than any forms of socialism or collectivism.

Much of Christian soteriology has been individualistic and juridical based on the logic that Jesus had to be divine in order to provide an adequate sacrifice for peoples' sins. Sin in this view is understood in personal, individual terms, and salvation is appropriated entirely by individuals who then may or may not improve social conditions. In the twentieth century the knowledge of social systems has made it inevitable and necessary that Christians should understand evil at least as much in corporate structural terms as in personal, individual terms,[11]

---

[11] Cf. Taylor (1972): "It seems to me both legitimate and necessary to argue that in our day, and probably at all times, the 'powers' from which [people] need deliverance are embodied in many forms including especially the massive economic, political and cultural structures in which we find ourselves imprisoned" (p.141-142).

yet the classical paradigm of Christianity does not lend itself easily to concepts of salvation that deal with the corporate structures of evil.

There is no longer any doubt that poverty and wealth are to a large extent functions of social systems over which many of the individuals affected often have very little individual control. Traditional christology and the meaning of salvation inherent in it did not focus especially on the dire situation of the poor. Recent biblical and theological studies have rediscovered "God's preferential option for the poor and oppressed" that permeates the scriptures and have tried to find a basis for this in the life and teaching of Jesus. Such a God and such a Jesus are quite different from the God and Jesus of the traditional paradigm. The saving work of this God does not center on the problem of personal guilt or peace of mind but on bringing the rebellious and destructive powers of oppression into the righteousness and peace of the Reign of God.

Liberation theologians have made a critique of traditional theology which cannot be ignored. Christianity must change its basic paradigm or else risk becoming the religion of the oppressors, shunned by the oppressed who hear no gospel in the church relevant to their most urgent condition. A Spirit christology could help to relate salvation more directly to the unjust situation of exaggerated wealth and poverty.

*i) Left Brain Bias*

One other polarity that is becoming better understood in our times is the difference between people with practical and those with aesthetic, or mystical, orientations. Recent brain research has posited a difference between left and right brain functions that are reflected in individual people or in social structures which may have a bias in one direction or the other. Ashbrook (1984) has done pioneering work in relating brain research to theology. He has detected a left brain bias in Western Christianity. This means a bias toward rational, analytic, technical thinking with a deficiency in emphasis on the relational, imaginative, visual and mystical aspects of reality. This is not the place to expound Ashbrook's findings at length, but it is possible to say that if his account is accurate one can see that the traditional Logos christology, as it has been developed in the West, is a contributing factor to the distorted one-dimensional approach to reality that is typical of Western civilization.

The Logos need not be conceived as rationality of the left brain variety but in most periods of Christian history it has been so conceived. Logos christology "fits" together with the view that human beings are *homo sapiens* who are essentially constituted by their mental, rational abilities understood in the way in which the West has understood rationality. The Logos concept in Greek thinking was aligned with the Apollonian orientation rather than the Dionysian, and there has accordingly been a tilt in Western civilization towards Apollonian expressions of life and society.

In Christianity, in the West in particular, faith in the Logos Incarnate and the triune God of which he is the Second Person has tended to be conceived in terms of rational assent for certain propositions. This creates a bias against those whose orientation is more aesthetic or mystical as well as against those who are mentally handicapped and do not have the ability to appropriate the rational propositions necessary for salvation.

Ashbrook has shown how Eastern Christianity differs from that of the West, manifesting more right brain orientation in its theology and even in its church architecture. If Eastern Christianity shares the same basic paradigm with Western Christianity it would appear that the paradigm can not be held responsible for the debilitating biases in either left or right directions. The fact is, however, that Eastern Christianity is not so firmly christocentric as Christianity in the West, typically stressing the work of the Holy Spirit much more than the West has done. If the stress on Spirit has had anything to do with the "right brain" emphases in Eastern Christianity it reinforces the promise of developing a Spirit christology to redress the left brain imbalance in Western Christianity.

Ashbrook uses the structure of the human mind as a metaphor for the mind of God, suggesting that the fullness of God's mind would include analogous elements to those of the whole human mind, including both left and right brain functions. I would suggest that Spirit is a metaphor which is even more wholistic and inclusive than the metaphor of mind. Spirit includes all that mind is plus elements of body and world that are important analogies for the understanding of God. Spirit christology can be more wholistic than Logos christology, lending its influence more effectively for wholistic life. More of this in chapter III.

## *Cultural Reasons for a Paradigm Shift*

It is not only theology and biblical studies which have created the present crisis for the christocentric-trinitarian paradigm of Christianity. In fact, the theological and biblical crises have arisen out of the changing historical or cultural context. The world and our human understanding of it are vastly different from the way things were when the traditional Christian paradigm was formulated. It is necessary to look at some of the monumental historical and cultural changes that have made the modern world and modern people what we are. The analysis of some of the basic characteristics of modern culture will clearly suggest what creates the need for a paradigm shift in Christianity.

In the nineteenth and twentieth centuries there has been an intellectual paradigm shift, a basic change in the way reality is understood which is affecting every aspect of social and intellectual life, including religion and theology. The gist of the paradigm shift is the emergence of historical sensibility with certain characteristic features and attendant conditions. These include: pluralism, with the relativistic logical theory that goes with it; the awareness of the extent of ideology; the critical scepticism that attacks ideological tendencies; and a language-centred outlook in philosophy and other intellectual disciplines with consequent acceptance of the analogical, symbolic, metaphorical and mythical nature of truth. Gone with these changes are naive realism and absolute certainty about what is real or what is right. The correspondence theory of truth can no longer be simply assumed. If it is held at all it must be surrounded carefully with many qualifications.

Human consciousness undergoes a tremendous shock as it realizes these changes. There are various reactions and responses to be seen in the contemporary world, ranging from fundamentalist dogmatism to "mere relativism" to structuralism and, perhaps, to what some observers see emerging in most recent years, a transformation of consciousness, a new mind:

> The great, shuddering, irrevocable shift overtaking us is not a new political, religious, or philosophical system. It is a new mind — the ascendance of a startling worldview that gathers into its framework breakthrough science and insights from earliest recorded thought (Ferguson 1980, p.23).

*a) Explosion of Knowledge*

Paradoxically, the primary condition that unsettles the certainties of ancient knowledge and requires a new framework and new approach to their truth is a knowledge-explosion. Like a fire that changes sand crystals into glass which can then be blown into various shapes or broken into useless pieces, the flames of the knowledge-explosion are continuously working a transformation on existing truth, some to be reshaped, others to be removed. The fire was lit many centuries ago by Copernicus and Galileo and others and it has increased in magnitude ever since. The dynamics of the phenomenon are beginning to be understood. The framework of changing knowledge, the governing principles, key concepts, relevant theories and explanations have changed — in other words, the *paradigm* of truth has changed. Philosophers, sociologists of knowledge, literary critics, linguists and all scholars who are concerned about the epistemological bases of their disciplines, are coming to understand the new paradigm and some of its implications for their work. Theologians also are looking at the explosion of knowledge and drawing conclusions for theology, ethics and religion in all its aspects.

*b) Relational Thinking*

The spark for the fire of modernity was lit when Copernicus conceived of a new relationship of earth and sun and Galileo realized that it was the relativity of earth and sun to each other that distinguished the Ptolemaic and Copernican systems.[12] The relativity of the *two systems* to each other was also seen by Galileo as a fertile source of new understanding. It was the concept of relativity and its method of application as much as the new knowledge itself that drew the opposition to Galileo of those in authority. They could see the crisis such thinking causes for absolute truth. Much that was fixed and certain before, with this new kind of thinking became mobile and relative. Explanations of the nature of things could no longer be given without taking account of their relatedness to other things.

This complexification of knowledge led to rapid expansion of knowledge. The result eventually was the emergence of distinct sciences including historical science which was aware as never before of the comparative and relative influences in different periods of history. A

---

[12]Driver (1981, pp.61-74) describes this development of the concept of relativity. I owe much of the analysis to him.

new concept of logic was conceived by Hegel to cope with the new idea of reality as historical. Dialectical logic acknowledges the continuous change inherent in reality and tries to organize the understanding of changing reality into successive positive and negative stages in an accumulative process.

*c) Awareness of Ideology*

Marx combined the concept of dialectic with the question *cui bono?*, in whose interest do changes come?, and who benefits from the explanations of knowledge? The awareness of ideology as a set of ideas with power to serve vested interests has become common and has contributed to the "hermeneutic of suspicion" or critical scepticism that characterizes modern intellectual life. Marx and Freud saw the presence of ideology in religious ideas, and since that time there is, for theologians, no escaping the question "in whose interests?" any more than for anyone else. Liberation theologians have shown how traditional theology can serve the interests of the established economic and social powers. Even theological truth, it is clear, has to be discerned in its relationships to other systems of knowledge and power.

*d) Systems-Theory*

We now see that reality consists of many systems, or at least our knowledge of reality is organized in systems — physical, biological, psychological, sociological, economic, religious and many other subsystems within the larger systems. Every system has its own set of ideas that may be ideological. The many systems interact in very complex ways creating some harmony, as in the ecological systems, and much disharmony and evil as we can also see in the ecological systems. In acid rain, for example, economic systems clash with biological and geological systems. Social customs, psychological forces and economic interests combine to produce alcohol and nicotine addictions that harm our biological systems. And so on. Every system has its power and so do the sets of ideas that define the systems. In a sense, then, every set of ideas has an ideological tendency. People typically employ the power of systems and their sets of ideas for purposes of some kind of gain. Conversely, the power of the systems and their ideologies to a great extent control human affairs and account for the conflict and destruction and alienation that constitute evil.

*e) Pluralism*

The co-existence of systems of various kinds is the basis of pluralism. The popular view of pluralism as individuals each having his or her own ideas on any given subject fails to see that ideas have power of their own, not merely the power that we give them when we subscribe to them, but power that comes from the system to which the ideas belong. An individual person may not be fully aware of the systematic connections of the ideas he or she espouses but the connections exist nonetheless. Ideas, like the realities which they denote, exist in complex patterns of relationships — in systems which have organization and power. Pluralism is the situation in which a multiplicity of systems with the particular sets of ideas that describe them exist in active relationship to each other.

*f) Relativity and Field Theory*

The relating of systems in pluralism is the relativity that characterizes modern thinking. Such relativity or relating of systems and sets of ideas can be denied or ignored only by a willful refusal to see what is there to see. To deny the relativity of ideas is no longer possible without excluding oneself from one of the main discoveries of the human race. To do so is comparable and related to the kind of thinking seen in the Flat Earth Society. It must be stressed, however, that to affirm relativity as a universal condition of truth does not necessarily imply "mere relativism," the conclusion that there can be no adequate criteria of evaluation that make one set of ideas more authentic than another. To affirm relativity does not require the resignation of all values but it does require openness and a "critical" mentality which is prepared to consider all related factors in an issue.

The awareness of relativity in the modern world was radically developed by Albert Einstein in his "special" and "general" theories of relativity and in his unified field theory. Einstein demonstrated the relativity, the changing patterns of relationships, between the basic realities of mass and energy, time and space and velocity. In Einstein's view discrete objects are subordinated to the idea of changing patterns of energy. In other words, objects are understandable only in the dynamic *fields* in which they exist. Knowledge of objects is therefore never *final* because the fields in which they exist continue to change in time. "Field" theory has now been applied in other disciplines beside physics. It is one of the basic assumptions of modern understanding of reality. When field theory is applied to language and knowledge the basic relativity becomes apparent.

The social relativity of knowledge is now understood. Sociology of knowledge explores the relations between knowledge and the power of groups in society. Epistemological relativity leads to the awareness that we live in language like fish in the sea. The structure and dynamics of language condition our relationship with reality immensely — not totally, I believe, because even if there is always a language "filter," so to speak, on the reality that gets through to us, reality precedes language and remains to some degree independent of language. As Nicholas Lash has expressed it "[Humanity] is not constitutive of truth, but ... truth ... is constitutive of [humanity]" (Goulder (ed.) 1979, p.230).

*g) Comparative Religions*

In studies of religion the awareness of relativity introduces a comparative approach that sheds new light on whatever is compared. Churches and even theological schools may continue to exercise "tunnel vision" and not look at any comparisons or relationships between Christianity and other religions but travel or the media and the increasingly cosmopolitan nature of society will inevitably expose the majority of people to other religious systems. The shrinking of the world to a "global village" has made it unavoidable for people to relate to those of other religious beliefs. The growing awareness of the unity and interdependence of humanity, as epitomized by the "earth-rise" picture taken by astronauts from the moon, makes it highly desirable to change, if necessary, the basic paradigm of our religion in response to the new situation of pluralism and relativity in which we find ourselves.[13]

*h) Implications of Cultural Crises*

As I hope to show in this book, changing the paradigm need not mean departing entirely from our original tradition. On the contrary it can mean a recovery of elements in our tradition which for various reasons were minimized or suppressed in the past in favour of other emphases which were originally foreign to the biblical tradition. Changing the paradigm of Christian theology can be a radical proposal in the best sense of returning to the roots of our tradition. (The word "radical" comes from the Latin word *radix,* root).

The crisis, then, that arises for the prevailing paradigm of Christianity out of our modern culture of pluralism and relativity includes the necessity of relating the Christian set of ideas about God and the world to other religious ideas. This entails acknowledgment that epistemologically, Christian ideas can make no stronger claims to truth than other religions can make.[14] The criteria for evaluation of religious ideas will have to be largely practical. Christians will have to cease "pulling rank," so to speak, by claiming absoluteness for our versions of the truth but excluding all others from the same possibility. This traditional position is rightly seen as a double standard in the light of modern epistemology.

The crises of modern pluralism also require relating theological ideas to the sets of ideas or ideologies of other systems in reality. When sociology, psychology, biology, linguistics or philosophy, to mention only a few contemporary systems, are related to theology it can produce far reaching changes in our traditional sets of theological ideas. It can also revitalize and enrich theology and engender renewal in the life and mission of the church. The relationship of liberation theologies to socio-economic analyses surely has much to do with the vitality of the basic Christian communities in Latin America or in the feminist movement worldwide.

The crux of the crises is the issue of absoluteness which is bound up with the claim of Jesus' deity and with the claim of inerrancy of the scriptures. Many Christians have accepted the cultural and historical relativity of the scriptures and renounced the idea of inerrancy as being

---

[13]Cf. Tillich (1963): A theology which does not deal seriously with the criticism of religion by secular thought and some particular forms of secular faith, such as liberal humanism, nationalism and socialism, would be *"akairos"* — missing the demand of the historical moment. ... Again I must say that a Christian theology which is not able to enter into a creative dialogue with the theological thought of other religions misses a world-historical occasion and remains provincial (p.6).

[14]Burbidge (1977) shows that faith is basically a commitment to an ultimate criterion of truth and action which is actually received as a "miracle" or "gift" (p.73) rather than as a result of logical necessity. Even though faith may subsequently be subjected to rational, critical examination it is initially and finally an "uncaused cause" in our behaviour and thinking or else whatever caused it would be our real faith and the ultimate criterion of life. Segundo (1976) makes a similar point: "Real life for a human being presupposes a nonempirical choice of some ideal that one presumes will be satisfying. It is this ideal, chosen ahead of time by nonempirical standards that organizes and gives direction to the means and ends used to obtain it" (p.104). (See also Segundo (1982,) pp.3-27). Because faith is a "nonempirical choice" or a miraculous "gift" there is no absolute logical proof of one "god" over another. As far as logical necessity is concerned, alternative traditions of faith meet as equals. It is true, as Segundo says, that faith operates as an "absolute" factor in a person's life (1982-p.19) because it determines life and thought for the person. But "absolute" in this sense does not guarantee that the object of the faith is "infinite, perfect. or metaphysical." Whether the faith is true or not remains logically unprovable. Faith is logically a risk.

an unfruitful and even destructive approach to the scriptures. The issue of Jesus' deity is under increasing strain from the intellectual paradigm of the modern world.[15] The church is being dragged "kicking and screaming" to address the anomaly and anachronism of its prevailing paradigm — not that it should simply adopt the paradigm of the prevailing cultures. It should look for a paradigm that is accountable not only to secular knowledge but also to the broadest and deepest understanding of the experience and scriptures of our tradition. Our tradition, *pace* Barbour, is not simply identical to the prevailing paradigm of theology. It is a rich and varied repository of experience and understanding that allows for many possibilities in shifting the currently operative paradigm.

*Summary of the Crisis*

In *The Human Face of God,* (1973) the late Bishop John A. T. Robinson posed the question "How do we put [the mystery of God in Christ] on the map of our thought-world?" (p.12). The traditional christocentric-trinitarian paradigm of Christian theology is having great difficulty remaining on the map of the contemporary thought-world. The thought-world of biblical scholars is discovering the theocentricity of the Bible and its witness to Jesus himself, including the risen Jesus, which questions the christocentricity of traditional Christianity. The weakness of the New Testament basis for the doctrine of the Incarnation of the Second Person of the Trinity is becoming increasingly clear and the question arises with mounting force whether an alternative model for christology, perhaps one based more in the synoptic gospels rather than the *Gospel of John,* might not be a more authentically biblical christology.

The conviction is growing, too, that christology, like other basic doctrines of our faith, should be grounded and safeguarded primarily in the scriptures, including the Hebrew scriptures, rather than in decisions of the church councils. The accelerated learning about Jesus in our times has discovered a person inimical to any earthly absolutes, a parabler, an ironist, a monotheistic iconoclast who can only with absurdity be turned into an absolute icon himself.

The question has been raised if the doctrine of God's redemptive work should no longer be tied to a single historical person and event, as the doctrines of creation and fall were once but no longer mistakenly thought to be tied. The question is: should God's redemptive activity not perhaps also be seen as a universal activity of God which is distinctively or even definitively, but not exclusively, seen in the single person and event of Jesus of Nazareth?

The exclusiveness of seeing Jesus as the only, absolute once-for-all saviour is now known to have contributed to the anti-Semitic horror story which is part of the often unacknowledged history of the church. Others have felt excluded from God and salvation because of the exclusive way salvation in Christ has been interpreted. In the modern thought-

---

[15] Aldwinckle (1982) recognizes the problem: "Have we now reached a point when the Christian churches and the individual believer must be prepared for a radical change in our understanding of what the Christian faith is and what it implies? The doctrine of the Incarnation is on the line" (p.199). Aldwinckle's book is dedicated to the purpose of answering the question in the negative.

world the claim to absoluteness and exclusive authenticity is seen to be ethnocentrism, a divisive, primitive and undesirable trait.

The absolutist claims for Jesus have also been seen to be used as a basis for justifying hierarchical order in church and society. The traditional victims of the hierarchies, women, racial groups, the poor and the politically oppressed are calling for new explanations of Jesus' saving significance which not only cease to support the oppressors but speak more directly to the conditions of evil that cause oppression.

The individualistic views of sin and salvation which were primary factors in the development of official christology are being challenged by the awareness of the structures of evil in the systems that constitute the world. Needed is a paradigm of Christian faith which will serve as a hermeneutical key to relate the biblical witness to the pluralism of alienated systems and their ideologies, their sets of ideas, for therein lies the root and locus of evil that needs salvation as we understand it in our time. Amidst all these questions is one very widely acknowledged certainty, namely, that Jesus of Nazareth was a human being in every sense of the word.[16] In the modern thought-world he could have no convincing significance at all if he were not a real human being. We are quite sure that all the persons who have walked the paths of history were human beings. The Incarnate divine person of the Logos does not fit into the map of this thought-world. Yet we are equally sure that "God was in Christ reconciling the world." This incoherence generates a severe crisis in christology, a crisis that shakes the very framework or paradigm of Christianity.

It is time for a change in the disciplinary matrix of theology, time for a change in the key concepts of incarnation and salvation. It is time for a change in the interpretation of the "standard exemplars" of the Christian paradigm, the life, teaching, death and resurrection of Jesus and the two central sacraments which epitomize the explanation about Jesus. It is time to look for new data in the scriptures and experience of our tradition, and to accept some new assumptions such as the one about the humanity of Jesus.

In this time of changing the paradigm there will have to be repudiation of some traditional theories and beliefs such as the ontological Trinity and the eternal deity of Christ but there may be equivalent gains in the explanation of former anomalies such as the absence of femininity in the Godhead. There will be many overlapping assumptions between the old and new paradigms; much of the language of the new will be the same as that of the old; much of the "data" in the scriptures and in tradition will be the same. Most important of all the community of faith will be the same community. A change of paradigms has happened before in the Christian tradition and it could happen again.

---

[16]Schoonenberg (1971), for example, observes that "it is always desirable in discussion to use what is most certain as the point of departure. ... Here the best point of departure ... is the humanity of Jesus" (p.66).

## The Promise of Spirit Christology

It is my conviction, shared by a few other contemporary theologians, that Spirit christology is the most promising one in sight with which to respond to the crises that we have been considering. There are different conceptions of what Spirit christology should be like and we will look at some of them in due course. Not all who look hopefully to the development of Spirit christology would agree, either with the analysis of the crisis as I have done it or with the formation of the christology that follows. Yet we might agree on some of the reasons why Spirit christology is an alternative whose time has come.

Walter Kasper, for example, is thoroughly committed to upholding the traditional christology of Chalcedon and he does an excellent job of explaining it in a favourable light, but he still believes that "a pneumatologically defined Christology can in fact best convey the uniqueness of Jesus Christ and his universal significance" (Kasper 1976, p.252). Philip J. Rosato, S.J. suggests some developments on Kasper's model in light of his analysis of the failings of Ebionite Spirit christology (1977, pp.423-449). After adding up the strengths and weaknesses of Spirit christology, Rosato concludes that the former outweigh the latter, especially if certain steps are taken to correct the weaknesses. He, like Kasper, is determined to avoid renouncing any of the main constraints or doctrines of official *Logos* christology.[17] Since this is the case, it is not convincing to me that his particular version of Spirit christology will in fact facilitate dialogue with the Jews and people of other faiths or ideologies as he speculates that it might.[18] An exclusivist, absolute divine Jesus will still be seen as a product of ethnocentrism, regardless of whether the divinity is explained in terms of Spirit or Logos. We will look more closely at Rosato's and Kasper's arguments in Chapter VI when the two main alternative kinds of Spirit christology are compared and contrasted.

Don Cupitt is prepared to be much more radical than Kasper or Rosato in rethinking the bases for his Christian life, explicitly accepting philosophical constraints and not feeling as obligated as Kasper is to affirm Chalcedonian conclusions. Because Cupitt finds the "theistic philosophy of spirit" to be central and essential for understanding God and humanity he concludes that Spirit christology is the appropriate one to espouse. He asks "why choose one [religion] rather than another? I accept the one which, it seems to me, embodies the idea of spirit in its central myths more perfectly than any other, namely Christianity." (1976 p., 118).

For somewhat similar reasons, as well as for more biblical and theological reasons, Paul Tillich proposed a Spirit christology in his

---

[17]Congar (1983, vol.III) concludes that "This type of Christology [eg. Kasper's or Rosato's] in no sense contradicts the classical Christology that has been developed since Chalcedon" (p.165).

[18]Rosato's intention is excellent. Cf. Rosato (1983): "At a time when it is imperative to lead modern persons to the credibility and practicality of faith in God as Spirit, a Christian pneumatology in dialogue with the social sciences yields perceptions of various independent concepts of the presence of divine spirit in human society itself, and thus places religion and pneumatology in a global and communitarian context from the outset" (p.263).

*Systematic Theology,* Part IV "Life and the Spirit." However, he did not develop it as much as he might have, since the main christological development in his *Systematic Theology* was a Logos christology which he fully expounded in Part III "Existence and the Christ."

The most substantial Spirit christology that I am aware of is that of G.W.H. Lampe in *God As Spirit* (1977). Lampe argues for a monotheism of Spirit and says that "The model of 'Spirit' seems especially suitable for christology and for interpreting man's whole experience of encounter with God" (p.12). The advantages of the Spirit model of christology, as Lampe sees it, include the following:

> ... it lends itself less readily to any hypostatization, and to the consequent implication that the deity encountered in Christ and in ourselves is an intermediary, so that God immanent is ... inferior to God transcendent ... . Spirit, too, seems better able to express the truth that God's interaction with human persons ... takes place at every level, involving not only the intellect but the will, the emotions, and the subconscious.
> ... Spirit carries with it a greater connotation of freedom and of personal volition than 'Logos' ... for 'the Spirit blows where it wills' (p.116).

We shall be referring to Lampe's work again.

The promise that I see in Spirit christology will be explored systematically in the chapters ahead. At this point it is possible only to summarize the promise under the same categories, biblical, theological and cultural that were used to look at the crisis in christology.

*Biblical Reasons*

There are strong biblical reasons for developing Spirit christology as the basis for an alternative to the traditional theological paradigm. If a fundamental shift in Christian thinking has to be made it is highly desirable that the Bible should be the basis on which the change is made. It can be argued that the Bible is a book about Spirit from beginning to end. In fact there may be no other metaphor that is used so frequently and consistently throughout the entire Bible.[19]

If a new metaphor is to become the root-metaphor for Christian theology it is important that there be some commonly accepted source from which the scope and limits of the metaphor can be drawn. The Bible records a long historical development of the understanding of Spirit which can provide controls or limits on the kinds of meaning that can be attributed to the root-metaphor as well as providing rich content of meaning for the term. With a Spirit christology one ought not to

---

[19]Congar (1983, vol.I) points out that "the word *ruah* occurs 378 times in the Old Testament" (p.3). Despite this number it is sometimes claimed that Spirit is not a very significant term in the Hebrew scriptures. Such a claim is based on the even more prominent place that Spirit has in the New Testament. Hanson (1973) for example, says that the Old Testament references to Spirit "do not, all put together, amount to anything remotely approaching or even anticipating the Christian doctrine of *the* Holy Spirit" (p.116). (Italics his). Detailed studies of Spirit in the Hebrew scriptures, however, do not support Hanson's claim. Montague (1976), for example, while acknowledging a very significant progress in thinking about the Spirit in the New Testament, nonetheless shows that the Hebrew understanding of Spirit presents us with a "truly impressive view" (p.126).

wander intentionally or inadvertently away from the basic biblical tradition. As David Tracy observes: "Attentiveness to the reality of the classic alerts all Christian theologians to note the singular fact that they are not called upon to invent a new religion" (Tracy 1981, pp.372-3). The Bible is the classic of Christian tradition and it is important that Spirit christology can be developed by theologians being attentive to our classic.

Besides providing the material content of the metaphor of Spirit, the Bible also supports the specific model of Spirit christology in a variety of ways. There is a clearly eschatological connotation of Spirit in the Hebrew scriptures and an explicit linking of the concept of Messiah with Spirit. In the New Testament, as Pannenberg concedes, "probably the oldest attempt to express God's presence in Jesus was characterized by the concept of the Spirit" (Pannenberg 1968, p.116). There appears to be a growing consensus among New Testament scholars that, as Schillebeeckx puts it, "it is highly probable historically speaking, that Jesus understood himself to be the latter-day prophet" (1979, p.306). There is no question that Spirit is the dynamic presence of God in the prophets. Reginald Fuller expands on the point: "It is the unexpressed, implicit figure of the eschatological prophet which gives a unity to all of Jesus' historical activity, his proclamation, his teaching with *exousia* ('authority'), his healings and exorcisms, his conduct in eating with the outcast, and finally his death in the fulfilment of his prophetic mission" (1969, p.130). Furthermore, Schillebeeckx shows that the common christological titles of Christ, Son of Man, Son of God and Son of David in the New Testament were affected decisively in their basic meanings by the earliest "prophetic-sapiential" tradition which saw Jesus as the one "filled with God's Spirit" (1979, pp.441-515).

As we shall see in Chapter IV there is an immense amount of evidence in the New Testament directly linking Jesus and God's Spirit.[20] The idea of Spirit christology is strongly present not only in the synoptic gospels but in other parts of the New Testament as well.[21]

Apart from the direct, explicit linking of the Spirit with Jesus throughout the New Testament there is an important indirect connection made through the interpretation of the image of God. In the New Testament the concept of image of God is used in three ways: christologically, soteriologically and anthropologically. Jesus is identified as the true image of God.[22] Human salvation is conceived to consist in recovering the image of God.[23] And finally, the New Testament once

---

[20] Kasper (1976, p.16): "Scripture sees the Spirit at work at all stages of Jesus' life."

[21] Cf. Taylor (1972): "Jesus' continuous and total possession by the Spirit was, together with his resurrection, the ground on which the apostles came to be convinced that he was not only Messiah but Son of God. His unique unity with the Father was, as they saw it, both given and attested by his unique relation with the Spirit. One tradition clearly associated his special endowment by the Spirit with his birth. ... Another view connected Jesus' special relation with the Spirit with his baptism ... . But the strongest line of teaching was St Paul's who found the Spirit's unique action upon Jesus most particularly in his resurrection" (p.86).

[22] "He is the image of the invisible God" (Col 1:15). "Christ who is the likeness of God" (II Cor 4:4). "He reflects the glory of God and bears the very stamp of his nature" (Heb 1:3).

[23] "And we all, with unveiled face, beholding the glory of the Lord, are being changed into his likeness from one degree of glory to another; for this comes from the Lord who is the Spirit" (II Cor 3:18). Again, "[You] ... have put off the old nature with its practices and have put on the new nature, which is being renewed in knowledge after the image of its creator" (Col-3:9-10); and "those whom he foreknew he also predestined to be conformed to the image of his son" (Rom 8:29).

or twice alludes to the idea of image as it was understood in the Hebrew scriptures, namely, as the essential nature of all human beings (Jas 3:9).

The connection between Jesus and the Spirit through the concept of image is established if one understands that image of God in the Bible consists of the relationship of human beings to God through the presence of God's Spirit in and with people.[24] In other words, if the biblical concept of humanness is founded on the idea of humans being the image of God, which means having the capacity to enter into covenantal relationships with God in the Spirit, then Jesus as the image of God and as a real human being must be understood also in terms of his relationship with God in the Spirit.

At this point one cannot show in full detail that humanness as the image of God in the Hebrew scripture is conceived in terms of Spirit, but the case can certainly be made.[25] Furthermore, if Jesus is understood as the image of God in terms of the Spirit being present with him, then Jesus' soteriological significance in terms of his mediating the Spirit to people makes good sense. Salvation in or through Jesus has to do with people receiving the Spirit and attaining thereby some "measure of the stature of the fulness of Christ" (Eph 4:13). In short, Spirit christology facilitates an integration of biblical christology with biblical anthropology and soteriology. These and other theological reasons for a Spirit christology ensure that one does not simply fall into the genetic fallacy and assume that the earliest biblical christology is necessarily the best.

*Theological Reasons*

Spirit may be uniquely capable of serving as the common metaphor for God, Christ, humanity and creation. We will explore the meaning of Spirit later on in Chapter III. If it can serve as a metaphor referring to God, Christ, humanity and creation it will prove to be most useful in relating the doctrines of creation and redemption. Sallie McFague points out that "the most fruitful metaphors are the ones with sufficiently complex grids to allow for extension of thought, structural expansion, suggestions beyond immediate linkages" (1982, p.39). "A model must be *both specific,* in order to refine concepts and make distinctions and comprehensive in scope, in order to include wide ranges of experience" (1982, p.71). It will be seen in due course that Spirit as a root-metaphor and the Spirit model of christology meet these criteria of fruitfulness.[26]

---

[24]Hendry (1957, p.115). makes the point that the presence of the Holy Spirit in human beings should not be thought of as God being present *in principle* but rather only as reflected freely in the created image. He speaks of human spirit as the image of God's Spirit but, since the human spirit is mainly sinful God cannot be thought to be present to the human spirit in principle. This view does not take account of the biblical idea of God's presence as Spirit giving life and vocational skills and other gifts which precede, to some extent, the free responses of human beings. It can, therefore, be said that God is present with human beings in principle if it is understood that God constitutes and sustains human existence by God's free willing of it. This does not prejudice the possibility of humans freely responding to many aspects of God's grace and it acknowledges God's creative and prevenient grace on which all creatures depend for their very being.

[25]Cf. Newman (1983, pp.25-31).

[26]Robinson (1962) argues that the richness of modern understanding of Spirit is the result of the Spirit being in the forefront of inquiry since the Reformation. "It is no exaggeration therefore, to say that these recent centuries have done for the doctrine of the Holy Spirit what earlier centuries, particularly the fourth, did for the doctrine of the Son of God." (p.220).

Spirit in the Bible can be seen to include a very wide range of experience and yet it has specific meaning which "feeds" the concepts and distinctions used in connection with it.

The fact that Spirit is clearly metaphorical is itself a distinct advantage over Logos which is primarily a concept rather than a metaphor. The meaning of Logos for the Greeks was not derived from characteristic human experiences in the way the meaning of Spirit was for the Hebrews. Logos was a conceptual abstraction derived from rational analysis. It might be argued that the Hebrew metaphor, Word, which was translated as Logos in the Septuagint was derived from experience of God and that some of that metaphorical background was attached to the New Testament and later Christian uses of Logos. However, the Greek conceptual meaning of Logos certainly overshadowed and outweighed the Hebrew experiential component in Logos if there was one, at the time when the Logos model of Christ was developed into an ontological theory of the triune being of God.

The point of advantage in using metaphors rather than concepts for explanations about God is their aniconic nature which is essential for speaking about God. Metaphors, like the symbols they describe, are explicitly inadequate for referring literally or absolutely to God, as well as adequate in certain respects. Their inadequacy, if acknowledged, prevents them from becoming idols of God, claiming for themselves the perfection or absoluteness that rightly belong only to God.[27] Concepts, on the other hand, can be assumed to be claiming adequacy in their denotations and connotations, and can more easily be idolatrous in their reference to God than metaphors can. It belongs to the very nature of metaphor to be somewhat imprecise as well as valuably suggestive, and it is an advantage not a disadvantage, for the basic language about God to be imprecise in some respects rather than spuriously claiming precision. The advantage is religious as well as theological. Metaphors point to the religious experience upon which theological reflection is founded.

Another advantage of Spirit theology and christology as metaphorical theology is that it clearly allows for the possibility of other religious communities having authentic experiences of God which are also metaphorically describable. As metaphorical theology, Spirit theology cannot have absolutist pretensions. It has to acknowledge that other metaphors based on other experiences may communicate aspects of the reality of God which it is inadequate to convey by virtue of its intrinsically limited potential. As we shall see in the next chapter this methodological "poverty" is entirely appropriate for Christian theology which is *theologia crucis*.

Neither should metaphorical Spirit christology be susceptible to becoming the basis for hierarchical thinking of one sort or another, as Logos christology was and is. Driver comments wryly that "a hierarchical principle cannot make very much of a reality like Spirit

---

[27]Ruether (1970) cites Gabriel Vahanian's thought: "It is the work of the Holy Spirit constantly to shatter this tendency of man to turn his culture into a God" (p.178).

which is impossible to locate" (1981 p.107). Without a propensity for sponsoring hierarchy, Spirit christology may meet some of the concerns of feminists and others who have shown that traditional theology has supported their oppressors. Sallie McFague points out that "at the heart of patriarchalism ... is a subject-object split in which man is envisioned over against God and vice versa. God is man's superior Other and woman in this hierarchy becomes man's inferior other" (1982, p.148).

In Spirit theology and anthropology there is no clear cut subject-object split, no hierarchy of orders, because the transcendent is immanent, "closer than hands and feet and nearer than breathing." The traditional hierarchy has cost women and others very dearly in terms of being oppressed and in terms of giving resistance to oppression. Driver observes that "we may expect the price to go even higher before we get a paradigm shift in the culture" (1981, p.145). If there could be a paradigm shift that would remove the hierarchical tendency in Christianity it might strengthen the newly emerging one in the culture.

As well as not being an active part of the problem of oppression, Spirit christology may be positively part of the solution. The traditional Christian paradigm has tended to reduce the understanding of evil to individual sins because salvation was conceived primarily in individual terms. A new paradigm based on Spirit theology could provide a hermeneutical key to relate the biblical witness to the modern understanding of systems and ideologies. We will look at this possibility in Chapter V.

The biblical understanding of powers and principalities was, in fact, an understanding of the systemic and ideological nature of fallen creation. The problem of evil understood in these terms is a spiritual problem that is larger than individual sin. God's work of salvation as the restoring of creation to the Reign of God and the fulfilling of the earth by judging and healing its systems can be understood in a Spirit theology in which Spirit is seen as the constitutive reality in both creation, humanity and Christ as saviour.

*Cultural Reasons*

The biblical understanding of powers and principalities was also an awareness of what we now call pluralism, the multiplicity of organizations and centres of power coexisting in relationships with each other. Spirit is the Reality which can relate pluralistic powers in accordance with the purposes of God. Spirit is the relational Reality which realizes the Reign of God amidst the many centres of power ranging from individuals to nations and transnational agencies. Spirit is, therefore, very germaine to ethics and can help achieve a theology that is oriented to orthopraxy as well as orthodoxy. The ethics that issues from a Spirit theology and christology may be less inclined to the kind of legalism that is endemic in traditional Christianity. An ethics of Spirit might lean less towards cultural imperialism and more towards conceding the spiritual authenticity of some ethical mores in other cultures.

Not least important as an advantage in Spirit christology is the wholistic character of Spirit compared to the rationalistic bent of traditional Logos christology. Logos theology has at times been richly inclusive of the emotional, affective and volitional aspects of humanness. Irenaeus' concept of Logos was such an interpretation, but, in the main, Logos has been conceived as the rational element in God and the corresponding faculty in human beings. Spirit, unlike Logos, can include the unconscious and bodily elements in humanness which, as we know from Freud and other psychoanalyts, require healing or salvation as much as the conscious, rational part of us does.

Gabriel Vahanian makes the observation that "the Church cannot understand itself unless the language of its self-understanding speaks to the world and unless the world itself can use the same language" (1966, pp.xi-xii). One of the great advantages of using the terminology of Spirit in theology and especially in christology is that Spirit is a metaphor found in many different religious traditions as well as in philosophy and the sciences.

Spirit is a term of which most human beings make some use and have some idea of what it means. Not that all would necessarily agree on what it means, but the term at least provides a basis for discussion and sharing, a point for dialogue in which all participants have something to contribute as well as receive. While it may be true, as Tracy concludes, that "we now seem to find ourselves in a situation ... where there is ... no language game where anyone can find refuge from the conflict of the radically pluralistic present" (1981, p.351), it is also true that there is at least one "language game" in which people of radically different traditions can begin to "play" albeit with the risk of conflict. The language of Spirit is the only language in sight with any promise of being a *lingua franca* with which people of different intellectual and religious traditions may begin to converse together about certain unseen but nonetheless real elements of their experience.

Tracy agrees with numerous other observers of the post-modern situation that there is a rediscovery of the uncanny occurring for people from widely different parts of the current intellectual spectrum. The sense of uncanniness appears to be arising as some awareness of the positive and the hopeful in a situation of intense awareness of what is exceedingly negative and foreboding. The modern "hermeneutics of suspicion" leads towards nihilism and experience of the Void or Abyss in which all meaning and certainty is destabilized. Paradoxically in the experience of the Void people may experience what Donald Evans calls "reality-assurance" (Evans 1979, p.32), the acceptance of meaning, reality and value in spite of all that challenges them.

As Don Cupitt has experienced it, "the Void can become the Ineffable and can arouse (noncognitive) worship" (1982 p.66). This experience of affirmation through intense negation is akin to the experience of mystics in all ages. Marilyn Ferguson sees it as the basic experience that is creating in our time a new consensus or conspiracy ("breathing together") among the most able intellectuals and interpreters of reality (1980, p.23f.). Tracy points out that "the journeys to and from the experience of the uncanny in the contemporary situation are as diverse, often as conflicting, as the classical paradigm" (1981, p.362). He concludes: "Conflict is our actuality, conversation is our hope" (p. 363).

Conversation among the members of a pluralistic world would be assisted if there were frank recognition on all sides that the language appropriate to discussion of the Ultimate Reality of God is less-than-absolute metaphorical language. Conversation would be assisted if it could begin with exploration of the common experience of the Void and the inexplicable uncanny Reality that emerges from that experience. And conversation would be assisted if representatives of the ancient religious traditions which have long known the mysterious Presence in the Void could find some common terms in their traditions, if there are any, to begin exploring in order to build common understanding and common commitment for the sake of peace and righteousness on earth.

The metaphorical terminology of Spirit is surely one of the most likely candidates to be a common language among people of diverse traditions.[28]

Christians can use the language with integrity only if it is consistent with the basic paradigm of Christian tradition. At present this is not the case. The language of the Spirit which blows where it wills is fundamentally anomalous to a paradigm which claims absoluteness, finality, metaphysical certainty and exclusiveness for itself. Christians could use the language of Spirit with integrity if the metaphor of Spirit became the root-metaphor of the Christian paradigm and if the central model of Christian tradition — the model of Christ — were interpreted in terms of Spirit.

A Spirit christology as the basis for a Christian metaphorical theology would enable Christians to have dialogue with others who know the Spirit, and especially with Jews,[29] without our having the hidden pretension of possessing absolute truth. The pretension has to be hidden, if it exists, because there can be no genuine dialogue when one party claims that their version of the truth is totally and absolutely right. The traditional Christian paradigm has such a claim explicitly built into it. It is time to change that claim.

*Conclusion*

Changing our traditional paradigm should not be regarded as a departure from Christian tradition but rather as a development of it that is appropriate for the present context of life. "Meanings change not wrongly and deplorably but rightly and laudably in each new context of faith ... . Critics who dismiss all 'Christian deviation' as signs of loss of faith are, quite simply, missing the heart of the matter" (Slater 1978, p.94-95). As Sobrino (1978) points out: "The reformulation of Christology in a new situation is nothing else but an expression of faith in the universal significance of Christ" (p.348).

---

[28] Cf. Cupitt (1976): "God as universal unknowable spirit is a common focus for the spiritual aspirations of all [people]" (p.117).

[29] Cf. Ruether (1972): "It is around such an interpretation of God's *shechinah* that Christianity might be able to reestablish with Judaism some new dialogue about the meaning of 'incarnation'" (p.10).

## Chapter Two
# METHOD IN CHRISTOLOGY

*Introduction*

An immense variety of methods and approaches in modern christology calls for decisions on which elements should be included in the method of a Spirit christology. Walter Kasper (1976, pp. 17-18) discusses three major christological approaches at the present time: those with a cosmological perspective, e.g. Teilhard de Chardin; those with an anthropological approach, e.g. S., Ogden, D. Soelle; and those with the perspective of universal history within the framework of theodicy, e.g. Pannenberg. Fiorenza (1980, pp. 81-89) finds seven or eight different theological methods in christology since Vatican II: those influenced by the philosophical ideas of German idealism, those focused mainly on concrete political and social praxis, those applying social analysis to interpret Jesus, those influenced primarily by literary criticism or historical criticism or process philosophy or feminist concerns or psychological interpretations. The question is: which if any of these methods or perceptions should be emphasized in the development of Spirit christology?

It is quite clear that Spirit christology does not fall simply or entirely under one or other of the above mentioned perspectives. It will be cosmological in certain respects and anthropological in certain respects. It will not be centred on any concept of *heilsgeschichte* or salvation history, if that idea is conceived to pertain exclusively to the Judao-Christian histories, but it will certainly be responsible in basic ways to the Hebrew and Christian traditions. The version of Spirit christology developed here will not be singularly influenced by the philosophy of German idealism or by process theology. It will relate to political and social praxis, feminist concerns, psychological and sociological interpretations and will be open to influence from literary and historical criticism among other important contemporary influences.

*Revisionary*

Schubert Ogden (1982, pp. 11-19) sees many of the different modern christologies falling into one broad category of "revisionary christology" which is characterized by at least three traits: it seeks to explain the person of Jesus by "some hypothesis about the nature of his person, his qualities, his mode of being, his relation to God, and so on"; it is primarily concerned about the historical Jesus as the one whom christology seeks to explain; and it affirms that Jesus is the Christ because the man Jesus realized the conditions necessary for him to be truthfully called the Christ, i.e. perfection of one kind or another. Is Spirit christology, we may ask, a revisionary christology? It would appear to be so, although the term "radical," meaning returning to the roots, would seem more appropriate than the term revisionary.

*From Below and Above*

Another popular distinction that has been much used to classify christological method is the distinction of christology "from below" and "from above."[1] The former start with the human aspects of Jesus and move towards an affirmation of the divinity whereas christologies "from above" start with the firm conviction that Jesus is divine and move toward some explanation of his humanness. Does this distinction have any value for the present undertaking?

Theologians are still divided on the subject. Sallie McFague argues that "Jesus as a parable of God means starting from 'below'" (1982, p.49). She notes "there is little doubt but that this was the way that the early Church arrived at its confession of Jesus as the Christ" (p.49). Schillebeeckx agrees that "the New Testament presents a 'Christology from beneath'" (1979, p.570) but then argues that he does not like to use this terminology because "the alternative of christology either 'from below' or 'from above' is a spurious modern dilemma" (1980, p.432). His reasons are that "the best way into the distinctive nature of Jesus of Nazareth ... is indeed not to approach him either from a given idea of what 'being God' means or from a preconception of what 'being man' — and thus being-a-human-person — really entails" (1979, p.604). Kasper agrees that the terminology is inadequate. "A christology purely 'from below' is therefore condemned to failure [because] Jesus himself understands himself 'from above' in his whole human existence" (1976, p.247). Ian Barbour seems to me to put the question in an accurate perspective when he says:

> There is a greater influence in religion than in science "from the top down": from paradigms, through interpretive models and beliefs, to experience. But the influence "from the bottom up" starting from experience, is not totally absent in religion (1974, p.124).

Spirit christology will not begin with any high assumptions about Jesus' divinity but it will assume that the Spirit of God was in Jesus and it will bring to the understanding of Jesus some preunderstanding of the Spirit as revealed in the Hebrew scriptures, as well as in Jesus' own life and death and resurrection. On the other hand, Spirit christology will begin with the assumption that Jesus is a complete human being which, I believe, is the point Sallie McFague and John A.T. Robinson and other modern christologies have wanted to affirm.

*Manifestation and Proclamation*

David Tracy (1981), following Paul Ricoeur, makes a distinction between manifestation and proclamation as classical forms of religious

---

[1] See, for example, Robinson 1973, pp.32-33, or O'Collins 1983 p.113.

expression which can be seen to characterize christologies as well as theologies in general. Manifestations, typically recurring in ritual, myth or symbol, engender a radical sense of participation in or belonging to the primordial sacred power of the cosmos. Thus, theologies or christologies with a "mystical priestly-metaphysical-aesthetic emphasis" are of the manifestation type. Proclamation typically occurs in kerygma, parables or event and creates a sense of non-participation, a sense of being a discrete responsible self, dependent but separated and estranged from God. Thus, theologies or christologies with a "prophetic-ethical-historical emphasis" (pp. 303ff.) are of the proclamation type. Tracy makes it clear that the two types are not mutually exclusive any more than word and sacrament are mutually exclusive in most Christian churches. As different kinds of religious expression, however, manifestation and proclamation can decisively shape christologies, depending on which is given major emphasis.

*Left and Right Brain Type*

James Ashbrook sees a connection between these two kinds of religious expression and right and left brain functioning. In these terms, christology can be marked either by left brain dominance which tends to be concerned about the ethical, logical, analytical and historical, with a redemption orientation, or by right brain dominance which is imaginative, relational, mystical and visual, with a creation orientation. Again, the two tendencies are not mutually exclusive (Ashbrook 1984, p26). They can however, be in real tension. Schillebeeckx (1979, pp.29-30) observes that:
> Inside the churches, too, the traditional ... Christology has fallen apart in our time ... on the one hand a total emphasis on the man Jesus as inspiration and orientation for working, not uncritically but committedly, to achieve a better world here on earth ... , on the other hand, a total emphasis on the God "Jesus Christ," the Lord exalted to his Father's side, who is alive and active among us even now, is celebrated in the liturgy and sheds upon us the Spirit as pledge of an eternal life to come, ... Two types of Christianity based on two types of Christology ... . Each would do well to acknowledge the Christian status of the other.

These two types appear to correspond to the distinction between theologies of proclamation and manifestation. Should Spirit christology emphasize manifestation or proclamation, left or right brain tendencies? Or better, how can Spirit christology adequately embrace and reflect both kinds of classic religious expression? There will certainly be an attempt to do so in the Spirit christology that is developed hereafter, even if Jesus is not called God in the same way in which some "manifestations" do.

*Praxis*

Tracy observes that liberation and political theologies, as a third distinct type of theology, may include both manifestation and proclamation but then "move on into the realms of action and history, of performative, personal, social and political praxis" (1981, p.390). Their concern is not only to be bearers of a word or seers of a manifestation but even more doers of the word in history. There is obviously a close affinity between political and liberation theologies and theologies of proclamation, in particular "left brain" types of theology. In any case they have presented a challenge to traditional theologies which cannot be ignored.

Robert McAffee Brown (p.1978, p.60f.) distinguishes six differences between liberation theology and traditional theology, including a different starting point (the poor), a different interlocutor or person to whom the theology is addressed (the nonperson), a different set of tools (the social sciences), a different analysis (the reality of conflict), a different mode of engagement (praxis) and, in total, a different theology in which reflection as the "second act" follows the commitment to praxis in the cause of the poor. How, one wonders, would a Spirit christology relate to these elements of liberation theology?

Analogous to the differences between the methods of liberation theologies and traditional theologies are the different approaches to societal change in the philosophies of Hans-Georg Gadamer and Jurgen Habermas. Gadamer believes that the disclosive power of classical thought retrieved by hermeneutics and communicated in rhetoric is sufficient to effect change, whereas Habermas argues for the necessity of an instrument for critique of ideologies because society is typically under the sway of systematically distorted communication, manipulated by powerful forces for their own vested interests. If Spirit christology is to communicate the message and power of salvation and effect some change in our society it should include an instrument for ideological critique as liberation theologies do, as well as the hermeneutics of retrieval of our scriptural tradition and the "hermeneutics of suspicion" which is the critically sceptical approach of all modern scholarship. Spirit christology will aim to serve the ends of orthopraxy as well as the purposes of kerygma and proclamation. Jozef van Beeck (1979, pp.306-307) reminds us:

> We must advert, in the case of each christology to its *function*, to what it attempts to *do*, to the way it purports to change people and situations. Many christologies, however — especially the more abstract, conceptual ones — do not explicitly betray their performative function: still, all have one, even though it may seem at times almost entirely extrinsic to the christology taken at face value.

The Spirit christology developed here will try to be as explicit as possible about its "performative function." Tom Drivers' concern has been heard: "It will not do to establish our christology first and then figure out its ethical implications" (1981, p.X). The ethical issues in a pluralistic world where organized powers co-exist and contend will be in view from the outset, although a full development of the topic awaits a later book.

*Metaphorical and Dialectical*

The metaphorical nature of theology is another contemporary idea that cannot be ignored. It arises out of the understanding of language and literary criticism. The language of Spirit is metaphorical and this affects what is said about Jesus as one who was "full of the Holy Spirit" (Luke 4:1). If, for example, the presence of God in Jesus is understood metaphorically as the presence of Spirit, then, as Sallie McFague points out, one cannot assume to claim "identity between the human and the divine" (1982, p.18). Metaphors by their very nature imply and entail discontinuity as well as continuity between "tenor" or principle subject (in this case God's Spirit) and "vehicle" (in this case Jesus as the Christ). The nature of metaphorical theology and of Spirit as a root-metaphor will be explored in the next chapter.

Just as there is a dialectical nature of "is and is not" in metaphors and symbols, so also one can call "dialectical" the coexistence of manifestation and proclamation, of myth and parable, of creation orientation and redemption orientation, of orthodoxy and orthopraxy, of "from above" and "from below," of a hermeneutics of both retrieval and suspicion. Dialectic implies the mutual dependence and close interrelatedness of the apparently polar opposites. It allows for a dynamic interaction, a process of movement back and forth, between opposite constraints of undeniable legitimacy. Dialectic is not a methodological "flip-flop" but a realistic way of relating in productive tension elements which are very different, even opposites, because reality and truth are better accessible to us if both elements are acknowledged rather than if either one or the other is denied for the sake of neatness or static finality. The dynamic character of dialectical process tends to make it difficult to arrive at complete and closed solutions or explanations, but it is better to have all the relevant elements in the attempted explanation than to simplify by excluding some real factors. Hence, I have tried to indicate some of the main constraints that will be honoured or expressed in the process of developing a Spirit christology. The shape of the process or method remains yet to be proposed.

*The Method*

There are four stages in the method which I am going to follow. I have come to this understanding of christological method over a number of years of teaching christology and of being influenced by a long succession of christological books. Van Beeck, in particular, fixed some elements of the method firmly in my convictions. Recently, David Tracy (1981) confirmed for me the four stages in christological method by his brilliant analysis of the four moments that are involved in the interpretation of any classic text.

The first stage in the christological method here is to examine the nature and content of relevant preunderstanding. "The interpreter of the classic comes ... with a certain preunderstanding of the subject matter" (Tracy 1981, p.118). The second stage is to consider the "realized experience" of Christ, the "claim to attention ... on the subject by the classic text." In theological terms, the second stage is to consider the character of the faith in Jesus as the Christ which gives occasion for doing christological work at all. This faith occurs in the church and is mediated by recollection of Jesus as known in the scriptures and traditions of the church.

The third stage is to "employ some model of dialogue to indicate the appropriate kind of response to the realized experience of the classic" (p.120). This is the stage of systematic reflection which builds on the basis of preunderstanding and experience of Jesus as the Christ mediated by historical recollection. Needless to say there are a number of important questions to be clarified about how recollection and reflection are done appropriately.

The fourth stage in christological method is to relate the model as developed in recollection and reflection to the "entire community of inquirers" (p.120) which, in the case of a theology of salvation, includes both the community of the church members and the larger community of all human beings who may not be actively inquiring about Christ but who nonetheless are in need of, and are possibly seeking, some kind of salvation.

In this chapter on method each stage of the method needs to be looked at critically. Then, in subsequent chapters the stages themselves will be carried out, except for the last stage which will be dealt with in a subsequent study.

## *Preunderstanding*

Some theologians have been reluctant to acknowledge that christology is affected by any prior knowledge. They try to affirm that christology comes before all other knowledge and should remain independent of any cultural or philosophical understandings. As Kasper sums up the question, "One either sees as Rahner requires, Christology as lying within the God-world relation, or like Karl Barth, one explains the God-world relation within Christology" (1976, p.21). Barth would not concede that any preunderstanding, philosophical or even theological, was operative in his own christological efforts. He believed that christology should influence all other knowledge of God and the world, rather than vice versa. Barth criticized Tillich severely for his method of correlation in which the questions which theology answers are to be discerned by listening to the current intellectual analysis of the world and its problems, the "creative self-interpretation in all realms of culture" (Tillich 1951, p.63). To Barth, Tillich's method amounted to letting the world write the agenda for theology, a dangerous practice which could subvert the gospel to the vested interests of the world. Tillich, on the other hand, insisted that "God's answers" as revealed in the scriptures were not secondary to the cultural questions but in a circular, interdependent relationship with them so that the answers influence the questions, as well as vice versa. He accused Barth, in turn, of casting the gospel like a stone without making any effort to package it in contemporary concepts that the hearers might understand.

Tillich's position on the interdependence of theology and philosophy in theological method appears to have more validity than Barth's claim for a completely autonomous christological method. It is simply not true that christology is written as it were, on a *tabula rasa,* a clean sheet with no presuppositions or prior knowledge affecting it.[2] Barth's own theology was clearly influenced by philosophical traditions, even if he disclaimed them. Barth was correct in warning of the danger of acculturated theology but incorrect in refusing to acknowledge the interdependence of theology and other human knowledge.

Kasper refers to Wiederkehr's proposal that the relationships of theology and philosophy be conceived as "an ellipse with two focal points" (1976, p.21). This sounds much like Tillich's position. In the development of christology, as in any theology, the knowledge of the world (philosophy) must be conceded to be a formative influence along with what is revealed. "There is no escape from history and language ... and all linguistic meanings are human social products" (Cupitt 1982, p.4). The language used in christological formulations has its history and its meanings which are presuppositions and preunderstandings brought to christology and not simply derived from it, although the terms may be decisively influenced by the christology in the process of being used for the christology. We do not come to begin our christology "naked" of all language and understanding. There is no "innocent eye" (McFague 1982, p.79) which can see Jesus Christ without the filters or lenses of our previous knowledge and experience that colour and shape what we see. Better we try to examine and be aware of the preunderstanding that influences our christology than to deny its existence.

*a) The Human Condition*

Of all the knowledge we have at our disposal what should be considered to be directly germaine to christology? If Tillich was right one element of preunderstanding to be considered is the diagnosis of the human condition done in the light of knowledge of God (revelation) from our tradition. Tillich quotes from John Calvin's *Institutes* (I, 48) to support this contention:

> The knowledge of ourselves is not only an incitement to seek after God, but likewise a considerable assistance towards finding [God]. On the other hand it is plain that no [one] can arrive at the true knowledge of [oneself] without having first contemplated the divine character, and then descended to the consideration of [one's] own (1951, p.63).

We come to christology with some preunderstanding of ourselves and of God.[3] This preunderstanding will take the form of questions about ourselves and about God as well as some accumulated knowledge about

---

[2] Cf. McFague (1982): "Whether religious or nonreligious, everyone who encounters Jesus as a parable of God does so with preconceptions of God." (p.50). Cf. also Boff (1978): "... When we comprehend we always go to the object with a precomprehension derived from our milieu, education, and the cultural ambience we breathe. Nevertheless, we ought to distinguish very clearly between precomprehension and preconception. ... [the latter] judges the object and does not let itself be judged by the object (p.38-39).

[3] Cf. Ogden (1982): "There are two other questions to which the christological assertion is also intended to give an answer at the same time that it is intended to assert who Jesus is. On the one hand, there is the question 'Who is God?' understood as asking about the ultimate reality upon which we are each dependent for our own being and meaning as human persons. On the other hand, there is the question 'Who are we?' ... Unless one were already asking about one's own identity and the identity of the mysterious ultimate reality ..., one neither would nor could ask the question 'Who is Jesus?'" (p.28-29).

ourselves and about God. Questions about ourselves will involve presuppositions about all of humanity and the world and the cosmos. They will also be specifically pointed at the situation to which we think the saving significance of Jesus may have or should have the most bearing. Hence, liberation christologies begin with the questions about the poor and oppressed. In any case, the understanding and concern about evil and suffering and wrong is in a sense prior to christology, as well as subsequently influenced by christology. "Resistance to all forms of evil and suffering, in whatever guise they appear among us is then the precondition for ... an authentic faith in God and sincere confession of Christ" (Schillebeeckx 1979, p.616).

*b) Knowledge of God as Spirit*

The activity and revelation of God did not begin with Jesus nor, for that matter, stop with Jesus. We bring some understanding derived from the Hebrew scriptures and from our own experience and possibly from other sources in our world. In this respect we are similar to Jesus himself who brought to his self-interpretation, whatever that was, a knowledge of God derived from the Hebrew scriptures, his own experience and the cultural traditions of his time and place. Specifically, then, for the development of Spirit christology we need to examine our preunderstanding of God and Spirit and our understanding of the world and humanity interacting with Spirit. We need to consider how God's Spirit is involved in creation, revelation and recreation and how evil occurs in the creation. The understanding of Spirit will be derived primarily from the scriptures interpreted in light of experience and contemporary knowledge of humanity and the world.

This "preunderstanding" of Spirit and world will be worked out in the next chapter. At this point a sketch will indicate something of the direction to be taken. God as Spirit will be seen as the power of life, the animating energy in the physical dimension, the power of "information" or memory in the evolutionary process which produces the systems of all kinds in the created world. Spirit is the power of faith, hope, love, courage and the power and meaning of vocation and the power of good ethos in human communities. God as Spirit is the power of words and wisdom as well as energy and love. Evil will be defined in terms of the conflict and alienation of the systems in the world. The dynamics of systems and their ideologies will be illuminated not only by scientific analysis but also by the biblical understanding of the principalities and powers.

At least two major advantages accrue from developing the preunderstanding related to christology in close dialogue with biblical sources. First, one may reduce the risk feared by Karl Barth of importing alien philosophical categories and ideas into theology and christology which preempt the central meaning that might originate in the historical tradition of the community of faith. When the Logos-Incarnation-Trinity paradigm of Christianity was being formulated some of the central ideas did not come from the Hebrew religious tradition of Jesus but from cultural sources belonging to other religious and philosophical traditions. Unless one is to opt for wide open syncretism or enthusiasm in which root meanings can be grafted into Christian theology from any source whatever, there is surely value in developing root meanings as much as possible in consonance with the distinctive understandings of scriptural traditions. It is true that "we are not limited to the received tradition nor to scripture in our search for authentic christological names" because "our process is the same as that which went on in the writing of the New Testament and has continued ever since in Christian literature, preaching, and teaching" (Driver 1981, p.26). However, our freedom from scripture and tradition is only similar to that of the writers of the New Testament if we, like them, have a primary commitment to scripture.

The question of the significance of the canon cannot be explored at this point except to affirm, in the tradition of Reformed theology, a considerable commitment to the canon of scripture. One does not have an absolute commitment to the canon of scripture because that would mean idolizing it and denying or ignoring understandings which conflict with parts of scripture but which are in honesty undeniable for modern people. The profound appreciation, however, of the understandings of God and humanity and the world that emerged in the Hebrew religious tradition impel one to work out one's basic ideas on these subjects in close conjunction with that tradition. We will consider the question of the canon more fully when we look at the stage of "recollection" in christological method.

Another advantage of recovering, if possible, the biblical understandings as root meanings in a christological paradigm is that one may remain close to the ideas which Jesus himself had about God, humanity and the world. To be sure, those ideas will inevitably be interpreted and expressed differently in our linguistic and cultural context.[4] Despite the best efforts to retrieve the mind of Jesus there will be differences between what we think and what he thought. If we do not try for consonance with Jesus' thinking and do not recover with some degree of accuracy the use of some of the main terms and metaphors which were employed by Jesus and his original interpreters there is a good possibility that we will invent a new religion instead of participating in the tradition to which Jesus belonged. Why we should want to belong to his tradition rather than some other is the issue in the next section.

### The Starting Point for Christology: Religious Experience

We start to seek a logic of Christ, an explanation of the saving significance of Jesus of Nazareth, because we care passionately about him. Christology is not a disinterested academic exercise in historical research.[5] It is a quest impelled by faith, a search for adequate expression

---

[4]Cf. Hodgson (1971): "The task of christology in the first instance is not merely to repeat the faith of Jesus or the dogmatic norms of the tradition but rather to bring this faith to expression anew in ways that determine and direct our own existence.

\* \* \*

We can say again what came to expression in Jesus only by saying it differently. Within the continuity of content must be acknowledged discontinuity of form of expression" (p.42-43).

[5]Cf. Hodgson (1971): "Participation in the contemporary occurrence of the Christ-event is the fundamental 'prejudice' with which historical thinking about Jesus must begin" (p.41).

of the truth about one who has been experienced in such a compelling and vital way that the experience can only be called a religious experience.

What is religious has to do with what is ultimately real and important, what we call God. Tillich spoke of the religious as that for which we have "ultimate concern." Tracy sees religion as having to do with what we sense pertains to the whole of reality. The religious is not just one perspective among others, such as economic or political or aesthetic; it is the perspective which includes and embraces all other perspectives. It is the perspective of the whole of reality, the ultimate and infinite reality beyond all finite perspectives and including all finite realities. Religious experience entails an experience of the mystery at the limits of the known, at the horizon of all there is to know.

In the case of the experience of Jesus which starts christological endeavour one has an experience of conviction that here is the ultimate in authentic human being, here is one who participates in the mystery of the Ultimate, here we can say no other, so help us God, but that this Jesus is of supreme importance to us and to the world as we understand it. Of all the prophets and holy people we know or have ever heard about, Jesus, we believe is the very limit of what we can conceive as good and Godly and worthy to be known and proclaimed. His significance we are convinced is religious, not merely historical. He is of Godly significance, which is to say that when we care about him and adopt his way of living we are at the same time caring about the will of God for human life.

Such an experience of religiously caring about Jesus is the point at which christology begins. Christology, therefore, is an activity that goes on in the church where people care in this way about Jesus. In the language of the earliest disciples Jesus is thought to be the Christ of God, and it is Christians who do christology. If the experience of caring religiously about Jesus were absent the study of him would not properly be called christology. *"Christology deals with Jesus as the basis of the confession and the faith that he is the Christ of God"* (Pannenberg, 1968, p.21). This begs the question, for the moment, of what "the Christ of God" means; but whatever its meaning it is clearly a religious ascription which says something about God as well as about Jesus. It does not necessarily mean that Jesus is God — in fact it clearly does not say that. It says that Jesus is the "anointed one" of God, one chosen or designated or "sent" by God to accomplish certain of God's purposes. The confession and the faith that Jesus is the Christ are religious, i.e. directed to God even if the focus is on Jesus.

Theologians who have come to the conclusion, in accordance with the orthodox paradigm of the Christian religion, that Jesus *is* God will say that the starting point of christology is "the phenomenology of faith *in* Christ" (Kasper 1976, p.28) (Italics mine). Others, such as Tracy or Driver, will hold more accurately that faith is basically theocentric, a relationship between people and God. One might then speak of faith in God *through* Jesus Christ but, strictly speaking, one should not speak of faith in Jesus, if one means by faith what one means when referring to faith in God. We commonly use the term faith in many ways and even in totally secular contexts, such as "I have faith in my old car," but when we say "I have faith in God" it means something quite different. Faith in God is not conditioned by this or that caveat. It is not contingent upon any historical facts. We would not in faith say "I will be loyal to God as long as the money keeps coming in" or "I trust in God, if there is one."[6]

If we had faith in Jesus we would have to say something like "I have faith in Jesus if he was like the reports we have received about him" or "if he was not a Zealot as some scholars say he was." Faith in Jesus would necessarily be a matter of wilfully guaranteeing certain historical events and interpretations which might, in fact, not be as we think they were. Faith in God is not falsifiable by any historical events, although certain types of experience such as suffering or affluence may cause people to lose faith. Faith may be turned off, so to speak, by being diverted to some other object but in itself it is not conditioned by this or that historical contingency. Faith is an utter trusting of what is unconditioned and uncaused and inexplicable or ineffable. It is like walking on seventy fathoms of water, trusting one's life to the mystery of the deep which has been disclosed to us in various ways as trustworthy and benevolent.

According to the second of the Ten Commandments faith in God cannot be directed to any images of God, even though God is disclosed in things we can see as well as hear, such as pillars of fire, columns of smoke, plumblines and people. "The subject (some would say object) of Christian faith is not Jesus of Nazareth but God" (Driver 1981, p.29). In his analysis of faith Tracy agrees:

> Faith is, above all and prior to any articulation of specific beliefs, a matter of fundamental disposition and orientation involving the responses of both real trust and genuine loyalty to the object of faith. For the Christian *that faith is always directed to God,* the God of Abraham, Isaac, Jacob and Jesus Christ (1981, p.47) (Italics mine).

Tracy goes on to say that as part of their trust and loyalty to God Christians focus on Jesus as God's representative. It is an incalculable blessing to receive the disclosure of God in Jesus Christ, and those who know Jesus and care passionately about him find their faith in God to be very much, if not entirely *through* Jesus — not entirely, because there are other people both before and after Jesus in whom God has been present and disclosed. The disclosure of God in and through Jesus is of such immense, decisive significance for those who have experienced it that they are constrained to call him the Christ of God or other titles that indicate his singular importance. Christology is the intellectual process of critically examining the significance of Jesus for faith in God. It is the academic discipline of exploring what of God is typically disclosed in Jesus, what are the characteristic experiences of faith that people have in encounter with Jesus as the Christ.

---

[6]Cf. Frankl (1975): "Either belief in God is unconditional or it is not belief at all. If it is unconditional it will stand and face the fact that six million died in the Nazi holocaust; if it is not unconditional it will fall away if only a single innocent child has to die" (p.15-16).

God is presumably free to "speak" to faith or "show" to faith any number of things, but over the centuries the community of disciples of Jesus have recognized certain experiences as being characteristic of what God discloses through Jesus. The characteristic experiences of faith for Christians have been celebrated in liturgy, religious instruction, and church life. There has been a discernible consensus in the Christian community over the years about what are the central elements of the faith experienced in the encounter with Jesus. The consensus has not been total. There are many variations and many different explanations, but what Tillich called the "Catholic substance" of the Christian faith can be traced and studied. In so far as that faith has a connection to Jesus it is the proper object of christology inside the Christian community, even if the explanations arrived at in christological work are subsequently used in proclamation or dialogue with those outside the church. The church is the place where the experiences of God in Jesus Christ occur and such experiences are what give occasion for working out the logic of Christ. "It remains the realized experience which must serve as the first word and the final criterion of relative adequacy in any attempt at both understanding and explanation" (Tracy 1981, p.113). Barbour concurs:

> Both the cognitive claims of religion and its living practice must be grounded in experience.... A return to the experiential basis of religion is important for its renewed vitality in practice, as well as for a sound epistemology in theory (1974, p.8).

Christology as a function of the Christian community is concerned about both the renewed practice of faith and a sound epistemology.

*Three Focal Points*

What then are the main characteristic expressions of God in the typical encounters with Jesus in the church community? There are three focal points, namely the life, death and resurrection of Jesus that have given rise to experiences shared widely, even universally, in the Christian community. Each focal point, or what might be called classic event, has engendered many different experiences with many possible interpretations. The specific kinds of experiences people have in relation to the three focal points in the history of Jesus and the kinds of interpretations rendered for those experiences depend at least in part on the kinds of questions and circumstances people bring to the encounter with Jesus. There is a very real sense in which the world does at least partly write the agenda for revelation. A better way of saying the same thing is to say that God meets people where they are and discloses something or "says" something related to the needs and questions which they think are most significant at the time. As Tillich once said "nothing is as irrelevant as the answer to an unasked question." God does not indulge in irrelevant disclosures. God's disclosures may be surprising and may create awareness of significant questions and issues so it is not true that the world entirely writes the agenda for God's disclosures. God comes to the real situations and circumstances in which people find themselves, and people experience the presence of God as directly relevant to the significant issues and concerns which they perceive in the world.

The experiences of God in relation to Jesus, then, vary in relation to the changing contexts of people in history. The interpretations of God's disclosures in Jesus also vary accordingly. However, the focal points in Jesus' history do not change and these focal points by their very nature tend to produce similar kinds of experiences, even if people are in quite different contexts. The events of Jesus life, for example, including his actions and teachings, in so far as it is possible to retrieve them historically, tend to produce similar understandings of what Jesus was like. We are talking here about a very rough consensus, of course, because historical retrieval on the basis of the very limited amount of evidence and the kind of evidence that we have of Jesus' life is not likely to produce unanimous interpretations or responses. It is true nonetheless that there is considerable consensus on some things, such as that Jesus associated with people who were generally despised in his society and that Jesus both advocated and himself practiced mercy toward those whose needs of one kind or another were dire. The encounters with these and other aspects of Jesus' life tend to create similar religious experiences in people of widely different times and places. The experiences will be similar at least to the extent of being profoundly significant experiences of judgment or affirmation which decisively affect the thinking and feelings of the persons involved. "To encounter Jesus, whether in the flesh or through the New Testament pictures of him, has always been liable to be a turning point in anyone's life, a crisis of salvation or judgment" (Hick 1977 p.172). People have experienced such profoundly significant meanings in connection with each of the main focal points of Jesus' life, death and resurrection.

The religious experiences related to the death of Jesus are many and varied as we shall see in a later chapter, but there is also a very common tendency for the cross to be the occasion for people to experience God's judgment on what is wrong with the world and to experience God's call to self-giving similar to Jesus' self-sacrifice. In Jesus' crucifixion is seen the kenotic humility which is cited in the early Christian hymn in Philippians 2:5-11. "Christ Jesus ... did not covet equality with God as a thing to be grasped but emptied himself and became obedient unto death, even death on a cross." In going to the cross Jesus manifested what the prophet Micah said God requires of people, namely, "to do justice, and to love kindness, and to walk humbly with your God" (Micah 6:8 RSV). The encounter with this aspect of Jesus' death creates a crisis of judgment on any circumstances in which such justice and kindness and humility are transgressed.

As a powerful sign of appropriate humility before God and before one another, the cross has direct bearing on theological method, including christological method. The cross is the sign of the principle of human limitation and finitude, the sign of mortality, the sign that humans are not God because they do die and are finite and fallible. In theological method, therefore, the experience of the cross becomes a self-critical principle which acknowledges that Christians and their words and ideas and actions are like "earthen vessels" (II Cor. 4:7 RSV) that can be broken and replaced. This self-critical principle in theology and life is what Paul Tillich called "the Protestant Principle." It is by no means only protestant but is so called because of the historical protestant objection to claims of infallibility by anyone in the church.

In christological method the way of the cross implies the principle that all formulations are reformable and not absolute or perfect. Humility in our dialogue about Christ requires acceptance of the fact that all our ideas and words are only human ideas and words which cannot claim divine authority for themselves or grasp "equality with God." Christians in dialogue about Christ are, as D. T. Niles so classically put it, "like one beggar telling another beggar where to find food." The cross is the principle of our methodological poverty.

Christians who deny themselves and take up the cross and follow Jesus accept the weakness, poverty and possible mortality of their ideas and theological formations. The way of the cross as it pertains to forming and exchanging ideas, even ideas about God or Christ, is a way of humble, vulnerable love of God and one's neighbour. It is a way of faith which walks in the presence of the *mysterium tremendum* and *mysterium fascinans* which we encounter in Jesus going to his death.

There is a sense in which the resurrection has priority over the other two focal points if one understands the resurrection to be the event which enables people to have a contemporary encounter with Jesus at all. In other words, if encounter with Jesus is not merely a matter of remembering Jesus in the past and being moved by the meaning or the stories about him but more than that, a personal encounter of some kind in which Jesus is deemed to be present in some way, then it would appear that it can only be the risen, "living" Jesus who initiates experiences of himself in the present. Driver contends however, that "one of the oldest tensions within Christianity, reflected in the New Testament itself ... [was] whether Christ was and is an active agent in the real world or only the subject of an internal process called 'faith'" (1981, p.6). We will look at the question of Jesus' resurrection and the place of the Spirit in relation to it in more detail later on.

No matter how it is explained, it would still seem to be true that the resurrection has a priority in the genesis of Christian religious experience. Without the resurrection experience of the early disciples, whatever that experience was, it is unlikely that we would even have heard about Jesus of Nazareth at all. The resurrection was singularly significant for the emergence of a Christian church in the first place, although the other two focal points were also very significant. Van Beeck insists that the resurrection experience of the early disciples conditioned everything they remembered or recorded about Jesus. Hence, any subsequent experiences we may have which are focused on Jesus' life or death are already affected by the influence of the resurrection on the New Testament records which facilitate those experiences of Jesus' life and death. "The witness' sayings must be considered, not primarily as discernments that convey their involvement in shared human concerns but as statements that make their point to the extent that they succeed in representing Jesus Christ alive and present" (1979 p.259).

This appears to me to be an extreme and unwarranted claim. Some of the New Testament records about Jesus are certainly rhetorical in nature but some are also reports of what Jesus said and did regardless of whether he was subsequently raised by God from death. It is better, I think, to see the three focal points of Jesus' life, death and resurrection as each being capable of giving occasions for religious experiences, rather than to subsume the first two under the influence of the resurrection to the extent that Van Beeck does.

The resurrection is characteristically experienced by people in the church as a powerful initiative by God pursuant to the tragic event of Jesus' death. The resurrection casts Jesus' death in a different light changing, if not removing, the nature of its tragedy. It thereby creates hope for people in the midst of other tragedies in other times and places. Thus, the religious experience of God's raising of Jesus is typically an experience of hope, although there can be much other meaning in it as we shall see.

The resurrection is for many Christians the sign that in spite of limitations and even mortality human beings can participate in the Reign of God which is truth and righteousness, beauty and love. The power of the resurrection is the power of God to impart life in mortal persons, to bring goodness out of imperfect conditions, to fill earthen vessels with glorious treasure, to justify sinners, to raise up what is fallen, to call into service and to sanctify those who, like Isaiah, are ones "of unclean lips" who "dwell in the midst of a people of unclean lips" (Isaiah 6:5 RSV). The resurrection signifies the possibilities of God which exist in spite of creaturely impossibilities.

In christological method, as in all christological work, it is the power of the resurrection which provides for the possibility of truth and ethical expression in spite of the finite ethnocentric, "hypothetical" nature of theological statements. Theological formulations, like other human activities, can be "justified by grace," affirmed and used by God in spite of their shortcomings.

The life, death and resurrection of Jesus are, thus, the focal points out of which the religious experiences of Christians come which are the raw material, the starting point, for christological work. One focal point or another may attract the concentrated attention of one theologian or another. In the end, however, the experiences connected with all three must be explored if christology is to be adequate. "The event of Jesus Christ, as most theologians eventually acknowledge, is expressed with relative adequacy only in the full range of the symbols cross—resurrection—incarnation" (Tracy 1981, p.426). Incarnation is a problematic term but it cannot be taken to mean less than the presence of God in the life and teachings and actions of Jesus.

*Holy Spirit in Christological Method.*

In the history of Christian theology there has been a long and continuous consensus that the Holy Spirit is actively involved in any contemporary religious experiences having to do with Jesus. The New Testament writers themselves explained their Christian experience in these terms. In John 14:26 Jesus is reported to say that "the Holy Spirit, whom the Father will send in my name, he will teach you all things, and bring to your remembrance all that I have said to you." Again, in John 16:13-15, "When the Spirit of truth comes ... He will glorify me, for he will take what is mine and declare it to you. All that the Father has is mine; therefore I said that he will take what is mine and declare it to you." These passages clearly suggest that the teachings and actions of Jesus' life will be remembered or reanimated for people by the activity of the Spirit. St Paul's theology clearly indicates his belief that Jesus' death and resurrection are similarly reanimated for people when they encounter Jesus at these points "in the Spirit."

There is no question, therefore, of there being any kind of christology whatsoever without the involvement of the Holy Spirit. Since any faithful encounter with Jesus occurs "in the Spirit" there is a sense in which all christology is Spirit christology. Hence, "the religious event of the experience in the Spirit of the Christ is the constitutive reality mediated through the traditions in all christologies (Tracy 1981, p.317). The Spirit, however, has most commonly been conceived to be only the vehicle or medium of our experience of Jesus rather than the very presence of God in Jesus which is the "object" of any experiences of real faith we might have in connection with Jesus. The Spirit in Christian experience has consistently been interpreted to be a subordinate factor which only facilitates the more important factor of getting to know Jesus. The Spirit in this view is more like the telephone lines than like the person to whom we are speaking on the telephone. When the Spirit has such secondary importance in a christology it is not accurate to call such a christology Spirit christology.

Spirit christology is one in which the very person of God who is encountered in Jesus' life, death and resurrection is the Spirit of God. Whenever God is present, be it in nature or in prophets, in Jesus or in followers of Jesus, God is present as Spirit. Our christology, which accepts this premise, will try to work through the implications that are in accordance with this foundational understanding of God.

If the disclosures of God in the life, death and resurrection of Jesus are disclosures of God as Spirit then it is fair to assume that they are not entirely different in kind from the disclosures of God as Spirit which have occurred elsewhere in human history. Regardless of the question of God's self-disclosure in other religious traditions, Christians can hardly deny that the God disclosed in Jesus was also disclosed as Spirit in the history of the Hebrew people prior to the time of Jesus.[7] Marcionite attempts to relegate the disclosures of God in the Hebrew scriptures to a secondary and even inauthentic status have rightly been discouraged in the Christian community, albeit not always vigorously or consistently. In practice much Christian theology has been formulated as if the disclosure of God in Jesus Christ were of an entirely different order

---

[7]Macdonald (1927) quotes Novatian as follows: "the Spirit promised in the Gospel is not a new Spirit, nor even newly given ... one and the same Spirit dwelt in the prophets and the apostles" (p.79).

and kind from the ways God has been disclosed elsewhere. A Spirit christology might correct this misperception and explore the nature of God's self-disclosure in Jesus in explicit comparison with the nature of God's self-disclosures elsewhere. The question of which criteria might be used to resolve contrasts between Christian peoples' experience of God and other peoples' will be looked at presently.

At the moment it may be useful to look briefly at how characteristic experiences of God in connection with Jesus' life, death and resurrection compare with the general types of religious experiences which have been identified in studies of religion. Religious experience has been classified in various terms, but there is a discernible consensus about the basic nature of religious experience.

## *The Nature of Religious Experience in General*

When people encounter God in their experience they typically have a complex or dialectical experience involving both negation and affirmation. Classifications of religious experience almost invariably propose terms to represent both of the basic elements. Accounts of religious experience which ignore or deny one element or the other (often it is the negative element which is overlooked) are unconvincing caricatures of real encounters with God. Over the centuries and around the earth there have simply been too many recurrences of the dialectical (negative-positive) experience of God to doubt that authentic religious experience has both elements. As a human phenomenon, faith entails the experience of both promise and judgment, a sense of participation in ultimate reality and a sense of separation, a rejoicing in awareness of the right and a lamenting consciousness of wrong.

*a) Manifestation and Proclamation*

Paul Ricoeur, followed by Tracy and others, has classified these two moments or forms of religious experience as "manifestation" and "proclamation," the latter being the "negative" expression of non-participation or distancing from the object of the religious experience, while manifestation is the experience of participating positively in the Ultimate Reality as known in the religious experience. The two elements cannot be entirely separated from each other, although different religious traditions can emphasize one more than the other, thus producing what Tracy calls "trajectories" of manifestation or proclamation (1981, pp.376 ff.). The two forms of religious experience are actually dialectical and mutually dependent elements of a single kind of event, namely the event of faith, but the distinction between the two moments or elements of religious experience is real and important.

Rudolph Otto in *The Idea of the Holy* spoke about the *mysterium tremendum* and *mysterium fascinans* as the two elements in the experience of the Holy. The "tremendous" mystery is Ultimate Reality encountered as awesome and fearsome in its implications for people. The Real proclaims Itself as much beyond what presently is, by comparison negating what is and calling it to become what it might be. To know the "tremendous" mystery is to feel the distance or separation between what we are and what is Ultimately Real. To know the "fascinating" mystery is to feel embraced and affirmed within the Ultimately Real. It is to be drawn into reunion with the Mysterious Whole who embraces all things. The experience of *mysterium fascinans* is an experience of love and blessedness, of comforting well being and satisfying beauty. The experience of *mysterium tremendum* is a realization of (unfulfilled) purpose, a conviction of meaning to be achieved, a call to obedience.

*b) Mystical and Numinous*

These two basic elemental aspects of religious experience occur in relation to both mystical and numinous religious experiences. The terms mystical and numinous refer to another pair of basic distinctions which have been discerned in human religious experience. Mystical experience is apophatic, that is, an experience of the Ineffable through the *emptying* of meaning. Mystical experience is characteristically achieved affectively by an ascetic discipline or, theologically, by a *via negativa,* a way of approaching the Ineffable Truth by saying what it is not. Numinous experience, on the other hand, is meaning-laden experience in which the Mysterious Reality communicates meaning in the imaginative activity of the person's experience. Numinous experience is kataphatic — an imaginative event in which symbols convey aspects of the meaning of Ultimate Reality. The nature of symbols as distinct from metaphors and myths will be developed in the next chapter. Here it can be said that they are vehicles of numinous religious experiences which, like mystical experience disclose the tremendous and fascinating mystery of God.

*c) Rational and Attitudinal*

Urban T. Holmes (1980) provides a phenomenology of prayer which shows another pair of factors that are also involved in religious experience. Apophatic or kataphatic, mystical or numinous experiences are also related to the speculative or rational, and the affective or attitudinal, propensities of human beings. Thus, mystical or numinous experiences are typically expressed in either affective or speculative terms and certainly have to do with both the mental and attitudinal aspects of human existence.

The structure or phenomenology of religious experiences then, can be seen to involve a number of basic elements. By adding the tremendous and fascinating aspects of divine Mystery to Urban T. Holmes' proposed phenomenology we are able to represent the dynamics of religious experience in a diagram as below.

**The Speculative or Rational Capacity for Expression**

**The Tremendous and Fascinating, Mystical or Apophatic Experience**

**The Tremendous and Fascinating, Numinous or Kataphatic Experience**

**The Affective or Attitudinal Capacity for Expression**

All four poles of the diagram are inseparably present in any religious experience. The numinous has some dimensions of the mystical in it and vice versa. Both are both tremendous and fascinating or, in Ricoeur's terms, both entail both proclamation and manifestation. And both the rational and attitudinal capacities of human beings are expressed in the expressions of religious experience.

The point of developing this model for understanding religious experience is to have appropriate terms for describing specifically Christian experience as the raw material or starting point of christological reflection. God as Spirit has been experienced in many religions in the ways indicated in the above model. In Isaiah 6, for example, the religious experience of the prophet has been seen by many interpreters to be a classic example of encounter with God, involving the tremendous and fascinating aspects of manifestation and proclamation as well as the mystical and numinous experiences expressed both rationally and affectively.

The experiences that Christians have in encountering God as Spirit in Jesus Christ are similar kinds of experiences. The dual or dialectical aspects of judgment and promise are typical of Christian experiences of faith. The experience of the power of God in the resurrection of Jesus is characteristically a positive experience of affirmation, forgiveness, promise and hope. It confirms identity as a participant in God's Ultimate Reality, giving comfort and a sense of the goodness and benevolence of God. The experience of the way of the cross is more typically an experience of the judgment of God on the earth and everyone in it, including Christians themselves who sense their failure to participate fully in the Reality of God, identifying with those disciples and others who crucified Jesus and did not participate in the meaning and purpose of God which Jesus proclaimed.

Cross and resurrection cannot be separated in authentic Christian experience.[8] The risen Christ is the one who was crucified — and vice versa. The Christian sacrament of baptism epitomizes the inseparability of the cross and resurrection when it reenacts dying and rising by the believer going down into the water and emerging again to new life through Christ. Baptism by sprinkling loses some of the symbolism but, according to St Paul in Romans 6:3-11, the meaning of baptism consists of this reenactment of the inseparable cross and resurrection of Jesus. The religious experiences which Christians have in connection with the life and teachings of Jesus could also be shown to entail both manifestation and proclamation, both fascinating and tremendous experiences in dialectical relationship.

Similarly, too, Christian experiences of God in the life, death and resurrection of Jesus could be shown to be both mystical and numinous.

---

[8]Tracy (1981) warns against the danger in Spirit christologies of neglecting the cross. "The resurrection emphases of all pneuma christologies, from early Judaic Christianity through many Orthodox christologies to Kasper in our own period ... need to expose themselves further to the stark contradiction of the cross and the negativities—personal, social, political, historical and natural—of our and every situation" (p.314).

Christians are wont to speak of the mystery of the incarnation or the sacred mystery of the cross and the resurrection. The ineffable nature of God is experienced even as the purposes and personality of God are disclosed in the encounters with God in Jesus.

Christology begins at the point of expressing the religious experience of God encountered in the history of Jesus. That expression is not only rational; it can and must also be affective or attitudinal. Christology is a matter of praxis as well as doxa. In fact it should be both. The Spirit who is encountered in Jesus is a wholistic Spirit who includes both the rational word and affective relations as inseparable and necessary elements in the grace which faith receives and expresses.

In christological method, as already indicated, one necessary step is accurate recollection of the history of Jesus. Such recollection is equally important for affective or attitudinal expressions of the experience of God in Christ as it is for the more often emphasized rational expression of the logos of *Christus*. We turn now to the matter of appropriate recollection or retrieval of the history and traditions of Jesus as the Christ.

## Recollection of Jesus in Scripture and Tradition.

The intention of this section is not to do the actual work of recollecting the history of Jesus from the scriptures and tradition. This will be attempted to some extent in subsequent chapters. The aim here is to examine this step in christological method and discern some of the main aspects of the recollection or retrieval process. This necessarily very brief treatment of the relationship of christology and biblical and historical studies will touch on the issues of how retrieval is done, what are some of the main difficulties in the process and, finally, the importance or "authority" of what is retrieved for christological reflection.

*a) Historical and Literary Research*

Recollection or retrieval of the historical Jesus is done using all available methods of historical research. Whatever can be known about Jesus using the accepted methods of scholarly historians must be brought to light and considered by the theologian even if the results of historical study produce findings which are problematic for theology or christology. It is unthinkable that any recoverable truth about Jesus of Nazareth should be either ignored or suppressed for the sake of protecting christological formulations, whether traditional or revisionary. Furthermore, it has become increasingly clear that the New Testament records which provide evidence for the history of Jesus are also works of literature. The understandings and methods of literary criticism and linguistic analysis must also be brought to bear on the scriptural records. These, too, may shed light on the historical Jesus.

Historical and literary research, however, are not simple processes which produce incontestable, factual accounts of what happened or what was said in the past. Subjective factors which historians or literary critics bring to their work, make a degree of relativity inevitable in assertaining and interpreting what was said and done in the past. The subjective factor precludes any possibility of the historical records being considered as absolute. "Faith cannot escape the relativity of history and of historical judgment" (Driver 1981, p.7). Wiles agrees: "On no showing can the records of [Jesus'] life have absolute significance for us; [but] on any showing to which the name of Christian could conceivably be given his life would remain of substantial importance for us" (Hick (ed) 1977, p.8).

Historical research of any kind is inevitably a kind of hermeneutical or interpretive circle in which the discoveries about the past influence the thinking of the historian and the thinking of the historian influences the way in which the discoveries about the past are discerned and interpreted. This circular process is particularly inevitable in the case of theologians who begin their christological work with some kind of commitment to the singular importance of Jesus. Their theories about the historical Jesus are liable to be "value-laden." This understandable tendency toward bias implies a need for exceptional rigour by the theologian in exercising critical caution in the retrieval process. The possibility of pious self-deception is very real.

In the past hundred years or so an immense amount of attention has been given by Christian scholars to the methods and possibilities for recovering historical truth about Jesus. The outcome of the search has produced a widespread consensus on the kinds of difficulties there are in the undertaking and a less firm consensus on whether enough historical truth can be established to serve as raw material for what is said about Jesus in christological formulations.[9]

The difficulties of historical research on Jesus include not only all the ones which any historical research has to cope with but some which are peculiar to the particular nature of the New Testament writings that provide much of the source material for the research about Jesus. The writers of the New Testament were themselves highly biased or "value-laden" in the way they reported the events of Jesus' history. They expressed their interpretation of the significance of Jesus using ideas derived from a wide variety of contemporary traditions which are very difficult for the modern historian to disentangle and understand.

Moreover, the New Testament authors were not historians of the sort that exist today who try to be as disinterested as possible in their presentation of historical events. The New Testament authors present their references to Jesus in what might better be called rhetorical form rather than historical accounts. Their rhetoric was addressed to the particular circumstances of the congregations for whom they wrote, and one of the continuing circumstances common to the early Christian congregations was conflict with the Jews in the synagogues run by the Pharisees. As a result, there is a lot of anti-Jewish polemic which colours the way references to Jesus were recorded. "In the gospels Jesus of Nazareth has, so to speak, vanished into the background of the polemic

---

[9]Tracy (1981), for example, does not believe "that 'the historical Jesus' (i.e. the Jesus retrievable through modern historical-critical methods), as distinct from 'the Jesus witnessed to by the apostolic witness' can prove an appropriate standard or norm for the tradition (*that* norm is the apostolic witness)" (p.239). I do not agree with Tracy on this point. More is said about this question at the beginning of Chapter Four.

between 'Israel' and 'Church,' a problem which in that form Jesus had never encountered and perhaps had never intended" (Schillebeeckx 1979, p.22).

At the same time, however, the authors of the New Testament were themselves Jews and their characteristic method of creating rhetorical arguments in support of their commitment to Jesus was to "prove" their case by ingenious references and allusions to the Hebrew scriptures. These references are also not easy for the modern historical researcher to discern and interpret accurately. Another complicating factor in the background of the New Testament was that Jesus almost certainly spoke Aramaic whereas the New Testament books were invariably written in the Greek language.

This brief description by no means exhausts the difficulties facing any historian who wishes to retrieve a reasonably accurate picture of what Jesus of Nazareth actually said and did. The process is extremely complex and fraught with possibilities of misinterpretation. It appears to some theologians that in the midst of these difficulties "Jesus vanished into the thin air of speculation" (Driver 1981, p.35).

*b) The Importance of the Historical Jesus*

As a result, some have concluded that the historical Jesus is not of primary importance in christological formulations.[10] Driver is particularly forthright in explaining the situation as he sees it.

> The eschatological orientation of Jesus and the Evangelists is so different from that of our culture that we cannot reconstruct from the documents a Jesus whose character and deeds we might understand as both credible and realistic — that is, a "historical" Jesus, ... . We should remind ourselves that the Christian religion has never depended on knowing Jesus "as he actually was." ... The church is not founded upon the particulars of a historical person ... but upon what has come to be called "the Christ of faith" (1981, p.34).

Driver develops his point at considerable length, speaking about "the captivity of Christ in the likeness of Jesus" (p.83) and about it being "a fundamental error, and a costly one, for theology to seek the truth of ... Christianity exclusively in Christ's past" (p.47). Driver believes that Christianity, in order to be ethically effective, has to begin to act on its own authority rather than continuing to give "lip service to Christ as norm" (p.53).

Don Cupitt similarly develops his account of Christ's saving work as "logically independent of the truth of any historical statements about Jesus" (1982, p.104). He justifies this method on the basis that the Christian way of life should in principle be self-authenticating, "intrinsically worth living just for its own sake."

There can be little doubt that the content of Christian faith and ethics

---

[10]Cf. Green (1977): "It is astonishing that while Graeco-Roman historians have been growing in confidence, the twentieth century study of the Gospel narratives starting from no less promising material, has taken so gloomy a turn in the development of form criticism that the more advanced exponents of it apparently maintain — so far as an amateur can understand them — that the historical Christ is unknowable and the history of his mission cannot be written" (p.123).

are inevitably influenced by present circumstances and contemporary ways of thinking. Rosemary Radford Ruether (1981) shows how the christologies of Hans Küng and Edward Schillebeeckx, which profess to be based on reliable historical understanding of Jesus, are in fact shaped to a considerable extent by their particular theological biases. Ruether concludes that "this hermeneutical circle between our contemporary values, concerns and faith-stance and our reading of the Bible is inevitable" (p.2).

The admission of a hermeneutical circle, however, appears to be quite different than the claims of Driver and Cupitt to be "logically independent" from the Bible. In a hermeneutical circle there is a dialectical logic of interdependence which operates between the Bible and contemporary believers. Within the circle the Bible may still be judged to have an essential role, even a primary role in maintaining the continuity of the Christian community and tradition through successively changing eras. It is possible to argue that when Christians either in enthusiasm or through neglect have departed from scriptural tradition then undesirable aberrations have developed in Christian history.

As a result of a prodigious amount of scholarly work on the New Testament writings, Hebrew scriptures and other ancient texts there appears to be a solid core of reliable historical information about Jesus. We shall be looking at some of this material in due course. The point at the moment is to reaffirm that recollection through historical retrieval does constitute an indispensable process in christological method, albeit not a simple one but a dialectical one. The historical material about Jesus is subject to ongoing study, with the possibility of new interpretations and new discoveries, and theologians will come to do their christological work under the influence of different situations and divergent, urgent concerns. Despite these complexities they will continue to encounter the figure of Jesus as one whom they care passionately about. "For reflection and life it is the historical Jesus who is the key providing access to the total Christ" (Sobrino 1978, p.352). People who care about Jesus will not do their christological reflection without seeking direction and confirmation from the best historical information available about him.

Even in the case of Driver and Cupitt it can be seen that their conclusions about Christian faith are accompanied by many references to the biblical Jesus although they claim independence from him. Cupitt affirms that "although the historical connection is contingent, we have found that it is valuable and should be cherished" (1982, p.104). Driver likewise acknowledges the value of scripture while insisting strenuously that it cannot be treated as an external authority for faith: "the scriptures are part of our memory bank. Without them we would suffer institutional amnesia and go mad" (1981, p.91).

If the recollection or historical retrieval process is conceived to be a hermeneutical circle there is, *pacè* Driver, a certain degree to which the scriptures and the historical Jesus are an external authority for faith and for theological reflection on faith. Driver contends that we give to the scriptures whatever authority they have.

The church needs now to learn a lesson of psychological maturity. It should ask of scriptures "Who gave you the authority to be our text of reference?" And it should answer: "*WE* did" (1981, p.90).

In a sense this is true; unless we acknowledge their authority they will not have any authority for us. It is not true, however, that we create the authority that we give to scriptures. We recognize it; we do not produce it. The scriptures by their intrinsic quality command our respect. They create the existential commitment to their authority. We do not really give it to them. *They* give their own authenticity to us and we receive it as authoritative for living. This is the case for the historical Jesus and for many other parts of the New Testament and the Hebrew scriptures.

*c) Discerning Authentic Recollections*

It is true that for many people there are parts of the scriptures which they have to repudiate or ignore because the intrinsic immoral quality of those passages, or their factual inaccuracy, or their theological impropriety do not warrant respect or create authority which can be recognized. Jesus apparently disregarded some of the scriptural injunctions about observances of the Sabbath for ethical reasons under particular circumstances. St Paul repudiated the commandment requiring circumcision.

One of the authoritative meanings received from Jesus by many Christians is his message, confirmed by St Paul and other New Testament writers, that God desires people to be free, like beloved children rather than slaves, to act in whatever ways they think will serve the purposes of love. This message as well as others from Jesus have usually been seen by Christians to have authority over other parts of the scriptures.

The council of I John 4:1-6 to "test the spirits" by reference to their confession of Jesus is advice which most Christians have accepted, even though it is by no means an easy principle to apply. Jesus himself does not have "absolute" authority in so far as his words and actions have to be interpreted and received as authentic for faith and life. The interpretation and reception processes involve subjective activities that are very much relative to the time and place and state of knowledge of the people concerned. The truth about Jesus is determined not solely by the scriptural words alone but by a complex mix of the scriptures with the conscience, reason and contextual situation of those who try to articulate the truth.

*d) Discerning Authentic Traditions*

The factors involved in determining authentic recollection of Jesus as part of christological method apply also to discerning authentic traditions in the history of the Christian community. These traditions are, as Cupitt said of the scriptures, "valuable and should be cherished" although they do not have the same weight of authority for theology and living as the scriptures generally have or as Jesus, even more, has. The theological and ethical traditions of the church are historically relative similar to the relativity of the scriptures. They are analogously difficult to retrieve with historical accuracy. The church, moreover, has had a tendency to suppress parts of its own history which were deemed unfavourable for celebration and remembrance. The Gnostic Christian movements, including their Christian writings have only recently been retrieved as part of Christian history. The horrendous record of Christian persecution of the Jews remains unknown to many Christians despite the excellent retrieval done recently by Rosemary Ruether and others. Despite the "distressingly human" record of the church in its history there are still large sectors of the Christian church which continue to elevate their theological and ethical traditions to a degree of authority almost equal to that of the scriptures. The criteria of reason, conscience and contextual circumstances, as well as the criteria of Jesus and the scriptures should be applied to Christian history rather than accepting its traditions uncritically. The traditions are authoritative only if they pass "the test of the spirits" including the application of that test by critical, conscientious reason.

The question of authoritative truth and critical reason belong not only to the process of recollection and historical retrieval but also to christological reflection itself, the process of formulating statements about Jesus as the Christ of God. We now turn to that stage of christological method.

## *Christological Formation as Theological Reflection.*

Christological method is not in actuality a neat four stage procedure moving from preunderstanding to realized experience through historical retrieval to reflective formulations and then to societal or ecclesiastical application. Rather, all these elements of the method operate simultaneously or dialectically — mutually influencing each other in ways that make them difficult to isolate. Tillich spoke about theological method as a circular process of correlation in which cultural or philosophical preunderstanding influenced the reflective formulations of theology which, in turn, from tradition in the past and faith in the present, influenced the cultural preunderstanding and the topical questions.[11] Method of this kind might equally well have been described as a "swirl." Some such circular process also operates in liberation theologies and other theologies that have strong apologetic or ethical orientations. The context influences the theology which affects the analysis of the context. The Spirit christology to be worked out here will have a complex "circular," for want of a better word, method too.

Spirit christology is a "model of dialogue to indicate the appropriate kind of response to the realized experience" (Tracy 1981, p.120) of God in Jesus Christ. The Spirit christology model is fashioned out of a three-way interaction between (1) a theology of Spirit from the scriptures, including the New Testament witness to Jesus and the Spirit, (2) a contemporary understanding of the pluralistic world with its patterns or structures of evil which pose the questions of salvation in our time,

---

[11]Cf. Hodgson (1971): "It is insufficient to start with our contemporary situation alone. ... Just as we move backward only by moving forward, so also we move forward only by moving backward. Each new form of christological confession must be tested and interpreted by reference to the common content of christology — God's redemptive deeds in the words, activity, and fate of Jesus (p.44).

and (3) a contemporary understanding of Spirit as a metaphor based on realities which are known empirically in our time.

*a) Symbols, Metaphors, Concepts, Models and Doctrines*

The task at hand in this methodological chapter is to look at the ways models function in christology and how they can be evaluated for truth or adequacy. In order to understand models it is necessary to speak of metaphors, analogies and symbols as well as concepts and doctrines. Models have been defined as "sustained and systematic" (Barbour 1974,p.16) elaborations of metaphors or "dominant, comprehensive metaphors with organizing structural potential" (McFague 1982, p.193). As "a systematic set of analogies" (Barbour 1966, p.217) a model is more extensive or comprehensive than a single metaphor, although a model may be based mainly on a single metaphor which could be called a "root-metaphor." In the case of Spirit christology the model is based primarily on the root-metaphor of Spirit which will be expounded in the next chapter.

In elaborating on metaphors, models combine them with concepts and develop them into doctrines or theories. There is a kind of pyramid-building process that begins with symbols being expressed logically in metaphors which are then combined with concepts and elaborated in models and finally expressed in doctrines. The process moves from experience through imagination in metaphor to abstract thought whose purpose is to clarify and perpetuate the initial experience.[12]

The experience of symbols is the starting point. Symbols are "non linguistic bonds uniting us to the cosmos" (McFague 1982, p.120, citing Ricoeur). Symbols are usually things in the natural or physical world which in moments of insight are seen to represent some aspects of other realities which cannot be empirically perceived in the ways in which the symbols are perceived. In the experience of the Hebrew people, for example, the desert wind *(ruach)* which was so familiar to them became a symbol for the unseen reality of God.[13]

The meaning of symbols for what they symbolize is expressed in metaphors. Hence, the Hebrew people could speak of God's presence as God's *ruach* or say "God is *ruach*" which is a metaphorical statement. As McFague explains, "symbols need metaphors for without them they are dumb; metaphors need symbols, for without them they lose their rootedness in life" (McFague 1982, p.120). A symbol is a concrete reality which "participates in" (Tillich 1957, p.9) other kinds of reality. Through the symbols we are able to experience dimensions or elements of reality that are not knowable by direct sense perception. Thus "symbols open up levels of reality which otherwise are closed for us" (Tillich 1957a, p.42). Wind or breath seen as religious symbols for example, disclosed

---

[12] Cf. McFague (1982) on Ricoeur's theory of interpretation: "The overall goal of interpretation is *to return to the experience* the primary language expresses. In the case of Christianity, Ricoeur describes this experience as ... reorientation to the ways of the kingdom of God" (p.121).

[13] Ramsey (1973) argues that language about God can be revitalized if we recover the kind of process of "cosmic disclosure" (p.13) that took place in the experience of the Hebrew people for whom "discourse about God developed in the context of a gale, wind ... providing us with specimen discourse about Spirit" (p.5).

the mysterious, holy Reality of God to the Hebrew people. A symbol such as a wedding ring points to the unseen but very real love and commitment which exist between the marriage partners.

Metaphors state the relationship between the symbol and what is symbolized. A metaphor thereby expresses in an imaginative way some hitherto unknown truth about something or someone by referring to another familiar reality. It transfers connotations from something that is well known to something that is not yet known. For example, when Jesus, according to John, said "I am the vine" he was saying something to his disciples about himself that was not yet known by proposing an image which was well known to his disciples. They were invited, as it were, to transfer connotations from their knowledge of vines to their knowledge of Jesus. Not all the connotations of the symbol are transferable; Jesus is obviously not like a vine in certain respects. A metaphor, then, entails the contradiction of implying that something is and is not like what it symbolizes. This ambiguity is constitutive of metaphors. It is what makes them different from literal statements. The tension between the "is and is not" in a metaphor can be creative. It invites the imagination to explore what the is, and is not, consist of. It allows some freedom to the knower to interpret what is known by the metaphor. It does not "nail down" the reality of which it speaks, although it invites development of understanding in concepts and systematic reflection.

Parables and myths are similar to metaphors in this respect. They are stories of different kinds which combine symbols and metaphors in more complex narratives. This is not the time for a complete analysis of myth and parable . Very briefly the difference between myths and parables is that myths use analogy to expand understanding of what "is" whereas parables use analogy to challenge what is thought to be true by revealing what "is not" the case. "Myth establishes world ... . Parable subverts world" (Crossan 1975, p.59). Because Jesus used parables so frequently we will be looking at their significance more closely when we do the step of historical recollection in Chapter IV.

Metaphors, then, articulate the existence of particular symbols or images that both reveal in some ways and do not reveal in other aspects the truth about something hitherto unknown.

Models by comparison, are more fully elaborated interpretive schemes which can apply in many contexts. Models are based on metaphors which are sufficiently complex to allow for numerous connotations of the symbol to be spelled out conceptually and then applied in various contexts. The model "God as Spirit was in Jesus Christ" will be developed to show that the various connotations of the metaphor "God is Spirit" and the connotations of the symbols which feed this metaphor provide useful concepts that can be widely and fruitfully applied in Christian theology.

In models, the root-metaphor and the concepts derived from it have a "symbiotic" relationship "in which the metaphors provide 'food' for concepts and concepts provide 'sight' for metaphors" (McFague 1982, p.119). In the case of the Spirit christology model the concept of incarnation, for example, may describe the presence of Spirit in human beings and, specifically, in Jesus of Nazareth while the root-metaphor of Spirit in turn provides content for what the term incarnation means as it is used in the model of Spirit christology.

*b) Contextuality*

In addition to the input from religious experience through symbols and the input of imagination which discerns the metaphorical meaning of the symbols, models also receive input or influence from the environment in which the model is being developed.[14] The environment includes the cultural, historical and social conditions which create the fabric, so to speak, of thought and experience into which the christological model is being interwoven. Christological models by definition have to do with the question of what kind of salvation the Christ facilitates, and the cultural, historical and social conditions to a large extent create the urgent questions about salvation. The christological model, therefore, is influenced in its development by the theologian's understanding of what kinds of salvation are needed in the particular cultural, historical and social conditions of the times.

The understanding of the environment may well be influenced by the experiences of God which the theologian and the community of faith have had in the past, but the understanding of the environment is also shaped by the contemporary academic studies and artistic interpretations of it. In the model of Spirit christology to be developed in this book the understanding of the various kinds of systems in our environment and the ways in which these systems conflict to produce evil will have a central place. God as Spirit will be understood in relation to the systems, and God as Spirit in Jesus will be seen as indicating the way of salvation in the environment where evil occurs as a result of the conflict of pluralistic systems of power and thought.

*c) Criteria for Christological Models*

The question of truth is not an easy one in the complex "swirl" of christological method which involves revelatory insights in the experience of symbols, imaginative selections of meanings in the formation of metaphors, contemporary and therefore changeable understanding of cultural, historical and social conditions as well as the difficult task of historical retrieval of knowledge about Jesus and the church's tradition of belief.

Perhaps the first criterion for a christological model is whether or not it is a dynamic hermeneutical process. A temptation that not all theologians resist is to avoid the uncertainties and risks of reinterpretation and creative reflection by simply repeating the doctrinal formulations of another historical, cultural and social era. By this means they may claim more certitude for the ideas they advocate by appealing to the authority of tradition, but such heteronomous certitude is spurious and

---

[14]Cf. Tracy (1981): "The Christian belief in the reality of the Spirit ... impels Christians to search anew for the 'signs of the times.' There interpreters find those 'discerning questions and possible answers' in the situation whereby they rearticulate and allow to live again (as a new expression of spirit christology in and to a new situation) the empowering and discerning event of God's self-disclosure in Jesus Christ" (p.310).

vulnerable to rejection by autonomous fiat. The real authority of tradition must exist *theonomously* in a fresh speaking of its meaning by the "living" word of God which is re-interpreted and re-articulated in the new environment. The process of repeating doctrines anachronistically, rather than interpreting them contextually, is not an authentic theological process if one believes in a God who continues to live as Spirit, whose "dwelling ... is with [humanity]" (Rev 21:3) and who declares "Behold I make all things new" (Rev 21:5).

David Tracy, following Hans-Georg Gadamer, claims that authentic theological hermeneutic has the character of conversation in which understanding happens in the "back-and-forth movement" between the sources which provide information relevant to the question under discussion (1981, pp.99-107). The elements of the experience of symbols, metaphorical expression, historical retrieval and contextual knowledge "listen" to one another as it were, and correct each other, reflect on the subject at hand and produce a model which at the very least includes the dynamic interaction of these component elements.

This method could be described as "Spirited." Unless a christological method is "Spirited," alive to the present environment as well as the historical origins of tradition, unless it is hermeneutical, including the living word of God in relation to the present world, it cannot be regarded as a "true" model. Truth, it will be observed, is not here thought to be simply a matter of correspondence with static reality but more as a dynamic practical occurrence corresponding to the will of God for a changing world.

The dynamic, contemporary character of christological models suggests a second criterion, namely, ethical judgment or conscience. There can no longer be any doubt that christological models are capable of causing harm. Rosemary Ruether's book *Faith and Fratricide* has shown the theological roots of anti-Semitism. In *To Change The World* and in other writings Ruether has shown how christology can influence the systems that perpetuate poverty and political oppression, injustice to women and environmental abuse. Ruether is not alone, by any means, in realizing the ethical implications of christological models. Van Beeck reminds us that all christologies have a "performative function"(1979, p.306-7). Driver cites Sartre's insight that "no perception and no concept arises in the human mind apart from the thinking subject's intentionality toward its neighbour and its world" (Driver 1981, p.21). Hence, he concludes, "Before we trust any theological doctrine we should ask what is its socioethical consequence" (p.22). The ethical criterion for any christological model should ask not only what harm the model may do but what good contribution it might make to human healing and social justice. Jesus' warning about false prophets applies to "false" christologies as well. "You will know them by their fruits" (Mt 7:20 RSV).

The fruitfulness of a christological model may refer not only to its ethical consequences but also to its religious adequacy in communicating the full meaning of God's saving work in Jesus. This criterion of religious adequacy suggests that one of the basic functions of christological models is to evoke distinctive attitudes and elicit self-commitment (see Barbour 1974, p.7). John McIntyre suggests several criteria for christological models including that models should "mediate Christ, his love, his forgiveness, his power and his truth; [should] sustain faith and renew it with the very life of Christ; [should] lead to fresh commitment to him for work to be done in his name, ... and [should] issue in sincere obedience to Christ and to his will" (1966, p.81). McIntyre is clearly very christocentric in his own faith but theocentric christological models should also effectively mediate the meaning and Spirit of Jesus.

The religious adequacy of a christological model is the extent to which it allows the life, death and resurrection of Jesus to be occurrences of religious experience for the followers of Jesus. Adequacy to the biblical witness to Jesus is one aspect of this religious adequacy. Another is the appropriate retrieval of the Christian religious experience of the community of believers over the centuries. The biblical witness and witness of tradition, as well as the personal experience of the believer provide *supporting evidence* for a christological model. Barbour maintains this is "the most important criterion" (1974, p.143). Others like Kasper would insist that among the various kinds of supporting evidence Jesus himself is "the ultimate criterion" (Kasper 1976, p.28), and the faith of the church is the secondary criterion. Kasper insists that "neither of the two criteria can be pitted against the other."

This ignores the very real possibility that a christological model may emerge which is supported by evidence from Jesus and from other biblical writers as well as by personal experience in a particular environment but which is not so strongly supported by the tradition of the church. In fact, as was shown earlier paradigm shifts have occurred in the history of the church and may occur again. If a christological model entails a paradigm shift its supporting evidence from scripture and experience may well be at variance with some of the traditions of the church.

The religious adequacy of a christological model includes another dimension which may be listed as a criterion in itself namely, the *extensibility of application* of the model (See Barbour 1974, p.143). The fruitfulness of a model is not only its ethical application and its ability to engender authentic experience which corresponds to the experience of Jesus and the church; fruitfulness can also be measured in terms of the extent of application and the extent of experience mediated by the christological model. If a christological model only "plays on one string" as it were, and applies only to one very limited aspect of human experience its religious adequacy will be correspondingly limited. If, for example, a christological model were developed solely on the basis of the colour of Jesus' skin it might be a very powerful and significant model for application in some specific contexts but it would not extend any significance to many other characteristically human contexts. On the other hand if a model is developed on a more profound understanding of Jesus it may extend the significance of God's saving activity in Jesus to many human situations. The more extensive the applicability of a model the more religious adequacy it may be said to have.

This raises the question whether any one model can be sufficiently adequate or whether complementary models are needed to extend the saving significance of Jesus as far as it might be applied. Certainly complementary models have always existed together in the community of faith. The New Testament has numerous christological models in it. A number of biblical scholars have shown that despite the diversity of models there was also substantial unity in the New Testament portrayal of Jesus and his saving significance.[15] Models, it appears, can be adequately complementary. In modern physics the principle of complementarity of models has been accepted. Barbour quotes the physicist Niels Bohr as saying that "a complete elucidation of one and the same object may require diverse points of view which defy a unique description" (Barbour 1974, p.75). McFague insists *"many* models will be necessary both to express and to interpret the complexity and richness of the divine-human relationship" (1982, p.127). Dunn concludes his study of *Christology In The Making* with a strong insistence that *"christology should not be narrowly confined to one particular assessment of Christ nor should it play one off against another, nor should it insist on squeezing all the different New Testament conceptualizations into one particular 'shape;' but it should recognize that from the first the significance of Christ could only be apprehended by a diversity of formulations which though not always strictly compatible with each other were not regarded as rendering each other invalid"* (1980, p.266-7).

The church, however, eventually developed the "two-nature" model as the authoritative model which became the foundation for the trinitarian orthodox paradigm of Christianity. Other models have had to conform to this paradigmatic model or be suppressed, as many models were suppressed during the christological controversies of the early centuries of Christianity.[16] Modern critical enquiry has shown how many non-religious factors were involved in the movements to suppress the diversity of models. This tends to support the widely held contention in our times that the church should allow various models to exist rather than suppressing them. Despite the existence of various christological models and despite even the need for different models it remains true that the adequacy of a model can be estimated partly by the criterion of the extensibility of its application. More adequate models have wider application even if they do not require the suppression of other models.

If the christocentric-trinitarian paradigm were replaced by the paradigm of a Spirit christology there would still be room for various models in christology. Spirit christology entails a relational unity between Jesus and God rather than ontological identity of Jesus and God. If the relational paradigm were accepted it would be possible to interpret the relation with various metaphors and models, such as ones that focus

---

[15] See, for example, Dunn (1977): "The fact is that *there was no one christology in first-century Christianity but a diversity of christologies.* ... Within this diversity however a unifying element is regularly discernible; namely, *the affirmation of the identity of the man Jesus with the risen Lord.* (p.226-227).

[16] Young (in Hick 1977) observes that: "An exclusive claim that the only way of understanding the nature of Jesus is in terms of a unique divine incarnation ... has obscured the potential richness and variety of christological images and insights ... . To recognize the possibility that diverse responses to Jesus Christ have equal validity may well be the only constructive way forward in a world which is beginning to value the enriching aspects of its variety and pluralism (p.14).

on grace or covenant as well as the relationship in Spirit. This is not possible within the paradigm of ontological identity. In this case only one model is acceptable, namely, the two-nature model, interpreted in terms of hypostatic union. Identity is identity. There have been various attempts to interpret the two-nature model, such as by using the concept of *kenosis*, but the two-nature model itself does not leave room for other models to exist.

A final criterion for christological models is logical coherence and the ability to survive the most penetrating analyses of critical reason. Even though christological models function religiously for persons within the community of faith they are nonetheless public and part of the intellectual milieu of society. They cannot with integrity ignore the intellectual questions and criteria of knowledge that are operative in the society. They cannot exist on the basis of special pleading which excludes them from the criteria of reasonableness that pertain to understanding in general. Contradictions and illogicalities are as unacceptable in theology as elsewhere.

At the same time, the criterion of coherence does not require the dynamic "conversation" among the component elements in a christological model to be finished and complete. Reality anywhere, including the Reality experienced in religion, is so profound and complex that it is not susceptible to "final" analyses that are beyond question or doubt. In fact, many contemporary scholars have found out that the all-out application of "the sceptical ... iconoclastic and critical Spirit" (Cupitt 1982, p.113) of modern intellectual enquiry leads to an experience of "the Void" in which the finiteness and relativity of all meanings are clearly experienced. Cupitt believes such a persistent application of the "hermeneutics of suspicion" is necessary and also consistent with Jesus' own iconoclastic and ironic stance. If such critical realism leads to an experience of the Void it may not prevent religious experience but on the contrary engender an authentic experience of God as Ineffable and trustworthy. Donald Evans similarly contends that the most certain experience of what he calls "reality-assurance," on which the attitude of fundamental trust is established, occurs in experiences of the Void rather than in positive explanations of the trustworthiness of ultimate reality (1979, p.32-34).

The point is that a thoroughgoing critical approach to all knowledge, including christological knowledge, is not to be feared for the possibility of it destroying faith. As Evans and Cupitt and many others have avowed, faith does not require protection from rational enquiry. On the contrary, the models that express religious faith need to meet the standards of coherence and reasonableness that apply to understanding in general. Tracy points out, however, that apocalyptic ideas which point to the end of earthly continuities are a healthy corrective to any pretensions that our current systems of thought are absolute, final, or beyond dissolution by the passing of time (1981, p.265f.).

Rationality with its demand for coherence is not an absolute. It is an instrument for clarifying the communication of meaning. This is as appropriate in christological work as anywhere else. Tracy points out correctly that the kind of rationality which is applied as a criterion of theological models should be the rationality "appropriate to the kind of disclosive publicness expressed in all classics" (1981, p.198). Other kinds of subject matter may require the use of other kinds of logic.[17]

---

[17]The complex question of comparing religious knowledge with scientific or historical or aesthetic knowledge is beyond the scope of this book. Ian Barbour has done it well in *Issues in Science and Religion* (London: SCM Press Ltd., 1966).

*Chapter Three*
# TOWARDS A BIBLICAL AND CONTEMPORARY THEOLOGY OF SPIRIT

*Introduction*

Some knowledge of God, of humanity and of the world necessarily precedes any encounter we have with God in the life, death and resurrection of Jesus. Christological method requires explicit acknowledgement of the preunderstandings that have direct bearing on the interpretation of the saving significance of Jesus. In the case of Spirit christology the most important understanding that precedes such interpretation is a theology of Spirit which expresses beliefs about what God is like and how God relates to the world and to humanity in particular.

This theology of Spirit includes a doctrine of creation and a theological anthropology. It also must include a basic understanding of what is evil in the world and what, therefore, calls for the redeeming or recreative, "saving" work of God in Jesus as the Christ. This is a very tall order for any book on the subject, let alone a single chapter in a book on christology. This chapter, accordingly, can only sketch the main outlines of a theology of Spirit which is needed to inform our understanding of what God does in and through Jesus as the Christ. It will deal first with the symbolic origins of the biblical understanding of Spirit, then develop a metaphorical theology of Spirit based on both biblical and modern understanding of humanity and the world, then suggest the conceptual framework in which evil and salvation can most appropriately be understood. The latter will be explored more fully in the chapter that deals with the soteriological (logic of salvation) aspects of Spirit christology. Finally, in this chapter some conclusions will be drawn about the doctrine of God as Spirit which have most immediate implications for what might be said about Jesus as the Christ.

The experience of symbols is the starting point for a theology of Spirit. Symbols are "nonlinguistic bonds uniting us to the cosmos" (McFague, 1982, p.120 citing Ricoeur). Humanity "first reads the sacred on the world, on some elements or aspects of the world ... manifestations of the sacred ... hierophanies where the sacred is shown in a fragment of the cosmos, which ... gets charged with innumerable meanings..."(Ricoeur 1967, p.10-11). Ricoeur explains how symbols emerge in immediate experience of the world, in oneiric or dream experiences and finally in poetic imagination.

In the biblical experiences of God as Spirit we can see all of these dimensions present. There is a rich variety of experience of Spirit that develops throughout the course of the entire biblical period of history.[1] My purpose here is not to treat these biblical symbols of Spirit in the chronological order in which they emerged but to gather up from across the many centuries of Hebrew and early Christian experience the main symbols from which the metaphorical biblical thought about God and humanity was derived.

In the ancient world it was widely held that the world consists of various forms of four basic elements: air, fire, water and earth. All four were the source of experiences of Spirit.

Because symbols are primarily events of experience, it requires some imagination to reconstruct the kinds of experience in which elements or aspects of the world became symbols of God's presence as Spirit for the biblical people.

*Biblical Symbols of Spirit.*

The word for Spirit in the Hebrew language is *ruach* which means moving air. The Hebrew people were never far from the experience of the desert where the wind is a fascinating and terrifying reality. It blows the sand into everchanging shapes and horizons, creating and recreating the face of the earth from day to day. It is a force to be reckoned with; at its fiercest the *ruach* of the desert can be deadly dangerous. No living thing can stand against its power. The mighty blast of the *ruach* was said to have blown back the Reed Sea to allow the Israelites to cross over in their exodus from Egypt. The desert wind was a most prominent feature in the life experience of the Hebrew peoples, the prevailing energy in their physical environment, awesome at times in its creative beauty, eerie at times in sound and fury, helping, thwarting, caressing and chastising. No wonder that the *ruach* of the desert suggested much of the meaning of God to those who lived close to it!

The *ruach* of the desert was closely involved with the clouds of the sky. The wind is invisible except when it takes the form of clouds or mist which can be seen, but paradoxically cause other things to be unseeable. The invisible God "who makest the clouds thy chariot, who ridest on the wings of the wind" (Ps 104:3) was frequently experienced in the symbol of cloud, as of wind. In the Bible generally, there is a "strong emphasis on metaphors of the ear as compared with those of the eye" (Frye 1981, p.116). Clouds and mist are acceptable symbols for the presence of the invisible God because while they are visible to some extent they are thoroughly opaque and hide any reality within them.

Wings are also associated with wind. The wings in the desert belonged notably to the wild eagles and semi-domesticated doves. The power of

---

[1] Cf. Robinson (1962), in referring to the idea of God in the Hebrew scriptures, says: "Where God is present, He is always active, and no word gathers up His activity more completely than this word *ruach*"(p.17).

eagles' wings to lift and soar, and the fierce protection the mother eagle's wings provide for her eaglets inspired awe and fascination. The *ruach* of God was said to hover over the waters in creation like the loving and powerful hovering of a mother eagle over her infants in the nest. The untrammeled dove that freely lights on a person's shoulder became a symbol for the descending of God's *ruach* to be present mysteriously and beautifully in special ways with rare individuals.

The moving air of the desert was different only in degree from moving air that marks the presence of life in the throats of animals and people.[2] Breath was also called *ruach,* and breath is scarcely less fascinating and awesome than the desert wind. Where does it come from? Why do creatures without it die? The Jewish philosopher Aquila is reported to have strangled some camels and then asked the emperor Hadrian to set them on their legs again, thereby proving to the emperor that the world is based on "ruach" or "spirit" (*The Jewish Encyclopedia* 1916, p.447). Breath is so consequential for creaturely existence that it is easily seen to have Godly significance.

Like the desert wind the moving air in peoples' throats may not be silent. It produces words and sighs, songs and cries. Knock the *ruach* out of people and they have nothing to say. The mysterious moving air in peoples' throats is creative of meaning; words are like the shapes that the desert wind produces in the sand — they determine the landscape of personality, expressing the feelings, attitudes, intentions, and will that mould the character of actions and relationships. The throat which is the organ of *ruach* in breathing and speaking was considered to be the locus of individuality, what others have called soul or personality *(nephesh).*

Like the wind that winnows, separating chaff from grain and facilitating the production of food the *ruach* of breath with its words expresses the discernments of wisdom and judgment that are also fascinating and sometimes terrible, nurturing people with words of promise and insight, searing them with words of anguish and condemnation. The words of the prophets and wise ones of Israel were seen as the product of the metaphorical *ruach* of God (Cf. Zech 7:12).

Scarcely less important than air as a symbol of God and closely correlated with it was fire and its derivative symbols of light and heat. The desert sun and moon and lightning storms are awe-inspiring for the most secular of minds. For the Hebrew people who were extraordinarily open and sensitive to the mystery of God they were powerful symbols of the presence and certainty of God. Air and fire are closely related: fire moves air upwards creating clouds of smoke, and wind or breath make fire burn higher, increasing the light and heat. Heat is present in breath and in the body as long as it is alive. The fire of lightning comes with the *ruach* of the storm and when the sun goes down there is often a lull or a change in the wind before the moon comes up. The celestial fires that order the sequence of day and night

---

[2]Cf. Robinson (1962): "Whatever else the Spirit of God may mean in the Old Testament, it means the difference between life and death, it means vitality" (p.13).

are inseparable from the *ruach* of God. God is present in the fire of the burning bush before Moses, and the Spirit of God descends on the disciples at Pentecost in "tongues as of fire, distributed and resting on each one of them" (Acts 2:3) accompanying "a sound ... like the rush of a mighty wind." Light and heat are as fascinating as the wind and sometimes as formidable. When Yahweh finally addresses Job he asks, among other things, "Have you commanded the morning ... and caused the dawn to know its place? Where is the way to the place where the light is distributed, or where the east wind is scattered upon the earth? (Job 38:12,24). The creation of the world itself began with air and light, "two symbols of 'spirit'" (Frye 1981, p.124).

Again, for people of the desert there is perhaps an exceptional awareness of the elemental importance of water in the total scheme of things. Water, like wind and fire, was experienced as a symbol of God's Spirit. Rain comes with wind and lightning in the storm and causes the miracle of growth. It, too, has the potential of danger in it, if it comes at the wrong time or in too much quantity, as in a flood. The water of springs and rivers are precious blessings for animals and people alike. The throat that breathes also thirsts and lives as much by the water it swallows as the air it breathes. Thus, the Spirit was often spoken of as being "poured" out like water and "filling" people. The element of water is the main constituent in blood in which heat, movement and water combine to signify life in most creatures (Gen 9:4). In trees the life depends on the sap (Ps 104:16 KJV) and the sap or resins or fluids of certain trees and plants were used, and are still used, in the church in anointing or healing rituals in which the Spirit of God was thought to be present. The fluid of the grape produces wine which is also still experienced as a symbol of the presence of the Spirit in the Christian tradition. "All were made to drink of one Spirit" (I Cor 12:13).

Throughout the Bible "the distinction between living water and dead water is of primary importance" (Frye 1981, p.145). The proximity of the people of Israel to the Dead Sea no doubt reinforced the fact for them that some waters support life while others do not. Life begins in the waters of the womb and continues to be dependent on life-giving fluids from the first suck of mother's milk to the last sip of water or wine before death.

From New Testament times until now new life was thought to come with baptism in water which is also a baptism in the Holy Spirit. Jesus, according to John, offered "living water" of eternal life, while in the vision of the Revelation to John "many men died of the water [of wormwood], because it was made bitter" (Rev 8:11). Water that nourishes or poisons, refreshes or drowns, is inherently fascinating and fearsome, a fitting symbol for the experience of God who has power over life and death and who works in mysterious ways the wonders of life to perform.

The experience of God's Spirit in connection with water was not far removed from thinking of Spirit as some kind of material substance. The Greek conception of *pneuma,* the word used to translate *ruach,* was very much as a kind of substance or matter that permeates the whole cosmos and has particular influence in human beings (Heron 1983, p.32). For the Hellenists "power is conceived of as a substance" (Schweizer 1960, p.18) and the powerful Spirit of God is no exception. Schweizer points out that "this Hellenistic substance-concept was of course indebted to primitive concepts which occur just as much in the O.T. as anywhere else; ... but only in Hellenism did it become normative for theory about the spirit" (1960, p.56n.). Robinson suggested that in the story of the Spirit with Moses and Elijah being shared to other people "the energy is so materialistically conceived that it can be transferred from one to another" (1962, p.16). *The Jewish Encyclopedia* (1916), however, claims that "the materialistic view of the Holy Spirit" in the New Testament writers "assumes a form fundamentally different from that of the Jewish view in certain respects" (p.449).

In any case, in the later parts of the Bible bodily and material substances are used as metaphors of the Spirit. Paul speaks of the "spiritual body" (I Cor 15:44), and the *First Letter of Peter* exhorts the readers, "like living stones be yourselves built into a spiritual house" (2:5). St Paul at one point alludes to a current legend that the rock which Moses struck (Num 20:17) to get water for the people of Israel in the desert subsequently followed them in their migration to the Promised Land, providing water all along the way (I Cor 10:4). Paul says "The Rock was Christ" and in accordance with his custom of identifying the heavenly Christ as Spirit, calls it a "spiritual rock." In Deuteronomy 32:4,15,18, Moses calls God "The Rock" and in several other places in Hebrew scriptures others refer to God as "Rock." (e.g.2 Sam 22:2; Ps 28:1; Isa 17:10). In his prophecy about the ultimate deliverance of Israel, Isaiah combines several of the symbols we have been exploring:

> Behold, a king will reign in righteousness.
> Princes will rule in justice.
> Each will be like a hiding place from the wind
> a covert from the tempest
> like streams of water in a dry place
> like the shade of a great rock in a weary land. (32:1-2).

This will take place when "the Spirit is poured upon us from on high" (vs.15).

Air, water, fire and earth, the elemental realities of the universe, as they have often been thought to be, together with a wide variety of symbols derived from these four elements were the symbolic occasions for biblical people to experience the Spirit of God. Each symbolic element is inherently mysterious in its own way, combining fascinating possibilities of blessing with fearsome possibilities of danger. "No image is inherently good or bad ... which it is depends on the context (Frye 1981, p.148). This means that the experience of God as Spirit in any symbol is not predictable. The Spirit, as it were, takes its own initiatives to instill the experience of *mysterium tremendum* and *mysterium fascinans,* the numinous encounters with the Sacred, which influence human destiny so decisively.

We have quite different views of the universe from those of the biblical people, but because so many of their symbols of the Spirit were ordinary elements of every day life we can and do have similar experiences of the Sacred. The Spirit which "blows where it wills" (John 3:8) can and does encounter people now in the elements of nature and humanity that have fascinating and terrifying potential for people. Many modern people living in urbanized contexts may have relatively fewer encounters with the elements of nature than did the people of biblical times. But even a casual reading of the Bible and especially of the New Testament will show that the experience of the Spirit for biblical people was by no means solely or even mainly a kind of nature mysticism. While the four natural elements were the initial symbols of the presence of the Spirit the derivative and related human symbols of words, attitudes and community ethos account for the vast majority of biblical references to the Spirit.

A contemporary theology of Spirit can and should be founded on symbolic experiences similar to those reported in the Bible. The task of theology is to reflect systematically on the experiences of symbols, expressing their meanings metaphorically and organizing the content of the understanding as logically and comprehensively as possible. We turn to that task now.

*An Outline of a Metaphorical Theology of Spirit.*

Theologians who have attempted to develop theologies of Spirit that are both thoroughly biblical and fully modern have chosen quite different categories or concepts to form the main outline or structure of their theologies. H. Wheeler Robinson discerned "five outstanding suggestions of the term [Spirit] which emerge in the course of its long history through four languages and literatures" [Hebrew, Greek, Latin and English] (1962, p.24-25). The five were:
(1) wind-like energy
(2) the *creative activity* of God
(3) the whole *physical life* of human beings "usually regarded on its higher side" (p.25)
(4) the *personalized idea* of divine energy associated with Jesus Christ
(5) the Greek philosophical use of pneuma which "covered the idea of *divine immanence,* thus linking itself with the use of the term in modern philosophy" (e.g. in Hegel).

John V. Taylor (1972) was heavily influenced by Martin Buber and developed his theology of Spirit on the basis of five aspects of personal activity that are engendered by the presence of the Spirit. The five activities of Spirit are:
(1) urging every creature to *higher consciousness* and personhood
(2) creating occasions for spontaneity and *responsible* choice
(3) calling out from people *self-oblation* and sacrifice
(4) letting loose the springs of *creativity* in people
(5) setting people *free.*

Paul Tillich was primarily a theologian of the Spirit although he is often not regarded as such because his first two volumes of *Systematic Theology* (1951 and 1957) focused on Being in its essential and existential aspects. The third volume (1963) developed the theology of Spirit which embraces the ideas of the first and second volumes and sets them in their intended perspective. Tillich understood spirit (small "s") to be a dimension of life which is the most inclusive ontological category that unites essential and existential being in actuality. The divine Spirit (with a capital "S") is understood on the basis of being analogous to the ontological spirit in creation and especially in people. The divine Spirit, also called Spiritual Presence, has a relationship of "mutual immanence" with the human and created spirit. Divine Spirit, then, is present and active in every time and place where everything actually exists but can be resisted or received by the human spirit with the corresponding results of destruction or fulfillment. The content of the divine Spirit when manifested in human spirits is faith and love, and its characteristic functions are the self-integration of life (morality), the self-creativity of life (culture) and the self-transcendence of life (religion). The divine Spirit is present fragmentarily in individuals and communities, "latently" or by anticipation in pre-Christian religions, "manifestly" in Jesus as the Christ and in the church. In all morality, culture and religion the divine Spirit works to create order in the first place and then to overcome destructive ambiguities and estrangement by the recreation of New Being.[3]

The theology of Spirit that will be outlined in this chapter will obviously owe much to the insights of the three theologians mentioned above, as well as to many others. It will not, however be an attempt to compile their main ideas. In accordance with the theological method described in the last chapter the theology of Spirit suggested here will try to be in spirited "conversation" with the biblical symbols of Spirit as well as with other theologians and with the context of modern thinking, especially about the nature of evil. The theology outlined below has seven basic terms: energy, information, imagination, discernment, attitude-virtues, vocation and ethos.[4]

*Energy*

The Bible has an understanding of God's Spirit as a power that is deeply and universally active in the world and especially in people.[5] The power of the Spirit includes the mysterious power of life itself. Job said that "the *ruach* of the Almighty gives me life" (33:4). Animals also live by the *ruach* of God. As we saw earlier the Spirit is thought to have the kind of power experienced in the wind, the lightning and the moving waters of the earth. In human personality the Spirit can be an awesome power that causes ecstatic behaviour, tremendous strength (Samson) and blazing anger (I Sam 11:6). It is thought to be the power of resurrection (Rom 8:11) and of creation in the first place. "When

---

[3]Cf. Tillich (1963, pp.11-162).

[4]Cf. Pannenberg (1985): "The concept 'spirit' ... is not to be understood in terms of consciousness. It is to be understood rather, as that which alone makes possible both consciousness and subjectivity (in the sense of the unity of conscious life) and that, at the same time, makes possible the unity of social and cultural life as well as the continuity of history amid the open-endedness and incompleteness of its processes" (p.520). Pannenberg owes some of his basic ideas on spirit to Barth (cf. p.522).

[5]Cf. Taylor (1972): "The Holy Spirit is just as likely to speak through our bodies as through our minds" (p.50). "There is more of Dionysus than Apollo in the Holy Spirit" (p.50).

thou sendest forth thy Spirit, they are created; and thou renewest the face of the ground" (Ps 104:30).

According to our modern understanding of physics we might say metaphorically that God's Spirit is the energy that fills the universe. Energy is a fascinating and potentially terrifying reality in our times. However little we understand it, contemporary people have a sense that energy is the most basic and pervasive reality there is. "Einstein is the great symbol for a new realization that matter, which up to the twentieth century had been the great bastion of the objectivity of the world, was an illusion of energy" (Frye 1981, p.14). Energy is thus what makes everything live and move and have its being. Energy is the farthest horizon we can see when we look microscopically or telescopically at ourselves or the universe. No energy, no universe. No energy, no life. If we relate our mythical and discursive language at all we might well think of energy when we read Psalm 104:30 "When thou sendest forth thy Spirit [as energy] they are created."

Energy by itself however, is an insufficient metaphor for what God as Spirit does in the creation of the universe. Energy is structured or else there is chaos. As Paul Tillich defined it, spirit is the unity of power and form. A contemporary word for the formative, as opposed to entropic processes, in the universe is information.[6]

*Information*

The structures we can discern in creation are as fascinating and awesome as the energy which they order. Genesis I speaks of light, darkness, firmaments, waters, land, plants, creatures and people. We have come to think of the structures in creation in terms of systems of organization.[7] Atoms, molecules, cells, tissues, organs, bodies, species and ecosystems are some of the terms we use to describe the elementary organization of energy as we know it. We organize our knowledge of the organization in creation into systems: physics, astronomy, chemistry, biology, anthropology, philosophy, psychology, sociology, aesthetics, politics, economics, ecology and a plethora of other systems and sub-systems, each representing a complex set of ideas that refer to some part or aspect of the order in the universe. The discovery of the cellular structure of

---

[6]Cf. Campbell (1982): "The view arose [after World War II] of information as an active agent, something that ... 'informs' the material world. ... Thus information emerged as a universal principle at work in the world, giving shape to the shapeless, specifying the peculiar character of living forms and even helping to determine, by means of special codes, the patterns of human thought. In this way, information spans the disparate fields of space-age computers and classical physics, molecular biology and human communication, the evolution of language and the evolution of man" (p.16). Again: "Contrary to the entropy principle which implies that order is the exception and confusion the rule, information theory asserts that order and sense can indeed prevail against disorder and nonsense. From the simplest forms of organic life to the words used to express our most complex ideas, from our genes to our dreams ... virtually everything around us follows the simple rules of information." (Introduction on the dust cover).

[7]Cf. Taylor (1972): "For nearly twenty-five years a theory of 'systems' or of 'organizing forces' has been quietly built up. It is closely related to the insights learnt from sociology, business management, cybernetics and computer science but the theory has received its greatest impetus in the field of biochemistry. ... A cell is a system. ... An organ is a superior system ... . Organic life, therefore, is seen to be a towering hierarchy of systems ... in which each system autonomous in its own right at one level, takes its place as a sub-unit in another system at a higher level." (p.28-29).

DNA, the organization which informs the organic development of human beings, illustrates with its potential for genetic engineering the fascinating and awesome character of the elemental ordering of reality.

The systems of creation are what the New Testament called the principalities and powers. These have often been regarded only as the agencies of evil in the universe but the Bible portrays them as the necessary ordering authorities of life and creation which have rebelled from the sovereignty of God and become what we would call "cancerous," that is, unruly, conflicting, destructive, imperialistic, colonizing, violent forces which threaten the well being of the world and creatures. There is no doubt that we must look at the systems if we are to have anything like an adequate understanding of the evil in the world to which the hope of salvation in God will apply. It is also true, however, that we in our time have to look at the systems if we are to have any adequate understanding of the creative, ordering, work of God in the world.

The biblical authors, who thought in terms of principalities and powers, angels, thrones, dominions, elements, authorities and such, had a similarly ambiguous estimation of the ordering agencies in creation. God, in their view, has delegated the ordering of creation to subordinate authorities who typically usurp God's ultimate authority to themselves and become idolatrous, contending with each other for power and control rather than serving God and the creation in their God-given responsibilities. In the original creation and in the creation when it is consummated or fulfilled the powers are under the reign of God doing what they were intended to do. As Colossians expressed it: "in [Christ] all things were created, in heaven and on earth, visible, and invisible, whether thrones or dominions or principalities or authorities — all things were created through him and for him ... and in him all things hold together" (Col 1:16-17). The Greek word for "hold together" is *synhesteken* to which the word "system" is etymologically related. Hendrik Berkhof and, more recently, Walter Wink have confirmed the often forgotten positive significance of the principalities and powers. Berkhof says:

> Paul observes that life is ruled by a series of Powers. He speaks of time (present and future), of space (depth and height), of life and death, of politics and philosophy, of public opinion and Jewish law, of pious tradition and the fateful course of the stars. Apart from Christ man is at the mercy of these Powers. They encompass, carry and guide his life ... they are all our "guardians and the trustees," the forces which hold together the world and the life of [people] and preserve them from chaos.
>
> \* \* \*
>
> The state, politics, class, social struggle, national interests, public opinion, accepted morality, the ideas of decency, humanity, democracy — these give unity and direction to thousands of lives. Yet precisely by giving unity and direction, they separate these many lives from the true God. (Berkhof 1962, p.22; 32-33).

Walter Wink in a "thoroughgoing examination of the use of the terms for power in all the relevant literature of the period and in the New Testament" (Wink 1984, p.X), summarizes his findings as follows: "these Powers are the good creations of a good God, but some of them have 'fallen' becoming more or less evil in intent and may even be set on the destruction of humanity" (p.104). Wink believes that "we cannot dispense with the particular mythic language of heaven and the spiritual and the Powers" (p.143). He proposes to revive the biblical thought by "juxtaposing the ancient myth with the emerging postmodern (mythic) world view and asking how they might mutually illuminate each other" (p.104). In a seminal passage he indicates what the results of such a process might be.

> What I propose is viewing the spiritual Powers not as separate heavenly or ethereal entities but as the *inner aspect of material or tangible manifestations of power*. I suggest that the "angels of nature" are the patterning of physical things — rocks, trees, plants, the whole God-glorifying dancing, visible universe; that the "principalities and powers" are the inner or spiritual essence, or gestalt, of an institution or state or system; that the "demons" are the psychic or spiritual power emanated by organizations or individuals or subaspects of individuals whose energies are bent on overpowering others; that "gods" are the very real archetypal or ideological structures that determine or govern reality and its mirror, the human brain; that the mysterious "elements of the Universe" *(stoicheia tou kosmou)* are the invariances (formerly called "laws") which, though often idolized by humans conserve the self-consistency of each level of reality in its harmonious interrelationship with every other level and The Whole; and that "Satan" is the actual power that congeals around collective idolatry, injustice or inhumanity ... (p.104-105).

It is obviously naive to think that the biblical writers were naive about the organizations and systems that operate in the creation. Their pre-scientific awareness of the way things are consisted of a profound variety of meaningful distinctions, including some that are missing in a one-dimensional scientific world view, some that we need to recover. Most important of all is the idea of God's Spirit as the creative agent who provides not only the energy but the organizing patterns or "information" for what exists, including the subordinate agents of all kinds.

Information that organizes patterns of energy can also be called memory. DNA, for example, is sometimes referred to as the memory that determines the development of cells and organisms. Spirit not only contributes information or intelligibility to everything but also empowers the recollection or extension of information in memory.

*Information as the Word*

The biblical term for the information that orders everything is *Word*. "By the *word* of the Lord the heavens were made" (Ps33:6). "And God *said* 'Let there be light'" (Gen 1:3). The association of word (Hebrew:*dabar;* Greek:*logos*) with Christ in *Logos* christology has ensured that the biblical idea of the Word of God as the creative and redemptive agent is very familiar in Christian thought. The hypostatization of *Logos,* however, and its identification with Jesus of Nazareth has led to trinitarian thinking which is a basic divergence from Hebrew thinking about the Word of God.

In Hebrew thinking and, indeed, in most of the New Testament, God's word is not hypostatized as an entity distinguishable from God in anything like the way in which the second Person of the Holy Trinity is distinguished from God the Father or God the Holy Spirit. In the vast majority of biblical thinking God's Word, Wisdom, Hand, Arm, Face and Spirit, among other things, are alternative ways of speaking about God's own presence, while implying at the same time that God is not to be thought of as entirely localized or domesticated.[8] Among these various periphrases used to avoid the suggestion that God is totally mundane it can be argued that the term Spirit has priority in the Bible and that the Spirit is thought to bring the Word rather then vice versa.

Spirit was for the Hebrew people a more wholistic metaphor for God than any other. As such it was the most suitable term for referring to the reality of God. When the author of John 4:24 has Jesus say to the woman of Samaria "God is Spirit" it is a statement that corroborates, and is corroborated by, the thinking of the vast majority of biblical authors. Spirit is the most suitable term to describe the reality of God because it can signify both God's presence with power and meaning and God's invisible, ineffable transcendence.

The Word of God as a metaphor is very valuable to convey the idea of God's will or intentions or mind, but it is not as inclusive or wholistic a metaphor as Spirit. It was reasonable, therefore, that biblical authors should think of the Spirit bringing the Word or think of the Word as a particular aspect of God who is Spirit.[9]

There is a lot of biblical evidence to confirm that this was in fact the way in which the metaphors of Spirit and Word were thought to be related. Because most Christian scholars have been influenced by the christocentric-trinitarian paradigm in which the *Logos* has tended to have priority over the Spirit the clear biblical evidence of the reverse relationship of Word and Spirit has gone largely unacknowledged. The close connections between Word and Spirit have been widely noted, of course, but the tradition of thinking of both Word and Spirit hypostatically as discrete entities or "persons" has stood in the way of seeing that Word is in fact a function of God who is Spirit. Word is produced by God as Spirit and is one of several aspects of God's activity and being that can be distinguished.

To be sure, "Word" is one of the most frequently used terms in the Bible to refer to God's activity. It occurs in the Bible approximately as many times as the term Spirit does. Because it is a metaphor that particularly denotes meaning and intentionality it is extremely useful

---

[8]Cf. Taylor (1972): " In the parallelism of Hebrew poetry *ruach* and *dabar* are virtually synonyms" (p.58).

[9]Cf. Taylor (1972): "The Spirit represents the divine action in its total impact, while the Word represents the specific direction and form which the divine action takes at one point of time" (p.61).

for referring to the kind of personal God known in the Bible. "Speaking" is one of the main functions of a personal God who communicates with creatures who can also speak and listen.

The more universal function of creating intelligible order in everything that exists, and the less aural phenomena of empowering significant emotions or attitudes, are not connected metaphorically as closely with Word as they are with Spirit. Word is very appropriate as a metaphor in anthropocentric thinking that is also biased towards mental activity as the most significant activity in reality. But the Hebrew people were not as biased toward mental activity as the Greeks were. Their understanding of humanness was much more wholistic, emphasizing various bodily functions and organs such as throat, blood, heart, bowels, liver, and even kidneys. They did not emphasize brain or mind as having priority in the make-up of human beings. They acknowledged the significance of hearing and speaking as important functions along with other functions such as caring in the heart for justice, showing loving kindness from the guts or bowels and having the several characteristics of wisdom including good judgment from the kidneys.

God as Spirit comes to be present and engenders Godly activity in any of the several functions or aspects of human beings. The Spirit comes also to other creatures and to the inanimate world as power and meaning that animates, orders and gives life. Spirit contributes both power or energy and the information or intelligible order that together make creation and living creatures possible.

Biblical references to Spirit and Word confirm the dependence, as it were, of Word on Spirit.[10] David is reported to have said with his "last words" "The Spirit of the Lord speaks by me, his word is upon my tongue" (II Sam 23:2). Before Balaam uttered his oracle to the encamped tribes of Israel "the Spirit of God came upon him, and he took up his discourse" (Num 24:2). Ezekiel described his prophetic experience in terms of the Spirit bringing the Word. "And the Spirit of the Lord fell upon me and he said to me, 'Say, Thus says the Lord: ... '" (Ezek 11:5). The author of Zechariah expresses the general biblical view of the relationship of prophetic words to the Spirit when he speaks of "the words which the Lord of hosts had sent by his Spirit through the former prophets" (Zech 7:12).

It is true that the great prophets Jeremiah and Amos avoided referring to God's Spirit in connection with their prophesying apparently because they did not wish to be confused with contemporary ecstatic "prophets" whose frenzied extravagances were claimed to be inspired by the Spirit. Hosea who was approximately contemporary with Amos continued to speak of "The prophet ... the man of the Spirit" (Hos 9:7) and, as we have seen, Ezekiel, a contemporary of Jeremiah, certainly thought his prophesying was the work of the Spirit of God.

---

[10]Kaufmann (1980) disagrees with this claim. While admitting that "there is no biblical doctrine of the relationship between the word and the spirit" (p.101) he nonetheless says that "this primary revelation of the divine word is never considered to be an effect of the divine spirit" (p.98). Without citing the evidence he insists that "the word of God is not brought on by the spirit, the spirit is the by-product of the word" (p.100). The evidence, as seen below, appears to support a different conclusion.

The later Rabbinic tradition thought that the Spirit was the author of the Word of the Torah. "The expression 'holy spirit' ... becomes a commonplace among the rabbis to express the divine revelation which is found in the words of the Torah or on the lips of the prophets" (Montague 1976, p.113).

Nor was this relationship of Spirit and Word lost in the New Testament. The author of the letter to Hebrews when quoting from the Hebrew scriptures repeatedly refers to the Holy Spirit as the author: "Therefore, as the Holy Spirit says ... " (Heb 3:7, Cf. also 9:8 and 10:15). The synoptic gospels all include a message from Jesus to the disciples about the Holy Spirit helping them speak before the courts. "For it is not you who speak but the Holy Spirit" (Mk 13:11, Cf. Mt 10:20 and Lk 12:11-12). St Paul claimed "no one can say 'Jesus is Lord' except by the Holy Spirit" (I Cor 12:3). We impart the gifts of God he says, "in words not taught by human wisdom but taught by the Spirit" (I Cor 2:13).

For Paul the Spirit is not mindless power or raw energy. "For the Spirit searches everything, even the depths of God" (I Cor 2:10). In Romans 8:27 he refers explicitly to "the mind of the Spirit." He refers to the Corinthian converts as "a letter from Christ ... written ... with the Spirit of the living God" (II Cor 3:3). The Gifts of the Spirit in Paul's view include prophecy, teaching and exhortation among others (Rom 12:5-8). The Pauline author of Ephesians similarly prays that God "may give you a spirit of wisdom and of revelation in the knowledge of him" (Eph 1:17). The same author speaks of "the sword of the Spirit, which is the word of God" (Eph 6:17).

Even John, the great inspiration of *Logos* christology might have agreed with the idea that Word is derived from Spirit. "For he whom God sent utters the words of God, so measureless is God's gift of the Spirit" (Jn 3:34 NEB). The Spirit whom Jesus says will be sent by God to the disciples is called "the Spirit of truth" (Jn 14:17) who "will teach you all things" (14:26) and "guide you into all the truth for ... whatever he hears he will speak" (Jn 16:13). The author of the Revelation to John, if a different person, agrees that the Spirit speaks the word. "He who has an ear let him hear what the Spirit says to the churches" (Rev 2:7,11,17,29;3:6,13,22).

Very few biblical scholars or Christian theologians would deny a close relationship of Word and Spirit in the Bible or in the orthodox Christian paradigm. There is simply too much biblical evidence which cannot be ignored, and in trinitarian theology the principle of *circumincession* or *perichoresis* guaranteed the inseparability of the three Persons of the Trinity. The trinitarian thinking, however, with its emphases on and indeed origin in the idea of the Word Incarnate is not open or inclined to consider what is clearly there in the scriptures, namely, that Word comes *from* Spirit and not only with Spirit.

Theologians who focus attention particularly on Spirit are generally not content to think of Spirit as energy which acquires mind or moral character, strictly speaking, only when it is accompanied by the Word. John Vincent Taylor, for example, acknowledges that what the Hebrews encountered as Spirit "was not simply energy but also form, not simply drive but also direction; not only holy but also righteous" (1979, p.60). In his own theological construction Taylor sounds much like some Process theologians who think of Spirit as the cosmic power in evolutionary order: "As a believer in the Creator Spirit I would say that deep within the fabric of the universe, therefore, the Spirit is present as the Go-Between who confronts each isolated spontaneous particle with the beckoning reality of the larger whole and so compels it to relate to others in a particular way; and that it is he who at every stage lures the inert organisms forward by giving an inner awareness and recognition of the unattained" (p.31). H. Wheeler Robinson says "we include in the revelation of spirit in Nature, not only intelligibility, order and continuity, but also progress and beauty" (1962, p.83).

Tillich also certainly thought of Spirit as combining power and form. The triune God, in his view, is actually Spirit in which the other two 'persons' are united. Karl Barth, despite his famous christocentricity, has recently been shown to have a somewhat similar view of the Trinity in which the Spirit proceeding from both the Father and the Son constitutes the actuality of God as having communion between the other two 'persons' and with human beings. The God whom Christians experience directly is God the Holy Spirit, the divine "You" "both in the economy of revelation and in the immanence of His own being" (Rosato 1981, p.59). The question of the Trinity will be considered at more length in a later chapter.

The point here is that there is merit in conceiving of God as Spirit from which the "Word" of intelligible order, meaning and purpose comes forth to be present in the world. The *Logos* is part of the Spirit of God or, better, the Spirit includes both energy and the information which together are inseparable in the ordered creation. Robinson in a footnote comments that "It is interesting to speculate on the consequences for Christian theology if the Logos idea had been linked to the Spirit instead of the Son (1962, p.25 n). As we have seen, there is ample biblical basis for doing so. In fact there had to be strong contextual and cultural reasons in early Christianity for not continuing with the earliest prophetic-sapiential interpretation of Jesus as having the Word of God because he was filled with the Spirit of God. We shall look at this development of *Logos* christology in more detail in due course.

*Imagination and Discernment*

The Spirit not only creates the regularities of organized energy in the universe but also brings these intelligible realities to be known in the minds of sentient creatures. Knowledge, however simple or sophisticated, is a function of relationship. No relationship, no knowledge, whether one is referring to the knowledge that earth worms have of pebbles or that people have of each other. In human relationships the Spirit is present as an active participant making mutual knowledge possible. On the basis of the experience of meeting and knowing other persons in the Spirit it is possible to surmise that the Spirit is operative in all relating and all knowledge between sentient creatures. Analogous to the way in which the Spirit is experienced in human encounters, a similar dynamic process can be posited to exist in the events of knowledge that occur between other creatures.

Martin Buber was the great Jewish philosopher and theologian of Spirit in human relationships. He posited the presence of Spirit in "the Sphere Between" persons or between people and other knowable entities. The knower and the known are able to meet in the intimate encounter of knowing because the Spirit between them joins them in a relationship of giving and receiving, respecting and 'listening' in which true communication occurs.

> Spirit in its human manifestation is man's response to his You. ... Spirit is word ... . Spirit is not in the I but between I and You. It is not like the blood that circulates in you but like the air in which you breathe ... . It is solely by virtue of his power to relate that man is able to live in the Spirit (1970, p.89).

The function of mind to enter into knowing relationships has two aspects or moments that correspond to what is now recognized as right and left brain functions. These two moments of knowing can be called imagination and discernment or participation and distanciation.[11] They have also been described in terms of religious experience as manifestation and proclamation. In Buber's terms relationships are either I-Thou, an immediate subjective encounter with another who is present, or I-It, which is a less immediate, more detached knowledge of an object as if it were a thing of the past. Both "moments" of knowing are necessary but, for Buber, the I-Thou knowing relationship is the primary or prior one in which Spirit actively and truly illuminates reality to a knowing subject. Objective analytical knowledge follows afterwards, as concepts which follow images or symbols.

> Knowledge: as he beholds what confronts him, its being is disclosed to the knower. What he beheld as present he will have to comprehend as an object compare with objects, assign a place in an order of objects, and describe and analyse objectively; only as an It can it be absorbed into the store of knowledge. But in the act of beholding it was no thing among things, no event among events; it was present exclusively. It is not in the law that is afterward derived from the appearance but in the appearance itself that the being communicates itself (1970, p.90).

The sets of ideas by which we analyse and discern reality in its many forms are the substance of objective knowledge. Prior to objective knowledge is the moment of imaginative encounter or immediate participation of the knower in what is manifested of the known[12] True

---

[11] Rahner (1968) speaks of imagination as "the foundation and root of all sensibility" (p.305).

[12] Cf. Taylor (1972): "The opening of our eyes toward other people ... also is the gift of the Spirit" (p.21). "This ability to see the truth of the other [person] — we call it empathy today" (p.21). I think empathy (the "feeling with" others) presupposes imagination, if the feelings are to rise to conscious understanding. Imagination precedes understanding and also precedes ethical decisions pertaining to the future. Cf. Segundo (1984): "We do not concretely choose between values, but between imagined representations of possible satisfactions" (p.18).

rational discernment and real wisdom depend on the continuing activity of the Spirit to renew and refresh the relationship between knower and known. Buber warns of the danger of treating the world and its inhabitants as things, utilizing them, "conquering" and controlling them conceptually but not truly knowing them, because they can be truly known only as You or Thou through living encounters in the Spirit. "The fear of the Lord is the beginning of knowledge ... [and] wisdom" (Prov 1:7; 9:10). It is necessary to "take off one's shoes" so to speak, in reverence, in order for true discernment to occur, in order for imagination to be truly creative rather than fantasy. Such reverence is a form of love. Love as Buber said, is to step into the presence of the other and listen (1970, p.131). In the Spirit of love true meeting occurs between knower and known. The Spirit brings creatures into relationship and knowledge occurs.[13] The Spirit of energy and information is also the Spirit of truth and the Spirit of love.

Tillich, like Buber, saw the relating Spirit of love active not only in the process of knowing others but also of knowing oneself. The two are inseparable. Persons are "constituted" as persons in the encounter with other persons in the Spirit of love. Tillich called this process the "self-integration" of persons (Tillich 1963, p.38f.). Individual identity is established and found in the process of relating to others. The relating events, which bring about the integration or centering of individuals as persons, are occasions of moral significance too, for morality can be broadly defined as the character of responsible relationships between people and the others in their world. In living, responsive relating to others as You, not as It, there is always the moral imperative to accept the others as ones who are entitled to be themselves, as even oneself is so entitled. There is a presupposition and imperative that the other be given just treatment in the encounter of knowing and relating to them. As Buber said, "Love is responsibility of an I for a You" (1970, p.66). Knowing, in the presence of the Spirit, entails moral responsiveness. The Spirit of truth which is the Spirit of love is also the Spirit of justice.

In the Bible the Spirit who facilitates imagination and discernment was understood to be the author or originator of at least four different kinds of knowledge: law, wisdom, prophecy and apocalyptic. Imagination and discernment were involved in each kind of knowledge in different ways. This can be seen by a brief survey of the four types of knowledge.

Law generalizes about the morality or justice in social relationships, and thereby aims to create and preserve social order. As such it tends to be "covenantal" rather than "cosmogonic." That is, it pertains primarily to the specific social orders it is intended to uphold, although biblical law also occasionally pertains to the treatment of strangers and sojourners or even enemies who are encountered by the covenanted people.

Because the justice in relationships is an implication or imperative of the relating Spirit of love and truth "all law is concerned with the mediating of holiness" (Thompson 1978, p.151). Laws, accordingly, deal

---

[13]Cf. Frankl (1975): "Love alone enables the loving person to grasp the uniqueness of the loved person. In this sense love has a significant cognitive function, and certainly this was appreciated by the ancient Hebrews when they used the same word for the act of love and the act of knowledge" (p.36-37).

not only with matters of social justice but also with cultic matters such as sacred time (Sabbath), sacred place (Mt. Sinai) and sacred offices (prophets, priests and kings). Laws can be categorical statements relating to immediate encounters. "Thou shalt not steal" is an immediate implication of any I-Thou encounter. They can also be casuistic or conditional such as the *lex talionis* (an eye for an eye) which entails some application of an abstract principle of proportional justice. Both imaginative immediacy and analytical discernment are involved in the formation of laws.

The same is true of wisdom, although it tends to be "addressed to the detached consciousness and the critical wit" (Frye 1971, p.298). It nonetheless has an empirical basis in immediate experience, the proverbial laws and insights being "wrenched from the experience by a discerning eye" (Thompson 1978, p.162). It aims not so much for the maintenance of social order, although it has some of this concern, as for the happiness and fulfillment of individuals. Hence it can be described as "the individualizing of the law" (Frye 1981, p.125). Wisdom is oriented to the future in as much as it poses possibilities of prudent behaviour, but it is strongly geared to the past in its commitment to traditional values and laws.

In the most mature Wisdom literature of Ecclesiastes and Job, conservative wisdom is transcended by critical freedom. Koheleth, the preacher, the chief editor of Ecclesiastes, critically discerns the temporal relativity and impermanence of all the things that are sometimes deemed to be permanent and absolute. Koheleth appears to experience the Void or emptiness ("Vanity") that many people have known as the outcome of the "hermeneutics of suspicion" in our time. Like them, too, the experience for Koheleth is not ultimately negative because the pure, vulnerable trust that the experience of the Void can engender is an experience of the Spirit of Wisdom. Ultimately, Wisdom advocates an immediate encounter with God who speaks "out of the whirlwind" (Job 38:1). "Trust in the Lord with all your heart, and do not rely on your own insight" (Prov 3:5). "Walk in the ways of your heart and the sight of your eyes. But know that for all these things God will bring you into judgment" (Eccl 11:9).

Because discernment does involve the individual's decision, no matter how informed it is by tradition and precedent there is always the possibility of error and the possibility that time will change the form of knowledge. St Paul expressed this insight of wisdom in connection with his discernment of the significance of Jesus Christ.

> For it is the God who said, "Let light shine out of darkness" who has shone in our hearts to give the light of the knowledge of the glory of God in the face of Christ. But we have this treasure in earthen vessels, to show that the transcendent power belongs to God and not to us (II Cor 4:6-7).

Wisdom, like philosophy (love of wisdom), typically takes a cosmogonic approach in the Bible rather than a covenantal approach. It is concerned about what is true and good and beautiful anywhere and anytime, not what is especially so for the covenanted people. It is not in conflict, however, with the covenanted law but, rather, complements it with a more universal vision.

The prophetic sayings in the Bible are typically the inverse of Wisdom sayings in that they are predominantly the expression of intense immediate experience rather than analytical, generalized observations of detached and critical reflection. The prophets speak their particular knowledge to situations of crisis in the context of their own covenanted society. The form of their utterance does not show "carefully constructed logical development" (Thompson 1978, p.181) but "shocking juxtaposition of images which wrenches first one and then another emotion from the reader." Prophets are poets who sometimes compose hymns or laments as well as speaking in metaphorical images. Their themes are consistently judgment and promise. Despite the intensity and passion of their pronouncements there was, nonetheless, some cool-eyed analysis in their accusations of injustice. Their messages of hope consisted of announcing the possibility of "return" and restoration of well being for people through the divine good will.

Finally, the Bible includes apocalyptic sayings which are a development of prophetic expression. Apocalyptic is born of the experience of "unrelieved exile" (Thompson 1978, p.205) in which the crisis confronting the covenanted people is seen in cosmic perspective as a universal battle of God with the empires and powers of the world. The message of apocalyptic begins in the immediate experience of life as trouble-laden and culminates in a vision of the victory of God in heaven beyond this world. The apocalyptic authors devise a structure of thought "in order to bring a revelatory word to a cultural setting totally devoid of hope" (Thompson 1978, p.212). The word is that a complete metamorphosis of reality is about to take place or, in the case of the Revelation to John, has already taken place in a new beginning. The new beginning necessarily entails the complete destruction of the present world. "What is symbolized as the destruction of the order of nature is the destruction of the way of seeing that order that keeps [people] confined to the world of time and history as we know them" (Frye 1981, p.136). Frye suggests that this destruction "is what the Scripture is intended to achieve." Apocalyptic is thus what Tracy calls "a minefield" (1981, p.306) or corrective for all other kinds of knowledge, reminding us that the Spirit who "blows where it wills" is ultimately a "whirlwind" beyond our analytical or imaginative grasp.

We are left alone with the best of Wisdom and Prophecy in pure vulnerable trust of the ultimately Ineffable, Unimaginable, Indiscernible *"Ruach"* in the Abyss or Void, waiting for the gifts of energy and order and meaning that come from beyond the reach of our wills or egos. Apocalyptic symbolizes the death to self that is necessary for the genuine relationship of love in which imagination and discernment are born. "The apocalypse is the way the world looks after the ego has disappeared" (Frye 1981, p.138). "We find in this act of dying the undergirding reality of love ... love meeting love in the abyss" (Holmes 1981, p.142). The outcome is that "Love fires the imagination." "As soon as we renounce the expectation of reward, in however refined a guise, for virtue or wisdom, we relax and our real energies begin to flow into the soul" (Frye 1981, p.124). The real energies are the energies of the Spirit of God.

*Attitude-Virtues.*

"But the fruit of the Spirit is love, joy, peace, patience, kindness, goodness, faithfulness, gentleness, self-control" (Gal 5:22). The New Testament authors, especially St Paul, expound in great detail the effects of the presence of the Spirit in human personality and in human community.[14] The work of the Spirit in animating and organizing reality and in making knowledge possible is closely related to what are often called the "spiritual" aspects of human personality. Modern psychoanalytic thinkers deal with the "spiritual" aspects of personality under the category of "attitudes." Their analysis of attitudes is a valuable set of ideas to enlist as an ally in constructing a biblical and contemporary theology of Spirit. There is considerable coincidence of terms and meaning between what the Bible calls the fruit of the Spirit in human life and what psychoanalysis identifies as the life-enhancing attitudes.

Donald Evans (1979) develops an analysis of what he calls attitude-virtues and their corresponding opposites, attitude-vices. He believes that religion is primarily a set of attitudes and morality is primarily a set of virtues. Religion and morality, by these definitions, are universal to human beings because no one exists without some kind of attitude-virtues or attitude-vices. If one sees that attitude-virtues are the work of the Holy Spirit in human personality, as the New Testament clearly shows, it follows that all human beings are "religious" in the sense of being involved in a relationship with the Spirit of God. This is the fundamental meaning of the biblical idea of people being created in the image of God. Humans "image" or mirror God by having the character or qualities of God's Spirit reflected in their attitudes.[15]

The New Testament in several places refers to Jesus Christ as the image of God (Col 1:15, Heb 1:3, II Cor 4:4) and refers to human fulfillment as "the old nature ... being renewed after the image of its creator" (Col 3:9-10) or being "conformed to the image of his Son" (Rom 8:29). It is clear that St Paul understood the renewal of the image of God in people to consist of their receiving and struggling to express the Spirit of God who was the Spirit of Christ. He says: "We all, with unveiled face, beholding the glory of the Lord, are being changed into his likeness from one degree of glory to another; for this comes from the Lord who is the Spirit" (II Cor 3:18). Many Christian scholars have assumed that the Lord to whom Paul refers here is Jesus, but James D.G. Dunn has made a convincing case that it is the same Lord, Yahweh, before whom Moses took off his veil (1970a, pp., 309-320). The theological

---

[14]This aspect of the activity of the Spirit is not uniquely seen in the New Testament. Heron (1983) says *"ruach* [in the OT]... functions at the level of persons to mould their attitudes and behaviour"(p.6).

[15]Frankl (1975) testifies to the saving efficacy of attitudes which eyes of faith (including Frankl's) can see to be the work of God as Spirit. "It is through attitudinal values that even the negative, tragic aspects of human existence, or what I call the 'Tragic triad' — pain, guilt and death — may be turned into something positive and creative" (p.125).

significance of this point will be taken up again in a later chapter. Whether the Spirit here is thought to be the Lord God or the Lord Jesus Christ, in either case it is clearly the Spirit who works to fulfill the image of God in people. The qualities of the Spirit which are given to people are, we will see, substantially the same as what Evans calls attitude-virtues. According to the New Testament, various kinds of love, faith, hope, freedom, humility, joy and courage are some of the qualities of the Spirit that fulfill human life. The life-enhancing attitude-virtues that Evans analyses, borrowing from various psychoanalytic thinkers, include the same qualities of personality.

This is not the place to attempt a comprehensive treatment of the qualities which Spirit contributes toward the fulfillment of human personalities. In this outline of the theology of Spirit it is possible only to point to some of the main ones in order to give some idea of this particular aspect of the work of the Spirit of God in the world. Some of the qualities of Spirit that are operative in the human functions of imagination and discernment have already been mentioned. The love and justice that are prerequisites for knowing others in the Spirit of truth are the same qualities that are important for relating to oneself and others for purposes other than knowledge. Some of the other qualities of the Spirit in human personality such as humility and trust can also be seen to be operative in the relationships of knowing. The Spirit cannot be "parcelled" into neat segments of different kinds. As Barth claimed in his exposition of the divine attributes, all the attributes of God are inseparable. The various "perfections of love" and the "perfections of freedom" are substantially one.

In Evan's analysis of life-enhancing attitude-virtues the unity of all good attitudes hinges on the basic attitude of trust which itself includes five constituents (assurance, receptivity, fidelity, hope and passion) and is also presupposed and actively involved in the other seven basic attitude-virtues i.e. humility, self-acceptance, responsibility, self-commitment friendliness, concern and contemplation.

We have already spoken very briefly about the "pure, vulnerable trust" that is given in the experience of the Void and which is the opening of the self to all the energies and meanings of the Spirit. Evans sees one aspect of such trust to be "reality assurance," the confident acceptance that reality is fundamentally meaningful and worthwhile (trustworthy). "Acceptance means being open to life energies, cherishing their many manifestations, welcoming into one's inmost being the myriad forms of love and joy, beauty and creativity, harmony and radiance, mystery and presence, meaning and passion" (1979, p.27). In New Testament terms such an attitude of acceptance is, perhaps, "the narrow gate" (Mt 7:13) that leads to life.

Conversely, the refusal to trust may be the "unforgivable" sin that shuts out the Holy Spirit and thereby precludes the coming of other gifts or attitude-virtues. If so, it would appear that the "unforgivable" sin can be "visited" from the parents to the children "to the third and the fourth generation of those who hate [God]" (Ex 20:5). "Basic trust," the psychoanalysts tell us, is first mediated to a child by the trustworthiness of his or her parents. If children do not find the first people they encounter in life to be trustworthy and, as a result, develop personalities with an attitude of distrust, along with the whole configuration of other life-diminishing attitudes that tend to go together with distrust, it will be very difficult for such children to become trusting persons later in life, and they may well pass on their distrust to their own children. The vicious cycle of distrust begetting distrust can be broken only by a decisive conversion, a *metanoia,* which reverses a person's basic stance in life or basic attitude as a person. Such conversion is a real possibility. It can happen through repentance and forgiveness, which are also gifts of the Spirit. The dynamics of salvation or healing of deformed personalities and systems will be considered more fully in Chapter Five.

The ways in which basic trust influences some of the other attitudes can be mentioned only very briefly. Receptivity is "a syndrome of stances: gratitude, confirmation of others, and generosity" (Evans 1979, p.49). These are obviously impossible without the element of trust. In the absence of trust this "syndrome" is replaced by another consisting of wariness, resentment, hostility and miserliness.

Fidelity, another aspect of trust, is a faithful commitment which is steadfastly continued despite the anxieties or doubts that may arise. This, too, is a gift of the Spirit as well as a struggle of will. "For through the Spirit, by faith, we wait for the hope of righteousness" (Gal 5:5). The opposite of fidelity is idolatry in which some substitute good [or god] is sought with unmanageable craving or addiction. Despair may be the outcome of disappointing idolatry.

Passion is "trustful openness" (Evans 1979, p.85) to intense feelings that rise in the body-self, whereas its opposite, apathy, is thoroughly wary of them, repressing them in favour of "safe" neutrality. Passion may allow painful or even "negative" feelings to be expressed in the trust that "nothing ... can separate us from the love of God" (Rom 8:39, NEB). Without some such trust a person cannot have "wholeheartedness, enthusiasm, and empathy" (Evans 1979, p.103), three forms which passion can take.

Humility also involves trust. It is "a realistic discernment and acceptance of both what I cannot do and what I can do" (1979, p.111). It is the opposite of either unrealistic self-humiliation or unrealistic self-aggrandizement, both of which are stimulated by anxiety. Self-acceptance in spite of guilt is a familiar attitude to protestant theology which has emphasized justification by grace through faith. Self-rejection or self-punishment fails to trust that "You are accepted," as Tillich's famous sermon put it.

We have already mentioned responsibility as one aspect of the open, receptive attitude which characterizes I-Thou relationships. Self-commitment, another basic attitude, entails trusting that one's own life and personal identity are meaningful and important, warranting appropriate commitment in all the main expressions of one's being. The opposite of self-commitment is dissipation which does not take one's self seriously but scatters one's energies incoherently in dilettantish or similar behaviour.

Friendliness is the willingness to risk the self by entering into "I-Thou" relations of love. Anyone who is willing to be vulnerable in openness and good will towards another person has also to have the attitude of basic trust. Otherwise one will remain self-isolated behind a protective barrier of role playing, or else treat the other as an object for one's own purposes.

Concern is another variety of love, in which good will is directed towards those who have some obvious need of help. Concern can be pastoral or prophetic, the former directed towards individuals such as children or adults in distress, or the latter directed towards social institutions or ecological issues. The trust involved here is similar to that in self-commitment. If one cares and risks to take initiative one has to "sin boldly" as Luther said, and trust that God can use one's efforts for good. The opposite of concern is self-indulgence in which one is sentimental about one's own conditions and reserves one's own affluence or influence for self-benefit.

The final attitude-virtue that Evans describes is *contemplation.* It, too, is a variety of love, the capacity "to celebrate the sheer existence of people and things" (Evans 1979, p.149). This is the supreme attitude of trust in the worth of what exists. It is a religious attitude in the narrower sense of the term, meaning a relationship to what pertains to the Whole of Reality. It is a stance of worship and prayer, standing as it were before the Holy One who unifies cosmic reality. In an attitude of contemplation one can appreciate Elizabeth Barrett Browning's well known poem.

> Earth's crammed with heaven
> And every common bush afire with God.
> But only he who sees takes off his shoes —
> The rest sit round it and pluck blackberries (1900, p.372).

The opposite attitude to contemplation is self-consciousness or a self-preoccupation that again sees the rest of reality mainly in terms of the possibility of personal advantage.

By emphasizing trust as he does, Evans may appear to depart from the New Testament emphasis on love as "the greatest" of the gifts of the Spirit. Evans' analysis, however, clearly affirms that the varieties of love are the "supreme goals in human life" (p.160). The emphasis on trust is a realistic acknowledgment that, as Tillich said, "faith logically precedes love although in actuality neither can be present without the other" (1963, p.129). Trust and love are inseparable. They are two sides, as it were, of the one coin of the Spirit. This metaphor is, of course, inadequate because the Spirit present in personalities has more than two "sides."

An analysis of attitudes such as Evans has done provides some illuminating distinctions to understand what the New Testament calls faith, hope and love. Faith and love, if not hope, are terms capable of many interpretations and various meanings. This is not the place to try and explore different interpretations which theologians and others have given to them. The point I wish to make here is that faith and hope and love and courage and humility are some of the ways in which the Spirit of God empowers people. These gifts of the Spirit might be summed up under the category of grace, a term which St Paul, in particular, used most frequently to describe the contribution of God as Spirit in human life. Grace provides the qualities of mind and heart that we now call attitude-virtues. Grace, in Paul's view, also provides the power and meaning of another essential element in human fulfillment, namely, vocation.

*Vocation.*

The Spirit not only gives the power and structure of attitude-virtues to personality but also, according to Paul, gives the power and meaning of particular talents that constitute the vocational purpose of individual lives. "Having gifts that differ according to the grace given to us, let us use them ... prophecy ... service ... teaching ... exhortation ... he who contributes ... he who gives and ... he who does acts of mercy" (Rom 12:6-8). In another place Paul gives a similar list and concludes: "all these are inspired by one and the same Spirit who apportions to each one individually as he wills" (1 Cor 12:11). Paul is by no means unique among biblical authors in seeing individual talents and vocations as being the result of the Spirit present in people. In Exodus 31:1-11 there is the account of Bezalel and the other skilled artists and craftsmen who were appointed to make the tabernacle and its furnishings. "The Lord said to Moses 'See, I have called by name Bezalel ... and I have filled him with the Spirit of God, with ability and intelligence, with knowledge and all craftsmanship, to devise artistic designs ... for work in every craft ... and I have given to all able [people] ability, that they may make all that I have commanded you'" (Ex 31:1-5). According to this passage it is possible to conclude that the work of the world's people, which entails countless vocational skills and abilities, is empowered and enabled by the gifts of the Spirit of God.

In the story of the creation of people in the image of God (Gen 1:26-28) biblical scholars have discerned a vocational purpose in the meaning of image. The purpose is the stewardship of the earth and its creatures on behalf of God. The "dominion ... over all the earth" mentioned in Genesis 1:26 is understood finally in terms of the selfless loving service seen in Jesus who is deemed to be the true image of God. Service is the purpose that St Paul sees for the gifts of the Spirit that he talks about. In his letters the varieties of charismata are so wide ranging — from singing to celibacy to healing, for example, — that it would be arbitrary to exclude any vocational gifts that are not mentioned. The question of skills used for evil purposes can be approached only with some understanding of evil in view. The nature of the diabolical or demonic is considered in a later section.

Apart from the idea of the Spirit giving people general kinds of vocational gifts, the Bible speaks of the Spirit as the effective agent in the anointing of those whom God calls to very special and particular vocations. In I Samuel 10:1-9 we read of Samuel anointing Saul, the first king of Israel and saying, "the spirit of the Lord will come mightily upon you, and you shall ... be turned into another man." Similarly when

Samuel anointed David, "the spirit of the Lord came mightily upon David from that day forward" (1 Sam 16:13). The Servant of God in Isaiah's Servant Songs who will be chosen (or was chosen) to "faithfully bring forth justice" (Isa 42:3) is empowered by the Spirit. "Behold my servant whom I uphold ... ; I have put my Spirit upon him" (Isa 42:1-2). Jesus (in Luke 4:18-19) is reported to have understood his own vocation in terms borrowed from Isaiah 61:1-2. "The Spirit of the Lord is upon me, because he has anointed me to preach good news to the poor ...." In John 20:20-23 Jesus is reported to give the gift of the Holy Spirit to the disciples immediately after giving them a vocational purpose. "As the Father has sent me, even so I send You." For the New Testament church, and indeed for the church in all ages, baptism of the Spirit is an event of vocational definition, as it was for Jesus himself. The corporate vocational purpose of the people of the covenant brings us to the last term to be proposed for this outline of a theology of Spirit.

*Ethos*

The *Concise Oxford Dictionary* defines ethos as "characteristic spirit of community, people, or systems." The Spirit of God is present and active with power and meaning in groups of people as well as in the personalities of individuals. The Hebrew people and the Christian church have certainly affirmed this to be true, although they have not always allowed that the Spirit is present in other social groups besides themselves. The ethnocentric or ecclesiasticized view of the Spirit that is found at times in the Bible or in the church should not prevent a theology of Spirit from affirming that all communities, peoples or systems have the Spirit of God in them, however fragmentarily. The particular experiences that the people of Israel or Christians have had of the Spirit working in their respective communities can be explored as indicative of the ways in which the Spirit is active in other communities as well. Protestant theology for the most part has been willing to acknowledge that the church is, like individual Christians, *simul justus et peccator* and *semper reformanda*. The Catholic church and some Catholic theologians have questioned the validity of the church's claims to infallibility. The view in this outline is that if the Spirit did not come fragmentarily to social groups, including the church and the people of Israel, it would not come at all. A total or perfect presence of the Spirit in any community can only be posited as an eschatological possibility. As long as communities have human beings in them who are free in some sense and capable of resisting grace there will always be room for growth in the Spirit.

Ethos, then, is a word which can appropriately be used to speak of how the Spirit is present in communities, peoples and systems. As the Spirit provides the energy and information or patterning for all the created universe, including every dimension from the inorganic to the human personality, so too it can be seen to be the power and meaning that creates and enlivens social groups. Sometimes, to be sure, the Spirit appears to take a demonic form in the "principalities and powers." This question of the demonic will be addressed in the following section.

The vocational purposes given by the Spirit to individuals are typically seen to be part of the larger vocational purpose belonging to the community and people as a whole. Thus, Bezalel and the other crafts people, as noted, were called to exercise their skills in the service of the community whose vocation is centred around their worship in the tabernacle. Ezekiel speaks about God giving the house of Israel "my Spirit" in order that Israel will be able to fulfill their God-given vocation. "And the nations will know that I am the Lord, says the Lord God, when through you I vindicate my holiness before their eyes" (Ezek 36:23).

The New Testament church saw itself as the vanguard of God's redemptive work in the world which was directed to "make disciples of all nations" (Mt 28:19). This vocation was guided and empowered at every stage by the Holy Spirit, ever present and intimately involved in the church's life and mission. In Acts we have pictures of the Holy Spirit helping to pick Saul and Barnabas for a particular mission (Acts 13:1-4), forbidding the church at one point "to speak the word in Asia" (Acts 16:6-7), and participating in the decisions of the Jerusalem council (Acts 15:28). The Spirit was clearly thought to be active in the vocation of the church, as in Israel's vocation.

In other communities and social groups besides the church or Israel it is possible to affirm that, in so far as their *raison d'être* is not destructive but serves some good purpose in the total scheme of things, its power and meaning come from the Spirit of God. Paul Tillich had such a vision of the Spirit's work. "Wherever it is fragmentarily actual the Spiritual Presence is at work — through or in opposition to the churches or outside the overtly religious life" (1963, p.264).

The prophet Joel proclaimed that God would pour out the Spirit "on all flesh" (Joel 2:28). Lampe points out that St Paul's emphasis on Christ as the Second Adam indicates that "the object of the Spirit's creative work is not the Church as an end in itself; it is humanity as a whole" (1977, p.178). The metaphor Kingdom of God is finally unthinkable if it means only a small segment of humanity or the universe, and the metaphor of God reigning as a sovereign suggests that the economy, the education systems, health systems and so on, all have a God-given purpose which the communities, peoples and systems in the "Kingdom" are called to serve. The Reign of God is effected by God as Spirit present in the ethos of the peoples, working in and through the vocations of all the groups as well as individuals within social structures.

The Bible is particularly clear in saying that redemptive organizations are established by God's Spirit. "Not by might nor by power, but by my Spirit, says the Lord of hosts" will the new temple of Israel be established (Zech 4:6). Paul asks the Corinthians "do you not know that you are God's temple and that God's Spirit dwells in you?" (I Cor 3:16). *The First Letter of Peter* exhorts the readers "like living stones be yourselves built into a spiritual house" (I Pet 2:5). The author of *Ephesians* echoes the theme: "the whole structure ... grows into a holy temple in the Lord; in whom you also are built into it for a dwelling place of God in the Spirit" (Eph 2:21-22). The Pauline metaphor of body is also dependent on the idea of the Spirit bringing the body into existence. "For by one Spirit we were all baptized into one body ...

and all were made to drink of one Spirit" (I Cor 12:13).

In this outline of a theology of Spirit the power and meaning of Spirit have been considered from the point of view of the various positive, creative, good things that God as Spirit does in the universe and especially in human existence. Very little has been said about the existence of evil powers and meanings except to suggest that it is to the doctrine of principalities and powers that a biblical and modern theology of Spirit might look to find an appropriate set of ideas to speak about evil in relation to the work of God as Spirit. Some understanding of the working of evil is part of the preunderstanding that is brought to christology as well as developed in it and from it. The question of evil, then, must be addressed at least to the extent of indicating some of the main ideas that will be operative in subsequent soteriological and christological formulations.

*The Spirit and the Demonic*

The organization and order which God as Spirit gives to created beings is understood in our time in terms of the systems that characterize the many aspects of reality from the inorganic to the ecological. These systems express fascinating and awesome energy and information that we experience symbolically as the power and meaning of God as Spirit. The same systems, however, are capable of expressing power and meaning that, far from being symbolic of God, might better be described as diabolic, a word which comes from the Greek *dia-ballo* meaning "mislead" (Cf. Holmes 1981, p.128). The systems in creation often appear to be diabolic or misleading in the sense that they are not leading towards the good for which they were presumably created, but towards evil. Diabolic, of course, in English means "having to do with, proceeding from ... the devil: fiendish, atrociously cruel or wicked" *(The Concise Oxford Dictionary).* The systems as we know them appear to be devilish in certain respects, atrociously cruel, destructive and wicked, expressive of demonic, evil power and meaning rather than the power and meaning of God.

The problems this presents to people are twofold: (1) the practical problem of how to reduce, control or alleviate evil, so that suffering may be diminished, and (2) the theoretical problem of how to understand the origin of evil and the dynamics of its occurrence in relation to the power and meaning of God (Cf. Schilling 1977, p.29). Both problems are pertinent to christology, the logic of the saving agent of God.

However, the saving significance of the Christ has more to do with the first problem than with the second problem.[16] "For God sent the Son into the world, not to condemn the world but that the world might be saved through him" (Jn 3:17). The Christ does not primarily contribute an analysis of the workings of evil powers, although these can certainly be seen in relation to his life and death. Christ is primarily significant

---

[16]Cf. Boff (1978): "For Jesus, evil does not exist in order to be comprehended, but to be taken over and conquered by love" (p.119). Cf. also Sobrino (1978): "The quandary of theodicy must be resolved in praxis rather than in theory" (p.36).

as a revelation about how evil is dealt with practically when God's sovereignty is restored in the systems. The analysis of evil in creation may well be deeply affected by the revelation of God's saving work in Christ, but some analysis of evil, like some thought about God, is brought to the work of christology as well as derived from it.

The very first thing that has to be said about the theoretical problem of evil is that there are no completely adequate analyses or explanations of evil. Most people who have wrestled with the problem seriously have acknowledged that there is a mysterious quality about the occurrence of evil that is very much analogous to the mysterious quality of God's presence as Spirit. In fact, people have experienced evil in connection with wind, fire, water and earth in ways so similar to the ways in which Spirit is experienced symbolically in connection with these elements that evil is known as evil *spirit*. A demon is an evil spirit.[17] The demonic has a spiritual quality analogous to the quality of the divine. It is mysterious, fearsome and transcendent in the sense of being more than what we can fully understand or control. It certainly does not have real beauty of holiness that attracts by its goodness but it has something of the quality of the holy as a numinous, mysterious reality which appears to have its own power and meaning and can be almost personal in its capacity to take its own initiatives. Cancer or drought that causes starvation or killer hurricanes and tornadoes seem to be expressions of a demonic spirit at work in the universe.

In any case, evil has such a definite place in the world as we know it that one has to ask about its power and meaning in relation to God. Does evil have power and meaning apart from the energy and information provided by God as Spirit? Is reality fundamentally dualistic? Or is evil power and meaning polygenic in the sense of issuing from many origins? If the demonic were basically polygenic one would have to ask if the divine is also polygenic. The question of evil spirit is related to the questions of monotheism and polytheism. If the ultimate sources of power and meaning were thought to be dualistic it would amount to a kind of polytheism with two gods, one good and one bad.

According to the method in the present theology of Spirit the question of the demonic has to be approached first with reference to biblical understandings and then with reference to the modern ideas about the way things are. The Bible, being a collection of books written by many different authors over a long period of time, is not totally consistent even on such basic questions as monotheism and polytheism. At times in the Hebrew scriptures God appears to be portrayed as the highest "Lord of hosts" in a monarchic monotheism that virtually amounts to polytheism because of the hosts of lesser divine beings who have their place in the total scheme of things along with the highest God.

It can, however, be claimed with good grounds that the Hebrew people developed in the course of time an "exclusive monotheism" in which there is only one God who is present in the entire creation as Spirit,

---

[17]In Greek the word for demon, *daimon*, did not have the connotation of evil. It meant "divine Spirit."

Wisdom, Word or Glory. In exclusive monotheism there is no room for two or more cosmic spirits. If evil is spiritual it cannot be an independent cosmic spirit. Hence, we find evil spirits in the Hebrew scriptures being referred to as "sent" by God (Judg 9:23) or "from the Lord (I Sam 16:14).[18] "The Old Testament ... has anchored the demonic firmly in the Almighty power, that is to say, in the Spirit of God" (Schweizer 1960, p.6). Frye, however, observes that "Leviathan and Satan may be thought of either as enemies of God outside his creation or as creatures of God within it. In the *Book of Job,* and consistently only there, the latter perspective is adopted" (1981, p.194). The consistency of the Bible on the question is broken because evil spirit "is found eventually opposed to God and is hypostatized" (Schweizer 1960, p.6).

There is some ambiguity, therefore, between the increasingly strong exclusive monotheism in the Bible and the "limited dualism" in which Satan, originally a creature of God, acquires sufficient influence to engage God in a cosmic battle to determine the final outcome of creation. In apocalyptic thought God is seen as the winner of the final battle which helps relativize the powers of evil and make them temporary and limited opponents of God, not unlike rebellious human beings but on a larger scale.[19]

The understanding of principalities and powers as the larger scale creations in which evil is basically located can be related, as we have said, to the contemporary understanding of the systems in the universe. In a cosmology of systems the demonic is a function or malfunction of the systems. It is not an integrated or unified cosmic force like Spirit but is "legion" (Mk 5:9), that is to say, it consists of aspects of the many created systems but is not a single system in itself. The idea of a personified Satan as the chief ruler of all demonic spirits is an application of the royal metaphor which is convenient for classifying the many instances and forms of evil, but it must finally be demythologized if exclusive monotheism is to be affirmed. An ultimate dualism, as already noted, is polytheism.

The demonic, then, is something that happens in the created systems. Individual persons, it should be remembered, are themselves systems that participate in many other systems. Like typhoons, the demonic can be beyond our control and fearsomely mysterious, but it is not an evil god. It is an evil occurrence or evil aspect of the created systems. There is, therefore, hope that the Creator Spirit who gives energy and information to all created things can heal or restore evilly malfunctioning systems to their proper condition. The demonic is fundamentally parasitic, having its existence only because the systems already exist. The power

---

[18]Cf. Robinson (1962): "Originally the *ruach* is a non-moral energy which may issue in evil as well as in good, like the evil *ruach* that divided Abimelech and the Schechemites (Judges ix 23) or makes a husband doubt his wife's fidelity (Num v 14,30) or a people unfaithful to its God (Hos iv 12, v 4)" (p.15).

[19]Beker (1980) claims that such apocalyptic is the "coherent centre" of St Paul's thought. In Paul's theology "the major apocalyptic focus is, for him, those ontological powers that determine the human situation within the context of God's created order and comprise the 'field' of death, sin, the law, and the flesh" (p.145). Thus, in Pauline thought the principalities and powers are the locus of Satanic forces that cause evil and require the victory of God in Christ in order for salvation to be realized.

and meaning of evil is not from some independent source apart from God but is a distortion of the energy and information of God's Spirit.

In considering the theoretical problem of evil, therefore, it is valuable to realize that the good work of God as Spirit far outweighs or surpasses the amount of evil in existence. This is not to minimize the practical problems of evil which are horrendous, but it is to see the realities of God and evil in a more accurate perspective. Evil is a lot bigger than any individual human being but it is still creaturely, not Godly, which means there is still hope that God can overcome evil and restore the systems of creation to health and peace. Health and peace are operative words in overcoming evil because they infer wholeness and justice which are two of the casualties of evil when it occurs in the systems.

If we look at some of the particular examples of evil as we know it in our time it is possible to see something of how the demonic works, even if the demonic remains beyond our full understanding and control. In the physical or inorganic systems there is pollution of many kinds, like acid rain. Depletion is another kind of evil that relates to the inorganic dimension of the created world. In biological systems there are extinctions of species, addictions, disorders, illness, deformities. In the psychological systems there is guilt that can powerfully damage health. There is the fear of death and denial of death that Ernest Becker and others have documented so well. There are scape-goating, phobias, anxieties and psychoses. In the sociological systems there are racism, sexism, ethnocentrism and class conflict. In the economic systems there are disparities between North and South, rich and poor; there are inflation and unemployment. In political systems there are oppressive nationalism and denial of human rights. The examples are, of course, not exhaustive but they may give some idea of the way evil is related to the systemic organization of the universe.

To locate the demonic in the systems of creation does not imply that it does not also reside in the human heart. The *hubris* or *concupiscence* or sloth or any of the other sinful attitude-vices are clearly aspects of evil. They are, however, not simply individualistic in origin or function. Persons, we noted earlier, are constituted as persons in social relationships. The good or the evil that we have in our make-up as individual persons is not solely of our own creating although we are responsible for it and can struggle to liberate more goodness of the Spirit, as well as to control the influences of the demonic. As individuals we participate in a great many systems and the systems participate in us. The evil that is in our hearts is involved with the systems of which we are a part, and the evil in the systems is involved with the state of sin in our hearts. To some extent we help to make the systems idolatrous and demonic, and to no little extent the systems infest us with their evil. If we remember that the systems include psychological and sociological systems there is less danger of thinking of them as being totally outside the ambit of our personal responsibility.

What happens to corrupt the systems or principalities and powers, in the biblical view, is that they overextend their God-given authority and start acting as if they were gods. They are "rebellious" powers in the sense that they cease to serve the functions for which they were created and begin to serve their own ends, claiming independence from God and from other creatures and systems. They act like gods, too, in attracting the worship of human beings. In their immensely powerful place in the created order they pose as mysterious and fascinatingly transcendent. They elicit an idolizing response from people. The principalities and powers thus function as spurious "Spirits" calling people into vocations in their service, shaping the ethos of human communities, engaging imagination and affecting discernment, and offering energy and information to those who are willingly captive to their influence. The demonic "is the elevation of something conditional to unconditional significance" (Tillich 1951, p.140). The demonic is intrinsically idolatrous and idols are fundamentally demonic.

The upshot of the systems behaving as gods and being treated as gods is that they conflict with one another and rupture the peace and unity of God's "economy" or God's reign in creation. In acid rain, for example, one can see the conflict between the economic and ecological systems. The demonic and idolatrous forces in the economic systems disregard their appropriate limitations and claim more prerogatives than is their due, the result being a transgression on the domain of the ecosytems causing death and disruption. In the addiction of alcoholism one can see a whole cluster of systems in conflict. Our custom of social drinking, plus the economic power of advertising, plus certain psychological needs all combine in conflict with the individual's biological system and a web of sociological relationships in home and workplace. Individual and social life is torn apart whenever any of the systems assert themselves in ways that go beyond God's purposes for them. "A main characteristic of the demonic is the state of being split. ... A consequence of these splits ... is the state of being 'possessed' by the power which produces the split" (Tillich 1963, p.103). To the degree in which people are heteronomously possessed by demonic powers and meanings they correspondingly suffer a loss of freedom, and because they are no longer free they suffer a loss of the love that is the peculiar vocation of humanity, a loss of beauty and identity that come from the vocation of love, and finally a loss of hope (Cf. Newman 1983, pp.43-69).

The rule of the powers under their own aegis is not hopeful for humanity or the world because the systems by themselves do not have the necessary power and meaning to accomplish what only God can accomplish — justice among all the claimants for justice and peaceful coexistence among the pluralistic powers. If systems are treated like gods they invariably fail because they are not God and do not have the full power and meaning of God. They do not have what it takes to be God. Failure to be what they claim is as much an outcome of the demonic as is the inevitable conflict. The old story of King Midas gives a good illustration of how the powers conflict with each other and in the process show their weakness. Midas wanted economic power to be pre-eminent. He asked that everything he touched should turn to gold. When he got his wish he inadvertently kissed his beloved daughter who turned into solid gold. Midas' economic system was then in ironic conflict with his sociological and psychological systems. Gold proved to be incapable of being preeminent. It simply did not have what it takes to reign over all things. Instead of consummating or enriching Midas' life it tore his life apart. Marx, Freud and many others have shown the demonic propensities of money. It could be shown that any of the powers or systems in the world including religion can be equally destructive when they become demonic, functioning idolatrously apart from the sovereignty of God.

*Exclusive Monotheism*

The belief that there is ultimately only one God is characteristic of the Bible, both in the Hebrew scriptures and in the New Testament. This belief is or should be one of the presuppositions that is brought to the work of christology. There are different kinds of monotheism. Tillich distinguishes four kinds along with their "philosophical transformations," the analogous metaphysical systems that correspond in type to the various types of monotheism. While one must apologize again for the brevity of the treatment, it is necessary at least to name, and briefly to describe, the concept of God with which one approaches the interpretation of Jesus as the Christ.

The four types of monotheism in Tillich's view were: monarchic, mystical, exclusive and trinitarian, which correspond respectively to gradualistic metaphysics, idealistic monism, metaphysical realism and dialectic realism (1951, pp.228-235). Monarchic monotheism was referred to above as a kind found in early Hebrew religion where God is conceived to be "Lord of hosts" the "monarch who rules over heavenly beings, angels, and spirits" (p.226). This view of God is not consonant with the understanding of Spirit proposed here, in which God is conceived to be Spirit who is present and active wherever divine power and meaning are operative. There is no need to posit a hierarchy of divine agents if, as many biblical scholars affirm, the different modes of God's activity recorded in the Bible such as Spirit, Wisdom, Word, Hand, Face, Glory, etc. are intended by the authors to be thought of as periphrases which moderate the sense of God being fully exposed in one time and place. If the scholars are right, the main biblical view of God is not monarchic monotheism of an hierarchical sort.

A second type of monotheism is mystical monotheism. In this kind, God is thought to be so absolutely transcendent that the "ground and abyss" of God's reality are accessible only by ascetic discipline and are ultimately ineffable and inexpressible. While there is validity in recognizing the inexpressibility of God, this kind of monotheism is also not consonant with a theology of Spirit in which God's presence animates and orders everyday realities, illuminates in symbols and facilitates knowledge, empowers and informs attitude-virtues and community ethos, and calls individuals and social groups to their God-given vocations. God as Spirit is incarnational as well as transcendent, self-revealing as well as ineffable.

The third kind of monotheism described by Tillich is exclusive monotheism. This is "the elevation of a concrete god to ultimacy and universality without the loss of ... concreteness and without the assertion of a demonic claim" (1951, p.227). By concreteness Tillich means what I would call incarnation, God present and active in history. The God of the Bible is such a God, in intimate dialogue with people, in covenant relationship with the whole creation, taking concrete initiatives in history to save the Israelites from slavery in Egypt, "the Philistines from Caphtor and the Syrians from Kir" (Amos 9:7).The God of the Bible is universal and also incarnational in the sense of being in people and events in such a way that God "gives to all [people] life and breath and everything" (Acts 17:25), and "in [God] we live and move and have our being" (Acts 17:28).

God's claims on the world are not like demonic claims because they are claims for justice, which assures to everyone and everything their right to be what they are created to be. God's claim for justice is the form that God's love takes for all that has been made. This concept of God is the one that Jesus himself must have had if his knowledge of God was informed by scriptural tradition as well as by his personal experience. It is this concept of God that I wish to bring to christological interpretation. The big question, of course, is whether it must be supplanted eventually by a fourth kind of monotheism, trinitarian monotheism.

This question can be addressed adequately only after one's soteriological and christological formulations have been worked out. Historically, trinitarian monotheism emerged as a development after certain christological conclusions were affirmed. It was not originally a preunderstanding or presupposition of christological interpretations. Since the christocentric-trinitarian paradigm became the orthodox doctrine of the church, however, it is fair to say that most christological work has been undertaken with trinitarian monotheism as a preunderstanding. The political consequences of departing from the orthodox paradigm have been so drastic and have been publicly illustrated so vividly and regularly in the martyrdom of people like Servetus that it has, until very recently, been virtually unthinkable to approach christological thinking with a preunderstanding of God similar to that of most biblical authors, or of Jesus himself.

## *Summary*

From the swirling conversation among all the elements in christological method it is difficult to know when to stop or start in abstracting the content of preunderstanding that is brought to the conversation. The theology of Spirit is profoundly influenced by the New Testament and by Jesus himself, but it remains true that the understanding of God as Spirit did not start with Jesus or the New Testament. It is, therefore, realistic to acknowledge that a theology of Spirit is part of the preunderstanding that is brought to a Spirit christology.

In the theology of Spirit outlined here I have tried to be both biblical and contemporary because either biblical theology alone or a contemporary theology of Spirit alone would not provide an appropriate set of ideas with which to attempt an interpretation of Jesus as one in whom God as Spirit was singularly involved. Christology should not only be thoroughly rooted in the scriptural understanding of God, it should resonate with the understanding of God and the world which makes sense for contemporary people. Spirit must be seen to relate to our modern understanding of energy, information, epistemology, psychology and sociology or else it will remain a curious antiquarian subject that has little relevance for contemporary life.

The attempt to be both biblical and contemporary is confirmed as worthwhile when one discovers that the content of biblical understanding of God as Spirit is consonant with much of our contemporary understanding of reality and, indeed, contributes significantly to it.

The same is true for the biblical understanding of principalities and powers in relation to modern "systems theory." Biblical authors had a profound understanding of the corporate structures of both evil and good, and they clearly interpreted Jesus' saving significance in terms of those structures. We should do no less. However, we have to work out the meaning of Jesus' saving significance in terms of our own understanding of the corporate structures of reality, not in biblical terms alone, even if the biblical model is the decisive paradigm or exemplar to which we are committed.

Besides the theology of Spirit, the structures of evil and the concept of exclusive monotheism, there are no doubt other influential elements of preunderstanding that I have not acknowledged or examined in this chapter. I trust that what has been dealt with, albeit with regrettable brevity, will prove to be appropriate and related significantly to the christological formation that comes later.

## Chapter Four
## THE SPIRIT IN JESUS' LIFE, DEATH AND RESURRECTION

*Introduction*

Christology starts with an encounter with Jesus of Nazareth. People try to work out their ideas about the saving significance of Jesus as the Christ because they care passionately about him. They care about him because they know him to some extent. Some would say that christology begins with the Christ of faith but this would be inaccurate if it implied that such faith could come into being without Jesus of Nazareth.[1] If there had been no Jesus there would be no real Christ, only a product of mythical fabrication. Caring about Jesus is part of what faith in Christ means. If this is affirmed then one may say that christology begins with an encounter with the Christ of faith. If the Jesus who lived in Palestine were divorced from the Christ of peoples' religious experience, or vice versa, it is doubtful if there could be any real christology. Christology without Jesus would be ungrounded speculation or arbitrary fantasy. An account of Jesus without the caring about him that designates him as the Christ would be secular history and not faithful christology.

I recognize that to say this begs the question of the meaning of "Christ" and presupposes that Jesus can appropriately be called the Christ or Messiah. The fact is that whatever its original historical meanings and whether or not Jesus accepted the designation, the term Christ has consistently indicated more than anything else that those who have come to know Jesus through religious experience, mediated by the scriptures and the living traditions in the church, are constrained to acknowledge his unique significance for salvation, however the logic of salvation is conceived. What kind of salvation the term Christ stands for has varied widely in Christian history but the term Christ has always meant for Christians that Jesus of Nazareth is the one in whom and through whom salvation for human beings can be found.

Christological method, therefore, as we saw in Chapter II above, starts with the experience of God that occurs in historical recollection of Jesus as portrayed in the scriptures and other traditions of the church. The scriptures are, or should be, much more basic and foundational in the

---

[1] Cf.Tracy (1980): "Christianity without Jesus is no longer Christianity; the Christ principle without Jesus is always in danger of captivity to a personal or cultural mood. The Jesus of Christianity is the actual Jesus remembered by the church in the scriptures: the same 'dangerous memory' of the same dangerous Jesus is needed now"(p.243, n12).

recollection process than the interpretations in Christian tradition.

The formation and preservation of the canon of scripture is recognition of the very reasonable conviction that the knowing of Jesus and the religious experience of God's saving presence in him are better established on the "eye-witness" reports of Jesus' life, death and resurrection than on reports about him that were fashioned centuries later. Whether the authors of the accounts of Jesus in the New Testament were eye-witnesses of Jesus or not may now be open to question, but it is at least certain that the biblical accounts are much closer to being eye-witness reports than, say, the canons of the Council of Chalcedon in 451 C.E. The canonical writings are, with the possible exception of the *Gospel of Thomas,* the most reliable source-documents available to enable the recovery of what Jesus of Nazareth said and did in his life, death and resurrection. If the *Gospel of Thomas* or any other recently discovered writings were established by a universal consensus to be as authentic and reliable sources about Jesus as the canonical writings there would have to be an opening of the canon to include such writings or else an abandonment of the canon altogether in favour of a more sophisticated study of all the contemporary literature in the 1st. century C.E. which contributes to our understanding of who Jesus was and what he said and did.

The canon is not likely to be abandoned, at least by ordinary people, nor should it be abandoned. It is still the most reliable and basic material available for getting to know Jesus. If one cares about Jesus and is constrained to work out a christology, a logic of Jesus as the Christ who mediates salvation from God, then the starting point is still the information about Jesus and the interpretations of him that are found in the scriptures.

How one does historical recollection of Jesus in an authentic way in christology is no simple question, as we saw earlier. It entails using all the methods of historical and critical scholarship plus more recently developed methods of linguistic analysis and literary criticism. Furthermore, these scholarly methods operate within an hermeneutical circle in which a relationship of "mutually critical correlation" (Schillebeeckx 1981a, p.51) exists between what we find in the New Testament and our everyday lives. In short, our modern thought forms and experience influence the ways in which we encounter Jesus in the scriptures, and the Jesus we find in the scriptures critically influences the ways we think and experience life.

New Testament scholars are by no means unanimous in their understanding of how the New Testament information about Jesus is to be retrieved. Patrick Keifert suggests that there is a spectrum among the main positions to be found among New Testament scholars. The spectrum begins on one side with those who have a firm belief in the possibility of recovering accurate information about the historical Jesus and his historical context, by the use of historical methods. A second position is determined by the conviction that the New Testament authors themselves should be the focal point to which the retrieval process is directed, rather than the historical Jesus. A third position emphasizes the interaction of dialogue between the text and contemporary people; and the final position in the spectrum is held by those who eschew historical retrieval altogether and deal with the text strictly as a literary document interpreted entirely on its own terms. Keifert makes a proposal which I find convincing, namely, that "these various types of interpretation might be integrated for theological purposes" (1985, p.212).

Keifert thinks the linguistic paradigms (the third and fourth positions) should predominate. I believe that the historical paradigms (the first and second positions) should predominate. In my view, it is finally Jesus himself who commands interest and mediates an experience of God, even if it is extremely difficult to know Jesus through the prisms, so to speak, of the literary documents that give us information about him. I find those scholars to be convincing who claim that there is a substantial amount of trustworthy historical information about Jesus. At the same time, the literary documents that comprise the New Testament are undeniably sophisticated, profound and valuable in the ways in which they present their recollections and interpretations of Jesus. The pictures of Jesus which the New Testament authors give us also contribute to the understanding of Jesus that we come to know in the process of retrieval. If these pictures at times do not ring true to the historical Jesus whom we are able to find by using all the scholarly methods available (for example, if a New Testament author pictured Jesus as an anti-Semite), the pictures would have to be judged inauthentic in this respect in favour of what is known on more reliable grounds.

There is a lot of room for continuing debate and for judgments to change in this process of getting to know Jesus better, but it is clear to me that the name of the game, so to speak, is precisely getting to know Jesus better. This is predominantly an historical exercise and not a linguistic undertaking. To put it another way, the linguistic work which is certainly necessary and invaluable should serve the end of historical recollection rather then serving literary purposes as ends in themselves.

In this chapter, the aim is to explore the extent to which the Spirit of God can be seen to be operative in the life, death and resurrection of Jesus. In the hermeneutical circle which will function here, the modern thought and experience that will be in "mutually critical correlation" with what is found in the New Testament will be represented by the "biblical and contemporary" theology of Spirit that was outlined in the previous chapter. That theology of Spirit embraces what I see to be some of the key understandings of contemporary people about energy, information, bilateral mind processes, attitude-virtues, social ethos, and the virtually universal application of "field theory" or "systems theory" to every aspect of existence in the universe, including people. At the same time, the theology of Spirit also acknowledges that the Bible speaks about the same Reality of Spirit with its various functions and speaks about the same universe, albeit in different analytical terms. Hence, the contemporary component in the "mutually critical correlation" is, and should be, I believe, a "biblical and contemporary" system of thought.

The way in which this chapter will proceed is to follow the outline of the theology of Spirit as developed in the last chapter, asking at each stage what evidence can be found in the three focal points of Jesus' life, death and resurrection to indicate that God as Spirit was present and involved with Jesus of Nazareth.

*Energy and Information*

The involvement of the Spirit in Jesus' life is claimed by Matthew and Luke to begin with his conception. The main idea which the conception stories in these gospels are meant to convey is that God as Spirit is providing the creative power and form for the redemptive initiative in the Christ, analogous to the initiative provided by God as Spirit in the original act of creation. "The fundamental thought involved in the conception stories in their bearing upon the work of the Holy Spirit is legitimately derived from O.T. thought: the Spirit is *Creator Spiritus* in both creations" (Barrett 1966, p.23-24).

This conviction of the gospel writers that God as Spirit was involved in Jesus' life from its very beginning, accounting for the power that originated Jesus' life and the meaning which Jesus' life was to have, is not impossible to accept as a realistic description of the truth. The idea of a virgin birth may be considered to be a poetic or mythical way of expressing this conviction, and one need not and perhaps should not accept the poetic imagery as literal or factual truth. However, unless one is opposed to any idea of God's involvement as Spirit in the processes of life and history there is no reason, in principle, to reject the conviction of the Gospels that the Spirit, "the power of the Most High," did "overshadow" (Lk 1:35) Mary analogous to the way in which the Spirit was "moving over" (Gen 1:2) the waters, providing the energy and information for life in creation in the first place.

In the Rabbinic literature the idea is well attested that the Spirit as *Shechinah* is involved in every conception of human beings. "There are three partners in the production of the human being: the Holy One, blessed be He, the father and the mother" (*Niddah 31a,* cited by Barrett 1966, p.14). "Man will not be able to come into existence without woman, nor woman without man, nor both without the *Shechinah*" (*Gen. R.89.,* cited by Barrett). "When the husband and wife are worthy, the *Shechinah* is with them" (*Sotah,* 17a). Buber expresses a similar thought in poetic form: "When a man is intimate with his wife, the longing of the eternal hills wafts about them" (1970, p.151).

The stories about Jesus' conception by the Holy Spirit are not, however, making the Rabbinic point that all conceptions involve the activity of the Spirit. They are stressing that in the conception of Jesus the Holy Spirit was active in what we might call a providential way, "seeing to it" (*providere*) that the one is born who will be anointed to be God's redemptive agent, the Messiah. If one believes in God, it is not unreasonable to believe that God was active in a special way in the conception of Jesus, however that event happened biologically. This is not a matter of speculating about the details of genetic engineering undertaken by the Spirit. It is primarily a doxological response to what Jesus turned out to be. But at the bottom of the doxology is the belief that somehow God, present as Spirit in the conception of Jesus, accounts for the birth into this world of the extraordinary human being that Jesus was. By God's initiative and by God's design Jesus is given to the world. The energy and information of the Holy Spirit combine to start the redemptive work of God that was to be carried out by the Messiah in his life, death and risen presence. Nor does the energy and information of the Spirit cease to be operative with the event of conception alone. The Spirit contributes these elements to all the redemptive work in the subsequent life, death and resurrection of the Messiah.

The redemptive work of the Messiah is portrayed in the Synoptic gospels very much as a conflict between God and Satan, between the Kingdom of God and the power of Beelzebul. In the story of Jesus' temptation by the devil, in the miracles or signs that Jesus does, in the exorcisms, and in the story of the Passion itself, Jesus is shown to be in conflict with the powers of evil. In this conflict it is the power and mind of the Spirit which give Jesus the authority to exercise control over the demons or evil powers that oppose the Reign of God and disrupt and despoil the goodness of creation.[2]

In the cosmology of Jewish people at the time of Jesus evil was understood in terms of demons and the principalities and powers that we looked at briefly in the last chapter. Barrett notes that "in the Rabbinical literature ... we find a wealth of allusion to demons and their harmful activities ... . Demons were equally well known in the pagan world, and there is abundant evidence for belief in demon possession in both literary and non-literary texts" (1966, p.54). In accordance with this view of evil it was expected that the Messiah would deal with evil spirits when he came. Barrett cites numerous passages from the *Testament of the Twelve Patriarchs* and other sources to this effect (1966, p.58).

And Beliar shall be bound by him,
And he shall give power to his children to tread
upon evil spirits (Test. Lev. 18:11f.).

He shall redeem all the captivity of the sons of
men from Beliar and every spirit of deceit shall
be trodden down (Test. Zeb. 9.8).

And then his kingdom shall appear throughout all
his creation
And then Satan shall be no more
And sorrow shall depart with him (Ass. *Moys. 10.1).*

The Synoptics concur with this understanding of what will happen when the Messiah comes and portray Jesus primarily as the one who is engaged in the conflict with evil on behalf of the Reign of God and by means of the power of the Spirit of God.

In each of the Synoptic gospels the very first event in the active ministry of Jesus, after his baptism, is his time of temptation in the wilderness where he confronts the devil face to face in a kind of preliminary bout in which the fact of their conflict is attested and Jesus shows that the

---

[2] Cf.Gunkel (1979): "Jesus mighty deeds revealed the presence of the Spirit, the kingdom of the Messiah"(p.72).

devil can be overcome. In each of the accounts of the temptation it is the Spirit who "drove" Jesus (Mk 1:12) or "led" Jesus (Mt 4:1, Lk 4:1) into the wilderness for the encounter with the devil. In Luke's story "Jesus returned in the power of the Spirit into Galilee" (Lk 4:14) to begin his ministry. The ministry is defined immediately by Jesus in his first sermon in Nazareth when he quotes from Isaiah 61.

The Spirit of the Lord is upon me
because he has anointed me to preach good
news to the poor.
He has sent me to proclaim release to the
captives and recovering of sight to the blind,
to set at liberty those who are oppressed,
to proclaim the acceptable year of the Lord.
(Lk 4:18-19).

I shall be returning to consider this passage more fully at a later time, but it can be said now that it clearly illustrated the work of Jesus to heal and liberate people from their diseases, their bondage and their blindness, which in Jesus' time were thought to be the evil work of the devil, and it indicates the involvement of the Spirit in this work of overcoming the devil. The contribution by the Spirit of power and meaning to do the Messianic work of overcoming evil can be seen if we look at Jesus' miracles and exorcisms.

Exorcisms "were a signal instance of the power of the Kingdom of God in subduing the empire of the adversary" (Barrett 1966, p.68). According to Mark, Jesus answers the accusation that he casts out demons by the prince of demons with the logic that "no one can enter a strong man's house and plunder his goods, unless he first binds the strong man" (Mk 3:27). According to Matthew Jesus says "If it is by the Spirit of God that I cast out demons then the kingdom of God has come upon you" (Mt 12:28). In his version of this statement Luke refers to the "finger of God" (Lk 11:20) rather than Spirit of God, but as Barrett observes, "there is no real difference of meaning between finger of God and Spirit of God. ... Luke, no less than Matthew intends us to think of a divine might residing in Jesus, making him a 'pneumatic,' a spiritual person, and potent against evil spirits" (1966, p.63). In Luke 5:17, shortly after Jesus' first sermon in which he says that the Spirit is "upon" him, Luke says "the power of the Lord was with him to heal." This power is explicitly identified elsewhere by Luke as "the power of the Spirit" (Lk 4:14). St Paul, too, clearly classed the power to do miracles as one of the *charismata,* the gifts of the Spirit (1 Cor 12:10).

The power of the Spirit in Jesus enabled him to do a variety of miracles besides exorcisms. The New Testament sometimes used the term "power" *(dunamis)* as a general term to signify a mighty act done by the power of God. Thus, the people in Jesus' home district exclaimed "what *dunamis* are wrought by his hands!" (Mk 6:2). Sometimes the power *(dunamis)* in Jesus was seen to be almost like an electrical current that flowed out of him when he touched people to heal them. When the woman with the flow of blood touched Jesus in the crowd he turned to see her, "perceiving in himself that power had gone forth from him" (Mk

5:30). Jesus performed numerous healings by touching the persons involved, such as the leper (Mk 1:41), the two blind men (Mt 9:29) and the woman who "had a spirit of infirmity for eighteen years" (Lk 13:10-17). At one point Luke reports that "all the crowd sought to touch him, for power came forth from him and he healed them all" (Lk 6:19).

Dunn concludes that Jesus may have recognized his Messianic God-given authority because of "the visible evidence of the power of God flowing through him to overcome other superhuman power, evil power, to restore and make whole" (1975, p.47). Barrett also claims that the authority *(exousia)* of Jesus as Messiah is antecedent to the *dunamis* which he exercised. *Dunamis* is "kinetic energy" (1966, p.78) which issues from *exousia* "potential energy." In the story of the healing of the centurion's servant for example (Lk 7:1-10, Mt 8:5-13), the power to heal is clearly a result of the authority *(exousia)* that Jesus had and to which the centurion appeals. On two occasions Mark speaks of Jesus giving authority *(exousia)* to the disciples to exercise the power of exorcism and healing (Mk 3:15;6:7). This is reminiscent of the story in the Hebrew scriptures where the Lord "took some of the spirit that was upon [Moses] and put it upon the seventy elders" (Num 11:25). In Luke's account of Jesus' empowering disciples to go out and heal the sick and cast out demons he even says that the number sent out was seventy (Lk 10:1). This suggests that the authority and power to do God's work against the evil of Satan are the result of the presence of the Spirit of God.

The divine authority bestowed on Jesus also gave power to forgive sins (Mk 2:10, Mt 9:6, Lk 5:24) and to teach "as one who had authority" (Mk 1:22). Authority of this kind was the powerful and meaningful presence of the Spirit who could effect miracles and psychological healing through the spoken word alone. Jesus commanded the demons often by speaking directly to them, and because he had authority *(exousia)* they obeyed him.

The reaction of people to Jesus' miracles ranged from amazement (Mk 2:12,5:42,6:51) and marvelling (Mt 8:27,Lk 8:25), rejoicing (Lk 13:17) and glorifying God (Mk 2:12, Mt 9:8,Lk 5:26 etc) to fear (Mk 4:41, Mt 9:8,Lk 5:26 etc) and suspicion that Jesus was aligned with Satan (Mk 3:22,Mt 9:34). Barrett observes that these various reactions "attest in different ways the opinion that he was possessed of unusual ... spiritual power" (1966, p.86). There was no doubt that the early church believed it to be the very power of God present with him. In Peter's sermon on the day of Pentecost he introduced Jesus of Nazareth as "a man attested to you by God with mighty works and wonders and signs which God did through him in your midst, as you yourselves know" (Acts 2:22).

As Jesus' time of public activity began with a confrontation with Satan in the wilderness, and his entire ministry was a time of confronting demons in one form or another, so his Passion, the ending of his ministry, can be seen to be a climactic struggle with the power of Satan. In Luke's account the final sequence of events begins when "Satan entered into Judas, called Iscariot" (Lk 22:3). When Jesus foretold Peter's denial he said "Satan demanded to have you" (Lk 22:31). In all three Synoptic stories of the Passion the time in the Garden of Gethsemane is pictured as a tremendous spiritual struggle, even more intense than the original temptations by the Devil in the wilderness. Finally at Jesus' death darkness falls in a symbolic sign of Satan's apparent victory. We will return to the story of the Passion again, but for the moment it is enough just to see it as the conclusion of the same process that went on all during Jesus' ministry, namely, the conflict of God with the powers of evil in which the power and meaning of God's Spirit provided Jesus with the energy and authoritative purpose that overcame the works of Satan and promised peace and healing to all who would follow after him. The final conflict in the Passion, as we know, proves to be a victory for Jesus despite the initial appearance of defeat.

There is no way in which we will ever know for sure exactly what happened in the exorcisms, healings, and other miracles done by Jesus in his conflict with evil as it was understood in his day. In the withered hand that Jesus restored to wholeness did the bones grow suddenly to normal size (Mt 12:10 f., Mk 3:1 f., Lk 6:6 f.)? If not, what did happen? What actually changed so that the blind man Bartimaeus and other blind people could be made to see (Mk 10:46 f.)? When the dead were raised, including Lazarus, were there actually resuscitations of dead bodies? If not, what then took place? There is no doubt that these kinds of stories about Jesus were similar to miracle stories told about other eminent people in his time. It is therefore very likely that the stories about Jesus were designed, to some extent, to make the point that he was an extraordinary agent of God's salvation, even the long-awaited Messiah. Some of the miracle stories are quite apparently intended as allegories for homiletical or instructional purposes. Granting all this the question remains: can we understand enough about what Jesus was actually doing in his redemptive struggle with the powers of Satan to commit ourselves to continue the same struggle in our time? Can the work of his life be an occasion of religious experience for us, that is, an experience in which through knowing Jesus we receive the same power and meaning, the same Spirit who empowered and authorized his life-work? His miraculous accomplishments are extremely foreign to the ways in which the possibilities of energy and information are understood scientifically in our times. It is true that the limitations of science to understand all the real possibilities of energy and information can be seen to grow in direct proportion to what science has come to understand.

But perhaps it is not necessary to know the scientific details of what happened in Jesus' miracles in order to be assured that God's presence there as Spirit with energy and information is a possibility for us too, a possibility that promises some measure of victory over the powers of evil. As in the miracles of Jesus' conception by the Spirit and Jesus' resurrection in the Spirit, so in the miracles of his conflict with evil during his life, we may believe that God's power and purposes were somehow involved and actually effective.

*Imagination*

The picture that is given of Jesus in the Gospels is that of a person who is extremely perceptive, especially of other peoples' innermost thoughts and feelings. According to the understanding of the Spirit as the Go-Between who brings people into I-Thou relationships of intimate knowledge with each other it has to be said that Jesus lived consistently in the presence of this Spirit. If we say that imagination, as distinct from fantasy, is the ability to enter with the mind and feelings into the real situations of others, it can be said that Jesus had inspired imagination and empathy.[3]

He could look at Nathanael and say "Behold an Israelite indeed, in whom is no guile" (Jn 1:47), or at Simon, son of John, and say "You shall be called Cephas (which means Peter)" (Jn 1:42). These illustrate John's assessment of Jesus as one who "knew [people] so well, all of them, that he needed no evidence from others about a [person], for he himself could tell what was in a [person]" (Jn 2:25, NEB). Jesus knew who was to betray him (Mt 26:25) and that Peter would deny him (Lk 22:34). He looked at Zacchaeus and sensed a readiness to change (Lk 19:5) and "looking upon [the rich young ruler] loved him" (Mk 10:21) apparently empathizing with the tragic weakness of the young man's personality. On numerous occasions Jesus knew the thoughts of those who were hostile towards him and addressed the point of their hostility (Lk 6:8; Mt 12:25,22:18;Mk 2:8).

The recognition of Jesus' ability to know others almost uncannily has to be distinguished from the doctrinaire view which imputes absolute knowledge to Jesus by virtue of his eternal deity.[4] James Likoudis, for example, in criticizing the modern Roman Catholic catechism, *Christ Among Us,* claimed that Jesus, contrary to the view put forward in the catechism, "had total knowledge when was just a speck in his mother's womb" (1982). This opinion is similar to the medieval scholastic view of *scientia infusa* which held that the eternal Word had infused Jesus with all knowledge so that he "not only knows everything but knows everything in every possible way" (Schoonenberg 1971, p.123).

If Jesus is understood as one who lived profoundly in the Spirit of God and vice versa, his knowledge is not to be conceived in quantitative terms as a substance that was poured into him or imprinted indelibly in his mind like the patterns on a microchip. Jesus' knowledge was a product of his dynamic relationships with people and with God, relationships which entailed loving openness and self-giving, "stepping into the presence of the other and listening." His knowledge was a function of what we have called imagination, the grace of realistic empathy and solidarity with others, in which their true being and circumstances and possibilities are received, in the Spirit, into one's own consciousness. The quality of Jesus' imagination, in this sense is one of the awesome

---

[3]Cf. Boff (1978): "Perhaps in the whole of human history there has not been a single person who had a richer imagination than Jesus"(p.91).

[4]Cf. for example, Sobrino (1978) who acknowledges that Jesus had ignorance as any human being does. "Jesus' ignorance is not merely in matters of incidental detail. It goes right to the core of his own person and mission" (p.101).

and fascinating aspects about him which can be experienced as the Holy presence of God in him.

*Discernment.*

The Spirit also gives discernment which is the ability to abstract accurately from the immediate encounters of imaginal relating and apply the understanding so gained to other and future possible situations. In the Hebrew scriptures we saw the Spirit as inspiring law, wisdom, prophecy and apocalyptic. These kinds of discernment can also be found in Jesus and bear vivid testimony to the presence of God as Spirit in him. Yet another kind of discernment, however, had priority for Jesus: the discernment of the gospel.

*a) Jesus' Gospel*

"Now after John was arrested, Jesus came into Galilee preaching the gospel of God, and saying, 'the time is fulfilled and the kingdom of God is at hand; repent, and believe in the gospel'" (Mk 1:14-15).[5] The idea of God's Kingdom was the central aspect of Jesus' gospel message. "Of this there can be no doubt and today no scholar does, in fact, doubt it" (Perrin 1976, p.54). Kingdom, as a noun in English, suggests static, spatial connotations but the word used by Jesus had the connotations of a verb rather than noun, suggesting God's "*activity* in ruling" (Perrin 1976, p.55). The gospel that Jesus proclaimed was about the activity of God as Spirit which Jesus discerned in his own life and which he believed others could and would also experience. Jesus had received a call to announce and embody in his own person the coming of the age of the Spirit which he designated by the Messianic term Kingdom of God or Reigning of God. This Reigning of God would be a "decisive intervention in history" (Perrin 1976, p.60) which would bring great blessings for all who were prepared to accept it. Hence, it was a "gospel" i.e. good news about God's saving activity offered to any who would "repent, and believe."

It has been well established by New Testament scholars that the Kingdom preached by Jesus was the presence and activity of the Spirit of God. C.K. Barrett says "It is not too much to say that the spiritual might possessed and wielded by Jesus depended ... upon the relation of his ministry to the powers of the Kingdom of God" (1970, p.70). Dunn says *"The eschatological Kingdom was present for Jesus only because the eschatological Spirit was present in and through him:* in other words, it was not so much a case of 'Where I am there is the kingdom' as "Where the Spirit is there is the kingdom'" (1975, p.48-49). It follows, Dunn argues in a separate article, that Pentecost was the event in which the Kingdom came eschatologically for the church as it had come eschatologically to Jesus at his baptism (1970, p.36-40). The question of the relation of the Spirit (and Kingdom) in Jesus to the Spirit (and Kingdom) in the church will be taken up in another

---

[5]Cf. Sobrino (1978): "The most certain historical datum about Jesus' life is that the concept which dominated his preaching, the reality which gave meaningfulness to all his activity, was 'the kingdom of God'" (p.41).

place. Here it can simply be affirmed that the life of the Spirit which the church came to know so well and the life of the Kingdom that Jesus preached about are the same reality, namely, the activity of God present as Spirit governing the relationships of people both on an individual level and on a larger social and even cosmic level. "The message that sets the New Testament apart from the Old ... [is that] the Messiah has come; the age of the Spirit has opened; the Spirit itself [*sic*] is the power of the divine purposes centred in Jesus Christ, and radiating from him" (Heron 1983, p.39). Jesus preached this message as gospel, although for good reasons he muted the emphasis on himself as Messiah (the so-called "Messianic Secret"). He spoke relatively infrequently about the Spirit for the same reasons, namely, because "to have claimed a pre-eminent measure of the Spirit would have been to make an open confession of Messiahship, if, as seems to have been the case, there was a general belief that the Messiah would be a bearer of God's Spirit" (Barrett 1966, p.158).[6]

The occasions on which Jesus did speak of the Spirit and the unanimous way in which the gospel writers spoke about the involvement of the Spirit in Jesus' life, death and resurrection give compelling grounds for understanding the dynamic activity of God in Jesus synonymously in terms either of Spirit or Kingdom. If the substance of the Kingdom that Jesus preached as gospel is, in fact, identical with life in the Spirit[7] then the wealth of understanding of the Spirit in the New Testament books apart from the Synoptic Gospels and, indeed, in the Hebrew scriptures can supplement and enlarge upon the understanding of the Kingdom that we learn about from Jesus, as well as be tested by it. The gospel of God that Jesus preached contained both "what is new and what is old" (Mt 13:52). The decisive initiative of God in bringing the age of the Spirit was new; the kinds of activity that the Spirit does were old.

The gospel that Jesus preached and lived had to do with overcoming the powers of evil by living in close relationship with God in a covenant that required repentance and obedience but promised fulfillment and freedom and joy. The relationship with God that Jesus had was epitomized by his calling God "*Abba*" a term normally used in the intimate family relationship between children and their fathers. The "*Abba*" relationship was the "source and secret of [Jesus'] being, message and manner of life" (Schillebeeckx 1979, p.256). It was for Jesus, as for the church in due course a relationship created by the presence of God as Spirit.[8]

---

[6]Taylor (1972) suggests two additional reasons for the "comparative silence of Jesus about the Holy Spirit." "Believing that life-in-the-Spirit is the life of the end of the ages, his teaching about the Holy Spirit was bound to be wrapped up in metaphors of apocalyptic vision" (p.87). "Thirdly — though this can only be speculation — we have to ask how far one who lived totally and uniquely in the Spirit could himself be conscious of that Spirit. His whole attention was focused unchangeably on the Father" (p.88). Neither of these reasons seem to me to be as likely as the connection between the Messianic secret and talk of the Spirit.

[7]Cf. Driver (1981): "The gospel is a way of living ... the occurrence of a kind of relatedness so compelling in its 'promise' of things to come that it engenders expectation of a new age. ... It is the experience of community in awareness of the field of divine potential. It is the experience of the sacred power of life together (p.147-148).

[8]Cf. Taylor (1972): "The supreme and primary gift of the Go-Between Spirit is the abba-relationship whereby a [person] knows God as 'Thou, Father'" (p.176).

St Paul said, "When we cry "*Abba*! Father!' it is the Spirit ... bearing witness with our spirit that we are children of God" (Rom 8:16).

This close relationship with God as Spirit, as we have seen, provided Jesus with the authority and power to overcome evil in specific concrete situations. It presupposes a turning *(metanoia)* towards God or a returning that is accepted in forgiveness and love (cf.The Prodigal Son). It consists in trusting God to overcome evil ultimately, even if evil powers appear to gain the victory in the short run. We shall see this aspect of God's reigning relationship later on when the meaning of Jesus' death is considered. It has to be said now that the gospel of Jesus was not a *theologia gloriae,* a guarantee of simple success and uninhibited power. It was a message of power sufficient for peoples' weakness, a message of power present in weakness, the power of vulnerable love.

Since the Reigning of God is partly a matter of personal relationship with God it is pertinent to individuals who have to decide whether or not to orient themselves toward God and to keep the covenant with God. Perrin comments that "this concentration upon the individual and his [or her] experience is a striking feature of the teaching of Jesus, historically considered, and full justice must be done to it in any interpretation of that teaching" (1976, p.67).

True enough; but it is also true that the gospel is a message pertinent to social groups and social structures.[9] Perrin appears not to give sufficient recognition to the social meaning of the Reigning of God which has been found by other scholars to be at least as basic to the message of Jesus as the good news for individuals. In fact, the good news about overcoming the social and cosmic powers of evil has as its corollary the liberation and fulfillment of individuals, rather than vice versa. Kingdom, after all, is a political metaphor. The Spirit who constitutes the Kingdom created the social structure of the church as the people of the New Covenant, the New Israel, the "body" of Christ, the new "temple" in which individual members cooperate to do the work of God. While Jesus certainly stressed the significance and responsibility and infinite value of individual persons, it is necessary to acknowledge the corporateness of the categories with which he described the activities of God. The gospel was not primarily good news for isolated individuals. It was news about individuals living in community. It was the proclamation that God is active as Spirit re-uniting what has been estranged and divided by the demonic powers. The gospel of Jesus offered the possibility of being part of a covenant people. In the climax of his ministry Jesus is reported to have said that his own life-blood was the "blood of the covenant which is poured out for many" (Mk 14:24).

In recent biblical studies it is being acknowledged by many scholars that Jesus' message of the Reigning of God had intentional social, economic and political implications.[10] Cassidy (1978) has done a valuable

---

[9]Cf. Boff (1978): "The kingdom of God cannot be narrowed down to any particular aspect. It embraces all: the world, the human person, and society; the totality of reality is to be transformed by God (p.55).

[10]Cf. Schillebeeckx (1981a): "Even now we still hear some Christians proclaiming that Christian belief is purely a matter of the heart, of personal conversion, and that Jesus called us to conversion of the heart, to inwardness, and not to the reform of structures which enslave [people]. A closer analysis of the historical circumstances in which the Bible came into being will show us that this one-sidedness is un-Christian: it is only half of scriptural truth. ... Here [in Lk 22:25; Mt 20:25 f.; Mk 10:42 f.] the New Testament clearly recognizes that the life-style of the kingdom of God implies not only an inner renewal of life but also a renewal and improvement of social structures (p.58-59). Also Cf. Echegaray (1984, pp.89 ff.). Also Cf. Pawlikowski (1982): "The conclusion that needs to be drawn from the New Testament ... is that Jesus was a political activist who directly challenged the political power of the Temple priesthood. ... it is plain from the Gospels as they are, provided that we bring to bear a sufficiently sophisticated understanding of political power in Jesus' day" (p.100).

study of the social and political stance of Jesus as he is portrayed in the *Gospel According to St Luke*. Jesus' concern for the poor, the infirm, women and Gentiles, his attacks on surplus wealth, his advocating social relationships based on humility and service, his open criticism of political relationships of domination and oppression, his overt criticism of Herod and refusal to alter his conduct to placate him, his explicit attacks on the chief priests who were part of the political machinery in Palestine, the open attack on "those who sold" in the temple who were also controlled by the chief priests and probably paying them a percentage of their profits, his pointed insistence that what is rendered to Caesar should be judged by what is rendered to God, and his rejection and criticism of the violence that dominated political order under the Romans — all of these, Cassidy suggests, "cannot really be adequately grasped without reference to his faith in God and his understanding of God's purposes" (p.48). According to Luke, Jesus was not interested only in individual piety. His message of the Reigning of God and his own actions as representative of God's Reign "explicitly or implicitly call for radical modifications in these [social and political] patterns" (p.77). Accordingly, Jesus "posed a threat to Roman rule." "If large numbers of people ever came to support the new social patterns that Luke portrays Jesus advocating, and if large numbers came to adopt his stance toward the ruling political authorities, the Roman empire ... could not have continued" (p.79).[11]

Another perspective on the social, economic and political implications of Jesus' gospel as shown by Luke was given by Yoder (1972). Yoder claims that Jesus' first sermon in Nazareth gives "the platform" for his subsequent ministry. The quotation from Isaiah 61:1-2 as recorded in Luke 4:18-19 speaks very explicitly of social and economic matters. It announces good news for the poor, the captives, the blind, and the oppressed and proclaims "the acceptable year of the Lord." Yoder claims that "the acceptable year of the Lord" is a reference to the year of Jubilee which is described in Leviticus 25. According to this concept from Jewish tradition God requires that there be a major readjustment carried out in society every fifty years in order to set right what has gone wrong. Notably, people have become enslaved because of debts, the rich have accumulated more than their due share of society's wealth, the poor have become poorer to the point of hunger, and the strength of the land has been depleted by continuous cropping. The Jubilee year, therefore, was a call to periodic forgiveness of debts, redistribution of wealth, liberation of slaves and a year of leaving the land fallow. Yoder believes that Jesus was preaching that the Reign of God requires such down-to-earth adjustments in social order. When Zacchaeus was converted, for example, his first announcement had to do with the radical redistribution of his wealth. If Jesus did preach a message with such economic and political implications it would explain why he was such a threat to the established powers in his society. Nothing threatens the

---

[11] Frye (1981) comments that "if we think of [Jesus'] significance as prophetic rather than legal, his real significance is that of being the one figure in history whom no organized society could possible put up with" (p.132-133).

powerful more than a call for the redistribution of their wealth.

Jesus' teaching of the gospel and his own living of it cannot adequately be described in a few paragraphs or pages. The point of sketching its nature here is to carry through the search for evidence of God as Spirit in the life of Jesus. If the Spirit were not involved in the meaning of the gospel that Jesus proclaimed the basis for Spirit christology would be seriously weakened. It can be claimed, however, without any doubt, that Jesus' language of the Reigning of God could be transposed legitimately into language of God's active presence as Spirit. This is, in fact, what the early church did after it was no longer necessary to keep the Messianic secret. Jesus had spoken about the Spirit enough that the church could translate the gospel of the Reigning of God into the terminology of Spirit with confidence that Jesus' message was being faithfully continued. The term "Kingdom" as it was retained in the early church tended to refer increasingly to its future fulfillment of which the gift of the Spirit in the present was the *"arrabon,"* guarantee, or "first installment" (cf. Eph 1:14). For Paul and John and Luke the life of faith in the present was described primarily in terms of the presence of God as Spirit. This was consonant with the main emphasis in Jesus' preaching of the Kingdom. Perrin sums up: "In the teaching of Jesus the emphasis is not upon a future for which [people] must prepare, even with the help of God; the emphasis is upon a present which carries with it the guarantee of the future. The present that has become God's present guarantees that all futures will be God's future" (1976, p.205). The present as a guarantee *(arrabon)* of the future is present life in the covenant of God as reigning Spirit. This is the gospel that Jesus discerned, the gospel he lived and preached and died for.

*b) Jesus and The Law*

It was within the gospel covenant that Jesus also discerned the law of God which is "the law of the Spirit of life" (Rom 8:2). The imperative of law follows from the indicative of the gospel. Jesus' understanding of law has set a standard for western civilization that continues to measure statutes, ordinances, decrees and regulations wherever they occur. Because Jesus lived so closely with the Spirit of God he knew that love is the power of real justice and that love is the essence of the law. This was understood in the Hebrew scriptures and Jesus was reported to have quoted from them when he summarized the essence of the law in the two great commandments (Mt 22:37-40,Mk 12:29-31).

The difference that Jesus introduced to the understanding of law was in the conception of the extent of responsibility for application of the law. If the essence of law is love the question arises how far the obligations of love extend. This was the question posed by the lawyer who asked Jesus "And who is my neighbour?" (Lk 10:29) to which Jesus replied with the Parable of the Good Samaritan. It was also the question Peter raised when he asked "Lord, how often shall my brother sin against me, and I forgive him?" to which Jesus replied "seventy times seven" (Mt 18:21-22). Jesus extended the obligations of the law to the limits of love, subordinating principles of proportional justice, either distributive or retributive, to the Spirit of self-giving love. Thus, in the Parable of the Labourers in the Vineyard (Mt 20:1-16) the ordinary concept of fairness is upset by the idea that workers be paid according to their need rather than according to the narrower principle of proportional justice. Grace becomes the standard of law, and grace has no fixed boundary — it is a matter of acting in the Spirit of goodness as the father of the Prodigal Son acts. Good intentions and good results become the operative criteria in applying the law. Thus the offence of adultery extends to the lustful heart (Mt 5;28), and the laws of the Sabbath are not prohibitive of the works of healing (Lk 6:5-10);13:10-17,Jn 5:2-18) or acts of need (Mk 2:23-28), such as feeding the hungry. Positively speaking the "Golden Rule" sums up the matter of intentions. "Whatever you wish that people would do to you do so to them" (Mt 7:12).

It is clear that Jesus did not advocate dispensing with the obligations of law. According to Matthew he said "think not that I have come to abolish the law" (Mt 5:17). He was not antinomian, but he consistently relativized the status of written laws, emphasizing the priority of goodness and real justice over the limitations of written codes or accepted custom. In the Reigning of God, in which people are invited to participate, the demands of goodness are radicalized. The obligations to others correspond to the radical degree of love that God has for people. "In this expansion of man's horizons of obligation ... lay the revolutionary, new element of Jesus' ministry" (Kee 1971, p.638).

*c) Jesus and Wisdom*

In addition to discerning the gospel of God's Reigning and the law of the covenant of the Spirit Jesus also expressed wisdom in the tradition of the wisdom literature in the Hebrew scriptures. Certainly there were many in the early church who believed Jesus to be a representative or "envoy" of Wisdom — the Sophia of God who contributed the intelligible order to creation and the particular structures of the Torah, which wise people appropriate and apply.

Suggs observes that "the conception of Jesus as Wisdom's final prophet is quite central to Q's proclamation" (1970, p.28).He goes on to demonstrate that Matthew took the association of Jesus with Wisdom a step further to *identify* Jesus with Wisdom. In saying "Take my yoke upon you, and learn from me ..." (Mt 11:29) "Matthew has placed on the lips of Jesus a saying appropriate only to Wisdom, not Wisdom's representative" (Suggs 1970, p.96). Matthew, therefore, has a Wisdom christology and it is by no means the only example of Wisdom christology in the New Testament. Dunn (1980) does a thorough survey of the instances in the New Testament where Wisdom christology occurs, finding examples in Paul, John, Hebrews and Colossians, as well as Matthew and the earlier associations of Jesus with Wisdom in "Q" and in Luke. If one followed the principle of "where there is smoke there is fire" it would be perfectly safe to conclude that Jesus was a discerner and teacher of wisdom. The number of New Testament authors who saw Jesus in that perspective is considerable.[12] James M. Robinson affirms

---

[12]Cf. Sloyan (1983): "When Jesus of Nazareth, wonderworker and mystic, opened his mouth to teach, however, he was solidly in the wisdom tradition" (p.24).

that "it can be presupposed that some wisdom sayings were among Jesus' sayings from the beginning" (1971, p.112).

Some of the wisdom sayings of Jesus can be found in the Sermon on the Mount in Matthew and the Sermon on the Plain in Luke. In Gundry's commentary on Matthew he entitles the section of Matthew 6:1-7:27 "The Teaching of Jesus the Sage" (1982, p.100f.) and says that here "Jesus appears as the supreme sage, who teaches the wisdom of righteousness." His instructions take on the tone of O.T. wisdom literature. Schweizer says of the same section in Matthew, "the statements bear a marked resemblance to wisdom dicta that should be obvious to everyone" (1975, p.166). Perhaps there is no better example to select than Matthew 7:24ff.

> Every one then who hears these words of mine and does them
> will be like a wise man who built his house upon the rock;
> ... And every one who hears these words of mine and does
> not do them will be like a foolish man who built his house
> upon the sand.

The wisdom of Jesus in urging people to "do not be anxious about your life" (Mt 6:25), "judge not" (Mt 7:1). "do not throw your pearls before swine" (Mk 7:6), and do not hoard wealth "for where your treasure is, there will your heart be also" (Mt 6:21) has been part of the very vibrant tradition of Jesus' wisdom that has existed among Christian people in all ages. The self-authenticating truth of Jesus' wise sayings supports the idea that they originated in the activity of the Spirit within him.

### d) Jesus and Prophecy

Prophecy, in contrast to wisdom, is not a discernment of perennial and universal truths about the human condition; rather it is a passionate, concerned insight or action in particular crises and situations that call for judgment or action in light of the promises of God. Jesus was a prophet as well as a sage.[13] Indeed, there is considerable, if not unanimous, consensus among contemporary New Testament scholars that Jesus may have understood himself primarily as a prophet, the eschatological prophet of whom intertestamental Judaism had a lively anticipation.

There were two forms of such anticipation which related to the possible return of Elijah and Moses, respectively. Jesus is compared to Elijah and to Moses in various parts of the New Testament, although it is quite clear that he is not to be simply identified with them. If he was the eschatological prophet it was according to a revised version of the idea, not simply to either of the two popular versions. The *Gospel of John* repeatedly makes the point that while Jesus is like Moses in many respects he is greater than Moses, "for the law was given through Moses; grace and truth came through Jesus Christ" (Jn 1:17). In the story of the Transfiguration Jesus is seen to be with Moses and Elijah but the voice from the cloud clearly indicated Jesus' priority over them (Mt 17:5,Mk9:2ff.Lk9:28ff.). The story of Jesus' action in raising the son of the widow from Nain (Lk 7:11-17) was comparable to similar acts

---

[13]Dunn (1975) concludes firmly that "it is clear that Jesus regarded himself as a prophet" (p.82).

of Elijah (cf.1Kgs 17:17-24) and Elisha (2Kgs 4:18-38), and the people of Nain responded to Jesus' action by saying "a great prophet has arisen among us (Lk 7:16). There is a strong similarity, too, between the stories of Jesus feeding the five thousand and four thousand and the story of Elisha feeding the hundred men as recorded in II Kings 4:42-44. According to Luke 4:25-27 Jesus compared himself to Elijah and Elisha when he was preaching his first sermon in Nazareth.

Jesus appeared to class himself with the prophets when he said "a prophet is not without honour, except in his own country" (Mk 6:4,Mt 13:57,Lk 4:24) and when he said "it cannot be that a prophet should perish away from Jerusalem" (Lk 13:33). According to Matthew, Jesus spoke of giving his generation "no sign ... except the sign of the prophet Jonah" (Mt 12:39) although he qualified his prophetic status by saying "something greater than Jonah is here" (Mt 12:41) and qualified his status as sage by saying "something greater than [the wisdom of] Solomon is here" (Mt 12:42). No doubt these sayings are highly influenced by Matthew's theology but they do indicate quite clearly how the early church both classed Jesus with the prophets and claimed eschatological status for him. All that can be known of Jesus appears to corroborate this assessment of him and suggests that he likely thought this way about himself.

C. H. Dodd in an essay entitled "Jesus as Teacher and Prophet" (cited by Barrett 1966, p.94-95) listed fifteen points of similarity between Jesus and the great prophets of the Hebrew scriptures including his speaking with authority, sometimes in poetic form, his "pneumatic" traits such as visions and audition, his making predictions, his symbolic actions and his intimate communion with God, his preaching of The Reign of God, the ethical emphasis in his teaching, the similarity between his call for repentance *(metanoia)* and the prophetic "*shub*" (return), his special calling in a "pneumatic" experience, his consciously representing God, his mission to Israel, his sense of the historical importance of his life and death and his personal religion.

Schillebeeckx observes that Jesus in his preaching and actions consistently protests against "the gulf between theory and practice in Judaism ... the gap between 'orthodoxy' and 'orthopraxis'" (1979, p.244). This, for Schillebeeckx, "confirms one of the basic propositions of [his] book: in his life on earth Jesus acts, not in a messianic role but as the eschatological prophet from God — and that, according to one particular Jewish tradition, is equally 'messianic'" (p.245). After careful study of the models of latter-day salvific figures in Judaism Schillebeeckx concludes: "we are bound on analytical grounds to say that at primary source all four credal models start from the fundamental interpretation of the life of Jesus under the model of the 'messianic' that is, Spirit-filled, religious 'latter-day prophet'" (p.473). Walter Kasper concurs that "the best description for [Jesus] is 'prophet' (1976, p.69). "In fact it was most of all the Lord's own Spirit which was reflected in Jesus" (p.68).

Nothing confirms the presence of the prophetic Spirit in Jesus more than his social stance, his response to oppression and injustice, his concern for widows and children and labourers, his changing the status of women, his daring identification with the outcasts and despised people in his society, his criticism of the economic system that enslaved people for debt and that compromised even the Temple in Jerusalem. Jesus' predominant message of the Reigning of God was intrinsically a prophetic discernment of judgment and promise for the existing state of human relationships at both individual and social levels. Hence, the Spirit was upon him "to preach good news to the poor ... the captives ... the blind ... the oppressed." Out of the immediacy of his *"Abba"* relationship with God in Spirit Jesus discerned what was wrong all around him and what could be right in the Reigning of God in the world.

*e) Jesus and Apocalyptic*

A corollary of this prophetic discernment was Jesus' apocalyptic pronouncements. Apocalyptic is the cosmic extrapolation of prophetic judgment and promise. It goes beyond the range of immediate vision in space and immediate cognizance of time. "Of that day or that hour no one knows" (Mk 13:32), but the apocalyptic discernment expresses the ultimate victory of God over the destructive forces in existence which extend far beyond the limits of our vision. The extent of evil is so profound that its downfall will require an entirely new creation. Thus the Reigning of God, like the ruling of the powers, is declared to be ultimately ineffable and utopian. Any present approximations of either God or the demonic sources of evil are relativized. Fetishes, scapegoats and idols are all alike undermined.

There is a danger in apocalyptic thinking that the imagery of cosmic conflict and new creation will itself become absolute and thereby idolatrous and demonic, even if ostensibly doxological. We see this clearly in our times in the neo-apocalyptic millenialism that propagates views of the imminent destruction of the world based on calculations that centre on the founding of the state of Israel in 1948. This kind of apocalyptic is fundamentally (and this is the right word) inimical to the kind of apocalyptic that Jesus expressed in his preaching of the Reigning of God. The bottom line in Jesus' apocalyptic sayings was "The kingdom of God is not coming with signs to be observed, nor will they say, 'Lo here it is!' or 'There!' for behold, the kingdom of God is in the midst of you" (Lk 17:20-21).

Crossan (1973) and some others have pointed out that there are several kinds of eschatology that have been identified as the kind which Jesus preached. Albert Schweitzer concluded that Jesus advocated what might be called "consequent eschatology." In this kind the end of the world would come soon. Dodd saw Jesus teaching "realized eschatology" in which the new creation is a quality of life present already. A third kind, "progressive eschatology" combined the "already" and "not yet" of the first two kinds in a present-future tension. This has been a widely accepted understanding of Jesus' eschatology until very recently. Now another interpretation has been suggested which might be called "permanent eschatology."

In this view Jesus' eschatological preaching is not determined, as in the first three kinds, by the chronological view of time as a line running from the past through present to future. The apocalyptic new creation is not something that will happen in the future, imminent or otherwise, as opposed to happening in the present. Nor is it only a quality of life that can be realized in the present. The new creation, which is the Reigning of God, is present and in some sense realized as a new quality of life, but in such a way that nothing concrete in the present can be simply identified as God's Reign. The judgment and promise of God are *permanently* operative in relation to everything that exists. When God reigns God remains hidden even when present with power and meaning. God is, in other words, like *ruach,* wind, who "blows where it wills and you hear the sound of it but you do not know whence it comes or whither it goes" (Jn 3:8). God is essentially holy and mysterious.

This basic fact qualifies Jesus' apocalyptic thinking. In a sense, Jesus' apocalyptic thinking is the expression of God's holiness or "otherness" in relation to the concrete conditions of the world's existence. The apocalyptic of Jesus is the extension *ad infinitum* of his prophetic discernment of God's judgment of present circumstances and God's promises concerning them. The judgment discerned in relation to particular things or people is not absolute because it exists in the "earthen vessels" of a prophet's words and vision that are far exceeded by the infinite judgment of God. Similarly the promise of God discerned and proclaimed by a prophet in relation to particular things and people is not absolute because it is far exceeded by the promises of God. The promises and judgments, all the discernments of the Reigning of God, exist in "earthen vessels" which apocalyptic blows up in a puff of wind "to show that the transcendent power belongs to God and not to us" (IICor 4:7).

Jesus' apocalyptic represents a necessary dimension of his *"Abba"* relationship with God; it expresses the holiness of God that is real despite the intimacy of the relationship. When Jesus said "why do you call me good? No one is good but God alone" (Mk 10:18), he was expressing a similar point. Apocalyptic is prophetic discernment of good and evil relativized by the infinite truth of God in which good and evil go far beyond any human knowledge of it.

Crossan suggests that this kind of eschatology should be called "prophetic eschatology" to insure the distinction between it and apocalyptic which proposes the end of the world in chronological time (1973, p.25). I would propose calling Jesus' kind of eschatology "prophetic apocalyptic" as distinct from "predictive apocalyptic." It is important to see that Jesus' kind of eschatology is a kind of apocalyptic rather than mainly a kind of historiography. Dodd's and Bultmann's "realized eschatology" were closer to a real appreciation of Jesus' apocalyptic discernment than the other views which found a plan for human history as the basic component. Much as we wonder about the future of history and wish at times that we could be sure of the final outcome it is not accurate to find in Jesus' teaching any particular plan for the total process of chronological time. His apocalyptic discernment was not predictive, it was prophetic. It challenged all the absolutes and finalities that people perennially propose for their own purposes. In their place it announced the Reigning of God, the Holy One, the *Ruach* who is present with good power and meaning but who remains ultimately (i.e. eschatologically) mysterious in a tremendous and fascinating way.

Crossan believes that the analysis of Jesus' parables and aphorisms shows that Jesus was primarily teaching this "permanent eschatology" or what I am calling prophetic apocalyptic. He shows by painstaking exegesis that the parables primarily convey the message of "the permanent presence of God as the one who challenges world and shatters its complacency" (1973, p.26).[14]

Crossan calls this iconoclastic sensitivity "comic" eschatology. It is comic in the sense that any projected outcome of history is laughable seen in the light of the Holy Otherness of God. The laughter need not be "funny" but more likely "silent" (1976, p.32 *passim*) in recognition of the existence of pain before which one does not laugh. Nevertheless, the comic view accepts the world as a worthwhile "playing" by humanity, rather than as ultimate tragedy. "The silent laughter of comic eschatology is what binds us all most democratically together. It is the glad acceptance of a common fate, and, as such, it is love made visible" (p.32). Crossan accepts play (à la Huizinga) as "a supreme paradigm for reality" (p.28) and sees human language as "the only game in town" (my expression, not his). "There is no objective order except language itself" (p.180).

This does not appear to me to give sufficient recognition to the fact that God as Spirit is creating and renewing the world as well as challenging our human representations of world. Crossan is committed to the proposition that Jesus did not contribute to the formulation of law, wisdom or apocalyptic but only challenged all these with iconoclastic case parodies, antiproverbs, antibeatitudes, and comic eschatology. "The comic eschatology of Jesus involves an iconoclasm on all the major forms of his spiritual tradition" (1976, p.77). This is not the place to deal fully with Crossan's ideas, except to acknowledge the challenge they give to traditional thinking about Jesus and to acknowledge much value in them, especially in the idea of comic eschatology. At the same time, one has to say that preaching good news to the poor, liberty to the captives etc., is surely not a matter of "play" or iconoclasm alone but a real historical project albeit one that stands under the infinite prophetic apocalyptic judgment and promise of God.

If Spirit is seen as the ultimate paradigm of reality instead of play, one may affirm the reality of the creative expressions of Spirit in energy, information, imagination, discernment, attitude-virtues, vocation and ethos, or in whatever other terms one deems appropriate, while affirming the basic aniconic character of Spirit. To the contention that "there is no objective order except language itself" one has to insist that there is some kind of objective reality-out-there that corresponds, however indeterminately, to our discernment of it. People who are starving are not suffering from some version of a language deficiency although that

---

[14]Cf. Boff (1978): "Christ came basically to announce that God as well as human persons cannot be imprisoned within preestablished structures, whether social or religious. People must remain continuously open to the unexpected interventions of God. ... With Christ, all is shaken. With him the old world is finished (p.112).

may be a contributory factor. Law, wisdom, prophecy and gospel, when authentically discerned, are servants of reality-out-there. Apocalyptic can be an authentic discernment also when it reminds us of the inadequacy of our linguistic formulations and recalls us to hope in God's salvation beyond the limits of our temporal and spacial vision.

*Attitude-Virtues*

For many people it has been the personality of Jesus as much as anything else that has moved them to care passionately about him and to believe that God was in him.[15] Perhaps the centurion at the cross, who may have known or understood little else about Jesus except what he had seen of him in Jesus' last days in Jerusalem, was typical of those who have seen Jesus as a person and have been constrained to exclaim "Truly this man was a [or the] Son of God" (Mk 15:39).

There is no doubt a danger of psychologizing incorrectly when trying to recollect Jesus' personality. However, if we know enough about what Jesus said and did to regard him as a real historical person who can be a criterion for faith and life, it is not impossible to see what kind of person he was. It is possible to see what kind of attitudes he expressed in what he said and did. We define and analyse attitudes with our set of cultural ideas but the raw material of attitudes exists alike in all human beings as much as breath and the circulation of the blood do. Attitudes transcend cultural differences and can be seen for what they are despite the differing ideologies and cultural expressions of the people involved.

Attitude-virtues or good attitudes, we have said, show the presence of the Spirit of God in people. The evidence of the "fruit" of the Spirit in Jesus' attitudes is an important reason for having a Spirit christology. To look at this evidence of the Spirit in Jesus, I will, as in the outline of a theology of Spirit, follow Donald Evans' model of the structure of attitude-virtues.

*a) Jesus' Faith*

That Jesus had an attitude of fundamental trust is quite clear from what we know about him.[16] His prayer in Gethsemane "not what I will, but what thou wilt" (Mk 14:36) epitomizes Jesus' readiness to trust God to the point of death. With less trust he might have decided to "run away and come to fight another day." But he died as he lived, trusting in the Reigning of God. The story of Jesus walking on the sea of Galilee (Mk 6:45-52, Mt 14:22-33) was no doubt fashioned as a story "seeking to arouse faith" (Schweizer 1970, p.142), but it has given a lot of people a vivid image of the unshakable faith that Jesus had. In Matthew's version Peter represents most of us by comparison when he loses confidence and starts to sink.

In trinitarian theology there is some difficulty in acknowledging that

---

[15]Cf. Boff (1978): "The attitudes of Jesus ought to be followed by his disciples. They inaugurate a new type of human being and humanism, one we believe to be the most perfect that has ever emerged; and it has the capacity to assimilate new and different values without betraying its own essence" (p.77).

[16]Cr. Sloyan (1983): "The main thrust of Jesus' teaching was trust in God" (p.101).

Jesus had faith. If he himself was deity it is anomalous to think of him having faith in God anything like ordinary peoples' faith.[17] The communion among the three persons of the Godhead can only by a great deal of stretching be called a relationship of faith. In fact it cannot. This illustrates clearly the greatest difficulty about trinitarian theology, namely, its inability to treat Jesus' humanness with full seriousness. If Jesus cannot be conceived to have faith as other human beings do then he ceases to be human at all, no matter how dogmatically his humanity is affirmed.

If Jesus' full humanity is accepted with all that it implies then it is possible, indeed necessary, to see his trusting attitude as a component of his faith in God, as it is for others who believe in God. Jesus indicated that both "reality-assurance" and what Evans calls "satisfaction-assurance" were the fruits of his faith in God. The latter is the confidence that God will provide for physical life to go on, with sufficient satisfaction of what is needed.

> I bid you put away anxious thoughts about food and drink to keep you alive, and clothes to cover your body ... Look at the birds of the air; they do not sow or reap and store in barns, yet your heavenly Father feeds them.. You are worth more than the birds (Mt 6:25-27 N.E.B.) (Cf. Evans 1979, p.38)

Reality-assurance is the more fundamental trust that "life is worth living because it has already received the meaning and reality which are necessary for human fulfillment" (Evans 1979, p.23). The gospel of the Reigning of God, Jesus' central message and mission, is not least an affirmation of assurance that God provides the meaning and reality necessary for human fulfillment.

Out of his own trust in God Jesus was able to be receptive of others and generous in attitude toward those who were normally despised in his society. The story of Jesus and the woman who had been caught in adultery (Jn 8:1-11) shows the strength of Jesus' acceptance of those regarded as sinners and outcasts. In this case he deflected the punitive attack of the people who brought the woman before him by challenging them to consider the trust in God's acceptance of them that they depended upon. Jesus showed outstanding fidelity in this and other such instances because it was at great risk to himself that he acted in solidarity with the woman. She had been presented to him in order to trap and discredit him. He was already under strong suspicion and reprehension for having table fellowship with the wrong kinds of people. It took fidelity under the circumstances to hold steadfastly to the Spirit of acceptance that

---

[17]Schoonenberg (1971) affirms that Jesus had faith. He says: "Jesus understands himself always in relation to God, as Servant, as the Sent, as Son. This meant that he lived his life in surrender, obedience, and trust. Here is the place to ask the question of whether Jesus' attitude to God was one of faith. It is precisely through our acceptance of a limited and growing knowledge in Jesus that an affirmative answer to this question becomes probable (p.134-5). Cf. Boff (1978): "Faith for the Old and New Testaments is the power to say Yes and Amen to God ...; it is a continuous returning to and grasping on to God. According to this definition Jesus was an extraordinary believer and had faith. Faith was Jesus' way of life (p.113). Cf. also Sobrino (1978): "Of prime importance is the fact that [Jesus] himself was the one who first lived a life of faith in all its fullness ... he himself is the first and foremost of believers" (p.89).

he knew was theologically and spiritually right.[18] Moral courage is a good part of fidelity, and Jesus clearly had it on this occasion.

If Jesus had faith as other people have faith, he can also be seen to have had hope which is the aspect of trusting that arises in the face of despair. Hope is future oriented faith not to be confused with wishing or expecting. When the future looks like a "no-exit" situation and there is no light at the end of the tunnel except the proverbial headlamp of an oncoming train, despair is the temptation and hope is the "impossible possibility" based on the trust that "what is impossible with people is possible with God" (Lk 18:27). Hope is what Jesus had when he "steadfastly set his face to go to Jerusalem (Lk 9:51 K.J.V.) in full awareness of the likelihood that it would be fatal. Fatal, for Jesus, must have meant something like what fatal means for any thirty year old person. It raised the temptation of fatalism or some other version of despair and the possibility of hope, the belief against forseeable reality that unseen Reality will prevail for good. Hope is created by God, present in Spirit, as the power and meaning of the possibility of good in spite of evil. Prophecy, apocalyptic, wisdom, gospel and even law entail elements of hope in as much as they discern the promises of God in the midst of evil. Jesus can be seen to be full of hope.

It would hardly seem necessary to remember that Jesus was capable of the attitude of passion, except that it has been denied so frequently in Christian history in favour of a cold-blooded "Passion" in which Jesus acted out a role demanded by the transaction God is thought to require in order to forgive the sins of the world. Passion as an attitude is the moving presence of God as Spirit creating intense feelings along with sufficient trust to allow the feelings to be expressed. Self-justifying anxiety impels us to repress strong feelings in cautious apathy. We even make apathy into a cultural virtue, valuing "cool" detachment to the point of avoiding intensity of any kind. Jesus was a passionate person, if we judge by his tears over the city of Jerusalem (Lk 19:41), his fierce anger over the desecration of the Temple (Mt 21:12;Mk 11:15;Lk 19:45) and, finally, his cry of dereliction on the cross (Mt 27:46;Mk 15:34). In the latter, especially, can be seen the trust required of passion that calls on God even in moments of utter, mind-crippling anguish.

*b) Jesus' Humility*

Humility is sometimes considered to be the first Christian virtue, but again it has been illogical to attribute it to Jesus when he is considered to be essentially deity. There is a modern song that goes "O Lord, it's hard to be humble, when you're perfect in every way." Jesus might have sung this song if he were the kind of person that the tradition of the church has, for the most part, made him out to be. His humility in washing the disciple's feet and in accepting death on a cross can appear to be posing or gestures staged for effect unless Jesus was a real human being who was realistic about his limitations as well as his God-given significance.

---

[18]Sobrino (1978) stresses Jesus' fidelity: "Perseverance is another intrinsic feature of faith according to the Old Testament. Faith, in short, implies 'fidelity'" (p.103). Sobrino sees Jesus' fidelity as the aspect of his faith that enabled him to persevere through the Galilean crisis.

The implications of Jesus' saying "Why do you call me good? No one is good but God alone" (Mk 10:18) are seldom fully drawn out because of the *a priori* conclusion that he could not possibly have meant what he said. When Jesus advocated humility as he did on numerous occasions such as the times when he used children as examples (Cf. Mt 18:4; Mk 10:15;9:37;Lk 8:17;9:48) he was surely applying the criterion to himself as much as to others.[19] This was clearly the case when he said to the disciples "whoever would be great among you must be your servant ... . For the Son of man *also* came not to be served but to serve, and to give his life as a ransom for many"(Mk 10:43-44) (Italics mine). *The Gospel According To John* undoubtedly represents Jesus' humility faithfully when it has Jesus say "He who believes in me, believes not in me but in him who sent me" (Jn 12:44). Despite its "high" christology this Gospel could not lose sight of a fundamental quality of Jesus' personality, namely, his awareness that God is God and humans are human. This realistic appraisal of himself does not preclude his having a sense of "high" vocation, but it nonetheless constituted his genuine humility.

Jesus' question "Why do you call me good?" (Mk 10:18) raises the issue of Jesus' possible sinlessness and whether or not he had an attitude of self-acceptance in spite of some awareness of guilt. The *Epistle to the Hebrews* claimed that Jesus was "one who in every respect has been tempted as we are, yet without sinning" (4:15). Very few Christians have seen fit to differ with this description despite the difficulty of making sense of it in light of an understanding of human psychology, or of sin as an indelible part of social structures or, for that matter, in light of traditional Christian understanding of sainthood which recognizes saints partly by the depth of their sense of sin. The understanding of faith as the relationship in which one takes off one's shoes before God as Moses did and confesses as Isaiah did that "I am a [person] of unclean lips, and I dwell in the midst of a people of unclean lips" (Isa 6:5), also prompts one to ask "what about Jesus?". Was he *simul justus et peccator* like every other human being that can be conceived of, or must we conclude that he really was different in kind from every other person who ever lived?

The idea of Jesus as Second Adam and Image of God suggests that he reconstituted sinless humanness as it was, mythologically speaking, before the fall. The fall, however, can be understood not only mythologically but in a discursive, descriptive way utilizing the insights of psychology and sociology, in terms among other things of learning by mistakes and reflecting cultural biases. Even if Jesus never had to learn from painful personal failings, which is hard enough to imagine, it is even more difficult to see how he could grow up without participating in some of the distortions of his cultural milieu, assuming that such things as ethnocentrism or male chauvinism or certain institutions and customs like capital punishment or slavery are wrong. Jesus certainly

---

[19]Machovec (1976) notes that "before Jesus, nobody in the world imagined that childhood represented a human value or that it was an exemplar of humanity" (p.99).

is known to have challenged many wrong things in his society. Further, as many scholars have noted, there is remarkably little, if any, evidence in the Bible of Jesus having any occasion for remorse or any sense of guilt. The picture we get of Jesus is of one who is so full of the Spirit, so closely related with God whom he called "*Abba*", living so completely within the Reigning of God that there is virtually no trace of any human separateness from God or from other human beings that could be called the dynamics of sin as it is usually defined.

If the Gospels are what Philip Shuler (1982) calls "encomiums" or laudatory biographies it is not surprising that they do not contain much about Jesus' mistakes or failings, if he had any. In any case there are few, if any, signs in the Gospels that show Jesus coming to terms with his own short-comings and accepting himself in spite of things he had done that were wrong. One wonders about the time that Jesus arrived too late to help Lazarus before he died (Jn 11:1-44). The Gospel writer makes it appear that Jesus deliberately delayed going to Bethany in order that Lazarus would die and give Jesus occasion for doing a miracle for the glory of God. When Jesus arrived in Bethany he was reproached by Martha, and some of the Jews asked "Could not he who opened the eyes of the blind man have kept this man from dying?" (11:37). Jesus himself "was deeply moved in spirit and troubled" (11:33) and began to weep (11:35).This suggests the possibility of some remorse on Jesus' part. He had been told about Lazarus' illness and could have come sooner. Now when he sees the weeping Mary he realized the pain she might have been spared if he had come sooner. All this, of course, is speculation because the story is clearly fashioned for laudatory purposes. Still, Jesus' weeping under the circumstances hardly makes sense as grief for Lazarus' death, and one wonders if there is a trace here of an occasion when Jesus, either by omission or commission, caused unnecessary pain to another human being.

The Gospel records simply do not give evidence of Jesus having any sense of sin, except possibly for the question "Why do you call me good?". One does have to say that his teaching about God's forgiveness would be strange if he himself had never experienced it. It is also very difficult to imagine Jesus living without the necessity to "sin boldly" i.e. to act in situations where all the available options are undesirable in some ways, and there is no alternative except to confess one's imperfection and the imperfection of the world while trusting in the mercy of God.[20]

The question of Jesus' sinlessness is related to the logic of salvation and will be considered again when we take up that subject. For the time being it can only be acknowledged that historical retrieval does not show clearly that Jesus experienced guilt or forgiveness himself, although he certainly taught about them.

*c) Jesus' Self-commitment to God*

---

[20]Dunn (1973) argues that St Paul thought of Jesus as participating during his lifetime in the same ambiguous mixture of "flesh" and Spirit that makes his followers *simul peccator et justus*. "For Paul the earthly Jesus was the prototype of and example to the Christian caught in the overlap of the ages [of *sarx* and *pneuma*] — for it can hardly be argued that in Paul's mind Jesus' experience of the Spirit only began with the resurrection" (p.54).

It is infinitely less difficult to show that Jesus had the attitude of responsibility for himself before God and the self-commitment to follow through consistently with what he felt called to do and be. This vocational aspect of Jesus' life will be looked at in more detail shortly. Considered from the point of view of attitudes, there is no question that Jesus was responsive and responsible to the purposes he discerned for his life. We do not know much about what he did for the first thirty years of his life, except that Mark reports he was a carpenter (Mk 6:3), and Luke tells the story of his having some vocational awareness when he was twelve years old (Lk 2:41-52). We do know that when he was thirty Jesus began his public ministry and did not turn away from it until it was over. Among the elements of his personality that impelled him to take the course of life which he did there must have been a very strong sense of personal responsibility.

*d) Jesus' Self-giving Love*

There is only a fine line between the attitude of responsibility and the attitude of pastoral and prophetic concern. The latter is a variety of love for neighbours whereas the former is primarily love for God or some God-given purpose. In Jesus' case the two were inseparable. His love for God implied love for neighbour and his love of people demonstrated his love for God. Jesus' summary of the law in the two Great Commandments reflected his own attitudes. The Spirit of God who was in Jesus gave him the power to love the unlovable, to be a friend to the friendless and to care about the sinful world. Accepting the presence of that Spirit and its costly implications for his life was also an attitude of love on Jesus' part. He loved God and he loved humanity, and in both cases it was because of the Spirit of God within him.

Many theologians have seen in Jesus' self-giving love of God and humanity the most compelling evidence for his special saving significance, or even for his divinity. Pannenberg concludes that "Jesus is ... confirmed ... precisely in his having reserved nothing for himself in his human existence, in having lived entirely from God and for the [people] who must be called into his Kingdom" (1968, p.335). Macquarrie says "Christ's most utter self-abasement is also his ascension, when we recognize that God is in Christ" (1966, p.279). John A. T. Robinson, affirming the views of P.T. Forsythe and C. F. D. Moule, says "'the form of a servant' is not a derogation from ... the glory of God but precisely the fullest expression of that glory as love" (1973-p.208). In Moule's memorable phrase: "*Kenosis* actually is *plerosis*" (cited by Robinson (1973, p.208). The self-emptying *kenosis* (Cf.Phil 2:7) of Jesus in his love for God and humanity is the fullness *(plerosis)* of the presence of God as Spirit in him.

*e) Jesus and Prayer*

The catalogue of Jesus' attitude-virtues might go on indefinitely but I will mention only one more: his attitude of contemplation. The Gospels portray Jesus as a person who lived with prayer as a central part of his life. He frequently "went into the hills to pray" (Mk 6:46;Mt 14:23;Lk 6:12,9:28), including at the time of his Transfiguration. In Gethsemane he prayed before his arrest. He taught his disciples that "they ought always to pray" (Lk 18:1) and taught them how to do it. Jesus' style of prayer was not ostentatious public praying; in fact he cautioned against it (Mt 6:5-8), urging more prayer "in secret." By comparison with John the Baptist and his disciples, Jesus and his disciples appeared to be secular and irreligious. "The disciples of John fast often and offer prayers ... but yours eat and drink" (Lk 5:33;Mk 1:18;Mt 9:14). *The Gospel of John* apparently reflects Jesus' attitude on the matter when it has him say "God is Spirit, and those who worship him must worship in spirit and in truth" (Jn 4:24).

Prayer as the attitude of contemplation is more than the explicit words or postures of public or even private devotions although it certainly includes these, if we take Jesus as an example. Contemplation is an orientation of the whole of one's being to God and to God's presence in the whole of creation. It is to live in a thoroughly sacramental universe, aware of the "outward and visible signs of inward, invisible grace" in everything that exists. The attitude of contemplation is the doxological response of praise for the goodness that pervades all of reality, despite the evil that encroaches upon it. To live in contemplation is "the culmination" of other attitude-virtues (Evans 1979, p.152) because it means explicitly relating in trust to the Creator Spiritus, receiving and reflecting the qualities of good attitudes that we have mentioned: generosity, fidelity, hope, passion, humility, self-acceptance, responsibility, commitment, friendliness and concern.

Prayer is, in a sense, the door which opens to let God as Spirit be present with all the power and purpose that God can give. Yet prayer is itself a prevenient work of the Spirit not a "works righteousness." The attitude of contemplation, like the others, is first of all a gift or fruit of the Spirit and only subsequently the object of our disciplined effort. Jesus is important to those who care about him not least because he showed the way of a life of contemplation that is also a life of dedicated and active vocation. He showed how worship and work can be one.

*Vocation*

Up to this point we have been looking mainly at Jesus' life, including his personality and teachings, as one of the three focal points in which people encounter God's saving presence as Spirit in Jesus. The other two focal points, Jesus' death and resurrection, can also be seen as events in which God's presence as Spirit was the determinative factor that causes the events to be of saving significance for people.

Jesus' death was the climax of his life; as such its meaning was the meaning of Jesus' vocation. There are ways of understanding Jesus' death which separate its significance almost completely from the significance of his life and teachings. If his death is regarded primarily as a transactional atonement done to resolve the juridical dilemma of cosmic guilt it has little or nothing to do with what Jesus said or did before he was crucified. This doctrine of atonement and others will be considered further in the chapter on soteriology. It must be said now that any view of Jesus' death which ignores his life is not satisfactory because it does not take his full humanness seriously. Jesus was put to death for reasons that can be identified in his ministry and teachings. To ignore or minimize the reasons for his crucifixion is to ignore the historical person of Jesus and to disregard what he himself was committed to do and be. If Jesus' death is not to be seen as a tragically fated error or, worse, the killing of a good man staged by God, it has to be seen as the outcome of Jesus' vocation.

We have already touched in general terms on Jesus' vocation as preacher of the gospel of the Reigning of God, teacher of the law of the covenant and the wisdom of God, prophet of God's judgment and promise, and proclaimer of apocalyptic vision. His vocation can be seen in sharper perspective, however, when it is seen to lead him to the cross. His death clarifies and intensifies the meaning of his vocation. It also shows the way in which God's presence as Spirit worked in Jesus to accomplish God's saving purpose. To announce and live the way of God's Reigning was Jesus' vocation. It was at the same time to live in the way of the Spirit and the way of the cross.

We cannot be exactly sure when Jesus grasped the nature of his vocation with full clarity. It is likely that his vocational self-understanding developed in the course of his ministry and preaching. It may have begun to develop quite early in his life. *The Gospel of Luke* claims that Jesus had some awareness of his call to a special vocation when he was only twelve years old. Both Matthew and Luke say that Jesus' special vocation was made known to his parents and others when he was an infant or even at the time of his conception. Whatever the time of Jesus' initial call, whether or not it was communicated to him through his parents or through some other means, it is quite certain that he began to act on it when he went and received baptism from John the Baptist in the Jordan river.

Jesus' baptism was a time of vocational confirmation for him, or at least that is how it is portrayed in the gospel narratives.[21] In the first place the fact that he went and received baptism from John "meant that he was moving in the same circle of prophetic and eschatological concepts as the Baptist" (Barrett 1966, p.35). Jesus identified himself with John's concern about the imminent coming of the Kingdom of God and also with the ethical implications of the Kingdom that John stressed so vigorously. The way in which the story of Jesus' baptism is told in the Gospels makes it into a christological affirmation of Jesus' messiahship, identifying Jesus as the messianic Son ("Thou art my Son" Cf. Ps 2:7) and the elect Servant of God ("my Beloved; with thee I am well pleased" Cf. Isa-42:1;44:2).

This explicit christological understanding may be anachronistic at such an early stage in Jesus' ministry; it depends on whether or not Jesus had put together for himself the distinctive concept of the Messiah who was also the Servant. He must have had quite a well developed concept of his own role at this early stage in order to explain why he left his

---

[21]Cf. Congar (1983, Vol.III): "I would suggest that there were two moments when the *virtus* or effectiveness of the Spirit in Jesus was actuated in a new way. The first was at his baptism when he was constituted (and not simply proclaimed as) Messiah and Servant by God" (p.171).

former occupation and began a public ministry of preaching and healing. Further, he must have had a distinctive idea of the meaning of messiahship in order to explain the so-called "Messianic secret." If he preached consistently about the eschatological Reigning of God it is unlikely that he totally disavowed the idea of himself as Messiah but the fact that he did not want to be identified with the popular Davidic concept of Messiah means that he must have had another interpretation of messiahship as the criterion by which he rejected the prevailing popular view. The story of his baptism fits with this line of reasoning. It links the concept of Messiah and Suffering Servant in what became the uniquely Christian interpretation of messiahship, a concept that C. H. Dodd called "a piece of genuinely creative thinking" (1965, p.109).[22] If Dodd is right in saying that the Christian messianic interpretation "is an achievement of interpretative imagination which results in the creation of an entirely new figure" then it is most reasonable, I think, to give Jesus the credit for that achievement as Dodd does, especially since it has not been possible to trace its origin to any other particular person in the early church. If Jesus did, in fact, put together disparate strands of Jewish thinking into a new concept of Messiah and the way of the Kingdom of God, it is not unreasonable to assume that this vocational self-understanding had at least begun to take shape at the time Jesus began his vocation, i.e. at the time of his baptism.[23] The accounts of his baptism may not be very anachronistic, even if they are highly imaginative.

The story of Jesus' baptism tells of his seeing the Spirit descending upon him like a dove. This fits well with the idea that his baptism was a vocational confirmation for Jesus. Both the concepts of Messiah and Suffering Servant were firmly associated with the gifts of the Spirit in Jewish tradition. Isaiah 42:1 which is alluded to in the words that Jesus is said to have heard at his baptism, says "Behold my servant, whom I uphold; my chosen, ... I have put my spirit upon him." Barrett (1966, pp.42-44) shows that in later Jewish literature (i.e. I Enoch 49:3;Pss Sol 17:42; and Test Lev 18:2-14) the idea of the Messiah being anointed with the Spirit was also extant at the time of Jesus. We have no reason to doubt and good reason to believe that Jesus experienced the Spirit

---

[22]Dodd starts out from the questions "How do the New Testament authors use the Old Testament in their writing of the New Testament? Who uses them?" His hypothesis is that if two or more NT authors use the same passages from the OT then there must have been a tradition in the NT church of interpreting the meaning and person of Jesus by referring to those OT passages. Dodd finds fifteen passages (which he calls "testimonia") that are used by from two to five NT authors writing separately in different times and places. Dodd discovers that the ways in which the OT passages were interpreted were new and surprising; scriptures widely separated in meaning are brought together to create new concepts. "To have brought together, for example, the Son of Man ... and the victorious priest-king at the right hand of God, is an achievement of interpretative imagination which results in the creation of an entirely new figure" (p.109). Dodd asks "Who was responsible for it?", and notes that "the New Testament itself avers that it was Jesus Christ Himself who first directed the minds of His followers to certain parts of the scriptures as those in which they might find illumination upon the meaning of His mission and destiny" (p.110).

[23]Cf. Dunn (1975): "It is certain that Jesus believed himself to be empowered by the Spirit and thought of himself as God's son. These convictions must have crystallized at some point in his life. Why should the traditions unanimously fasten on [Jesus' baptism] if they had no reason for making the link and many reasons against it? ... The most probable reason therefore is that Jesus underwent a significant experience—significant in terms of his consciousness of sonship and Spirit — on the occasion of his baptism by John" (p.63).

throughout his ministry and thought of the Spirit as the power and meaning of the presence of God which constitutes the Reigning of God. The experience of the Spirit coming to him at his baptism and thereby starting his vocation as Servant-Messiah is quite reasonable and historically probable. If Jesus did not experience the "anointing" by the Spirit at his baptism it must have been sometime around the beginning of his active ministry because the Spirit was what his ministry was primarily about. The Spirit was what made the Kingdom come and be, so to speak, operative. Jesus' baptism may very well have been the occasion when the Reigning of God was realized for Jesus and he was empowered and called by God present as Spirit to begin his vocation in service of the mission of God's Kingdom.

Immediately after the inauguration of his work as eschatological Prophet or Messiah-Servant, or however he thought of himself at that stage, Jesus began to struggle with the main issues of his vocation. The story of Jesus' temptations in the wilderness can be seen as an account of Jesus wrestling with issues that were to recur again and again until the very end of his ministry.

The central issue was the way in which the Kingdom of God might come. If the Messiah is the agent or bringer of the Kingdom what policies should the Messiah follow in order that the Kingdom might be realized most effectively and most surely? The temptations were not merely directed toward the subversion of Jesus' personal piety by greed, power or pride, for example, but were challenges to his vocation, his very *raison d'etre*.[24] A wrong decision on one of the temptations could destroy the work Jesus was called to do. It could subvert the basic purpose for his being baptized and leaving his occupation as a carpenter. Worst of all, if Jesus chose the wrong policies to follow in introducing the Reigning of God, it could be an implicit contradiction to the Reigning of God. Instead of realizing and representing the Reigning of God Jesus might realize and represent the ruling of the Powers of Satan, the very thing from which the Reigning of God comes to save the world.

The temptations were a crucial struggle about the way of salvation. Yoder (1972) has described the different ways of salvation presented to Jesus by Satan as "the economic option" ("Command this stone to become bread" Lk 4:3), the "secular power option" ("The devil ... showed him all the Kingdoms of the world ... and said ... 'To you I will give all this authority and their glory ... if you ... will worship me'" Lk 4:5-7) and the "crusade option" ("And he took him ... to the pinnacle of the temple ..." Lk 4:9). These three options involve the economic, political and religious systems, all of which are legitimate and necessary for human life.

In his ministry Jesus did provide bread for people — and according to *The Gospel of John*, "When people saw the sign ... they were about to come and take him by force to make him King" (Jn 6:14-15). Jesus had clearly decided in the wilderness at the time of his temptations that

---

[24]Cf. Boff (1978): "The three temptations narrated by the Synoptics try to show how Jesus overcame the three types of messianism ..." (p.60). Cf. also Sobrino (1978): "In functional terms the temptation has to do with the concrete way in which Jesus will carry out his mission" (p.98).

this was not the way the Kingdom should come, so "he withdrew again to the hills by himself" (Jn 6:15).

The "political option" was a lively temptation, too. Jesus may have felt real affinity with the Zealot movement in Palestine. One or more of his disciples may have had connections with the movement, for example, "Simon who was called the Zealot" (Lk 6:15) and, possibly, Judas Iscariot whom "some have tried to associate with ... a group of revolutionaries who appeared in Palestine just before the Jewish revolt of A.D. 66-70, and who were known as Sicarii, meaning 'daggermen'" (Laymon (ed.) 1971, p.622). If Jesus' message about the Reigning of God had explicit political and social content, as it is thought by some to have, it must have been tempting to Jesus to use the "secular power option" to realize the political objectives. Jesus was apparently thought by the Romans to be a political threat so they crucified him under a sign reading "The King of the Jews," an object lesson for other political revolutionaries. The Zealots and possibly other revolutionary movements may have seen the Jesus movement as an ally. Jesus resisted being coopted for political revolution, however, because although the message of the Reigning of God had revolutionary implications the way of its coming was not by force of arms but by the power and meaning of the Spirit of God.

The "religious crusade" option may have been the most insidious temptation of all. When Jesus began to attract great crowds of followers and when he went into Jerusalem in a triumphant procession that took him to the Temple, it must have been a temptation to think of the Reigning of God in terms of a theocracy in which the Messiah would fulfil the popular expectations for the "Son of David." The people were certainly ready for a religious crusade. The alternative way of the cross seemed very uncertain by comparison. In the Garden of Gethsemane before he was arrested Jesus apparently struggled for the last time with the temptation of establishing a theocracy as the means to realize the Kingdom of God.[25] The alternative of trusting in God's Spirit to realize the Reign of God and suffering the violence of the Powers rather than organizing violent forces against them was, to the end, a walking by faith, not by sight.

Jesus had the faith. According to John 18:11, when Simon Peter took up the sword against the arresting party and wounded Malchus, Jesus rebuked Peter saying "Put your sword into its sheath; shall I not drink the cup which the Father has given me?" This saying has echoes of the prayer of Jesus in Gethsemane as reported by the Synoptic writers: "Father if Thou art willing remove this cup from me" (Lk 22:42;Cf.Mk 14:36;Mt 26:39). Earlier Jesus had asked the ambitious James and John if they were "able to drink the cup" (Mk 10:38) that he would have to drink. He must have seen the way of his ministry leading towards the cross and struggled repeatedly with the question of its necessity.

This temptation of a religious crusade was a life or death question

---

[25]Cf. Sobrino (1978): "The agony in the garden ... is the total absolute crisis of the logic of the kingdom with which Jesus commenced his public life" (p.99).

for Jesus and it would never have been easy to choose death. As the story of the struggle in Gethsemane shows, he obviously and naturally did not want to die. The options, however, were not in line with the Reigning of God as he knew it. Jesus' vocation was at stake. All that he had preached and stood for in his ministry was being put to the supreme test. The way of the Spirit which was the way of the Kingdom was turning out to be the way of the cross. Jesus' fidelity held constant; his trust persevered; he hoped in the face of despair; his commitment did not crumble; his prophetic and pastoral concern remained strong; he was upheld by the power of prayer, and "Through the eternal Spirit [he] offered himself without blemish to God"(Heb 9:14).

*Ethos*

Those who get to know this Jesus experience the ethos that is created by encounter with him.[26] Anyone who has been moved to confession by the awesome and fascinating Spirit that was in Jesus can understand first-hand the disciples who left their nets to follow him. They can understand Mary and Martha, Mary Magdalene, Joanna, Susanna and the many others who "provided for him out of their means" (Lk 8:3). The conversion of Zacchaeus makes sense. And the experience of the resurrection, the gift of the Spirit that created the church, appears to be in reasonable and understandable sequence, following the culmination of Jesus' life and ministry at the cross of Calvary.

If the resurrection/ascension and Pentecost are regarded as totally separate events from the death of Jesus or his life they become totally mythical and suspect of being arbitrary creations of religious fantasy. In other words, if the risen "Christ of faith" or the Spirit of Christ is divorced from the historical Jesus the result is simply the addition of one or two more divine figures or deities to the mythological universe. If the interpretation of the resurrection and ascension lose touch with what actually happened in the community of original followers of Jesus, or if the Pentecostal event is thought to happen without any necessary connection to the life and person of Jesus, then such a Christian faith is in danger of losing its historical roots.

What actually happened in the resurrection/ascension and Pentecost was the creation of the ethos of the church by the same Spirit who was in Jesus of Nazareth. The resurrection is what Schillebeeckx calls "The Easter experience: being converted on Jesus' initiative, to Jesus as the Christ" (1979, p.379). Schoonenberg is even more explicit: "The resurrection of Jesus is not a historical fact, it is one of the possible and therefore free ways to interpret what comes over us if we are seized by him after Jesus' death" (1971, p.158). Schillebeeckx does a careful and thorough analysis of the accounts of the early church in the New

---

[26]Cf. Lampe (1977): "Jesus, however, was not only the archetype of life in the Spirit, that is, life lived by faith answering to divine inspiration. He was also the source of its communication to others. ... Jesus became both the pattern of sonship and also the inspiration and power which can create in us a response analogous to his own, to the Spirit of God that was in him and is in us. The interaction of divine Spirit with human spirit presents itself to us, and takes effect within us, in terms of the character, actions and words of Jesus" (p.24-25).

Testament and finds that some sectors of the early church did not use the symbol of resurrection to signify their continuing to care passionately about Jesus and their belief in his gospel. "What is apparently the earliest creed expresses belief in the Jesus who is to return as judge of the world and (for the church) bringer of salvation, without any explicit mention of his resurrection" (1979, p.396). "In the three other early Christian creeds the resurrection is ... not an object of *kerygma*." "It is a ... question whether for some Jewish Christians the resurrection was not a 'second thought' which proved the best way to make explicit an earlier spontaneous experience."

There can be no doubt that the followers of Jesus had some kind of experience of him after his death and that this common experience created the ethos of the Christian church, even if the experience is articulated in various symbols, including resurrection, the breathing of the Spirit into the disciples (Jn 20:22), or the Pentecostal experience recorded in Acts 2:1-13. Schillebeeckx finds evidence that the experience of the risen Jesus was the experience of forgiveness for those disciples who had defected from his side at the time of his arrest and crucifixion (1979, p.390). The story of Jesus releasing Peter from his guilt and saying to him "Feed my sheep" (Jn 21:15-17) supports this interpretation. Perhaps the fact that there were different credal strands in the early church indicates that the encounters with Jesus after his death gave rise to various emphases, depending on the situations, experiences, needs etc. of the persons concerned.[27] The Easter experience of the women who stayed beside Jesus right up to his death on the cross may not have been primarily an experience of forgiveness. In any case, it seems doubtful if the experience of forgiveness could be the central significance of the resurrection. This matter will be taken up again when the question of the saving significance of Jesus' death and resurrection are more fully considered.

The main import of the Easter experience can be seen to be the realization that the Reigning of God which Jesus had announced and manifested in his life was still operative in spite of his death, and even because of his death. The way of the Spirit in Jesus was seen in perspective to be truly the way of the cross; and the symbol of resurrection affirmed that the Spirit and its way of the cross are truly the way of God's reigning on the earth. The death of Jesus did not end the Reigning of God in him; it manifested the Reigning of God. To believe in it, to see it for what it was, is to meet Jesus not dead but very much alive, "the power of God and the Wisdom of God" (1 Cor 1:24). To take into oneself and "internalize" the meaning of Jesus choosing to die as a faithful expression of the Spirit of God is to encounter Jesus as a living person, a live option for the deciding of one's own way of life. Jesus becomes "Lord and Christ" (Acts 2:36). The Spirit in him becomes the Spirit in us and we are joined with him and others in the *ethos* ("characteristic

---

[27]One wonders what are all the connotations in the mind of the Marxist philosopher Machovec (1976) when he writes "An atheist ... can readily admit that the moment when Peter discovered that Jesus was still victor, after Golgotha, was one of the greatest moments in history and human experience" (p.39). He appears to be close to the meaning of *Christus Victor*.

spirit" *Oxford Concise Dictionary*) of the Christ's community.

The Spirit that was Christ's was and still is the Spirit of God. The Christian community of that Spirit is not the only human community in which God as Spirit can be found, but it is a reliable paradigm of God's reigning in Spirit, so long as it remains true to the one whose vocation was to announce and live the way of God's Reigning. The one whom God anointed (*mashah* — hence Messiah) to be the agent of a renewed covenant of salvation continues to function in that capacity despite his death, even because of his death. In Jesus' life and death God as Spirit is encountered, and his vocation becomes the vocation of his community of followers. Ecclesiology is the extension of christology.

*Summary*

The task of historical recollection in christological method is a massive one that engages the best efforts of countless people in the church. It is a never-ending task because the knowledge explosion keeps producing new materials and new insights that alter our understanding of what happened in the life and death of Jesus and in the early church which first bore witness to him. In contemporary biblical scholarship there is an intense ferment of new theories and interpretations which are continuously being tested and their implications worked out. To do the historical recollection needed in a Spirit christology is a task far bigger than what we have been able to do in this chapter. Edward Schillebeeckx devoted the better part of the nearly fifteen hundred pages in his two volumes, *Jesus* and *Christ* to study of the biblical sources of christology. The few pages in the present chapter are just a rough map of a large territory. I hope, nonetheless, that they do indicate which way the wind was blowing in the life of Jesus and the early church. I hope that they provide a reliable, if incomplete, map of the real territory to be known in the study of the New Testament.

The focus has been almost exclusively on Jesus himself and the Spirit who was manifested in him as energy and information, power and meaning, inspiring the imagination with which he knew people and God, guiding the discernment with which he formulated gospel, law, wisdom, prophecy and apocalyptic. The personality of Jesus was seen through the lens of a modern understanding of attitudes. His vocation was seen as being anointed with Spirit to announce and embody the Reigning of God, and his vocation continues in the creation of a community of those who share in his ethos.

This attempt at historical recollection has not systematically studied the explicit christologies in the New Testament as represented by the wide range of christological titles. That massive task has been done by others, such as Schillebeeckx. If he and others are right, the earlier prophetic-sapiential understanding of Jesus had a decisive influence on the interpretations given to subsequent christological titles. This appears to confirm the place of Spirit christology as the very foundation of the Christian church, i.e. as the initial paradigm on which the church was established.

The purpose of this historical recollection has not been mainly to prove that Spirit christology can claim the authority of the biblical authors for its authenticity, however true that may be. The chief purpose has been to try and encounter Jesus in a realistic way by seeing him in the light of a biblical and modern theology of Spirit that does not do injustice to him or to the initial records of his historical existence but enables him and those who first bore witness to him to be communicated effectively to us, living as we are in a very different time and place. On the basis of what has been seen of Jesus in this process one can now go ahead and work out a logic of salvation, a logic of Christ, a logic of the church and other extensions of logic that can be guided and tested by the personality, vocation and ethos of Jesus as these have been recovered in the exercise of historical remembering.

# Chapter Five
# THE LOGIC OF SALVATION

*Sin and Evil*

Evil is what goes wrong in God's good creation; sin is what people do to cause evil or contribute to it; and salvation is the corrective for sin and for whatever evil is correctable. Some things and events in the created order appear to be wrong yet have no observable connection with sin. Typhoons that sweep up the Bay of Bengal and kill thousands of people in Bangladesh appear to be evil but their origins have no known connection with human beings. Some kinds of natural evil we have to admit we do not understand. Sin we understand somewhat better. Salvation is the possibility that sin can be overcome or prevented or remedied and that people can cope with evil of all kinds, in as far as it is within their capability to cope with it.

In Chapter Three evil was very briefly described in terms of the distortion of the systems in creation, the "principalities and powers" which God created to serve various functions in the ordering of creation but which become demonic as they claim too much authority and try to extend their aegis beyond their God-given functions. Nations, for example, are prominent systems that account for a great deal of the order in creation but which typically contribute incalculably to evil because they cease to express the power and meaning of God as Reigning Spirit and instead protect their own interests, becoming profoundly immoral and destructive as a result. Evil in this case is basically systemic, larger than any individual sins but also clearly dependent on individuals who sin. Evil is both individual and systemic.

Salvation, therefore, has to be seen as the corrective for both individual and systemic evil. If salvation is thought to be a matter pertaining only to individual persons it ironically participates in the tendency toward privatization which itself is a systemic evil in society. If evil is conceived to be totally systemic it minimizes individual responsibility and thereby undermines one of the traits that constitute the goodness of human beings as created by God. There is a dynamic inter-relatedness between individuals and the systems that order creation, and evil in order to be seen in an adequate perspective must be found to originate in both systems and individuals.

Evil in individuals, groups or systems can be understood as whatever works against or resists the working of God present as Spirit. Evil is whatever is profane, i.e. "outside the temple" (*pro-fanum*) where God is working; or evil is demonic in the sense of something functioning as divine which is not divine. In the theology of Spirit, as developed earlier, the contributions of the Spirit were expounded in a variety of terms. Spirit provides energy and information or memory that combine to create matter and all the dynamic and intelligible aspects of everything that is created. Spirit engenders imagination and discernment which make knowledge possible in its several forms including law, wisdom, prophecy, apocalyptic and gospel. It is God present as Spirit who moves with power and meaning in peoples' bodies and minds to create attitude-virtues. God as Spirit calls every created thing and person, every group and system to its vocation, its meaningful identity and purpose in the economy of creation. The Spirit, too, exists in groups and systems as their characteristic ethos, in as much as their ethos is good and not demonic and vicious. Evil is the negating or undermining or distortion of what God as Spirit does to create and sustain the world.

Each of the contributions that Spirit gives to make creation possible can be corrupted or distorted by individuals and systems. A few examples will illustrate the nature of evil in relation to the work that Spirit does.

Entropy is the normal process in which energy is converted in use from highly organized states to less organized states.[1] Over-consumption in an energy system accelerates the rate of entropy and results in a depletion of energy that is organized to be usable. The way in which petroleum fuels are being depleted is one of the best known examples in our time. The economic and social systems that promote uneconomical squandering of petroleum energy are accelerating the entropic process, the result being depletion of the usable energy, as well as disastrous pollution created by the unusable energy of smog. Another example of the abuse of God-given energy is nuclear weapons. We have reached such a state of distortion in the use of nuclear power that a simple human error, or even computer error, could result in total, instant entropy of the world's existing energy systems.

At the level of individual persons, the energy system in which the human heart is the central operating part is being corrupted to such an extent by stress and cholesterol that heart disease is one of the most frequent killers among all causes of death in North America. Drugs of many kinds can cooperate with the health-producing energy and information of the Creator Spiritus, but they can also be destructive misinformation that damages the human system. If drugs, whether socially approved or not, are consumed demonically or even profanely, with no deference to their God-given purpose, they become evil.

It is a fact of life today that everyone consumes drugs "blindly" without knowledge of them. We require the listing of drugs on the content labels of many foods we eat, but it is certain that there are numerous drugs, including carcinogens that everyone ingests simply by breathing, in most places of habitation. God alone knows the drugs that we are getting in the food materials we eat, such as meat or vegetables, that can have no content labels on them to give us a choice whether to use the drugs or not. This situation illustrates well the way in which systemic evil can influence individual participants without any apparently deliberate sin on their part.

At the social level in our contemporary world there are many kinds of misinformation that constitute evil. For example, any ideology or set of ideas that claims absoluteness for itself and requires its adherents to condemn all other ideologies and their adherents is demonic. Such

---

[1] Rifkin (1980) expounds the theory of entropy in detail and urges that its escalating effects be seriously addressed with a view to slowing the process as much as possible.

ideologies abound in our time not least in the resurgence of religious fundamentalism whether Christian, Moslem or Leninist. The result is extensive estrangement and alienation among people in a pluralistic world.

A failure to receive the Spirit who creates imagination can result in widespread "it-ism" in which other persons are regarded as objects, rather than known in I-Thou relationships as subjects to be respected and treated with justice. On the individual level it has been observed by people like Rollo May[2] that sexual relationships have become banal for many people because of the impersonal concern for technique alone or because of social values that sanction self-gratification without personal concern for the sexual partner. "It-ism" runs rampant in a world where terrorism is widely justified, unemployment is accepted as inevitable, massive starvation is blamed on a fictional food shortage and human foetuses or their mothers are regarded as expendable.[3]

Discernment of law, wisdom, prophecy and apocalyptic can also be distorted by individuals and systems. Totalitarian legal systems exist in the majority of the nations of the world. At the same time, individual anarchy is common wherever it is given space to exist. The promotion and consumption of pornographic materials in the so-called free societies is a ready example. A "pornography queen" interviewed on a Chicago television program exemplified the widespread belief that individuals can do whatever they fancy without guilt or shame as long as it is not explicitly illegal. Morality defined by the letter of the law amounts to a kind of spiritual anarchy. The absence of "the law of the Spirit" is profanity that constitutes evil, even if the evil is not illegal. The "wisdom" of the possessive individualism of our society is demonic wisdom. The way of life which it espouses is vitiated by an alienating double-standard in the consumption of the world's goods. It claims, as so many TV commercials say, that "I'm worth it" but does not state the corollary which is "regardless of the fact that it is impossible for most other human beings to enjoy similar benefits."

There are many prophets in our time, "charismatic" persons who claim divine revelation for themselves and establish cults of followers to provide the lucrative "perks" which false prophets typically claim as their entitlement. The success of so many spurious prophets may indicate a widespread need for prophetic discernment of the bewildering expressions of the Twentieth Century explosion of knowledge.

Prophetic judgment and promise extended to the absolute becomes apocalyptic, of which there is also no shortage of distorted versions in our times. Since October 22, 1844, when William Miller and his followers were proved wrong in their calculations of the apocalypse, most millenialists have been slightly more cautious in predicting a specific

---

[2] See Rollo May, *Love and Will* (London: Collins, 1972).

[3] Cf. Ruether (1972): "The culture is invalidated, not merely in its superstructure, but at its roots, and in its fundamental presuppositions. Walter Roszak identifies this fundamental pre-supposition as the 'myth of the objective consciousness' but I would prefer to define it, following Martin Buber, as that 'I-It' relationship which is the basic existential act that turns persons into things and makes all reality objectifiable and manipulatable" (p.29).

time for the end of the world. All have insisted that it is coming soon and all portray the event as an occasion when the vast majority of human beings and all other creatures will be destroyed in favour of a chosen few people who will survive in glory. It is difficult to imagine a more creation-denying set of ideas, and the possibility of this ideology being adopted by powerful world leaders who have the nuclear power to fulfill the apocalyptic prediction is appalling. Yet this demonic ideology exists under the name of Christianity. The discernment of Jesus Christ himself has been demonstrated time and again to be capable of demonic perversion. The devil is a notorious liar and the lies pander to individual and group interests, combining with other forms of evil to produce such demonic ideologies as apartheid and other varieties of the "chosen few" mentality.

In Chapter Three some attitude-vices were mentioned as the distortion or absence of various attitude-virtues that God as Spirit gives to people in varying measure. It is not necessary to name them again.

The violations against the Spirit of God can also be seen in our times in relation to the matter of vocation. Most human beings have vocations that derive a considerable part of their meaning from the ideologies of either capitalism or communism. The difference is not very significant since both are versions of what Mao called "world wide economism." Whether capitalism is private or state capitalism it is also now frequently a variety of a "permanent war economy." The vocations of people within the existing economies of the world are inevitably compromised to the extent that their labours support and contribute to the profane or demonic meanings of the economic systems in which they participate. Many who explicitly disavow those meanings nonetheless continue to enjoy the benefits of their systems at the expense of those whom the systems exploit. Northern participants in North-South dialogues have been shocked to be told "You are rich because we are poor." The seemingly innocent vocations of countless people of the North can in fact be implicated in the evil disparity between the rich of the North and the poor of the South and between the rich and poor within the North itself. The Spirit calls human beings to the vocation of stewardship over the resources of the earth, but other "gods," the principalities and powers, the systems, call people to serve other meanings. The result is massive systemic evil.

Finally, in groups and systems the ethos of peace, justice unity, truth and all the other virtues of the Spirit of God can be thwarted and displaced by evil ethos. The self-serving ethos of economism is a prime example, but classism, racism and sexism are other examples all too readily at hand.[4] Here as with the other aspects of the creative work of the Spirit no attempt can be made to mention all the forms of evil to be found, systemic or individual. Perhaps enough examples have been given to show the nature of evil as "against the Spirit" (Gal 5:17) and therefore against the Reigning of God. This may appear obvious to some readers, but unless this basic nature of evil is understood the logic of salvation can go astray focusing possibly on evil as only a private matter, not

---

[4] Ruether (1981) shows some of the logical connections between these social distortions and christology.

systemic, as it in fact is.

## *Biblical Logic Of Salvation*

The logic of salvation emerges when the understanding of evil as "against the Spirit" is brought together with the remembrance of God realizing the Reigning of the Spirit in Jesus' life, death and resurrection. In Jesus the nature of salvation is made known. He is the epitome and, therefore, criterion of all that the Bible reveals about salvation by God. This is the meaning of his being Messiah. In the next chapter we will look explicitly at how Jesus' identity may be described. Christological affirmations emerge from the logic and experience of salvation. They are spawned, as it were, by the event of God encountering people in a saving way in Jesus. In reflection on their experiences people employ terms such as Messiah or Final Prophet to signify the decisive and definitive character of the saving process they have experienced in the encounter with God in Jesus. Because the saving experience of God in Jesus can be determinative of the basic meaning and orientation of their lives, those who follow Jesus strive to find appropriate terms to describe his singular importance. His importance, however, is discovered first in the understanding and experience of salvation. Jesus first functions as the saving agent of God and then those who participate in the saving process work out appropriate ways to designate Jesus' identity as the one in whom God works for salvation.

In Jesus' life, death and resurrection both the theory and the practice of God's saving process can be known. The character of God's presence as Spirit reigning in the affairs of life has already been explored in the theology of Spirit and in the recollection of what God's Reigning was like in Jesus himself. The nature of God's saving presence in Jesus is continuous with the nature of God's saving work as known elsewhere in the biblical history. Jesus fulfills and epitomizes the Hebrew understanding of God's saving work rather than completely originating it. This is borne out by the fact that New Testament authors consistently used metaphors of salvation from the Hebrew scriptures to describe the saving significance of Jesus.

Thus, it is valuable to review some of the main metaphors of salvation and some theological tenets of salvation in the Bible in order to show more clearly what the nature of salvation in Christ is like. Then we will look at the practice of salvation as Jesus exemplified it. It is in the way of salvation more than anything else that Jesus makes an original contribution to the knowledge of God's saving processes. His way of salvation is what engages followers and what characterizes or should characterize the Christian community if it truly does follow Jesus.

*a) The Shepherd Metaphor*

The Bible has several metaphors of salvation that recur repeatedly. One is the metaphor of the shepherd. Salvation is like what a shepherd does for the sheep, namely *Yasha,* bring them into a spacious environment which is conducive to living and growing without hindrance. The deliverance from Egypt and leading into the Promised Land were God's *Yasha,* God's shepherding of Israel. The shepherd's saving function depends on the sheep trusting and following where the shepherd leads, and it is typically the case that those in most extreme circumstances of danger or need are most ready to trust and follow. Such persons have an "epistemological privilege" of seeing most clearly what kind of salvation is needed, and there is a "preferential option" on the part of the Shepherd "to seek and to save the lost" (Lk 19:10) and those in the most dire circumstances.

*b) The Judge Metaphor*

The condition of being lost or in danger is not necessarily geographical or physical, although it can be either. It is more usually the condition of being deficient in the life-giving qualities that the Spirit provides, as we have already seen. The state of deficiency for which there is also some responsibility gives rise to another basic metaphor, that of the Hebrew judges whose role it was to justify or "make things right" in matters of law. God is seen as the judge who acquits offenders against God's laws. The acquittal presupposes a "return" of the offender to stand trial, a repentance and acknowledgment of the full scope of the offense. The dynamics of this aspect of salvation, therefore, entail both full and true judgment by God as well as acquittal and acceptance by God. This metaphor of salvation deals with the element of human responsibility and guilt which is always a factor in the circumstances that need saving. Satan was originally conceived of as the one who accuses offenders before God. Offenses are not taken lightly, nor is the acquittal easy. The judgment is a serious matter. Sackcloth and ashes are a sign befitting the seriousness of the judgment. But God is gracious and wills to save offenders.

*c) The Redeemer Metaphor*

This is apparent in yet another metaphor in which God acts as *go-el* or redeemer to "plead their cause" (Jer 50:34) in the judgment. God is like a *go-el,* usually a relative or friend who acts on behalf of a person to save him or her from prison or slavery. The *go-el*, redeemer, may pay the debt to prevent the debtor from being imprisoned, or may serve as advocate to convince the judge that a person deserves acquittal. The redeeming work of the *go-el* is costly in terms of money or effort. In Isaiah 43:1-4 God is reported to say "O Israel: Fear not, for I have redeemed you; ... I give Egypt as your ransom ... I give men in return for you, peoples in exchange for your life." The cost of redemption can include the giving of human life.

*d) The Metaphor of Cultic Sacrifice*

The metaphor of cultic sacrifice also apparently entailed the giving up of something valuable as an indication of the earnest intention of repentance. Sin offerings and guilt offerings included bulls, rams, goats, lambs, pigeons or flour (Lev 4-6). In Isaiah 53 the metaphor is applied to a person. "The Lord has laid on him the iniquity of us all" (vs.6). God made him "an offering for sin" (vs.10) and "shall see the fruit of the travail of his soul and be satisfied" (vs.11). The sacrifice will "make many to be accounted righteous" (vs.11). This logic of satisfaction of God by sacrifice was open to a legalistic application that came under criticism from those who believed that God could be satisfied only by obedience (I Sam 15:22) or justice (Isa I:17;Amos 5:24;Prov 21:3) or steadfast love and knowledge of God (Hos 6:6), not by cultic sacrifices. In Matthew 9:13 Jesus is reported to say "Go and learn what this means: I desire mercy and not sacrifice." In Mark 12:33 a scribe is reported to have said to Jesus "to love [God] with all the heart ... and to love one's neighbour as oneself, is much more than all whole burnt offerings and sacrifices" to which Jesus replied "You are not far from the kingdom of God."

This correction of the logic of cultic sacrifice by the prophets and by Jesus himself requires that sacrifice, if part of the process of salvation at all, be seen as a sign of genuine obedience and love. It is wrongly conceived when treated as a self-serving technicality for appeasing God. According to Isaiah God says "I do not delight in the blood of bulls, or of lambs, or of he-goats" (Isa 1:11), and it is likely that God delights even less in the blood of a human being. The Jews eventually gave up the sacrificial system in favour of "return" through obedience and justice and loving kindness while Christians, ironically, continued to apply the logic of satisfaction by blood sacrifice to their interpretation of Jesus' death. It is a temptation to launch into a full scale critique of the Satisfaction Theory of The Atonement or the Penal Substitution Theory but that would be outside our present purpose. The point of recalling the widely mentioned metaphor of sacrifice in the Bible is to see it in its best light as a symbol of genuine repentance and love and to acknowledge the real possibility that one person's sacrifice of obedience can play a part in the saving process of others who are affected by it. Any juridical or substitutionary or penal connotations of the sacrifice metaphor are necessarily rejected on the basis that God is not manipulated by any such technicalities to judge in people's favour. God who "desirest truth in the inward parts" accepts only the sacrifice of "a broken spirit, a broken and contrite heart" (Ps 51:6,17).

*e) The New Life Metaphor*

In the Bible God is portrayed as interested not in legalities but in real fulfillment or transformation of individual and corporate life. The metaphor of new life became a central one for salvation in the New Testament. Its roots were in the Hebrew scriptures where new life in a renewed covenant was a prominent form of the prophetic hope for the people of Israel. Death, the opposite of life, was a correlative metaphor for the sin and evil that are overcome in salvation. The salvation that God accomplishes in Jesus is "eternal life" (John) or "life in Christ Jesus" (Rom 8:2), creating a "new creature" (II Cor 5:17) or "new creation" (Gal 6:15) or even a "new heaven and a new earth" (Rev 21:1). The initiation rite of baptism is interpreted by this metaphor of dying to sin and rising to new life in the Spirit of Christ (Rom 6:3-11).

*f) Metaphors are Complimentary*

The metaphor of salvation that Jesus apparently used most frequently was the political metaphor of God's active sovereignty. This metaphor addresses the systemic and corporate dimensions of evil and salvation in a way some of the other metaphors can not do. It has to be stressed, however, that the variety of biblical metaphors of salvation are complementary rather than mutually exclusive. Jesus may well have used all the metaphors mentioned here as the Gospels indicate that he did. The metaphors combined together give an idea of salvation as deliverance from dire, unhealthy circumstances for which one shares some responsibility and for which one needs to sincerely repent, trusting God for acquittal and the gift of renewed life in which God's active sovereignty in the Spirit creates freedom from the endangering powers that diminish and distort life.

## Biblical Tenets of Salvation

In addition to the central metaphors for salvation that convey some of the main aspects of salvation there are several theological tenets of salvation that are characteristic of biblical thinking on the subject.

*a) God Alone Saves*

The first is that it is God and none other who saves. "I am the Lord and besides me there is no savior" (Isa 43:11). (See also Hos 13:4). The idea of God as the only saviour is related to the first of the Ten Commandments: "I am the Lord your God who brought you ... out of the house of bondage. You shall have no other gods besides me" (Deut 5:6-7). The exclusiveness of God as saviour is also implied in the Great Commandment as Jesus is reported to have cited it. If God is loved with the whole heart and soul and mind and strength there is nothing left over to offer to any other saving power.

*b) Indicative Precedes Imperatives*

A second theological tenet of salvation in the Bible is that God's saving work is the prerequisite of human obedience rather than the goal of obedience. In other words, the divine imperatives are grounded in the divine indicative. "Save me that I may observe thy testimonies" (Ps 119:146). God's love establishes the covenant before the law of the covenant is given and God's love continues regardless of whether or not the law is kept perfectly. Salvation is a gift of God, not achieved by good works but calling for good works. Grace precedes human efforts in the process of salvation.

*c) Salvation is Historic*

Salvation in the Bible is mainly an historic process, changing the character of life in this world rather than being primarily aimed at salvation for life after death. For the Hebrew people the most memorable event of salvation was when "the Lord saved Israel that day from the hand of the Egyptians" (Ex 14:30). This historic salvation became the central feature of Israel's liturgies, creeds and religious festivals and shaped the kind of salvation promised by the prophets.

*d) Salvation is Future-oriented*

At the same time, the saving work of God was seen by most biblical writers to have an eschatological thrust. It pointed towards the future even as it recalled the past and celebrated God in the present. The saving God of the Bible is shown to be a God of promise who time and again, to Noah, Abraham, Moses and the prophets gives them promises and, after fulfilling the promises, in due course gives new promises. The promises eventually extend to include the whole world. The Spirit will be poured out on all peoples. Nor is this eschatological nature of salvation relinquished in the New Testament. The Reigning of God is present but its completion is projected apocalyptically to a cosmic victory of God over all the powers of evil.

*e) Justice is the Goal*

One of the most significant theological aspects of biblical thinking about salvation is its consistent, over-riding purpose to achieve justice as the realization of God's love for the world and especially for those who suffer most unjustly. As José Miranda shows conclusively, "In the view of the Bible, Yahweh is the God who breaks into human history to liberate the oppressed" (1974, p.77). There are literally scores of places in the Bible where God is shown to care about those who need help in order to realize the justice which is their God-given right. In fact as we saw earlier, Jesus defines justice in radical rehabilitative terms and in terms of human need rather than solely in the common terms of proportional retribution or distribution. Salvation in the Bible is fundamentally involved with the matter of justice conceived in the broadest possible terms as what people need in order to be fulfilled as the creatures God desires them to be. "The whole Bible is directed towards creating a world in which authentic interhuman relationship is possible and is a validity" (Miranda 1974, p.296).

## *The Way of Salvation*

What has Jesus to do with salvation? Does he simply refine or develop the concepts of salvation that began in the Hebrew religion? Or, on the other hand, does Jesus accomplish some redeeming transaction with God that applies by proxy to all other human beings? I believe the answers to the latter two questions are negative. Jesus has other saving significance than as perfecter of Hebrew religion, and the claims of him having universal *causative* efficacy for salvation are false because they are based on a juridical view of salvation rather than a dynamic, processive view.

The uniqueness of Jesus' contribution to the salvation of the world lies in his pioneering of faith as well as perfecting of it. His *modus operandi* or *modus vivendi* of salvation is what distinguishes Jesus as Savior more than anything else. Jesus' theology of salvation as the Reigning of God is, of course, very important and especially so in Spirit christology because the Reigning of God and the presence of God as Spirit are identical in substance. This understanding of God's active reigning in Spirit was not completely original with Jesus although his emphasis upon it constituted his distinctive message.

What was truly original and unique was the way in which Jesus *lived* the Reigning of God, embodying it in his own person and actualizing it in his own vocation. Jesus preached and manifested the way of the Kingdom of God and called people to follow him in that way of life. He formed and taught a group of disciples to live and preach the Reigning of God as he was doing, although they did not apparently do it very well until after the Easter experience radically authenticated for them the way of the cross that Jesus had taught and showed them. They then began to have the same *modus vivendi* or *modus operandi* as Jesus, and many of them went to their crosses much as Jesus had done.

It was Jesus' orthopraxy that constitutes his primary significance for salvation.[5] His way of the cross which was the way of the Spirit and the way of God's Reigning became the definitive meaning on which the church was originally founded.[6] Baptism to enter the church was explained by Paul as dying with Christ and being raised with Christ. Baptism was also understood as the sign of the gift of God's Spirit that made Jesus' way of life possible and operative for people. Salvation according to the early church was a way of life, and there is no doubt the way of life as they knew it was Jesus' way of life. The language of God's Reigning that Jesus used so much was transposed into language about a way of life in the Spirit, but there can be no doubt that the substance of life in the Spirit and life in God's Kingdom were and are the same thing.[7]

The language of Spirit became central to the church perhaps because they experienced Jesus with them in Spirit and they recalled that Jesus had taught them about the identity of the presence of the Spirit and God's Reigning. Maybe there was a certain amount of loss of nerve in the early church that led to the preference for the language of Spirit over the language of the Kingdom. The latter had helped to bring Jesus' life to an early end and might still have been provocative and more dangerous to use in the Roman empire than language of the Spirit which has less obvious political implications. Perhaps the language of Spirit, like the language of Messiah, was kept secret during Jesus' active ministry but blossomed into the open after his death because it had theological advantages that made it extremely useful. It certainly was highly utilized by Paul and other early Christians who showed little sign of timidity before Roman or any other authorities. Regardless of their theological language many of the early Christians followed the way of Jesus' life fearlessly and made the same sacrifice in the end that Jesus had made. It does not appear likely that they chose the language of Spirit in their theology for reasons of self-protection.

The way of salvation as Jesus taught and lived it can be seen to include conversion, regeneration, prophecy, law, wisdom and the way of the cross.

*a) Conversion*

The way of salvation that Jesus preached and lived begins with conversion, *metanoia,* a complete turning around of life that entails giving up the old way of life, adopting the values of God and doing the will of God in a new way of living.[8] According to Mark, Jesus started out

---

[5]Cf. Boff (1978): "Jesus shifts the center of gravity insofar as the criteria for salvation are concerned. It is not orthodoxy but orthopraxis that counts."(p.284).

[6]Cf. Echegaray (1984): "The practice of Jesus is thus to be seen as a concrete norm and as a practice that founds a community and gives birth to a historical, social, and spiritual tradition which is opposed to the inertial tendency of the empire. The 'already' aspect of the kingdom, which has taken a definite shape in the practice of Jesus, becomes the seed of a new organization of society through the operation of a dialectic that the world will be unable to suppress after the first Easter and which continues to point to the still unrealized fullness of God's reign" (p.96).

[7]Cf. Montague (1976): "In Acts the fact that the kingdom has begun is manifested on earth by the activity of the Spirit" (p.273).

[8]Cf. Newbigin (1969): "To be converted is to be turned round so as to recognize and participate in this [God's] coming reign" (p.98).

his ministry by announcing to people that the Reigning of God was accessible ("at hand") and urging them to "turn around" and believe the good news (Mk 1:15). The turning around that starts the way of salvation is a familiar theme in the Hebrew scriptures. One of the basic conditions or terms of the covenant that God made with Moses was that if the people of Israel found themselves separated from God because they had served other gods they might "return to the Lord ... obey his voice ... with all [their] heart and with all [their] soul; then the Lord [their] God will ... have compassion upon [them] (Deut 30:2-3).

Returning to God was and is the Hebrew way of atonement for sin understood as separation from God and God's way of living. The great prophets repeatedly called for people to return: "let the wicked forsake his way, and the unrighteous man his thoughts; let him return to the Lord, that he may have mercy upon him and to our God, for he will abundantly pardon" (Isa 55:7). "'Return faithless Israel,' says the Lord. 'I will not look on you in anger for I am merciful' says the Lord" (Jer 3:12). "Have I any pleasure in the death of the wicked, says the Lord God, and not rather that he should turn from his way and live?" (Ezek 18:23). "Return, O Israel, to the Lord your God, for you have stumbled because of your iniquity ... say to him 'Take away all iniquity; accept that which is good ... '. I will heal their faithlessness; I will love them freely, for my anger has turned from them" (Hos 14:1-4). "Rend your hearts and not your garments ... . Return to the Lord, your God, for he is gracious and merciful, slow to anger, and abounding in steadfast love" (Joel 2:13). "Return to me, and I will return to you, says the Lord of hosts" (Mal 3:7). Jesus' story of the Prodigal Son illustrates this understanding of the way of forgiveness as does the story of Jonah that is read each year by Jews on Yom Kippur, the Day of Atonement.

The examples of the doctrine of Return in the Hebrew scriptures could be multiplied many times. When Jesus preached the message of "Return and believe" there is no doubt that his Jewish listeners would understand and hear the echoes from their religious past. Unfortunately, Christians have not always heard it. In place of the message of forgiveness by returning to God the church has traditionally preached that forgiveness was achieved by the sacrifice of Jesus' blood on the cross. The good side of this doctrine has been that if people could believe it they could be assured that they were now forgiven and were acceptable to God. The bad side of the doctrine is the image of God that it presupposes, namely, as one who could be satisfied in any way by the sacrifice of human blood and as one who could not forgive without such a blood sacrifice. Another bad effect of the doctrine was the presupposition it has that the one sacrificed must necessarily be fully divine in order to have enough merit to satisfy God for the sins of the whole world. More of this later. Such calculating logic of forgiveness is far from the logic of salvation that Jesus shared with the main stream of Hebrew thought, both before and after his time. As we shall see, there was a sense in which Jesus' death came to be seen as a representative sealing of the new covenant of all those who return, in accordance with the model of covenantal renewal ceremonies in Hebrew religion. His death was his own supreme "return" in obedience to God and it is the epitome of the return adopted by all who follow him in his Spirit.

Return is a response to the gospel that precedes it. Unless one has some measure of hope and trust in God there is no logic in returning to God. There must, therefore, be some prevenient grace in operation before sinners repent and return. Such grace is implied in the parable of the lost sheep when the shepherd leaves the ninety-nine and goes "in search of the one that went astray" (Mt 18:12). Jesus exemplified such grace in his own person in eating and drinking with publicans and sinners, not as a strategy to convert them but because he genuinely cared for them. If they had not known his love to be genuine they would not have trusted him or his gospel.

Return, then is not a kind of works righteousness but a response to prevenient grace.[9] The grace leading to repentance is typically a combination of judgment and promise, the judgment convicting persons of sin and the promise assuring them of God's mercy on their return. Martin Luther perceived rightly that unless one heard the promise and was clothed, as it were, in God's mercy one could not even hear the truth of God's judgment. Without God's prevenient mercy the judgment of God would be a "consuming fire" (Heb 12:29).

It was the beauty of the Hebrew understanding of God that God's love was seen to precede the covenant and therefore embrace and underlie God's judgment on disobedience to the law of the covenant. "Those whom I love I reprove and chasten" (Rev 3:19). Jesus certainly did not have a less profound grasp on the nature of God's love. His understanding of the nature of God's justice as "rehabilitative" rather than strictly retributive corroborates his preaching of forgiveness by return. What God's justice requires is that people be actually changed and turned around in their way of life. This will achieve more good on the earth than any amount of penitential requirements for forgiveness. The one who is forgiven much loves much, as the story of the woman who anointed Jesus' feet in the house of Simon the Pharisee shows (Lk 7:36-50).

The Pauline doctrine of justification by grace through faith represents basically the same dynamic of faith as forgiveness by return. Paul stresses that God freely forgives people and regards them as if they were righteous while they are in fact not yet righteous, measured by the extent to which they have fulfilled the laws and purposes of God. Paul used the metaphor of the Jewish sacrificial system to claim that Jesus' death was a sacrifice that signifies the effecting of God's forgiveness. The point is the same as the Hebrew doctrine of return. Believing that you are forgiven by God is equivalent to believing that God loves you and will accept you if you return. The practical result is the same, namely, you are freed from the guilt of past sin and invited to begin life again in "the new Life of the Spirit" (Rom 7:6).

---

[9]Cf. Boff (1978): "Conversion should not be viewed as a precondition for the coming of the kingdom. It signifies that the kingdom is already inaugurated here. ... It is a gift offered freely to human beings. On the other hand it is their acceptance of that gift. This acceptance becomes real insofar as human beings collaborate in the work of inaugurating the kingdom through mediations of a personal, social, political, and religious nature: (p.287).

Sometimes Paul's doctrine of justification has been misinterpreted to be virtually identical with salvation understood not as a process of making right what is wrong but as a *fait accompli* that primarily has to do with being assured of a place in heaven. Such "angelism" is far removed from Jesus' gospel of the Reigning of God or Paul's theology of life in the Spirit.

*b) Regeneration*

Regeneration to a new kind of life is a second aspect of the way of salvation. To some extent regeneration occurs already in the moments of the prevenient grace that precede conversion and enable people to turn away from other gods and towards God as their hope in life. But there is a process of regeneration that goes on after conversion and continues throughout life in the way of salvation.[10]

Prayer is the activity or condition that both marks and facilitates regeneration. Like conversion, prayer is already a result of God's regenerating presence as Spirit, but prayer also opens the way for the fullness of the new life to continue to be realized. Life is an on-going process, and salvation as we see it in Jesus is a way, that is, an "advance in a certain direction" (*Oxford Concise Dictionary*) that requires on-going renewal and growth in order to meet the changing circumstances that are encountered.

Jesus exemplified the life of prayer that regenerated his own person as he "advanced" in the direction of the cross. Something has been said already about Jesus' "*Abba*" relationship with God. Schillebeeckx writes well about the centrality of it in Jesus' life and message.

> Whence does Jesus obtain the unconditional assurance of salvation to which his message of God's coming rule as final well-being for [people] so positively testifies? ...Such a hope ... is quite plainly rooted in a personal awareness of contrast: on the one hand the incorrigible, irremediable history of [human] suffering, a history of calamity, violence and injustice, of grinding, excruciating and oppressive enslavement; on the other hand Jesus' particular awareness of God, his *Abba* experience, ... an immediate awareness of God as a power cherishing people and making them free ... . It was to faith in this God that Jesus called [people] through what he said and did during his days on earth: that was the *raison d'etre* of his whole ministry" (1979, p.267-68).

Jesus not only proclaimed God as "cherishing and making ... free"; he himself lived in the strength and presence of this God. He met his temptations by praying; in clarifying his vocation he hears the voice of God; he cast out demons which "cannot be driven out by anything

---

[10]Cf. Berkhof (0976): "I personally believe that the word which best expresses the unity and the totality of the Spirit's work is the word 'regeneration'. The Spirit is the life-giver ... in redemption as well as in creation" (p.69). This is in considerable contrast to St Basil (in Schaff and Wace 1983) who maintained that the Spirit related to people only after they were purified from all sin. "Only then after a man is purified from the shame whose stain he took through his wickedness, and has come back again to his natural beauty, and as it were cleaning the Royal Image and restoring its ancient form, only thus is it possible for him to draw near to the Paraclete. ... shining upon those that are cleansed from every spot, He [the spirit] makes them spiritual by fellowship with Himself" (p.15).

but prayer" (Mk 9:29), he drew apart to solitary places to prepare for the crises confronting him; he is reported to have called on God in his time of most extreme anguish on the cross. "Anyone, therefore, who lives by Jesus and bases his [or her] life on him — while dismissing Jesus' *Abba* experience — is in fact wanting to live on a Utopian basis" (Schillebeeckx 1979, p.270).

The way of salvation that Jesus practiced was a life of continuous prayer — not primarily formal, ritual prayer but prayer that was a constant turning to God, trusting God, obedience to God in the kind of obedient service that love gives. If the cry of dereliction indicates anything of the style of Jesus' prayer it could also be an intense questioning of God when the logic of events was missing.

Jesus' prayer was the constituting activity of his way of salvation, the active acceptance of God's Reigning in his life and affairs, the opening of the door to allow the Spirit to blow in with all the power and meaning that the Spirit brings. Prayer is the primary activity of faith, the initial response to hoping in God, the first motion that expresses caring about God or God's world. It is like the first great gulp of air that a newborn child takes and like the successive breathing, hard or soft, that sustains the life until its death. If breathing in physical life is like praying in the way of salvation then perhaps it can be said that the Spirit who continually regenerates praying ones is like the oxygen in breathing that invigorates both mind and body.

Regeneration is the renewal of life by the Spirit present in those who have "turned" to God. The Spirit renews the energy and meanings in the convert. If sloth is one of typical signs of separation from God the way of return requires a new source of energy. The work of cooperating with God in the recreating of the world requires massive energies that can only come through waiting on God. "They that wait for the Lord shall renew their strength, they shall mount up with wings like eagles, they shall run and not be weary, they shall walk and not faint" (Isa 40:31).

The basic information that the Spirit brings along with new energy is the information of faith, namely, the knowledge that the world is God's and none other. All the systems and powers and principalities are seen in a new light as creatures of God with both promise and demonic potential. The intelligibility of everything changes in the return of faith when God becomes God and there are no other gods besides God.

Regeneration includes "the renewal of your mind" (Rom 12:2) as well as energy. In place of conformity to the misinformation of the self-serving systems in existence it causes one to be "transformed by the renewal of ... mind." The way of salvation is a way of continuing transformation of mind as one tries to love God "with all your heart and with all your soul, and with all your mind, and with all your strength" (Mk 12:30). Any who wish to enter the way of salvation without undergoing the wrenching upheaval of repeated renewals of their minds are in for some rude shocks. As a popular church banner put it: "The Sign of God is that we will be led where we did not plan to go." The God who says "Behold, I make all things new" (Rev 21:5) cannot be followed in the on-going process of salvation unless the new information that the Spirit brings is received in a transformation of mind.

Regeneration also entails a renewal of what we have called imagination, the ability to enter intimately into the realities of other persons and things, meeting them in the Spirit of love and justice who "goes between" in the process of knowing and who draws people into respectful and responsible relationships that make true knowledge a possibility. The way of salvation is a continuous regeneration of meeting and knowing that are both the expression of loving concern and the prerequisite for acting in love. The works of love require the knowing of truth if justice is to be realized.

Discernment, too, is regenerated continuously in the life of prayer in the Spirit. What the Reigning of God means as gospel, law, wisdom, prophecy and apocalyptic can be disclosed in increasing depth and perspective when one continues in the way of faith and prayer. We will look at these more closely in due course, as they comprise particularly significant aspects of the way of salvation.

The regeneration of attitude-virtues is one of the most important works of the Spirit because attitudes are really the basic stuff of personality. If salvation results in a "new creature" the attitude-virtues will certainly register the change. Distrust will be replaced by trust, anxiety by assurance, wariness by receptivity, despair by hope, apathy by passion. Pride or self-humiliation will be replaced by genuine humility, self-rejection by self-acceptance, irresponsibility by responsibility, dissipation by self-commitment. Self-isolation behind protective masks and role-playing will be displaced by friendliness that risks I-Thou relations. Self-indulgence will be replaced by pastoral and prophetic concern for others, and self-consciousness and self-centered narcissism may be overcome by a contemplative and loving relation to all that exists. Such massive transformation of personality does not occur in a flash or even completely for those on the way of salvation, but some movement in the direction of these changes is characteristic of the way of the Spirit when God reigns in human personality.

Vocation is also regenerated in the way of salvation. First, the basic human vocation of stewardship over the earth is changed from a mode of dominion that exploits and oppresses the creation to a mode of servanthood that loves and cares for what God has made and entrusted to human control. The understanding of this vocation can grow and change as peoples' circumstances and responsibilities in the world change. A new job means new work and a new understanding of how that work fits into the "economy" of God.

Vocation is regenerated, too, when new gifts of the Spirit are discovered and developed for the upbuilding of the human community or the community of faith. St Paul urged his readers at one point to "earnestly desire the higher gifts" (I Cor 12:31), the assumption apparently being that it is possible to receive new gifts for working as one proceeds along the way of salvation. When society or the church allows women, for example, the freedom to discover the full range of their vocational gifts it soon becomes apparent that regeneration in vocation is a real aspect of the way of salvation.

Finally, it would be a basic distortion of the regenerative work of the Spirit if it were presented only as happening in individuals and not in groups and systems. Communities of people who have returned in some measure to God experience the regeneration of their community ethos and community vocation. In fact, if God as Spirit exists typically "in the sphere between" as Buber and others have perceived, it may be true to say that regeneration in all the respects mentioned above is a function of interpersonal relationships, which is to say, a function of community. The biblical idea of covenant people, even in "remnant" suggests this fact — that God comes to people in groups even if the groups are very small. The reverse would then be also true, that people who return to God do so in and through the group which provides the traditions, language, vision, and support by which the "turning around" is made possible.

c) *Prophecy*

A third dynamic in the on-going way of salvation, as practiced by Jesus, is the process of working to change the world by the prophetic activity of judging it and discerning its promise. Prophecy is the result of encounter of the Spirit with evil. The evil in the world, as we have tried to analyse it, can be seen to reside in the demonic and profane systems and in the individual "hearts" that turn away from God to make idols of the systemic powers that be. Prophetic encounter with the principalities and powers entails both a clear-eyed discernment of what is wrong with them, and with the people involved in them, and an equally clear-eyed discernment of their promise, their rightful place in the Reigning of God in the earth.[11] This is not to presuppose a bland liberalism that holds that "everything has some good in it if we can only find it." It is not a reformist approach that assumes as a doctrinaire premise that any and every system, however corrupt or unjust, can be corrected by some gentle persuasion.

If Jesus is taken as the exemplar of what prophetic activity in the way of salvation should be like then it clearly includes denouncing in unequivocal terms what is against the Spirit. It includes calling for revolutionary changes in the ordering of societal systems including economic, political and religious systems.

It is not, however, a Utopian romanticism that operates on the assumption that present systems and powers could be replaced by a state of affairs in which there are no systems or subsidiary authorities between individuals and God. It is not like the Marxist Utopia in which the state will wither away and every person will be free of all organized restraints, able "to hunt in the morning, fish in the afternoon, rear cattle in the evening, criticize after dinner" (Marx in Fromm 1961, p.206).

According to the biblical view of things, God has organized the world

---

[11]Cf. Sobrino (1978): "The radicalness of Jesus' demand of discipleship is brought out by his insistent stress on the need for discernment. ... It has to do with discerning what the will of God is. ... So there are two stages in Christian discernment. The first ... has to do with a general determination of what is good and what is evil. The second and specifically Christian stage of discernment is concerned with the problem of the essential nature of the good that one is obliged to do" (p.130).

into systems that have a proper role to play in the ordering of chaos. Prophetic discernment calls the organized powers back to their right role in the Reigning of God. According to Jesus the rulers in the world are in accordance with God's Reigning only when they are "servants of all." While they continue to "Lord it over" people they are subject to prophetic denunciation and nonviolent resistance. Even Caesar has a possible place in God's economy of order in the world, but only under God. People are to "render to Caesar" only as much as they can also render to God. If it cannot be rendered to God then it should not be rendered to Caesar.

Some systems and powers in existence are so far removed from the ways of God, so profane and demonic, that prophetic resistance to them approaches total rejection. Slavery, apartheid, organized crime and the arms race are some examples ready at hand. Such totally demonic systems, however, can usually be seen to be cancerous additions to the basic systems needed to bring order out of chaos in human life. Apartheid, slavery, military expansion and even the Mafia are at base largely economically motivated. The prophetic denunciation of these demonic sub-systems of the economic order does not presuppose total rejection of all economic systems. Such a stance would fail to see salvation as historic and would not see the God-given possibilities for a good economy to help provide the necessities of life to all its participants.

The prophetic process in the way of salvation does not have recourse to any easy affirmation of the powers-that-be saying "Peace, peace, when there is no peace." Nor does it wash its hands, so to speak, and disclaim any interest or responsibility in the re-ordering of the basic organizations that make life feasible. Prophecy requires the "naming of the powers" the "unmasking" of their demonic pretensions and profane proclivities.

Sometimes, as Jesus and the great prophets of Israel showed, the resistance against the existing evil in the system required dramatic symbolic action. Jesus' action in "cleansing the temple" must have shocked the authorities into realizing very vividly the prophetic message that Jesus was giving.[12] They were not, however, open to the unsettling truth of Jesus' message or to the changes that would be required in order for their system to become just.

Prophetic activity is not essentially a Lone Ranger or Don Quixote ministry carried out by individuals operating alone against the powers-that-be, although at times individuals may have to act alone. The church and other communities with the Spirit in them have a prophetic vocation. In fact, individual prophetic ministries are subsidiary to the corporate ministries in which they originate. In God's economy of salvation, as we see it in the Bible, covenanted groups are the principal recipients of the presence of God as Spirit. The outstanding prophets and individuals with other singular ministries emerge in the covenant people and belong to a corporate tradition. In practical terms a corporate prophetic witness

---

[12]Cf. Frye (1981): "The casting out of devils is symbolically the same act as cleansing the temple" (p.157). The temple authorities may have realized this.

may also be more effective in confronting systemic evil.

Prophecy as an aspect of the way of salvation includes the on-going encounter of the Spirit with the evil in the individuals themselves who are "on the way." It is not only an activity directed at the systemic evil in the world. Prophetic ministry is received as well as given by faithful people and by the church as a system. The Spirit who judges evil and reveals good is outside the church in the world, as well as inside, and can come to the church and its members with prophetic truth from others. Life in the Spirit, the way of salvation, is a continuing revelation of promise and of wrong which is part of God's way of righting wrong both in the systems of creation and in the individuals who have returned and are on the way of salvation.

*d) Law and Wisdom*

It is not enough that judgment and promise are proclaimed in prophetic word and deed; the distortion of the created order has to be corrected. The chaos of evil has to be re-ordered. The world has to be 'returned' to the goodness God intends for it. Individuals and systems need to be sanctified, made holy and good, their demonic and profane dimensions changed. The way of salvation does not end with prophetic discernment; it also includes the discernment of law, the structure of justice in the created systems. Law is the form that social sanctification takes.

Those who have entered into the vocation of the Reigning of God have as part of their ministry the work of reforming the laws that order human relationships. They are called to discern the structures that would best serve the Spirit of love as it takes concrete form in just relations. Law is an aspect of all social systems, including the church itself. To change law is, therefore, a *political* task in the broad sense of the word. This means that the way of salvation requires corporate solidarity in order to accomplish the reforming of law. Any lingering privatization of religion should be dispelled in face of the work of discerning and reforming the laws that actually implement justice in the world.

The end or purpose of God's saving work is to change the world to realize justice for all people, and justice is served by law. It may also be subverted by bad laws. God's work of salvation in a sense culminates in the giving of just law. The Hebrew appreciation of Torah was a realistic perception of God's saving intentions. God formed a covenant people and gave them the law to ensure justice in their human relations. God has done the same for all groups of people. Law is one of the basic systems in creation that was created to be good but can, like any other principality and power, become demonic or profane. It needs the prophetic judgment and promise as much as any other part of the created world. And it needs to be re-created, renewed and reformed in order to realize the Reigning of God. This was and is true for the law in the Hebrew scriptures as well as for any other laws.

It is often unnoticed that St Paul regarded the Law of the Covenant as one of the principalities and powers which can be redeemed in Christ. Not all scholars agree that Paul simply identified Jewish law with the principalities and powers but all agree that there is a close relationship between Paul's view of the law and his theology of the powers. Caird says that "either Paul regarded the law itself as one of the powers or behind the law he perceived the existence of angelic beings who were responsible for the law's enforcement" (Caird 1956, p.44). He concludes, "There is much to be said in favour of both theories" but he favours the first theory. "Through the distortion of sin the law, which embodies a divine authority, becomes a destructive power." Schlier favours the second theory: "Indeed, according to St Paul, the influence of the wicked angels is asserted even in Jewish law" (Schlier 1961, p.27). Leivestad shows the many points of "parallelism" (1954, p.95) between the law and the cosmic powers. Berkhof unequivocally states that "doubtless Paul is thinking ... of the Mosaic law ... as a power which unites the Jewish people socially and religiously and simultaneously alienates them from God" (1962, p.37). Thus, Berkhof concludes, "Paul can view Jewish law and pagan regulations as essentially alike and both as overcome through Christ's cross." Walter Wink clearly agrees that the law was regarded by Paul as one of the Powers: "... the Law, the Temple, the State ... are unmasked, revealed as resisting the truly legitimate reign of God. All these Powers are now stripped naked by the cross for all humanity to see" (1984, p.79). The point of seeing law as one of the Powers or systems is not to condemn it absolutely, which Paul clearly did not do, but to see it as part of the creation that needs to be redeemed and renewed.

The law is what Caird and Schlier and Berkhof call one of the "subordinate authorities" (Caird 1956, p.83) in creation, subordinate to God but still having authority for people. This is equivalent to the position St Paul had on the law; it is "holy and just and good" (Rom 7:12) but certainly subordinate to the "law of the Spirit of life in Christ Jesus" (Rom 8:2). It also seems to be consistent with the position that Jesus showed *vis a vis* the law. Both Jesus and Paul had freedom in the Spirit to break certain laws when the serving of justice required it, but both acknowledged the authority of the law including the law of the "governing authorities" (Rom 13:1) and Caesar (Mk 12:17).

Thus, the discernment of law in the way of salvation includes both affirmation of existing law in as far as it is just, and resistance to law perceived to be unjust. Civil disobedience may be required for faithful obedience to the Reigning of God as Spirit. It may also be a kind of prophetic action to symbolize the injustice existing in a social system. Disobedience alone, however, is not sufficient to bring about the institution of better laws. There has to be creative vision and political effort in the way of salvation.

Wisdom is "the individualizing of the law" (Frye 1981, p.125), the application of the tried and true patterns of right to a person's particular circumstances. It requires a critical intelligence to discern what really is the best course of action. If wisdom is to be part of life in the Spirit it cannot simply go along with traditional customs or societal expectations. It has to be open and responsive to the leading of the Spirit. In the early church as described in the *Acts of the Apostles* the Spirit was thought to be involved in the very practical discussions of choosing which disciples would go to which place (Acts 13:1-4) or not go to a certain place (Acts 16:6,7). In sending down the decision of the Jerusalem Council to Antioch the leaders in Jerusalem said "It has seemed good to the Holy Spirit and to us to lay upon you no greater burden than these necessary things... (Acts 15:28). In this instance the Spirit's guidance countermanded certain prescriptions of the law while upholding other aspects of the law. Such freedom in the Spirit is as essential for discerning wisdom as it is for discerning law.

Wisdom as a function of individuals in the way of salvation can be described as personal guidance in life. Guidance is the receptivity to God's providential caring for each person. Jesus apparently sought such guidance in prayer and wrestled for it in his temptations. St Paul went to the Jerusalem council to test his own wisdom and what he had discerned to be the guidance of God in taking the Christian mission to Gentiles. Guidance can be both a matter of individual inspiration and a process of critical analysis and consultation with others. In the end an individual has to take responsibility for her or his own decisions and interpretations of what is the wise course of action.

Wisdom ultimately relies on the mercy of God to forgive its wrong discernments and even to take what is wrongly conceived and enacted and redeem it for some good beyond what is immediately visible. To follow wisdom in the way of salvation entails a certain amount of "sinning boldly" in circumstances when all the results of an action are not forseeable or when all the foreseeable actions are ambiguous, including the option of doing nothing.

*e) The Way of the Cross.*

The way of salvation that Jesus pioneered and perfected culminated in his crucifixion and resurrection. In the way of his death can be seen the ultimate, definitive characteristics of his way of salvation. The way of the Reigning of God is seen finally to be the way of the cross.[13] And despite the death of Jesus and his apparent failure to accomplish the changes in the world that his prophetic ministry was committed to achieve his resurrection revealed that the Reigning of God can and does come to the world through the way of the cross. The life in the Spirit of God that Jesus had before he was killed turned out to be inextinguishable. More than that, his dying mediated his life in the Spirit to his followers and continues to do so in a way that brings the Reigning of God in Spirit to people of the world in an on-going exponential process. Like a tiny seed that is planted and produces a huge, spreading and reproducing vine, Jesus' death brings about the coming of God's Reign that continues to come as the way of salvation, the way of the cross and the way of the Spirit.

The way of the cross is identifiable first and foremost in the narrative about Jesus' death and resurrection. As we saw in the last chapter, Jesus'

---

[13]Cf. Lampe (1977): "The Spirit which inspires love that 'seeks not its own' is the Spirit of Christ crucified, and the cross is its distinctive mark" (p.203). Cf. also Robinson (1962) on "the spirit of the Cross;": "no other name better expresses the fundamental relation in which one person stands to another ... according to Christian faith. The New Testament term for this central ethical relation of [person] to [person] is *agapé*" (p.33). Cf. also Sobrino (1978): "In the history of Jesus himself we find love taking the form of effective action at first and then the form of accepted suffering" (p.135).

vocation of Prophet-Messiah entailed a confrontation with the specific structures of evil in his society that reached a climax in his "cleansing of the Temple" in Jerusalem. At that point the opposition to Jesus was determined to eliminate him. He had to decide which course of action to take in order to be true to the Reigning of God as he understood it. There were at least three tempting alternatives that Jesus had struggled with during the course of his active ministry: the so-called economic option, the secular political power option and the religious crusade option. The temptation to follow one or more of these strategies was very real because of the legitimate aspects of each of them. Jesus cared about the economic conditions of people. How could he care about them at all and not be committed to changing the debilitating, life-shortening conditions of poverty that afflicted the ones who warranted the most concern? Jesus knew the important potential of political order to prevent social chaos and to implement laws that ensure some measure of justice in society. How could a corrupt political order such as the one in existence in Jesus' society not be changed without employing secular political power in opposition to the powers in control? Again, the power of religious conviction might be the basis for organizing a revolution that would re-order the economic and legal systems and accomplish the justice desired by the God of the Hebrew prophets and sages who was the God Jesus knew and served. As the opposition to Jesus closed in on him and threatened to eliminate him the question of if and how the Reigning of God that he was announcing might actually come became absolutely critical. It was a case of now or never if something was to be done to rescue and realize the mission on which he had been sent from the beginning of his ministry.

Jesus chose to go the way of the cross rather than trying any of the other alternative strategies.[14] The crux of the matter under the circumstances was whether or not to resort to armed violence. Without armed might, whether secularly or religiously based, there seemed to be no way to avoid the termination of what Jesus had been trying to do. But killing the opposition was inconsistent with the Spirit of love that was central to the Reigning of God as Jesus preached and lived it. It was an agonizing decision, reflected in the story of Jesus praying in the Garden of Gethsemane. According to Luke "his sweat became like great drops of blood falling down upon the ground" (Lk 22:44). He decided to submit to the violence of his opposition rather than resist them with violence. This was apparently not a decision compelled by necessity but a choice made in the Spirit of God, the same Spirit Jesus had expressed in his teachings about the law of God and in his personal attitudes towards sinners during his lifetime. The "Thou shalt not murder" of the Mosaic law was radicalized by Jesus to become applicable not

---

[14]Boff (1978) rightly points out that in choosing to do what he believed to be God's will Jesus "right to the end ... does not know exactly whether this implies merely great difficulties or death itself" (p.116). To say that Jesus chose the way of the cross is not to suggest that he chose death for its own sake or that he had a martyr complex or that he had a spirituality of self-victimization. He chose to accept suffering if it was the only alternative in order to remain faithful to his God-given vocation. "He shouldered it [death] as an expression of his freedom and his fidelity to the cause of God and human beings" (p.282).

only to the people of Israel, as it had been in the past, but to all people including one's enemies, and not only literally but spiritually, which is to say in the quality of attitude-virtues and ethos. Murderous intentions or actions, Jesus had taught, have no place in the Reigning of God. Whatever the chances of his mission being terminated by the violence of his opposition the Reigning of God could continue in Jesus only if he were not murderous towards his enemies. It looked like failure of the Reigning of God in either case: either in the termination by his enemies or in termination by himself if he resorted to violence. He chose to trust the way of God's Reigning as he knew it and let himself be taken by his enemies rather than flee from them or fight them with violence. The decision led to his utter desolation and death.

God, however, remained faithful and proved to be trustworthy. The dying of Jesus did not terminate the Reigning of God which Jesus had announced and lived. The power and meaning of the Spirit who was in Jesus entered into those who had known him and they began to live the life of the Spirit which is the Reigning of God. Jesus' death became a medium through which "in remembrance of him" the same Spirit that was his became alive and operative in those who remembered him. He became in the Spirit alive to countless people who loved him and believed that he represented God fully and accurately in the Spirit that was in him. The love for him, the caring passionately about him, has never stopped. He is still alive in the Spirit, still a mediator of the Spirit of God and the Reigning of God for those who know him and have answered the call to follow him. His way of the cross was not his annihilation but his exaltation. For those who have eyes to see, the way of the cross epitomizes what Jesus taught and lived, and it is the essence of the way of salvation.[15]

The event of Jesus' death and resurrection is a single event with two moments or facets. Neither makes sense without the other. His death without resurrection would probably have gone unnoticed as just one more of the countless number of unjust executions in history. Affirming his resurrection without remembering that he was crucified and why he was crucified is equivalent to forgetting that he was a real live human being. It is to dehistoricize him and make him just one more of the countless cosmic myths of human fabrication.[16] The death and resurrection have to be kept together if the reality of the way of the cross is to be grasped. The narrative of Jesus' life includes both his death and resurrection, and the point of the story is lost when either is left out.

The climactic event of Jesus' dying and coming alive in the Spirit is a story that has permitted a number of interpretations in Christian tradition and will no doubt be reinterpreted again and again as the

---

[15]Cf. Sobrino (1978): "Faith in Jesus attains its maximum radicality when we accept his path as normative and traverse it. The most radical and most orthodox affirmation of *faith in Jesus* is affirming that the *faith of Jesus* is the correct way to draw nearer to God and realize his kingdom, and then acting accordingly" (p.108).

[16]Cf. Sobrino (1978): "The worst temptation facing Christian faith ... [is] the temptation to forget that the Christ of faith is none other than Jesus of Nazareth" (p.381).

knowledge explosion continues and people see new aspects of the historical circumstances of the events or the literary character of the Bible. It is beyond the purview of this chapter to expound and analyse the various interpretations that have been given to Jesus' death and resurrection. The task here is to analyse some of the main features of the event as the climax of the way of salvation that Jesus pioneered in his entire ministry.

The way of the cross, as a part of the work of God in Jesus and others to right the wrong of the world, can be seen to have at least six distinctive characteristics. It is first of all an *active* process or endeavour, undertaken intentionally. It is not merely a reactive or a passive submission to the agents or powers of evil. Jesus was energized by the power of the Spirit, encouraged and empowered by the love that moved within him. As a result he actively engaged the problems and evils that he saw. The attitudes of both prophetic and pastoral concern and of self-involvement combined to make Jesus an active initiator and agent of change. He did not acquiesce to the overwhelming evil that he saw. He confronted it and acted to change it.

This indicates a second characteristic of Jesus' way of salvation: it was and is *subversive* of the existing powers-that-be. When Jesus' followers identify with idolatrous or profane ruling powers, whatever they be, or become such ruling powers themselves they have departed from his way of salvation. He was continuously subversive of the dominating structures in his society or in the individuals he dealt with, calling for justice for the oppressed, especially the poor, and casting out the demons that dominated individuals. If John Dominic Crossan is right in his interpretation of Jesus' parables, one of Jesus' main emphases in his teaching was iconoclasm and irony that punctured the pretensions of the absoluteness of prevailing social opinion in order to open minds to the possibilities of God's new creation.

Not only was Jesus' teaching subversive of idolatrous or profane ideologies, his actions confronted such systems of thought to create a crisis in which change had to be considered. His healing on the Sabbath is a case in point. Those who follow Jesus in his way of the cross might examine their theories and practice by the criterion of Jesus' subversiveness.[17] In his ground-breaking book *A Materialist Reading of the Gospel of Mark* (1981), Fernando Belo documents the extent of Jesus' subversive activity and teaching against patriarchy, political domination, putting kinship ties above all else, putting nation above all else, putting wealth above concern for the poor, and so on (See for example, p.245 ff). Jesus' preached and acted so as to subvert the ways of the world and the rationalizations that support them. The Reigning of God calls for real changes that will liberate those oppressed by the way thing are.

The third aspect of the way of the cross follows from the first two, namely, it entails having a strategy to accomplish the changes envisioned

---

[17]Cf. Sobrino (1978): "The realization of justice must necessarily entail a fight against injustice, for injustice will not disappear simply because one has a positive intention to establish justice as Jesus did" (p.125).

by the inspirited imagination and the prophetic and pastoral concern. Jesus did not go to Jerusalem by chance for his decisive encounter with the powers-that-be. He "set his face to go to Jerusalem" (Lk 9:51). The day before the incident of "cleansing the Temple" Jesus is reported by Mark to have gone into the Temple and "looked round at everything" (Mk 11:11). The dramatic action of the following day was apparently carefully thought out and planned in advance. In a larger sense Jesus' entire mission was a strategy of announcing and realizing the Reign of God. It was a strategy guided by prayer and the wisdom of the Spirit. It was informed by the discernment of the gospel and the law of God which is the law of the Spirit of life.

The strategy of Jesus' way of the cross was also a strategy of *nonviolence*. Few exegetes would deny that Jesus was nonviolent in practice; some would claim he was not necessarily nonviolent in principle. The latter insist that Jesus' iconoclasm would prevent him from making any law absolute, even the law "Thou shalt not kill." The freedom to discern the "law of the Spirit," they would say, is not fenced in by this or that absolute restriction that cannot be modified to meet the needs of particular circumstances. Certainly Jesus demonstrated such freedom from some of the laws of the Torah, and it is perhaps unwise to insist on what he would do or not do in other hypothetical situations. The ethical question of whether sometimes lives should be taken in order to save more lives can be extremely difficult. We do not know for sure what Jesus would decide to do in these cases.

We do know that he went a long, long way with his policy of nonviolence.[18] We know that given the choice between taking other lives to save his own and giving up his own to save the others he chose to give himself. It is hard to conceive of his agreeing with the counsel of Caiaphas, as John records it, that "it was expedient that one man should die for the people" (Jn 18:14) unless that man was himself.[19] Expedient loss of life is consistent with the Spirit of love when the life is given. When life is taken it is much more difficult to see the consistency with love, especially love for the life that is taken.

Fifthly, the way of the cross was a way of radical trusting, obeying and loving of God. Jesus' active, subversive strategies of nonviolent love for the world were born in his trusting and loving relationship with God and they continued there until Jesus' death. In fact, his death was the result of his trusting and obeying God in the time of supreme danger and temptation.[20] The Reigning of God requires such trust.

---

[18] Machovec (1976) says of Jesus' 'pacifism': "It is not primarily a matter of negative, passive pacifism ... but of living in a positive spirit recommended in the parable of the Good Samaritan (Lk 10:37). Then pacifism appears neither as flight nor as capitulation but as a form of total responsibility for others including enemies. It is not a question of 'non-activity' in the Buddhist manner, but of the introduction of a higher form of moral behavior (p.109).

[19] Frye (1981) comments that "any persecuting Christian is assuming that Pilate and Caiaphas were right in principle, and should merely have selected a different victim" (p.132).

[20] Cf. Rahner (in Rahner and Thüsing 1980, p.38): "It [death] is the one act of self-realization of freedom as a human being in which man disposes of himself entirely and inwardly (either for God or against him ) ..." Cf. also Montague (1976): "[In Mark's pneumatology] martyrdom, not miracles, is the ultimate testing of the Spirit" (p.252).

Whatever might be said in general about Jesus' sinlessness, it is a fact that in going to the cross Jesus was perfect in his obedience to God's Reign.[21] There is no greater love than "that a man lay down his life for his friends" (Jn 15:13). If he had shown less than perfect love there might not have been a crucifixion and the way of the cross would not have been disclosed as the way of salvation. As the *Letter to the Hebrews* put it, "it was fitting that [God] ... should make the pioneer of [human] salvation perfect through suffering ... , that through death, he might destroy him who has the power of death, that is, the devil, and deliver all those who through fear of death were subject to lifelong bondage" (Heb 2:10,14-15). Jesus' perfect obedience made it possible that the cross could become for human history the sign that "in everything God works for good with those who love [God] who are called according to [God's] purpose" (Rom 8:28).

The cross was a highly ambiguous mixture of good and evil as most events in history typically are. Through Jesus' trusting obedience and love, God was able to turn an evil event into a blessing for countless others. This was the epitome of the Reigning of God in history where virtually all events and all people are an ambiguous mixture of evil and good. The cross is the pre-eminent sign of God's mysterious providence whereby God can achieve good purposes in spite of the evil that seems to prevail in human affairs. Through the obedience and love of the one who was called according to God's purposes, God transfigured the significance of the crucifixion of Jesus and it became a means of grace for all who followed after him.

Finally, the way of salvation was eschatologically oriented. There has been much debate about whether or not Jesus was a "short-term" apocalyptic who thought the completion or culmination of God's saving work was *coming* soon, but there is little disagreement that he preached the coming of the Reign of God. His own ministry may have been vitalized by his apocalyptic hopes. The early church certainly was future-oriented, at least in the beginning, and it has never ceased to pray "Thy Kingdom come" which it believes Jesus taught his disciples to pray. Apocalyptic, as we noted in the last chapter, is the extension of the struggle of good and evil to an ultimate climax in which God overcomes evil completely. "[The apocalyptist] lives a hope that seems contradicted by the realities of [the] world but that is fed by ... faith in the faithfulness of the God of Israel and [God's] ultimate self-vindication" (Beker 1980, p.136). This is a utopian hope in the sense that its realization cannot be envisaged for a particular time or place.[22] When it becomes a matter of prediction it transgresses on God's freedom and becomes a destructive and false

---

[21]It is the trusting of God and doing God's will rather than suffering *per se* that characterizes the way of the cross. Cf. Sobrino (1978): "Christian spirituality is not formally a spirituality of suffering; rather it is a spirituality focused on the following of Jesus" (p.215).

[22]Cf. Sobrino (1978): "The phrase 'kingdom of God' is a utopian symbol for a wholly new and definitive way of living and being. It presupposes renewal in many areas: in the heart of the human person, in societal relationships, and in the cosmos at large. Today we ignore the last dimension because it clearly is bound up with cultural conceptions of Jesus' own age. It simply indicates how total the renewal is to be" (p.119). If our interpretation of principalities and powers derived from Berkhof and Wink is accurate, it is not meaningless yet to hope for the renewal of the cosmos.

ideology; but when it remains genuinely utopian it lends hope to those in the way of salvation. The way of the cross cannot exist without such "hope against hope."

*Comparative Overview*

Apart from a few remarks in passing, little reference has been made to the main soteriological theories that have existed in Christian tradition over the centuries. Now that the nature and way of salvation in this Spirit christology have been delineated a comparison with some other traditional views may further clarify the soteriology here. Rather than referring to the soteriological theories of specific theologians such as Anselm, Abelard or Calvin and doing the exposition of their views in full historical detail, I will compare the characteristics of Spirit soteriology with alternative characteristics that have been commonly identified as those of various traditional Christian views.

Salvation here is understood to be a process of overcoming evil with good rather than a once-and-for-all transaction done by Jesus at Calvary. It is a matter of the realizing or actualizing of the Reigning of God in Jesus and subsequently in followers of Jesus; it is not a matter of satisfying God's justice by the single meritorius act of Jesus' dying. The justice of God is conceived to be rehabilitative, served by the process of renewing individual and social life to be what God intends it to be; God's justice is not conceived to be primarily retributive, satisfied by an appropriate punishment or sacrifice. This processive salvation is dynamic rather than juridical.[23] It involves continuous change in the lives and in the world of those who live in the way of salvation. It is, therefore, historical salvation or salvation in history rather than "angelic" salvation which is concerned primarily with what happens after life. This processive salvation is positive and active in essence rather than consisting of a negative, punitive event or a death which is an end in itself. It is eschatologically oriented towards the complete overcoming of evil in the world, but it does not predict a time or place when this will occur. It has a utopian, prophetic apocalyptic rather than a literal, predictive apocalyptic.

In this processive view, Jesus is a "catalytic" saviour rather than a "causative" or "determinant" saviour who accomplished salvation as a *fait accompli* that must be appropriated in faith if salvation is to be possible any time and any place.[24] Jesus is not a "bottleneck" through which God's forgiveness must be received on the reasoning that there could be no forgiveness by God without the shedding of Jesus' blood. Jesus can occasion forgiveness by his gospel of "return" with its message of God's mercy, but he does not cause forgiveness to occur by means of a transaction between him and God.[25]

---

[23]Cf. Ruether (1983): "We need to think in terms of a dynamic rather than a static, relationship between redeemer and redeemed" (p.138).

[24]Russell Pregeant (1978, p.143ff.) develops a "catalytic" view of salvation in terms of process theology.

[25]Cf. Thüsing (Rahner and Thüsing 1980, p.83): "According to Hebrews, Paul and the gospel and first epistle of John, this 'blood' saves, not as the blood of Jesus shed in the past on Golgotha but rather as the community with Jesus living in the present insofar as he is the crucified and risen one in his identity."

As a catalytic agent or mediator of God's saving work in the world Jesus is not just an example to be followed but is alive in the Spirit, dynamically "inspiriting" his followers. Jesus' messianic role was clearly not over and done with when he died. In God's economy of salvation God continues to make Jesus a living and efficacious agent of salvation ever since his death.[26] In fact, his efficacy as catalytic agent of salvation increases in an exponential curve after he is no longer limited to one geographical place and time. The Spirit who was in Jesus continues to come to people through Jesus to realize salvation:[27] to call them to return to God, to regenerate their energies, to give them the information and memory of God's purposes, to renew attitude-virtues, vocation and ethos, to inspire prophetic and healing ministries, to reorder chaos by wisdom and law, and to empower active, subversive strategies of nonviolent love carried out in trust to the point of death, if necessary.

This process of salvation or way of salvation is not *"theosis"* or divinization; it is better termed humanization, the renewal of humanity in the image of God (Cf. II Cor 3:18). It is sanctification, the process of realizing both personal and social holiness or righteousness. Salvation so understood is not perfect or "entire" sanctification, except possibly proleptically. The Spirit who sanctifies is received partially and as a "down-payment" rather than in full perfection. The healing of peoples' blindness and the casting out of their idolatrous allegiances is an on-going process of growth in grace and wisdom and all the other benefits of the presence of the Spirit. To be filled increasingly with the Spirit of God should not be described as becoming divine because "no one is good but God alone" (Mk 10:18); the difference between God and creatures is essential to affirm. Identifying creatures with divinity is the root of demonic idolatry. To call salvation divinization is to flirt with the idea that creatures can become divine which, in fact they do only for their damnation, not salvation.

Similarly, although salvation is the Reigning of God, no particular individuals or corporate groups such as the church should be identified with the Kingdom of God. The earthen vessels that hold the treasure of God's glory should never blur the distinction between themselves and the one who graces them in Spirit. Since salvation by the Reigning of God in Spirit is healing of both individuals and systems, divinization is not an appropriate term for it. One can hardly speak of the divinizing of the entire world including its dust without departing drastically from the biblical idea of God.

This Spirit soteriology belongs to the *"Christus Victor"* tradition.[28] The principalities and powers or systems which are the main locus of

---

[26].Cf. Schoonenberg (1971): "Christ's being in heaven is obviously identical with his salvific power on earth" (p.154).

[27]Cf. Thüsing (Rahner and Thüsing 1980, p.85): "Jesus is always regarded in the New Testament as the one who made it possible for the believer to be in a situation of community with God in the present and in the future and, what is more, to have that relationship by virtue of the sending of the Spirit of God."

[28]Cf. Aulen (1969): "The central idea of *Christus Victor* is the view of God and the Kingdom of God as fighting against evil powers ravaging in mankind" (p.ix).

evil residing both in individuals and in the world are being "disarmed" and "publicly exposed" (*edeigmatisen*, Col 2:15), as God's Reign "triumphs" over them by the power of the Spirit. This happened in the life and death and resurrection of Jesus and it continues to happen when his way of salvation is followed by others. It is relatively clear how the way of the Spirit overcomes wrong in systems and individuals. This work of the Spirit has been described earlier. The prophetic activity, the ordering of chaos by law and wisdom, the renewal of attitude-virtues, etc. are the overcoming of demonic and profane powers by the presence of God as Spirit.

The question of guilt, however, needs particular attention because it has been claimed so often that guilt cannot be overcome without some atoning sacrifice. Guilt is the responsibility for wrong done in obedience to some commanding power other than God. When the power is named and disclaimed in the return to God that power is disarmed and its power is subordinated to the authority of God. The guilty one returns to an obedient and trusting orientation towards God. This requires restitution or reordering of the results of the wrong done in previous obedience to the idolatrous power. In addition to making restitution the responsibility of the forgiven one is to "go and do not sin again" (Jn 8:11). The point of forgiveness is to rehabilitate the person and reconcile the world to God's Reigning purposes. If the person who has done wrong has a change of heart, i.e. a change of orientation from loving idols to loving God, the joy of being accepted in that return prevails over the the feelings of guiltiness. The Prodigal Son is welcomed home in a feast of joy. He does not have to do any atoning act other than the return home itself. The fact that the sinner "was dead, and is alive; ... was lost, and is found" (Lk 15:32) is sufficient reason "to make merry and be glad." In spite of the clarity of Jesus' parable and the many statements in the Bible about "return" those who claim that forgiveness must require an expiatory sacrifice insist "Sin is so serious that forgiveness is no cheap sentimental welcome back." The welcome back of the Prodigal Son, however, need not be described as cheap or sentimental.

The logic of a necessary atoning sacrifice arose originally from the New Testament itself which seems to refer many times to Jesus' death as the action that enables forgiveness to be effected. There is no doubt that the New Testament authors used the metaphor of the Hebrew sacrificial cult to point to the singular importance of Jesus' death for salvation. However, in fact, the early Christians understood the sacrificial cult in a way which did not assume that forgiveness was *effected* by offerings of blood. Robert J. Daly S.J. (1978) shows that "It is precisely an *incarnational spiritualization of sacrifice* that is operative in the New Testament and the early church" (p.138). It was not the material blood or body of Jesus in itself that constituted the sacrifice acceptable to God; it was "the internal dispositions" of "obedience and love toward God, and of self-sacrificing love and service to and for the brothers and sisters" Hence, "Christian sacrifice was not a cultic but rather an ethical idea" (p.140). People are not forgiven because Jesus did the ethical activity that they cannot do for themselves. We are forgiven when we sacrifice as he sacrificed, when we love as he loved, when we return to the Reign of God from the reign of the powers.

For we do not offer animals in sacrifice; still less do we believe that the forgiveness of sins is tied up with certain sacrificial blood rites. But then *neither did the early Christians*. They were, in fact, reproached as irreligious by their pagan neighbours because they neither offered sacrifice nor worshipped in temples (Daly 1978, p.135).

The early Christian understanding of Jesus' death as a sacrifice, using the Jewish temple cult as a metaphor, is misunderstood when it is taken to mean that Jesus propitiated or appeased God by his death. Frances Young acknowledges that "the New Testament was written in Greek, to pagan converts and therefore it was only natural that the Jewish concepts lying behind the language of the New Testament should be misunderstood in a new cultural environment, and we can see that this clearly happened" (1975, p.73).[29] The fact that Tertullian, Anselm and Calvin, the three most prominent framers of the Satisfaction Theory and Penal Substitution Theory of the Atonement, were lawyers before becoming theologians may help to explain how the metaphor of legal satisfaction from feudal civil law and the metaphor of punitive satisfaction from criminal law should have come to hold such a central place in Christian tradition.[30] These metaphors from civil and criminal law have a basically different logic than the metaphor of cultic sacrifice from Jewish cultic law.[31] In the latter case it was understood that only God can save and God is not moved to do so by sacrifices of blood. The sacrifices were to show that the return to God had been made in Spirit and in truth. They "signed and sealed" the internal dispositions of the worshippers; they did not cause God to grant forgiveness.

How then could Jesus' death be called an expiation "for the sins of the whole world" (Jn 2:2)? Expiation means to make amends for wrong-doing. If Jesus is thought to be representative in some way of all human beings who have contributed to the horrendous wrong-doing in the history of the human race his obedience and loving trust of God to the point of death may be seen as the human race, through its representative, making amends to God by means of a complete and perfect "return" to God. If Jesus is thought to have such corporate representative status then his faithfulness may be said to make amends to God on behalf of everyone else. Such corporate thinking employs what Frye calls the "royal metaphor." According to this metaphor a sovereign such as the Emperor of Japan "stands for" the whole Japanese nation in certain

---

[29]Cf. Thüsing (Rahner and Thüsing 1980, p.82): "The New Testament soteriologies, which work with categories of 'sacrifice', are not sufficiently understood ... . They bear evidence of a soteriological aim that has not been sufficiently liberated from the narrow confines of a classical Church soteriology."

[30]Cf. Kelly (1978, p.177): "... Tertullian, whose legal outlook led him to emphasize the necessity of reparation for offences committed, ... transferred the idea to theology. Thus he has the theory that good deeds accumulate merit with God, while bad deeds demand 'satisfaction' — we observe the introduction of this important conception into Christian thought."

[31]Cf. Dillistone (1968): "An extremely limited and unhistorical view of sacrifice was made the determinative legal symbol to interpret the significance of the death of Christ" (p.199).

symbolic actions, for example, in his official apology for the wrongdoing of the Japanese in the Second World War. All Japanese can identify with the apology. The Emperor has made amends on behalf of all Japanese. Jesus' followers may believe he can stand for all human beings, and his complete return of obedience to the point of death is then thought to make amends to God for all the world's evil. This interpretation of Jesus' death is a "transactional" view of salvation which we have already rejected in favour of a dynamic "processive" interpretation. In the next chapter we will consider the ways in which it is legitimate to use the royal metaphor in connection with Jesus, but such corporate thinking must have its limitations when applied to human responsibility before God for the evil of the world. As God loves individuals God requires each person to be responsible for the wrong he or she does. God calls each individual, as well as groups and systems to return. Jesus' obedience and love cannot be regarded as a *substitute* for what each person must do. The idea of Christ substituting for us in his death is demeaning for him as well as immoral for us. Gerald O'Collins observes;

> There is less intentionality and more passivity apparent in the way we use the language of 'substitution'. This consideration alone should win support for speaking of 'Christ our representative' and not of 'Christ our substitute' (1983, p.34).

Because Jesus' self-sacrifice in life and in death pioneered the way of salvation for us we can say "he died for us" but it was not as a substitute for our own self-sacrifice in the way of the cross. In his life, death and resurrection he is the catalytic, inspiriting mediator for us of the way of God's Reigning. We can thank God in the Eucharist and at other times for the remembrance of Jesus pioneering our faith and at the same time we offer ourselves as living sacrifices. His blood was shed for us and he was a "ransom" for our salvation in the sense that without his sacrificial life and death we would not know the gospel of the Reigning of God. *The First Letter of John* makes clear what is the right emphasis in the logic of salvation. After speaking of Jesus as expiation and "advocate with the Father" the author says: "And by this we may be sure that we know him, if we keep his commandments ... . He [or she] who says he [or she] abides in him ought to walk in the same way in which he walked" (I Jn 2:3,6).

Expiation, then, despite its use in the New Testament is not a metaphor of salvation that can be easily used in an accurate way in our society. It is extremely susceptible to a juridical interpretation on the basis of metaphors taken from civil or criminal law which are entirely foreign to the original metaphor from cultic sacrifice. Spirit soteriology as developed here can emphasize the self-sacrificial character of the way of the cross both for Jesus and for any who follow him, but it will not employ the idea of expiation as substitutionary satisfaction of God, much less the idea of propitiation to appease an angry God.

The "processive" interpretation of salvation in Spirit christology is, finally, a kind of *imitatio Christi* view of salvation. As Tom Driver points out, there are inappropriate interpretations of what imitation of

Christ means, for example ones which are based on the simplistic question "What would Jesus do?" (1981, p.23). There are more legitimate ways to understand it. Schillebeeckx points out that the "call to the imitation of Jesus is a constant theme in the New Testament" (1979, p.222).[32] Imitation in the New Testament is not conceived simply as imagining specific actions that Jesus would hypothetically do in the circumstances confronting us. It is conceived more as a *following* (Cf.I Pet 12:21) in our time and place of the *way* of life that Jesus followed in his time and place.[33] Leonardo Boff states that "Christianity is concrete and consistent living in a christic structure, a living of that which Jesus of Nazareth lived ... " (1978, p.250). Jon Sobrino says in a similar way "[Jesus] reveals the very process of filiation, the concrete way in which human beings can and do become children of God" (1978, p.340).

A much narrower concept of imitation is proposed by John Howard Yoder. He claims that:

> There is ... but one realm in which the concept of imitation holds—but there it holds in every strand of the New Testament literature and all the more strikingly by virtue of the absence of parallels in other realms: this is at the point of the concrete social meaning of the cross in its relation to enmity and power. Servanthood replaces dominion, forgiveness absorbs hostility. Thus—and only thus — are we bound by New Testament thought to "be like Jesus" (1972, p.134).

Unless the "concrete social meaning of the cross" is interpreted to mean the whole content of the way of the Reigning of God in human life as realized by Jesus it must be judged to be too narrow an interpretation of what *imitatio Christi* entails. As we have seen, the presence of God as Spirit in Jesus produced a rich, many-splendoured way of salvation including prayerful regeneration and the gift of a wide variety of attitude-virtues as well as prophetic discernment, wisdom and the political Spirituality of the way of the cross. Yoder's point is legitimate in what it affirms but inadequate in what it excludes.

The way of salvation in Christ is, in conclusion, a definitive paradigmatic expression of salvation but it cannot be regarded as completely exclusive to Jesus or his followers. The Spirit of God was not and is not exclusive to Jesus or to Christians. Every aspect of the work of God as Spirit which constitutes the process of salvation could be found before Christ and outside Christianity. Jesus' unique contribution to the salvation of the world was to manifest the Reigning of God "in an absolute and exhaustive manner" (Boff 1978, p.248). Boff, Tillich, Rahner and many others in the history of Christianity have acknowledged that God as Spirit or Word is not restricted to Jesus of Nazareth or his explicit

---

[32]Dunn (1973) claims "there is the strand of *imitatio Christi* firmly embedded in Paul's thought—Rom.xv.2f., I Cor.iv.17, xi.I, 2Cor.viii.8f., Gal.i.10, Eph.iv.20,32-v.2, Phil. ii.5-8, Col.ii.6, I Thess.i.6; also Rom.xiii.14, Eph.iv.24 (p55). He quotes W.D. Davies who says that for Paul "every Christian is pledged to an attempted ethical conformity to Christ; the imitation of Christ is part and parcel of Paul's ethic" (p.55).

[33]Cf. Sobrino (1978): "The following of Jesus does not mean reproducing the historical traits or acts of Jesus; rather, it means reproducing the whole process in which he was involved" (p.126).

followers. As we shall see in the next chapter, in the New Testament the protological statements about Christ's pre-existence are basically intended to acknowledge that the way of God's working in Jesus extends to all times and places. In Jesus God's presence as Spirit is revealed in a categorical way and as the beginning of a dynamic, on-going, historical process which Jesus announced as the coming of the Reigning of God. We have seen something of the way of God's Reigning in Spirit in Jesus. We turn now to reflect on what can be said about the person and significance of Jesus himself.

## Chapter Six
# SPIRIT CHRISTOLOGY: AN INTERPERSONAL MODEL

*Introduction*

Out of its preunderstanding of God and the world, and from its recollections of Jesus, and in accordance with its newfound awareness of salvation as God revealed it in Jesus' life, death and resurrection the early church worked out its logic of Jesus as the Christ.[1] The same combination of factors are necessary in contemporary christology.[2] The early church derived its preunderstanding of God and the world from the Hebrew scriptures and from the culture of their time. Similarly, christologies today derive their preunderstanding of God from the Bible and from the culture of our time. The early church's understanding of the saving significance of Jesus emerged from a juxtaposition of their understanding of God and the world and the remembrance of what Jesus said and did. The early church had some eye witnesses of Jesus and his disciples from which to get the recollections of Jesus that informed and tested their christological reflections. Today we have a much more complex task of getting information about Jesus by careful scholarly study of the early church's christological writings.

The realization of the gospel that Jesus represented came as the "Easter experience," the life changing conviction that the way of God's Reigning, as Jesus had exemplified it, was trustworthy, a viable possibility for living, a reliable way of participating in God's dealing with the evil of the world. Jesus was the pioneer of this new initiative in God's saving work. The key to the gospel was the confirmation that Jesus' way of the cross was the authentic way of God's Reigning. This was the significance of the Easter experience. The crucified Jesus was not a dead issue. He was a live option. The Spirit of God who had made Jesus what he was in life and death was now making others to be like Jesus. The Reigning of God the Spirit was now coming to all who believed in Jesus' authenticity as the pioneer of God's way of salvation.[3] Jesus

---

[1] Kasper (1976, p.22) expresses a widely accepted consensus: "It can be shown that there are soteriological motives behind all the Christological pronouncements of the early Church. ... For that reason the scholastic separation between Christology and soteriology has to be cancelled."

[2] Cf. Congar (1983, Vol.III): "Christology should not be separated from soteriology. ... It is in fact almost true to say that Christology must be situated *within* soteriology, which embraces it;" (p.165). Cf. also Young (in Hick 1977): "Christological expositions are parasitic upon definitions and concepts of salvation" (p.13) and "In any attempt to rethink Christological belief the primacy of soteriology must be recognized" (p.30).

[3] Cf. Robinson (1962): "The Christian consciousness might be not unfairly described as the democratization of the prophetic consciousness through the gift of the Holy Spirit" (p.19).

was confirmed to the early church as Messiah, the one chosen and anointed by God to bring the ultimate saving initiative of God to the world. Moreover, because the Reigning Spirit of God was so closely identified with Jesus in his life and death the early church could for all practical purposes speak of the Spirit of God as the Spirit of Jesus. The Spirit of Jesus was synonymous with the guiding and empowering presence of God in living the way of the Spirit.

Despite the close involvement of Jesus in the new way of salvation, however, the early church remained theocentric and monotheistic in accordance with their Jewish theological background.The Spirit of Jesus was still the Spirit of God. Jesus himself was not God.[4] He was the Spirit-filled Messiah of God. It was only later when the church moved out of the Hebrew monotheistic religious milieu into the Greek polytheistic milieu that Jesus was deified. The doctrine of the Trinity was eventually developed to preserve a kind of monotheism in conjunction with the affirmation of Jesus' deity.

The deification of Jesus is now being seen as a highly problematic claim in the pluralistic context of the modern world. There are compelling reasons to develop a christology more closely akin to the earliest christologies of the still Jewish church. In those christologies the Spirit of God was the central operating Reality.

There appear to be two basic alternatives in developing Spirit christologies, depending on whether the relationship of Jesus and God as Spirit is judged to be interpersonal or intrapersonal.[5] An intrapersonal relationship between Jesus and God would presuppose that Jesus' identity as a person was the very identity of God. If Jesus somehow shared the identity of God's personality he could be said to have an intrapersonal relationship with God, assuming that God has only one personality, one centre of consciousness. The relationship between Jesus and God would be like a person talking to herself or himself rather than two persons talking to each other. The classical christocentric-trinitarian paradigm of Christianity has held this view, despite the use of the term "three persons" in one God. It is traditionally recognized in Western Christianity that the "persons" of the Trinity are not supposed to be conceived as three "centres of consciousness."[6] An "intrapersonal" model of christology has all the problems associated with affirming Jesus' deity.

An interpersonal relationship between Jesus and God the Spirit would presuppose that Jesus was a human being with his own personality, his own centre of consciousness, his own identity which, however Godlike, was nonetheless not the identity or centre of consciousness of God's very Self. This is the model of Spirit christology that will be developed

---

[4]Schoonenberg (1971) insists that "we should be understanding the entire data of the New Testament better if we replace the divine person in Christ with God's total presence" (p.123).

[5]This distinction is made by Arnold B. Come (1959), p.149. He explains in a footnote on p.195: "*Interpersonal,* to mean relation between two persons: *intrapersonal,* to mean that structure within a being that makes the being 'person'."

[6]Cf. Schoonenberg 1971, p.79. "consciousness and freedom are for Thomas and in Thomism deliberately eliminated from the Trinitarian concept of person. The divine persons have no individual consciousness and freedom, but realize in a relative way the consciousness and freedom common to all three."

here. The reflection on this model will proceed by comparing and contrasting the main characteristics of this interpersonal model with those of an intrapersonal model as it has been proposed by Kasper and Rosato and others who wish to develop Spirit christology along the lines of the classical "two nature" type of christology. The interpersonal model proposed here will be similar to G. W. H. Lampe's Spirit christology in some, but not all, respects.

The following chart indicates the structure of the comparison that will be made in clarifying the nature of "interpersonal" Spirit christology.

## Two Models of Spirit Christology

| Interpersonal Model | Intrapersonal Model |
|---|---|
| 1. "Jesus, full of the Holy Spirit" (Lk 4:1) | 1. "The Lord is the Spirit" (II Cor 3:17) |
| 2. Antiochene (Disjunction type) | 2. Alexandrian (Unification type) |
| 3. Full Humanity | 3. Full Deity |
| 4. Functional Presence of God | 4. Ontological Presence of God |
| 5. Different in Degree (incarnation) | 5. Different in Kind (Incarnation) |
| 6. Theocentric | 6. Christocentric |
| 7. Exclusive Monotheism | 7. Trinitarian Monotheism |
| 8. Historical Christ | 8. Cosmic Christ |
| 9. Provisionality (Proleptic) | 9. Absolute Finality |
| 10. Titles | 10. Titles |

*1. Starting Point*

The interpersonal model takes as its starting point the prevailing New Testament view of Jesus as a man "full of the Holy Spirit" (Lk 4:1). This view of Jesus has been explored in Chapter IV. The intrapersonal model appeals to isolated passages in the New Testament where there is a possibility of inferring Jesus' deity. For *Logos* christology no verse is more important than John 1:1, "And the Word was God." For intrapersonal Spirit christology perhaps the key verse is II Corinthians 3:17, "Now The Lord is the Spirit." The assumption is made that Paul here is referring to the risen Jesus as "the Lord." Dunn (1970) however, argues convincingly that the Lord referred to here is God.

The context of II Corinthians 3:7-18 is an argument by Paul about law and the Spirit in which he refers in verses 7,10,13,16 and 18 to the passage in Exodus 34:29-35 in which Moses veiled his face before bringing to the people of Israel the two tables on which the law was written and unveiled his face whenever he "went in before the Lord to speak with him" (Ex 34:34). Paul does a "Christian midrash" on this passage to make the point that like Moses we should take off the veil when we turn to God (vs.16), and God who is the Spirit will change us "into his likeness from one degree of glory to another" (vs.18). It is true that "through Christ [the veil] is taken away" (vs.14); Christ has opened up the new Reign of God present in Spirit but it is undoubtedly God to whom Paul refers as the Spirit into whose image people are changed—as Jesus himself was made to be the image of God by God's Spirit.

It is beyond the scope of this book to look at all the scripture passages used in support of claims for Jesus' deity but it can be said in general that if they are approached with the theocentric presuppositions of the Jewish authors there are very few, if any, that can be said to support the idea of Jesus' deity. We will look at some of the main ones presently. We referred earlier to Dunn's study of the idea of a pre-existent personal Christ in the New Testament and noted his conclusion that Jn 1:14 is "the only such statement in the N.T" (1980, p.24) of the explicit idea of the Incarnation of God in Jesus. Dunn, it should be remembered, has no intention of challenging the traditional paradigm of Christian theology. We will look at this again shortly.

*2. Antiochene and Alexandrian*

Besides the strong biblical support for an "interpersonal" logic of Christ's relationship with God, it can be shown that this approach resolves some of the dilemmas that have been endemic in the traditional approaches to christology. In the early centuries of Christian history the two major approaches to christology were the Antiochene, culminating its development in the Nestorian "heresy" and the Alexandrian, culminating in the Monophysite "heresy."[7] Interpersonal Spirit christology in which the starting point is an assumption that Jesus was a real human being is obviously more akin to Antiochene thinking which insisted on the full human identity of Jesus than it is to Alexandrian thinking which was primarily concerned to affirm the full deity of Jesus in unity with God. It would be inaccurate, however, simply to identify interpersonal Spirit christology as Antiochene.

The Antiochenes, despite their concern for Jesus' full humanity, shared with the Alexandrians the presupposition that Jesus must also be accorded full deity if the logic of salvation as they both saw it, were to be maintained. The logic of salvation in two respects required that the saviour be fully divine: (1) in order to make a sufficient sacrifice as expiation and propitiation for the sins of the whole world[8] and (2) in order to accomplish in principle the full divinizing (*theosis*) of humanity that could subsequently continue in Jesus' followers.[9] Both Alexandrians and Antiochenes, therefore, were committed to affirming the immutable and entire deity of Jesus. Their differences lay in understanding how the humanness of Jesus was to be conceived and how the unity of the two

---

[7]See Pannenberg (1968, p.291.) "Jesus ... from the very beginning was a superman, the God-man. This is the tendency of Alexandrian Christology. The Monophysite tendency is present here at its root. ... the problem of Monophysitism ... begins ... with Cyril and indeed is really present in Athanasius."

[8]For example, See Kelly (1978, p.385) quoting Basil, "It is only the God-man who can offer to God adequate expiation for us all.

[9]For example, See Kelly (1978, p.243) quoting Athanasius, "The word could never have divinized us if He were merely divine by participation and were not Himself the essential Godhead the Father's veritable image.

natures could be explained. The Antiochenes insisted that Jesus had a full human identity like any other human being. The Alexandrians were content to speak of the divine *Logos* as the real identity of Jesus. "Human nature ... for Cyril as for Athanasius [was] only the 'garment' of the Logos" (Pannenberg 1968, p.289).

The main problem with the Antiochene approach was its inability to explain the unity in Jesus' person of the full deity and full humanity that were both claimed for the Christ. The main problem for the Alexandrians was that "Jesus possessed no specifically human individuality" (Pannenberg 1968, p.291).

Interpersonal Spirit christology clearly affirms the specific human individuality of Jesus and also affirms that he was full of the Holy Spirit. It is unthinkable that any contemporary christology would not recognize that Jesus was a specific human individual. To do so would be to entertain a mythological view of Jesus that would be totally divorced from the discursive thinking about reality that characterizes the knowledge explosion of the twentieth century. To say that God as Spirit was present in Jesus is also, admittedly, a mythological statement but one, we would insist, that is not incompatible with contemporary discursive thinking about human beings. Spirit is a kind of reality that discursive thinking can acknowledge even if Spirit is not quantifiable or predictable and controllable, as other objects of discursive thinking usually are. People with the most thoroughgoing commitment to the contemporary methods of discursive thinking are still able to acknowledge the fascinating and tremendous reality of interpersonal and sacrificial love, the power of good ethos, the mysterious creative energy and information that "blows" through artists and people of more pedestrian achievement.[10] The God of total deterministic deism and theism may be dead, but the mysterious power and meaning of Spirit is not dead, despite the knowledge explosion and the controls it has given to humanity.[11] God as Spirit can come to the world and be in a fully human being like Jesus without creating an artificial crisis of incoherence for modern understanding such as occurs with the claim that Jesus is God.

Spirit does not create the problem for Jesus' humanness that the identity of the *Logos* in Jesus caused for the Alexandrians nor the problem of the unity of Jesus' person that plagued the Antiochenes. Jesus can be thought to be a human being in every sense of the word and still be "full of the Holy Spirit."

## 3. *Full Humanity or Full Deity*

---

[10] D.H. Lawrence, for example, an avowed humanist, testified to the experience that his poems were written "by the wind that blows through me." (quoted by Norman Pittenger 1974, p.22)

[11] Schoonenberg (1971) says: "It is precisely the modern crisis in our understanding of God, ... which refers us to the Spirit and Life-Giver" (p.186). Cf. Taylor (1972): The whole of our uneasy debate about the meaning of the word 'God' for modern man cries out, I believe, for a recovery of a significant doctrine of the Holy Spirit. That is where we must now begin our talk of God—God working anonymously and on the inside: the beyond in the midst (p.5). Cf. also Frye (1981): "[God] may not be so much dead as entombed in a dead language" (p.18). Frye advocates returning to metaphorical language. Spirit is a valuable metaphor for speaking of both God and humans. "The nearest to the purely metaphorical conception is perhaps the word 'spirit', which with its overtones of 'breath', expresses the unifying principle of life that gives man a participating energy with nature" (p.19).

Full humanness can be affirmed for Jesus in interpersonal Spirit christology because humanness is not compromised by the presence of God as Spirit. Humanness is fulfilled and completed by the presence of the Spirit.[12] The crux of the matter is the nature of human freedom. If freedom can be understood to continue uncompromised by the presence of God in Spirit then full humanness is possible while "full of the Holy Spirit." If the idea of humanness is understood in a dynamic, relational way the presence of the Spirit can be described as theonomous rather than heteronomous and be seen as facilitating freedom rather than reducing it.

The image of God which defines humanness in the biblical view can be understood as a processive structure or capacity that human beings have whereby they can mirror or echo the qualities and characteristics of God's Spirit. Since the metaphors of light and sound both involve "waves" — or vibrations — humanness can be described metaphorically as the capacity to receive the vibrations of the Spirit and to reflect them more or less fully. According to Hebrews 1:3, Jesus "reflects the glory of God and bears the very stamp of [God's] nature." Jesus was described by various New Testament authors as the image of God, and Paul called him the Last Adam, indicating that Jesus was a model of authentic humanness. The dynamic concept of image as "reflecting" God was used not only by the author of Hebrews as quoted above but also by Paul in II Corinthians when referring to the process of salvation. "We all, ... beholding as in a glass the glory of the Lord, are changed into the same image from glory to glory even as by the Spirit of the Lord" (3:18 KJV). Thus, both Jesus as the authentic human being and salvation as a means of human fulfillment are conceived in terms of the dynamic reception and reflection of the Spirit of God.

Receiving the Spirit is not a mechanical or automatic process as might be suggested by pressing the metaphor of a mirror too far. As we said earlier, some of the creative initiatives of the Spirit occur at the subconscious and unconscious levels of human personality, but much of what the Spirit does involves an intentional response on the part of people. For example, any of the attitude-virtues, such as the several forms of love cannot occur unless a person decides to express them. There cannot be love in the sense of "seeking the fulfillment of the other" unless there is self-consciousness and freedom. These basic characteristics are presupposed in the process of reflecting God as Spirit. Humans are determined or "programmed" to some extent, but they also have the capacity to transcend themselves, to step outside themselves, as it were, and decide which influences or values to receive and express and which to resist.

The freedom, the capacity to decide in favour of optional possibilities is never value-free. There is no possibility of acting *freely* without deciding on the basis of some value, purpose or criterion. To twitch compulsively

---

[12]Cf. Lampe (1972): "The Spirit may possess a [person] and in some measure unite his [or her] personality to God. Yet this is without any diminution of his [or her] humanity; rather it means the raising of his [or her] humanity to its full potentiality, the completion of the human creation by the recreating influence of the creator-Spirit (p.117).

or to sneeze involuntarily are not acts of freedom, although suppressing them might be. Intention is essential for freedom. Moreover, as Tillich insisted, "freedom *and subjection to valid norms* are one and the same thing" (1963, p.28) (Italics mine). To act in accordance with demonic or idolatrous influences is a kind of slavery, rather than freedom. Similarly, to act out of ignorance can hardly be called real freedom. True human freedom occurs when people act on the basis of true discernment, accurate imagination, virtuous attitudes, appropriate vocation and good ethos. In other words, people are truly free when they reflect the Spirit of God. Resisting the Spirit in acts of vicious attitude or evil ethos are commonly called "free" but the self-destruction and harm such acts cause to others entail a loss of freedom rather than a realization of freedom. The structure of freedom allows people to resist the Spirit of truth, goodness, beauty and justice, but freedom actually occurs only when valid norms are operative in the deciding process.

Positive freedom should be distinguished from negative freedom (See Newman 1983, p.32f.). The former is the capacity to reflect the power and meaning of the Spirit of God; the latter is the turning away from God to reflect other powers and meanings. In negative freedom we decide to act on the basis of invalid norms. We commit ourselves to ungodly purposes or values, thereby idolizing them and suffering their demonic influences. Negative freedom has the structure of freedom but the substance of bondage.

Much more could be said about freedom but the point is now visible: Jesus could be "full of the Holy Spirit" without losing any aspect of his humanity. On the contrary, because he was full of the Holy Spirit Jesus realized human freedom to such an extent that he could be called "the image of the invisible God" (Col 1:15) or "the last Adam" (I Cor 15:45). Unlike Alexandrian christology, in interpersonal Spirit christology there is no problem with a reduction of Jesus' individual human identity when the statement is affirmed that "God was in Christ." In principle and in fact the influences of the presence of God as Spirit do not compromise fully human personality.

Other traditional questions about Jesus' humanness have to do with the extent of his knowledge or possible ignorance, whether or not he had faith, and whether or not he was sinless. These questions were addressed in Chapter IV. There it was found that Jesus had limited and growing knowledge like any human being. As Luke said "Jesus increased in wisdom and in stature and in favour with God and man" (2:52). It was shown that Jesus had faith like other human beings and it was suggested that while the New Testament does not give any evidence of Jesus doing wrong or learning by his mistakes it would be strange if he could preach and teach about forgiveness to the extent he did if he had never experienced it himself. In any case he could hardly have escaped "sinning boldly," having to act in situations in which all the available options are to some extent undesirable, including the option of doing nothing. He also had to live as any other human being does in a society in which all the systems are distorted to some extent by demonic or profane alienation. If his knowledge was limited, it is likely that he had to learn the extent of the demonic and profane as he "increased in wisdom."

It may have been partly the logic of expiation and the strong traditional Jewish emphasis on sacrificial victims being "without blemish" (Lev 22:19) that led to the claim in the early church that Jesus was "one who in every respect has been tempted as we are, yet without sinning" (Heb 4:15). Certainly, later on as the logic of substitutionary atonement gained authority the idea of Jesus' sinlessness became indispensable. The transaction that Jesus was believed to have accomplished with God on behalf of the world to clear the way for God's forgiveness of the sins of the world depended on Jesus having sufficient merit, by virtue of his sinlessness, to expiate the sins of the world.

If atonement is conceived in processive rather than transactional terms, there is no logical necessity to affirm Jesus' sinlessness. It is not necessary to preserve the concept of his merit being transferred in the eyes of God to our cause. God's forgiveness does not operate on the basis of the transferral of Jesus' or anyone else's merit. It requires only the sacrifice of a "broken and contrite heart" and is given freely to those who repent and change their ways in a return to the covenant of God. In Jesus, God renewed the covenant of salvation, opening the way of God's Reigning in an archetypal way. This disclosure of "the mystery which was kept secret for long ages" (Rom 16:25-26) does not logically require that Jesus' was sinless for his whole life. Jesus could not pioneer the way of the Spirit, the way of God's Reign, the way of the cross, without being in the end faithful and obedient, but there is no logical necessity to exclude from Jesus' life some personal experience of the "return" which constitutes the way of salvation for everyone else who enters into the covenant of the Reigning of God. Perhaps he was "in every respect ... tempted as we are, yet without sinning" (Heb 4:15), but christological reflection does not require this affirmation for the sake of its logic of salvation.

Even if Jesus were thought to share to some extent in the corporate distortions of the systems of his society or were thought to have learned by his moral mistakes, as every other growing person does, it would not compromise the saving significance of Jesus as archetype and mediator of the way of God's Reigning.

Nor does the undeniable perfection of Jesus' love and obedience at the time of his death compromise his full humanness. Such perfect obedience in particular circumstances is possible for any human being, without positing absolute sinlessness in the person's entire life.[13] If this were not so, the way of the cross would not be a way open to others.

---

[13] John Wesley was convinced that the full gospel included the promise and possibility of any human being attaining to the perfection of "entire sanctification." By this he meant "a total death to sin, and an entire renewal in the love and image of God, so as to rejoice evermore, to pray without ceasing and in everything to give thanks" (cited by Bruner 1979, p.325). He qualified this view of Christian perfection by saying that "it is not absolute. ... it does not make a [person] infallible ... it is improveable. ... it is amissable, capable of being lost; ... it is constantly both preceded and followed by a gradual work" (Bruner 1979, p.329-330). The qualifications appear virtually to remove the perfection. It seems better to speak of individual actions or times of perfection in human life rather than to use the term "entire" which suggests absoluteness and unchangeability.

The good news of God's Reigning is that history can be changed through the love and obedience of those who are called to serve God's purposes. By the grace of God present in Spirit, human love and obedience can be perfect for the situation at hand. In this way the faithful sacrifices of obedience can "salt" what is otherwise rotten and "leaven" what is otherwise dead. Through the good that is given to otherwise evil situations by the sacrifices of the obedient, God is able to bring unimaginable benefits from terribly evil events. One of main benefits of the crucifixion of Jesus is precisely this gospel of God's providential Reign, in spite of seemingly prevailing evil. This would be no gospel if Jesus' perfect obedience were not possible for him and for us as human beings. The good news lies in the repeatability of the way of the cross. "[Jesus'] Sonship is ... a paradigm of all human response to the personal outreach of God. It can only be the archetype of Sonship, however, if it is the response of an authentically human personality" (Lampe 1977, p.142).

The necessity of affirming Jesus' full humanness for the logic of salvation is apparent in interpersonal Spirit christology. The dynamics of Jesus' interpersonal relationship with God are the dynamics of salvation for any human being. If Jesus were not human it would cast into doubt the question whether other human beings could participate in the Reign of God, which is the life of the Spirit, as Jesus did.

In intrapersonal christology the necessity of affirming Jesus' deity for the sake of the logic of salvation has always been paramount. Some of the reasons have already been mentioned. The logic of satisfaction or substitution of a fully divine sacrifice for the sins of the world is not part of the interpersonal Spirit christology nor is the idea that a divine agent must accomplish a once-for-all unrepeatable victory over Satan. Interpersonal Spirit christology can take seriously the words that John's Gospel attributes to Jesus, "he [or she] who believes in me will also do the works that I do; and greater works than these will he [or she] do, because I go to the Father" (Jn 14:12). The question has to be asked, however, what interpersonal Spirit christology has to say about the divinity of Jesus.

It has to be clearly stated that the presence of the Spirit in Jesus did not make Jesus in himself divine, any more than it makes anyone else divine when God is present as Spirit.[14] To speak about any human being as a divine person is to lose the distinction between Creator and creature. This either endangers monotheism with polytheism or amounts to idolatry which is, by definition, to treat a creature as if it were the Creator. To say that Jesus was not a creature is to forfeit any realistic affirmation of his humanness.

To speak mythologically about any human being is to lose touch with reality to some extent. Mythical speech is necessary and appropriate in speaking about God, even God present in human beings. But mythical language about a human being *per se* is not necessary and appropriate. It represents a reduction of the truth about that person rather than

---

[14]Cf. Dunn (1975): "Certainly it is quite clear that if we can indeed properly speak of the 'divinity' of the historical Jesus we can only do so in terms of his experience of God: his 'divinity' means his relationship with the Father as son and the Spirit of God in him" (p.92).

the fullest truth. When we sing mythically about Davey Crockett killing a bear "when he was only three" it is perhaps harmless fun. But if we insisted on it seriously it would be a tragic loss of truth about him. In the formation of the canon the church was wise to omit the spurious gospel that portrayed Jesus as an omnipotent and petulant God-child who turned a playmate into a withered cripple in a moment of pique. There is a discernible line between the "enconium" character of the canonical gospels and the outright mythologizing about Jesus that took place later on in church history.

I am not saying that all the miracles attributed to Jesus should be demythologized. Some of them, such as the feeding of the five thousand and four thousand, obviously have to be understood allegorically, if the author's intentions are to be perceived. Other signs that Jesus performed may well be possible in the kind of reality in which we live.[15] The point is that if Jesus did the miracles attributed to him it has to be understood that he did them as a human being, not as God. Jesus did some marvellous works of mercy, but those great works have little significance for humankind unless they signify a possibility for human fulfillment that is open to other people besides Jesus.

The attributing of Jesus' miracles to his unique divinity illustrates how his saving significance for people is reduced when his full humanity is displaced by divinity. Conversely, the gospel is increased when the power and grace of God that were present in him are promised to all who follow him into the way of God's Reigning. If that power and grace are realized in us we cannot be said to be divine. We are human and will always be human. That is the most realistic and appropriate way to describe us. The same is true for Jesus. The presence of God as Spirit in human beings, including Jesus, is a real divine quality, but it is not part of any human being's identity as such. "To deify the 'Servant-Messiah' ... is ... a misleading way of acknowledging the divine quality of the human character of Jesus" (Lampe 1977, p.138).

What about the "divine quality"? As the historical retrieval in Chapter IV clearly shows, interpersonal Spirit christology affirms a great deal about the presence of God in Jesus. All the characteristics of God's Reigning in human life are found in the life, death and resurrection of Jesus. There is no question in interpersonal Spirit christology of reducing the divine quality in Jesus. It is the divine presence in him that makes him have saving significance for us. If God were not encountered in and through Jesus we would not call him Messiah or care singularly about following him. He would not be a mediator of the Spirit or an occasion for engendering our faith in God. To deny the deity of Jesus is not to reduce the claims for God's presence in him. It is to clarify the difference between Jesus as a human being and God as Creating and Redeeming Spirit. Anything that can be said about the fullness of God's presence in a human being is said by interpersonal Spirit christology about Jesus.

---

[15]Cf. Dunn (1975): "Until we know more from research into telepathy and psychical phenomena the prudent scholar would do well to keep an open mind on many features of Jesus' 'charismatic' mighty works'" (p.74).

In fact, the possibilities of God's presence being fully in a human person are discovered and, hence, defined in Jesus. He is for us the standard by which God's presence in ourselves and other human beings is tested. As the chapter on recollection indicates, however, Jesus is not simply a phenomenon in the past to which we refer in order to check orthodoxy or orthopraxis. He continues as the mediator for encountering God in Spirit. "We have here both a pattern and a power, made available to us in one of our own kind yet coming to us from God (Pittenger 1970, p.144). More will be said about this later.

### 4. Functional or Ontological Presence of God.

The traditional terms used to describe God's presence in Jesus are functional and ontological. Intrapersonal Spirit christology insists, with the trinitarian tradition, on the deity of Jesus being ontological and not only functional. Some recent attempts at intrapersonal Spirit christology have recognized the functioning of God as Spirit in Jesus but still insist that the presence of the Spirit made Jesus ontologically divine in a way which the presence of God does not do for other human beings.[16] The logic is less than compelling. Rosato cites Schoonenberg with approval as follows:

> In Spirit christology as well [as *Logos* christology] the Spirit is connected with Jesus not only functionally but also ontologically, because function is the expression of being and being includes function. Nor can Jesus be divine only "adverbially" because "the human Jesus acting divinely" also is divine by the Spirit's presence pervading him (1981, p.177).

Pittenger addresses the same issue: "If this [filial obedience] is said to be only a moral union and condemned on that ground then one can only reply that in this respect the moral is the metaphysical" (1970, p.143).

If one has to say that the moral is the metaphysical or the functional is the ontological mainly in order to avoid departing from the established tradition of Jesus' ontological deity even though it is surely spurious logic which does not apply elsewhere except in Jesus' case, then perhaps it is time to call for a real change in the established tradition. Either we must say that God's functioning in Spirit makes the whole universe in which God functions divine and that God's grace in all human morality makes everyone metaphysically divine or else desist from making the claim in connection with Jesus. Better we say that God's functioning in Spirit makes no one divine since that is, in fact, the case.[17] Interpersonal Spirit christology can affirm all that the tradition has said about God functioning in Christ but cannot logically infer Jesus' deity from that functioning of God in him.[18] It is the functioning of God in Jesus that

---

[16]Kasper (1976, p.166) admits that "even in John's gospel the unity of action between Father and Son is not yet really conceived as metaphysical, but is understood as a unity of willing and knowing." However, he goes on to say "This functional Christology is itself a form of ontic christology."

[17]Cf. Ruether (1970) "To be human we must refuse to be God" (p.143). Ruether here is explaining Camus' thought. In Vahanian's thought she finds a corollary idea: "Only by not deifying and finalizing itself can the created image be a place of the disclosure of God" (p.178).

[18]At this point interpersonal Spirit christology disagrees with Arian christology which held that God raised Jesus to divine status because of his perfect obedience. "When therefore Arius describes Christ as 'God' *(Theos)* without the article, we have every right to read 'divine' *(Theios);* for he has in mind the scheme of a perfected creature who, after progress in virtue has been raised by the Creator to the status of a *huios,* understood to mean *Theos* (=*Theios*) (Gregg and Groh 1981, p.21).

has saving significance and promise for the future of the world. The ontological claims for Jesus' deity were founded on a basically unbiblical logic of salvation by substitutionary sacrifice or salvation by divinization. Jesus' message of salvation by repentance or return to the Reigning of God does not logically require the deity of the Messiah, the "final" prophet of God's salvation.

In fact, who can doubt that Jesus himself would have abhorred being made equal to God? Even the *Gospel of John* which begins with the claim that the Word "was in the beginning with God" and "was God" (Jn 1:1) reports that Jesus "cried out and said 'He who believes in me, believes not in me but in him who sent me'" (Jn 12:44). The same author has Jesus say explicitly "the Father is greater than I" (14:28). John's christology is recognized to be as "high" as any in the New Testament but even John does not make Jesus equal to God. It would be possible to show that the other New Testament authors do not make Jesus equal with God either. The Christian tradition of claiming no subordination of the Son to the Father is clearly not well founded in scripture. It is neither true to the scriptures nor true to humanity as we know it to maintain that Jesus was God in himself. Certainly "God was in Christ reconciling the world" but this was a functional identity of God with Jesus' person, not an ontological identity which requires the horrendously complicated trinitarian doctrine to avoid polytheism.

## 5. *Difference in Degree or Kind*

From the recognition of God's functional identity with Jesus it follows that Jesus is different from other human beings in degree rather than in kind, as the traditional Christian paradigm has claimed. More exactly, the point is that God's presence in Jesus is not different in kind from the way God is present whenever God graces human lives and historical situations.[19]

If the way of God's Reign that was realized in Jesus were not possible for other people then "the good news of the Kingdom" that Jesus preached would be untrue. The thought is unthinkable. Yet is it not possible that countless people have been relieved of the vocation of living the way of the cross because they were told that the Jesus who pioneered it was a different kind of being from them, and they deduced that his vocation was an entirely different kind from their own? The way of the cross, they might assume, is possible for a deity but undesirable extremism for ordinary people. Besides, their logic might continue, the obedience and life of the divine Jesus are a sufficient substitute for theirs,

---

[19]Cf. Robinson (1973, p.209-210). "If one had to choose, I should side with those who opt for a 'degree Christology' — however enormous the degree. For to speak of Jesus as different in kind from all other [human beings] is to threaten, if not to destroy, his total solidarity with all other [human beings] which we have regarded as unexpendable." Baillie (1948) advocated a kind of functional christology in which the divine element in Jesus was present by the same "paradox of grace" that functions in other human lives. He says: "If then Christ can be thus regarded as in some sense the prototype of the Christian life may we not find a feeble analogue of the incarnate life in the experience of those who are His 'many brethren', and particularly in the central paradox of their experience: 'Not I, but the grace of God'? ... Is it not the same type of paradox, taken at the absolute degree, that covers the whole ground of the life of Christ, of which we say that it was the life of a man and yet also, in a deeper and prior sense, the very life of God incarnate (p.129)?

and there is no real need for others besides him to live in the way of the cross. Is it not possible that the deifying of Jesus and its rationale of substitutionary satisfaction has encouraged the exploitation of "cheap grace"?

If Jesus is thought to be the same kind of creature as we are, his saying "if any man would come after me, let him deny himself and take up his cross and follow me" (Mk 8:34) cannot be discounted by finding in it a double standard, one for the divine Jesus and one for the rest of us. How could Jesus be the pioneer of our salvation if he were different in kind from us? Only if salvation is conceived in static, juridical terms rather than as the way of the Reigning of God could a different kind of saviour accomplish salvation for us.

Jesus, like any other human being, had his own unique vocation as well as sharing with many others in the vocation of God's covenant. There is a sense in which Jesus is different from all other people; he is the Servant-Messiah, the one chosen and anointed by God to do a particular work in God's economy of salvation. To those who have encountered the ultimate Reality of God in Jesus' life, death and resurrection the significance of his vocation as the Christ of God can hardly be overestimated. His way of salvation is a life-changing, world-changing event for those who hear his gospel and believe it. As the bringer of the gospel of God's Reigning, Jesus is singularly important and more will be said in due course about the "finality" and universality of this importance. This singularity of Jesus, however, is not deity; he was a human being, the same kind of creature that all human beings are.

The question of Jesus' difference from other human beings in degree or in kind is related to the interpretation one gives to the idea of incarnation, i.e. whether it is regarded as a metaphor applicable to any human being or whether it is regarded as a literal concept applicable only to Jesus. Interpersonal Spirit christology can affirm incarnation as a metaphor for the way of God's Reigning but not as a literal description of the origin of Jesus, considered to be a deity.[20] Incarnation understood as a metaphor signifies the belief that God is present in the world and in the lives of human beings. It affirms the immanence of God and suggests the freedom of God to take initiatives in the creation. The term is useful to convey the deep and close involvement of God as Spirit in human lives, but it has to be recognized that there are dangers in using the term.[21] Its long association with the idea of Jesus' deity has

---

[20] Wiles (in Hick 1977) speaks of "a looser sense of the phrase 'incarnational faith' by which it expresses the conviction that the physical world can be the carrier of spiritual value." He goes on to say that "a 'Christianity without incarnation' in the more precise sense of the word 'incarnation' would not be a non-incarnational faith in the much broader sense in which those words are so often used" (p.7).

[21] Tillich (1957) has a good discussion of the dangers inherent in the term "incarnation." "The assertion that 'God has become man' is not a paradoxical but a nonsensical statement" (p.94). Tillich points out that if one speaks instead of a divine being (i.e. the *Logos* or Son of God) becoming man one avoids speaking nonsensically but there are still two dangers involved: "first there is the polytheistic connotation of divine beings besides God, and, second, incarnation is interpreted in terms of a mythology in which divine beings are transmuted into natural objects or human beings. In this sense incarnation is far from being a characteristic of Christianity. It is, on the contrary, a characteristic of paganism in so far as, within it, no god has overcome the finite basis on which he stands.....The unqualified use of the term 'Incarnation' in Christianity creates pagan, or at least superstitious, connotations" (pp.94-95). Tillich finally concludes that it is "practically impossible to protect the concept from superstitious connotations" (p.95).

left the term with the lingering connotation of the displacement of fully human being. It also can contain the suggestion that God's presence, "incarnated" heteronomously subjects the human being to God's will and thereby compromises human freedom. The term incarnation can only be used to refer to the presence of God as Spirit if the way of incarnation is clearly understood as a gentle, inviting influence, not a dominating, irresistable force.

The incarnation of God in Jesus is the model for God's incarnation in all people. Jesus' relationship with God was a close "*Abba*" relationship in which God as Spirit provided energy, information, imagination, discernment, attitude-virtues, vocation and all the fruits of the Spirit but did not compromise Jesus' freedom or humanness. At this point the biblical understanding of God's presence as Spirit indicates what incarnation means.

On the symbolic basis of wind or breath, God as Spirit can be said to *inspire* people. On the symbolic basis of fire God as Spirit can be said to ignite, inflame or enlighten people with Godly power and meaning. On the symbolic basis of water God can be said to infuse or "pour into" people all the goodness of grace, and on the symbolic basis of earth or matter, God can be said to upbuild people into a spiritual dwelling place. None of these metaphorical ways of describing God's presence in human life suggest any displacement of humanness or reduction of human identity by reason of God's presence. If incarnation is used in conjunction with these metaphors it can be a legitimate and valuable term, but if incarnation is used *in contrast to* inspiration, enlightenment etc. as the term that signifies the absolute deity of Jesus which is of a different kind than the presence of God as Spirit in other people, it undermines the gospel of God's Reign which Jesus preached and lived. The idea of an exclusive incarnation in Jesus does not convey the good news that God as Spirit can come to be in any human being in the same way as God "reigned" in Jesus. The main message that Jesus preached and lived is thereby lost.

To deify Jesus by means of the concept of exclusive Incarnation was not simply a harmless exaggeration or innocuous mythicizing of him that took place in the early christological controversies. It was a marked departure from biblical thinking in favour of philosophical concepts that came from a Greek culture rather than Hebrew culture.[22] It changed the basic paradigm of the Christian faith and facilitated the entrenchment of a logic of salvation based on juridical presuppositions. It emphasized the masculinity of God and secured a place of privilege for the male hierarchy of the church. It insured an exclusive role for the church and its leaders as the dispensers of God's forgiveness, which could no longer be conceived to be possible outside the church.[23]

---

[22] See Frances Young in Hick (ed.) 1977, p.24. "The predominant framework of thought [in the Patristic period] was a sort of popularized Platonism with influences from Stoicism and Pythagoreanism. ... So naturally enough, it became the prevailing philosophical environment which dictated the presuppositions within which Christian theology was to develop."

[23] Cyprian appears to be the first to declare the notorious belief that "there is no salvation outside the Church" (*salus extra ecclesiam non est*). It was a corollary of Cyprian's claim that 'He cannot have God for his Father who has not the Church for his mother" (Kelly 1978, p.206).

Worst of all was that in claiming to reflect the New Testament exaltation of Jesus as the Christ, the "orthodox" theologians actually lost sight of the historical Jesus and developed a mythology about him that was inimical to his teachings and person as well as to the New Testament itself.[24] Herein lies the root of all the other negative results of the traditional claims of Incarnation (with a capital "I"). It failed to apply to itself the "test of the Spirits" recommended in the New Testament. The Christ who had come "in the flesh" (I Jn 4:2) was ignored in favour of a mythological figure who fortuitously, it seems, served the vested interests of those chiefly responsible for its design.[25] This might appear to be an excessively harsh judgment unless one remembers what has happened to the Jews and other "unbelievers," to women and "heretics" and the "heathen" as a direct result of the absolutizing of Christ and, by extension, the absolutizing of the church and its leadership in the orthodox paradigm of Christian faith.

Because of the danger of deifying Jesus by using the concept of Incarnation it is important to use other terms to signify the singularity of Jesus. Thüsing, a New Testament scholar, suggests that the idea of God's "sending" of Jesus, or mission of Jesus, is the central one used in the New Testament and that this idea might be a better foundation for christology than the idea of incarnation. He asks:

> Should a Christology from above (or a descendance Christology) perhaps not be traced back to the idea of mission rather than the idea of incarnation? ... This might make a Christology from below possible (Rahner and Thüsing 1980, p.110).

He concludes that "this concept [of mission] provides an adequate safeguard for the special saving significance of Jesus" (p.167).

If Thüsing is right, an interpersonal Spirit christology would be on firm biblical ground when it sees Jesus' God-given vocation as the basis for his exaltation and singularity. Jesus' uniqueness was not ontological but vocational. His being chosen and anointed and sent to be the Servant-Messiah was what makes him singularly important. His carrying out of this vocation faithfully in the power of God as Spirit is the reason why he is exalted by God and by us. His special saving significance lies in what he does and who he is in his vocation, not in any ontological difference between him and us. His being the Servant-Messiah was and is contingent upon God as Spirit working in him; it is the "working" that matters. As Goulder suggests, Jesus' *homopraxis* with God rather than *homoousia* "was the understanding — so far as our documents

---

[24]Cf.Sobrino (1978): "If a Christology disregards the historical Jesus, it turns into an abstract Christology that is historically alienating and open to manipulation"(p.353).

[25]Frances Young in Hick (ed) 1977 writes: "The course of doctrinal controversies [in the Patristic period] was shaped not merely by the inherent quality of the arguments used, but by personalities and politics. Suffice it to give a simple reminder of how Cyril's attack on Nestorius is related to the political struggle between the ecclesiastical power-centres of Alexandria and Constantinople. ... it is significant that Cyril compromised in the Formulary of Reunion once Nestorius was out of the way. ... rightly or wrongly, deep emotions and profound intolerance stirred up councils, churches and armies of monks into horrific attacks upon one another, and to the excommunication and exile of upright and sincere church leaders. It is a distressingly human story."

take us — of Jesus himself and St Peter" (in Hick 1977, p.62). This "christology of agency rather than of substance" is truer to the scriptures and avoids the pitfalls of deifying Jesus, as Incarnation christology does not do.

The vocational singularity of Jesus can be described in terms of Jesus' representative function. As the Servant-Messiah Jesus represents God, notably in revealing the way of the Reigning of God which is the way of salvation. This entails representing all the aspects of the presence of God as Spirit, including the love which forgives and suffers the results of all the negative freedom that inflicts misery and death in human history. Because Jesus accurately presents or represents the presence of God as Spirit we can experience and know in him that God suffers with those who suffer. We can know the law of God's love, the wisdom of God, the saving purposes of God, and the ultimate hope in God. Jesus' discerning of law, wisdom, prophecy and apocalyptic represent various aspects of God's Reality that have saving significance for the world. Jesus' representative work as Servant-Messiah reveals and thereby facilitates and effects God's reconciling the world to God's Reign. Of course Jesus is not the only one who does this; his vocation in the broad sense of living the covenant with God is shared with many others, including the members of the church, but his exclusive vocation as pioneer, archetype, ultimate criterion and supreme exemplar of God's Reigning as Spirit is what constitutes his singular saving significance. Because of his God-given vocation as Christ, he represents God with a degree of authenticity that no one else can have.[26]

## 6. *Theocentric or Christocentric*

The idea of God present functionally in Jesus in the same kind of way in which God is present to all people, but in a different "degree" allows interpersonal Spirit christology to be theocentric rather than excessively christocentric. If the New Testament is as thoroughly theocentric as contemporary biblical scholars are claiming that it is,[27] contemporary christology should be consonant with that theocentricity. This will require a change from the extremely christocentric orientation of the traditional Christian paradigm. The change should not mean stopping the close and frequent attention we give to Jesus as the human Christ.[28] Rather, it will mean changing the ways in which we think about

---

[26]Cf. Robinson (1973, p.193-194) summarizes the christology of the author of the *Gospel of John* as follows: "Christ is the very 'exegesis' of the Father, (1.18), and indeed himself *theos* (1.1,18), because *as a man* he is utterly transparent to *another* who is greater than himself (14.28) and indeed than all (10.29). ... It is the same conception of filial obedience in terms of which the Synoptists represent Jesus as having his call."

[27]Cf. Thüsing (Rahner and Thüsing 1980): "A theocentricity in an ascending line was not only expressed by the Jesus of history, but also by the risen Jesus. This is a fact that is often overlooked. It is, however, rooted in New Testament datum" (p.92)."Paul's soteriology is theocentric, because his Christology is" (p.95). "John's thoroughly theocentric Christology" (p.96). "In Hebrews too, *pistis* is applied above all to the earthly Jesus and this *pistis* is standing firm and continuing in relationship with God. This *pistis* of the earthly Jesus ... is also transposed ... to the level of the risen Jesus" (p.96). "[Jesus] also lives in orientation towards God by involving his own in his own theocentric orientation towards the Father. ..." (p.106). Cf. Beker (1980): "Paul is an apocalyptic theologian with a theocentric outlook" (P.362).

[28]Cf. Rahner (1968): "Anthropocentricity and theocentricity in theology are not contradictories but strictly one and the same thing seen from two different aspects, and each aspect is unintelligible without the other. That theology should be anthropocentric does not contradict it being most rigorously theocentric. ... [This] is contrary to the view that it is possible to speak theologically about God without at the same time saying something about man and vice versa (p.xvi-xvii).

Christ. It will mean more following of Christ in his theocentric orientation rather than treating Jesus as if he himself were God. A theocentric Christianity would strive to reflect the Reigning of God as Jesus did rather than emphasizing the praise of Christ as an end it itself. The glorifying of Jesus is, in fact, possible only by the imitation of his relationship with God. There is no doubt that the Jesus portrayed in the Gospels called for this imitation or following of him in serving God and the world. If Jesus taught his disciples "when you have done all that is commanded you, say ... 'we have only done what was our duty'" (Lk 7:10), it is very possible that he was reflecting the attitude he himself had about his servanthood.

Excessive glorifying of Jesus can mean, by default, a reduction in the praise of God and, at the same time, a reduction in the reconciling Reigning of God. When Jesus Christ becomes "our God" and inordinately the focus of our worship and thinking it builds barriers between ourselves and others who believe in God. A *theologia gloriae* of Christ and the church can become a destructive principality and power in history rather than a reconciling, healing influence. Jesus is reported by John to have said "I, when I am lifted up from the earth, will draw all [people] to myself" (Jn 12:32). His way of the cross, the way of self-giving obedience, love and trusting of God is what will draw the world together. A *theologia crucis* is fundamental to appropriate christology. The logic of Christ must not, by doxologies to Jesus, divert the emphasis on God's Reigning in Jesus' way of the cross. This is to miss the point of Jesus' being "lifted up from the earth." From what we know about Jesus it is possible to imagine him saying to the church "never mind all the extravagant praise about me; just get on with the work and worship of God. That is what I lived and died for. Imitation after all, is the finest form of flattery." In fact, John's Gospel has Jesus say "I do not seek my own glory" (8:50).

Imitation of the way of the cross can only be theocentric or else it is not imitation of Jesus at all.

## 7. *Exclusive Monotheism or Trinity*

"There does indeed come a point where Christology reaches a fork in the road: to choose the route of the Unitarians or that of the Trinitarians" (Schillebeeckx 1979, p.657).[29] This statement is basically accurate, but I believe the choice is more exactly stated in terms of exclusive monotheism and trinitarian monotheism. The term Unitarian may have, for some people, the connotations of unbiblical, sectarian, philosophical, even un-Christian which could never be applied to New Testament authors, for example, or to the Hebrew scriptures, whereas it is certainly not impossible to describe virtually all the biblical authors

---

[29]Lampe (1972) notes this choice for Spirit christology: "The threefold distinction may be retained, God in his transcendence (or the being of God) being distinguished from God 'reaching out towards' and addressing (or God's Word) and from God operating immanently and influencing, inspiring and possessing (or God's Spirit). Or, on the other hand, it may be thought sufficient to distinguish between God as transcendent Spirit and God as immanent Spirit". In his later work Lampe chose the latter option.

as believers in exclusive monotheism. To contrast trinitarian thinking with unitarian also suggests that tritheism is what trinitarian means, since it appears that the oneness in the unitarian concept is what is at issue.

While confessing that he sees "no solution at all" in it, Schillebeeckx admits that "it may be that a Unitarian Christology has not always been sufficiently understood ... , for ... everything said about the Trinity is constantly alternating between a 'modalism' more or less devoid of content and a 'tritheism' that says only too much, while the attempts to dodge this Scylla and Charybdis lapse into more or less rarified insubstantial, purely verbal distinctions" (1979, p.657). The proposal in this interpersonal Spirit christology is that exclusive monotheism is a solution to many of the problems of trinitarian thinking, including those referred to by Schillebeeckx with his commendable candour.

In recent years numerous theologians have reaffirmed the value of trinitarian thinking, even while they have questioned other aspects of traditional Christian beliefs. It is fair to say, however, that in most cases the reasons why trinitarian thinking is espoused are not because of the deity of Jesus but for other speculative, philosophical reasons. Originally, in the history of the development of the Christian doctrine of the Trinity the conclusion that Jesus was "of one substance" with the Father led to the recognition that the Holy Spirit too, was a fully divine person, making some explanation necessary of the threeness and oneness of God. This led theologians like Augustine to propose ingenious metaphors of the Trinity such as the unity of memory, understanding and will or the unity of lover, beloved and love. The trinitarian theologizing moved away from the explicit consideration of Jesus' humanity and divinity to such questions as the relations of the three divine Persons, *circumincession* or *perichoresis, communicatio idiomatum,* the difference between procession and generation and the question whether the Spirit proceeds from both the Father and the Son *(filioque)* or from the Father alone. In christology the process became extremely "transcendental" and Jesus of Nazareth, the human being, was largely superceded by the cosmic Second Person of the Holy Trinity.

In recent times the humanity of Jesus has become of central concern to most theologians, but this has not impinged very deeply or widely on their trinitarian thinking because they have accepted basically philosophical or speculative reasons for reaffirming the Trinity. Very few theologians have both affirmed the full humanity of Jesus and accepted the implications of it for their doctrines of God. Some philosophical reason is usually found to justify trinitarian belief, even if trinitarian belief was originally justified only by the confession of the full deity of Jesus of Nazareth.[30]

---

[30]Hodgson (1944) explicitly affirms the validity of using philosophical reasons for establishing the doctrine of the Trinity. In reviewing the debates among seventeenth and eighteenth century unitarians and trinitarians Hodgson admits that *"on the basis of argument which both sides held in common* [namely, appeal to the scriptures], *the unitarians had the better case"* (p.223). Hodgson argues that philosophical reflection on the total empirical results of the life of Jesus can legitimately and truly produce the doctrine of the Trinity, even if it is not explicitly found in the scriptures. "Christian theologians seek by rational reflection to grasp and expound the doctrine of God entailed by the empirical factor of this self-revelation. This means philosophical thinking, and philosophical thinking is the attempt to order empirical evidence in accordance with the canons of rational thought" (p.174). It may be doubted, however, how "empirical" the process is when Hodgson says that "the doctrine of the Trinity is the projection into eternity of the essential character of that earthly life [of Jesus], arrived at by thinking away the accidents incidental to the conditions of earthly existence" (p.9).

A few examples will suffice to illustrate the point. Tillich agreed that "the Christian doctrine of the Trinity is a corroboration of the Christological dogma [the assertion that Jesus is the Christ]" (1951, p.250), but insisted that the presuppositions of the Christian doctrines of Christ and Trinity are to be found in the idea of God as Spirit, conceived as the unity of power and meaning. "God is Spirit, and any trinitarian statement must be derived from this basic assertion" (1951, p.250). For Tillich, "the analysis of 'life' in Hegel's early writings" (1951, p.234) determined his idea of God as Spirit and confirmed in his mind that "the classical German philosophers ... were right (and so were most classical theologians) in using the dialectics of life in order to describe the eternal process of the divine ground of being" (1963, p.284). Tillich's explanation for the necessity of trinitarian thinking, which also included recognition of "the tension between the absolute and the concrete element in our ultimate concern" and "the threefold manifestation of God as creative power, as saving love, and as ecstatic transformation" (1963, p.283), was as convincing and profound as any to be found in modern theology, but the question "what does this have to do with Jesus of Nazareth?" remains largely unanswerable. Trinitarian thinking for Tillich was obviously not derived from his thinking about Jesus. The opposite is clearly and explicitly the case, and if Tillich was right in his historical claim most classical theologians were similar to him in this respect.

Tom Driver is another example who, while calling for a change in the basic christological paradigm, nonetheless insists on the necessity of trinitarian thinking "as a philosophical concept relevant to life in general, and as an ethical concept assisting Christians to decide what is good (1981, p.97). For Driver "trinitarian thought is a corrective to all forms of dualism" (p.97-8) and "is implicit in any relationship that is understood as personal" (p.98). It is certainly not the deity of Jesus, or anything about Jesus, for that matter, which impels Driver to affirm the Trinity; it is the philosophical conviction that "in every relation of one to one, a third element is present" (p.102). Again one might well agree with this philosophy of relationships but why, one has to ask, does it have to be projected onto God and why should Jesus of Nazareth be implicated in the advancement of this philosophical principle? Since Driver does not affirm the deity of Jesus one also has to ask of him "how can you talk of a Christian doctrine of Trinity without including Jesus in it as one of the three divine Persons?". What happens to the human Jesus in these philosophical explanations of "dialectical realism"? Either he is transmuted into a cosmic principle or he is quietly left out of the talk about the Trinity.[31]

---

[31]Cf. Robinson (1962, p.204): "There is nothing arbitrary in the Christian doctrine of the Trinity. ... It is the specialization within the Christian consciousness of that experience of God which is also found in the concentric circles of personality, history, Nature, beyond Christian life." Rosato (1983, p.267) prefers the triad Creator-Recreator-Transcreator or Fashioner-Refashioner-Transfashioner, explaining that "One root, like fashioner or creator, is repeated three times so as to indicate the unity not only in divine being itself but also in divine revelation while two different prefixes are added in order to explain the threeness within the Godhead which must be posited because of the three different roles the one God assumes in the drama of salvation." Hebblethwaite (in Goulder 1979, p.93) indicates another typical reasoning for the doctrine of the Trinity. "It resolves that impass in pure monotheism which results from conceiving of God on the analogy of an isolated individual." He notes that "Lampe claims that there is no need to project relationship into God ... but this makes creation necessary to God, if God is to enjoy the fullness of being as love."

Moltmann (1981) has written perhaps the most significant and influential book on the Trinity in recent years. He claims that his "social" doctrine of the Trinity is biblically based stemming from the suffering of God as seen notably in the event of Jesus' crucifixion and stemming also from the biblical narrative of the relatedness of Father, Son and Spirit. We will look at these claims in more detail presently and find that the biblical foundations for the doctrine of the Trinity are not, in fact strong.

In Moltmann's theology of Trinity there are speculative factors that are determinative despite his claims of biblical foundations. His most basic concern is that the idea of God should be "social" and thereby model loving relationships for the benefit of the organization and functioning of human society. Out of this concern he attacks traditional Western trinitarianism which he considers to be basically monotheistic and, therefore, "monarchian" (p.191) and "patriarchal" (p.165). "There will be a modern discovery of trinitarian thinking when there is at the same time a fundamental change in modern reason—a change from lordship to fellowship, from conquest to participation, from production to receptivity" (p.9).

These are undeniably noble goals, as are the elimination of patriarchalism and political domination of all kinds, but it is questionable whether hoping for these changes can justify making God into a model social community. It is pure speculation that a model social Trinity is needed in order to bring out these changes in human society. It is quite possible that the doctrine of God as Spirit might serve these purposes more effectively and with far better biblical foundation than such trinitarian thinking.

The "social" doctrine of Trinity has serious problems avoiding tritheism, as we shall see, and leaves substantially unanswered the question why the number of Persons in the divine society should be limited to only three, especially when the Bible could easily provide other candidates, such as the female Sophia. In trinitarian thinking which does not start from the deity of Jesus, as the Christian doctrine did in its historical development, the number three in the Godhead becomes inexplicable except on speculative or philosophical grounds.

If trinitarian thinking does take Jesus into account it has to affirm his pre-existence and this causes insurmountable problems for the affirmation of Jesus' full humanness. Knox (1967) stated the problem unequivocally:

> We can have the humanity without the pre-existence and we can have the pre-existence without the humanity. There is absolutely no way of having both (p.106).

Schoonenberg makes the same point: "Whoever assumes a pre-existent divine person in Jesus places this person outside his history and to the degree that one sacrifices the human personhood of Jesus to his divine person, Jesus' history is robbed of its actual source, the personal decisions of the man" (1971, p.117-118). Little wonder that contemporary trinitarian theologians do not as a rule base their trinitarian logic on the pre-existence of the person Jesus; it means sacrificing his humanness. The conviction about Jesus being fully human is simply too strong now to be denied. Whether the doctrine of the eternal Trinity is based on Jesus' pre-existence or not it necessarily implies Jesus' pre-existence. The alternative is to separate the cosmic Christ from the historical Jesus, in which case the Christ becomes an abstract mythical fabrication, one among countless other mythical creations in the history of religions, and Jesus becomes a temporary adoption of Christ rather than the real Christ himself.

Schoonenberg faces this truth and opts for a "becoming Trinity" (1971, p.85), acknowledging that "on a Trinity in God from eternity and by necessity we as creatures cannot make any statements, either in the affirmative or in the negative" (1971, p.86). Schoonenberg accepts the claim made by most trinitarian theologians that "in the 'salvific-economic Trinity' we know the 'immanent Trinity'" (p.82), but holds that what we know in the salvific economy of God does not justify saying "that God is 'already' threefold in his pre-existence" (p.83). This traditional conclusion, he says, is made "consciously or unconsciously via a concept of God's immutability that is open to criticism" (p.82-83). Hence, the only way in which God could be an immanent Trinity is through "becoming triune by a historical decision of himself" (p.86).

Schoonenberg, to my knowledge, does not explore the logic of the "becoming Trinity" to any great extent, leaving the idea mainly in footnotes (1971, p.83-86) and in one article in *Tijdschrift voor Theologie* 6 (1966). On the face of it the idea might make sense of "economic" trinitarianism but it does not commend itself as a serious claim for believing in the immanent Trinity. If God could change God's essential being from unity to triunity in order to be revealed in Jesus and the Spirit why, one wonders, might God not change again, perhaps into an immanent pentad or hexad in order to be revealed in the five or six major world religions in a pluralistic age. The speculations about God changing in essential being invite the ludicrous. It is time to wield Occam's razor when the immanent Trinity is based on the idea of God changing God's basic identity.

Nevertheless, Schoonenberg has to be commended for taking seriously both the humanness of Jesus and the recent exegesis of the New Testament statements about Jesus' pre-existence. The latter, as Schoonenberg honestly admits, cannot be understood in a temporal sense to mean the existence of the person of Jesus prior to his actual historical existence. The protological statements about Jesus in the New Testament are not, as we shall see momentarily, a legitimate basis for developing trinitarian theology. "The pre-existence theology — or rather, the pre-existence philosophy, for its inspiration is middle Platonism" (Schoonenberg 1971, p.55), was primarily "speculations of Origen" which influenced the theological framework of the Council of Nicaea. In developing trinitarian theology on the basis of the "pre-existence" or protological statements in the New Testament, Origen and those after him departed in fact from the scriptural meanings of those statements and imposed upon them "pre-existence philosophy" derived from middle Platonism. The church has been lumbered with a pre-existent Christ and pre-existent Trinity ever since. Recent exegetical studies have shown that these ideas are foreign to the New Testament.

We turn now to consider the question of the biblical evidence for trinitarian monotheism. We will be able to see, I believe, that the evidence supports exclusive monotheism rather than the doctrine of a pre-existent Trinity. In considering the evidence it will be necessary to rely on the judgments of established New Testament scholars rather than doing the exegesis of scriptural passages here. To do the actual exegesis would require more space than this book could provide.

Dunn's work (1980) has already been mentioned. He devoted an entire book of over 400 pages to examining issues related to the question "What does it mean to speak of 'the pre-existence of Christ' in the N.T.?" (p.6). We have already cited his main conclusion that "here [in Jn 1:14] we have an explicit statement of *incarnation,* the first, and indeed only such statement in the N.T." (p.241). However, Dunn's belief that the Prologue to John expressed the idea of a pre-existent *personal Logos*-Christ is contested by others. Caird (1968) is cited by Robinson (1973) as follows:

> The Jews had believed only in the pre-existence of a personification. Wisdom was a personification, either of a divine attribute or of a divine purpose but *never a person.* (Italics mine) ... Neither the Fourth Gospel nor Hebrews ever speaks of the eternal Word or Wisdom of God in terms which compel us to regard it as a person. If we are in the habit of crediting them with such a belief in a pre-existent person, and not just a pre-existent purpose, it is because we read them in the light of Paul's theology (Caird 1968, p.79).

Robinson comments on this statement saying, "I do not regard Paul as an exception. I believe he appears to be so only because we read him in the light of later theology" (1973, p.179n.). Dunn, of course, agrees with Robinson about Paul and all other New Testament authors except John. "With Matthew there seems to be no thought of pre-existence involved; and in the Pauline letters and ... Hebrews, also, the thought is primarily of Christ as the eschatological embodiment of the wisdom of God ..." (Dunn 1980, p.211). Dunn notes further that "Within Judaism including Hellenistic Judaism ... there is no evidence that such talk of God's (pre-existent) wisdom ever transgressed Jewish monotheism" (p.210). One has to doubt, therefore, Dunn's own conclusion that "it is only in v.14 (fourth stanza) [of John 1] that we go beyond anything pre-Christian" (p.242). If Caird and Robinson and Thüsing and others are right, John did not transgress Jewish monotheism either. None of the New Testament writers did.

The protological statements in the New Testament, that is, "statements about Jesus' pre-existence, incarnation and mediation of creation" (Rahner and Thüsing 1980, p.166), can be understood "on the basis of Judaeo-Hellenistic speculation about personified and pre-existent wisdom"(p.166).[32] They are a way of expressing and safeguarding the

---

[32] Dunn (1973) speaks unequivocally of the Pauline use of the idea of pre-existence: "The pre-existence of Jesus is an inaccurate description of the Pauline theology. In Paul the only really explicit references to pre-existence come where Paul identifies Jesus with pre-existent Wisdom (I Cor. viii. 6, Col.i.15ff.; cf. 1 Cor. i,24,30). Strictly speaking it is Wisdom alone which is pre-existent: Jesus was the man that Wisdom became (so also probably, Phil.ii.6f.; cf. John i.14)" (p.59).

unique saving significance of Jesus. However, in the synoptic tradition of Judaeo-Christian Palestine "these statements about Jesus' pre-existence were not needed to safeguard the unique aspect of Jesus. ... they can be replaced by the concept of Mission" (Rahner and Thüsing 1980, p.166). On the basis of either the Synoptics, then, or the rest of the New Testament, "to take a Christology of the [pre-existent] Son as a point of departure for a contemporary Christology of pre-existence would be a misunderstanding of the New Testament" (p.167).

Robinson was probably right when he suggested that speaking about the pre-existence of Jesus may be "so misleading as to be unusable today" (1973, p.144). It is helpful, nevertheless to realize, for example, that the authors of Col 1:15-17 or Hebrews 1:1-3 were not referring to the temporal pre-existence of Jesus but were speaking of Christ "in Wisdom terms in relation to the creation of the world" (Dunn 1980, p.207). According to this identification of Christ with Wisdom "it is the act and power of God which properly speaking is what pre-exists; Christ is not so much the pre-existent act and power of God as its eschatological embodiment" (Dunn 1980, p.209).

There was a sense in which the New Testament authors believed that Jesus, like the people saved by Jesus, existed from the beginning as ideas in the mind or plans of God from whence they were "sent" or "called" (Cf.Rom 8:29-30) to fulfil their destiny in the world. In a providential sense, then, Jesus as well as any servant of God was pre-existent in God's foreknowledge.[33] Indeed, "in a sense, therefore, all creation is pre-existent in that it subsists from eternity as an idea in the mind of the creator; but the concept ... is applied more particularly to chosen agents of God's eternal and unchanging purpose" (Lampe 1977, p.120). This concept of pre-existence, of course, does not imply trinitarian theology.

Besides using or misusing the protological statements in the New Testament as a basis for trinitarian thinking some theologians claim there are explicit statements about Jesus' deity that support or require the development of trinitarian doctrine. Kasper says "scripture ... itself ... designates Jesus Christ not only as Son of God, but as God" (1976, p.168), albeit "only in comparatively few and late passages." He cites the prologue of John, Thomas' confession "My Lord and my God" (Jn 20:28) and 1 Jn 5:20, "He is the true God and eternal life." This scanty evidence does not support his highly tendentious claim that "the biblical statements about Jesus as true God then are clear and unambiguous" (p.171). Kasper's fellow Catholic, New Testament scholar Thüsing, disagrees with his interpretation on all three texts. On John 1:1 Thüsing explains "'Logos' here is not the second mode of subsistence of the Trinity, but God's revealed word." On Thomas' confession he says that it attributes

---

[33]Cf. Kasper (1976, p.174): "Today therefore the immediate source of the New Testament pre-existence statements is again sought mainly in the field of the Old Testament Judaism. Here — as distinct from Gnosticism — we find an historical way of thinking. According to the ideas of Old Testament Judaism, people and events important for salvation history exist in an ideal or — especially according to apocalyptic ideas—real way even before the creation of the world in the plan or in the world of God." Cf. also Rahner and Thüsing 1980, p.172.

to Jesus "a unity with God in the sense of Jn 14:9ff., that is, that the one who sees him sees the Father, in other words, that Jesus is transparent to the Father as his revealer." And of 1 Jn 5:20 he says that it is "the only text in which Jesus may perhaps be called God" but his own belief is that "it is the Father who is meant in 1 Jn 5.20b" (1980, p.180). Thüsing's admission that the New Testament does not call Jesus God could be matched by that of many other biblical scholars. [34]

Moltmann has two distinctive arguments which he claims provide a biblical basis for his doctrine of the Trinity. The first has to do with the suffering of God seen pre-eminently in the cross of Jesus.

> Anyone who starts from the experience of suffering and who perceives the mystery of the world in God's own sorrow is compelled to talk about God in christological terms. And he inevitably thinks of God in trinitarian ones (1981, p.40).

It seems ironic that Moltmann should make such a claim while acknowledging that the monotheistic Jewish theologian, Heschel, was one of the first people to develop a theology of the divine pathos. Moltmann also cites early rabbinic theology and the kabbalistic doctrine of the *Shekinah* in support of his claim. They taught about God's sufferings and self-humiliation in the cause of Israel's salvation (p.27-28). Moltmann sees in these Jewish views of a suffering God the idea of self-differentiation in God which points towards the re-unity of God, thereby making a "trinitarian" movement within the living God.

Certainly the biblical idea of God is that of a living God who suffers and otherwise responds to human beings and other creatures. But surely it is straining the implications of the living God of the Hebrew scriptures to insist that God must be triune in order to be alive and capable of suffering with the world! And surely it is not only ironic but inaccurate to acknowledge the Jewish understanding of God's suffering with the Jewish people and at the same time claim that "we can only talk about God's suffering in trinitarian terms. In monotheism it is impossible" (p.25). This appears to be a case of "conversion by redefinition." Monotheism is redefined to exclude the Jews and trinitarianism is redefined to include them. What comes out quite clearly despite Moltmann's intentions is that it *is* possible for a monotheistic Jewish concept of God to talk about God's suffering.[35]

The second distinctive argument Moltmann gives for finding "the biblical beginnings of a doctrine of the Trinity" is that "the history of Christ is already related in trinitarian terms in the New Testament itself" (p.64). By this Moltmann is referring to the fact that "*the New Testament talks about God by proclaiming in narrative the relationships of the*

---

[34] For example, see Vincent Taylor, "Does the New Testament Call Jesus God?" *Expository Times*, 73: pp.116-118, 1963.

[35] Young (in Hick (ed.) 1977, p.36-37) asks the question explicitly "How might I find out that God shares my grief and suffering ... ?" She answers her own question: "Surely I am most likely to be convinced of this, not by a single, isolated and unique occurrence, but *by repeated experience* ... . *The Book of Daniel* speaks of the sufferings of persecuted Jews ... . Potentially if not actually what is expressed here is universal insight into the suffering of God's faithful, a suffering which tells of God's suffering. This insight is hinted at in many places in the biblical tradition, in the experiences of Jeremiah and the poetry of Isaiah 53. ... Jesus is not the only evidence for the suffering of God."

*Father, the Son and the Spirit, which are relationships of fellowship and are open to the world*" (Italics his). There is not, of course, any talk in the Bible about fellowship between the Father and the Spirit or between Jesus and the Spirit; and fellowship is a strange word to use to describe the relationship between Jesus and God "the Father," even if that relationship is an intimate one. Moltmann's use of the term fellowship is consistent with his claim that in the Kingdom, as Jesus proclaimed it, "there are no servants; there are only God's free children. In this kingdom what is required is not obedience and submission; it is love and free participation" (p.70). This point requires some major qualifications[36] in view of the fact that the term "obey" and "obedient" are used dozens of times in the New Testament, including in the early Philippian hymn that speaks of Christ becoming "obedient unto death" (2:8). The idea that the relationship of Jesus and his followers with God is a "fellowship" that does not entail obedience is scarcely true to the scriptures, but even if it were, it is difficult to see why this should require trinitarian theology for its adequate expression.

Moltmann mentions James 2:23 calling Abraham "the friend of God" (1981, p.220) and says he is "the first of God's friends." Apparently Abraham should have had a trinitarian theology, too, in order rightly to describe his relationship with God. Moltmann says at the outset of his book that he is "particularly concerned to bring Judaism and the testimonies of the biblical Jewish faith into the discussion with the biblical Christian faith" (p.XV), but it seems a strange way to seek "common ground" with the Jews by repeatedly declaring the inadequacies of their monotheistic faith. The fact is that Jewish exclusive monotheism was and is able to include the ideas of God's intimate relationship with people and God's suffering with people without becoming trinitarian, as Moltmann so strongly insists.

The biblical ideas of God's suffering and relating intimately with people do not require the doctrine of the Trinity for their "correct interpretation." The Reigning of God does not require a trinitarian interpretation simply because it is reign of love instead of irresistible force. Monotheism in the Bible or elsewhere cannot be simply equated with monarchism or hierarchical patriarchalism. As Frye points out,

> With the rise of empires ... we get a kind of monotheism.
> This is, however, an imperial monotheism, quite different from
> the revolutionary monotheism of the Bible. (1982, p.93).

Not all monotheism, as Moltmann contends, "requires abject servitude" (p.192) so that a doctrine of the Trinity must be developed "as a theological doctrine of freedom." A monotheism of God as loving Spirit can, as we have already seen, ensure human freedom without subjecting God's person to a philosophically inspired split into three.

---

[36]Boff (1978) claims that "as far as we can judge, the word 'obedience' (and its derivatives), while occurring eighty-seven times in the New Testament, was never used by Christ" (p.92). Boff admits there are some debatable verses in which Jesus is shown using the word (p.305, n.11). In any case, he qualifies his point: "We do not mean to say that Jesus made no harsh demands. Obedience for him is not a question of fulfilling orders, but a firm decision in favour of what God demands within a concrete situation." Free participation (Moltmann) is not quite the equivalent of "fellowship.".

There have been a variety of trinitarian doctrines in Christian history and a variety of non-trinitarian Christian schools of thought.[37] It is tempting to enter into discussion of the finer points of difference in all the variations, but space does not permit it. The distinctions between Lutheran, Reformed and Catholic positions on the *genus majestaticum* concept of *communicatio idiomatum* must be left to others to deal with. One has to keep firmly in mind Rahner's warning against "the danger of wild and empty conceptual acrobatics" (1970, p.48). Only the most general and widely accepted characteristics of the Eastern, Western and social doctrines of the Trinity can be mentioned. The point of this exercise is to see some of the major unresolved and, perhaps, unresolvable problems of trinitarian monotheism and to show by contrast that interpersonal Spirit christology as a form of exclusive monotheism is a worthy alternative.

The tendencies toward disjunction and unification that marked Antiochene and Alexandrian christologies respectively also characterize Eastern and Western doctrines of the Trinity respectively. "Eastern Theology has as its basis the three Persons of the Holy Trinity, whose unity it then proceeds to explain .... On the other hand, Western Theology has as its basis the unity of God and proceeds from this to understand the three Persons in the Holy Trinity" (M. Fouyas, cited by Alfs 1984, p.28). The three domes typically seen on Greek Orthodox churches, compared to the single spires on many Western churches graphically illustrate the different theologies.

There is a tritheistic tendency in the Eastern Trinity because the distinctness of the three Persons makes unity in the Godhead problematic. The Father is the source of the Son and Spirit and appears to have an hierarchical priority even though the three Persons are claimed to be co-equal. The separated derivation of the Spirit from the Father "can lead to making the Spirit independent of the Son" (Kasper 1976, p.258) and can allow the Spirit to have a more prominent role in religious life and thought than is usually the case in the Western church. However, the separateness of Spirit and Son can also lead to an imbalance in the Godhead of two transcendental divine Persons over the one historical Son and give rise to mystical tendencies in the liturgy and life of the church.[38] Jesus' gospel of God Reigning in the world can be muted or etherealized in apophatic religious experience. [39]

The tritheistic, hierarchical, ethereal tendencies in Eastern trinitarianism can all be seen as serious threats to the essential character of biblical religion which emphasizes the oneness of God and the saving work of God *in the world*. Interpersonal Spirit christology, by contrast, is clearly monotheistic and focuses on God's presence in the world. By seeing God in Christ as the definitive or classic instance of the work of God as Spirit in the world there can be no tendency to etherealize religion

---

[37] Alfs (1948) provides a useful analysis of different versions of Trinitarianism and Non-trinitarianism.

[38] Kasper (1976, p.258) observes that "the eastern view can lead to ... a mysticism ... which often enough is indifferent to the Church as an institution and to the world."

[39] Lossky (1976) expounds and defends at length "that apophaticism which constitutes the fundamental characteristic of the whole theological tradition of the Eastern Church" (p.26).

and thereby miss by default the main significance of Jesus' gospel.

Western trinitarian theology has not actually been much more monotheistic than the Eastern versions, although it is true that there has been perhaps a stronger affirmation of one substance in the Godhead. In the West there has been a strong christocentric tendency that has virtually created a Binity in the Godhead. The Spirit has often been seen as a function of the other two Persons and, hence, less important or less prominent than they are. Augustine's influential metaphor of Trinity as Lover, Beloved and Love casts the Spirit as the *nexus amoris*, the connecting love of the other two who are indisputably Persons. The full personhood and full deity of the Spirit was late in being affirmed, and there has been notorious difficulty in making any distinction between what the Risen Christ does and what the Spirit does. "The attempt to refer the analogical term 'spirit' to a 'Third Person', and to recognize a distinctive role or function of the Holy Spirit, has never been really convincing" (Lampe 1977, p.43). The lack of emphasis on the Spirit has tended to confine the vision of God's saving activity to Christendom and encouraged an imperialistic approach to people of other traditions. At the same time, the christocentric character of Western theology has tended to strengthen the claims of the church to be the only authentic saving agency, Christians being designated as "the people of God."[40]

Recently the conception of a "social" doctrine of the Trinity has gained ground in Western theology. Karl Barth, among others, advanced the idea that the loving relationships among the three Persons of the Trinity account for the possibility of God being loving in eternity before anything was created to be loved.[41] Moltmann insists that the community or family of loving Persons in the Godhead is an essential model for loving relationships among human beings and claims that this social doctrine of the Trinity is absolutely necessary to avoid a doctrine of God which spawns sexism and hierarchical domination among people.[42] The idea of a community of God utterly abandons the possibility of thinking consistently of God being one, although Barth and Moltmann would deny being polytheistic. Bishop R. P. C. Hanson describes Barth's idea of the Trinity as "one mode of being God loving himself as another mode of being God, and being united in love of himself as yet a third mode of being God" and comments that "this does not make sense and

---

[40]Kasper (1976, p.258) says: "The western systematic insistence on the *filioque* can lead to a one-sided Christocentrism. The Church is then viewed one-sidedly from the point of view of the Incarnation as *Christus prolongatus*, ... as Christ's continuing life. Its goal, then, is to take root in the world and permeate the world even to the point of attempting to dominate it." Driver (1981, p.106) observes: "The result [of the *filioque*], whether intended or not, was to subordinate Spirit to Christ reinforcing the linear conception of the First, Second, and Third Persons. This ordering subverted trinitarianism with a hierarchical principle that ... ruins it. ... The hierarchical principle that has long contaminated trinitarianism has many bad effects."

[41]Hebblethwaite (in Goulder (ed) 1979, p.93) makes the same argument.

[42]Eg. Moltmann (1981, p.198): "The Trinity corresponds to a community in which people are defined through their relations with one another and in their significance for one another, not in opposition to one another, in terms of power and possession." Again, "It is only when the doctrine of the Trinity vanquishes the monotheistic notion of the great universal monarch in heaven, and his divine patriarchs in the world, that earthly rulers, dictators and tyrants cease to find any justifying religious archetypes any more" (p.197).

is indeed the *reductio ad absurdum* of Augustine's doctrine [of *nexus amoris*]" (1973, p.132—133). The same criticism would apply to Moltmann's version of the Trinity which is even more tritheistic than Barth's and the *nexus amoris* even more emphasized. Moltmann accuses Barth's version of being "a late triumph for Sabellian modalism" (1981, p.139).

Rosato (1981) stresses another reason for having a social doctrine of the Trinity. His concern is twofold: first, that Christ should not be seen, as Barth does, to account for all the saving activity of God, thereby limiting the Spirit to the "noetic function" of revealing Christ to people, whereas the Spirit should be seen as "active in other religions and in secular movements so as to effect new salvific initiatives" (p.164); and second, that the "originative" concept of the Trinity in which all salvific work is "elected" or predestined in Christ from the beginning should be corrected by an "eschatological" model because the former "causes man's role, as a free agent distinct from Jesus Christ and as a partner in the Father's encounters with him through the Holy Spirit, to lose its own salvific importance" (p.168). In other words, both the Spirit and human beings lose their independent roles in God's saving work when the Trinity is conceived in the traditional Western christocentric way. A social doctrine of the Trinity would allow for more independent functioning of all three Persons including the Spirit "who throughout time is also active wherever the Father's gracious love creates a new salvific encounter between Himself and man *beyond the Word*" (p.165) (Italics mine). The idea that the Spirit, or the Father for that matter, is active "beyond the Word" departs from the axiom of Western trinitarian thinking that "the external operations of the Trinity are indivisible" (Gregory of Nazianzus, cited by Lampe 1977, p.225). It also suggests a separation in the "one substance" of the Godhead. It leaves the Godhead with no remaining principles of unity and establishes a tritheistic Trinity which could more exactly be called polytheistic.

Rosato's concern for a more adequate concept of the universal work of the Spirit is commendable, but he fails to see that such a view of the Spirit demolishes the unity of the Trinity. If Christ's work is not cosmic and universal in complete unity with the work of the Spirit and the Father then God's unity is fractured. The problem with affirming a universal, cosmic Christ, however, is the necessity of saying that good people from other religions, including Jews before the time of Christ were and are actually Christians in some way even if they do not know it. This contention is increasingly difficult to accept in our time because it appears to be egregiously ethnocentric.

Interpersonal Spirit christology provides a good solution for Rosato's concerns. In fact, Rosato's description of his own solution could almost be a description of interpersonal Spirit christology. "It would mean interpreting the definitiveness of Christ as a truly new eschatological breakthrough and universal opening of the Father to all [people] through the same power active in Christ but also beyond Him, that is, through the Spirit" (p.165). If the Spirit can be said to be in Christ and beyond him it is difficult to see why God should not be conceived as monotheistic

Spirit. Rosato in theory favours an intrapersonal relationship of Christ and Spirit within the oneness of God but he departs from the traditional accepted implications of one personhood in God by dividing the external operations.

In the social doctrine of the Trinity as Moltmann and Rosato propose it, the one personhood of God is conceived in accordance with Hegel's "communitarian" concept of person (Rosato 1983, p.267) according to which "the more one enters into community, the more one is oneself." Hegel's concept, however, unlike Moltmann's or Rosato's, does not presuppose more than one centre of consciousness in the person. Moltmann goes to great lengths to insist that the trinitarian persons must be thought of as distinct centres of consciousness in order to avoid the traditional monotheistic character of the Western doctrine of the Trinity. "To represent the trinitarian Persons in the one, identical divine subject leads ... to the reduction of the doctrine of the Trinity to monotheism" (1981 p.18), with the result that "the personal God in eternity corresponds to the bourgeois culture of personality" (p.139) and provides "a theological reason and religious justification for the modern bourgeois world's cultivation of the individual" (p.155). This reasoning can be flatly rejected as unreasonable. To say that oneness in God causes "the culture of narcissism" (p.5) is unconvincing, to say the least, and totally unnecessary in view of the oneness of God as known in the Bible. If it were convincing, the most reasonable solution would be to opt for straightforward polytheism. Moltmann virtually does this except that he wishes to have his cake and eat it too, by limiting the number of divine Persons to three and claiming, but not explaining adequately, their unity as three.

Moltmann insists that *perichoresis* (or *circumincession*) is what accounts for the unity of the Trinity, but he appears to contradict himself in the process. Karl Adam defines the traditional concept as follows: "Circumincession in the Trinity starts from the permanent possession of a common nature and reaches its climax in the active animation of this possession of a common nature by the three divine persons" (1957, p.265). Moltmann rejects the idea of "a homogeneous divine substance" (p.17) because it "leads ... to the disintegration of the doctrine of the Trinity in abstract monotheism"; but in his explanation of *perichoresis,* "eternal love" is what makes the three Persons one. Love is a dynamic function of "circulation" or "perfect and intense empathy" (p.175) among the three Persons. Why it should not also be conceived of as the "animation of this possession of a common nature" (à la Adam, above) is impossible to see. Moltmann "has his cake" in denying one substance in the Godhead and "eats it, too" by claiming that love is what makes the Godhead one rather than "three different individuals" (p.175).

In fact, Moltmann's three Persons of the Trinity are three different individuals, or at least the first two Persons are. At one point he admits that "the trinitarian Persons are unique. They cannot merely be defined by their relationship to their common nature" or else "the limitation to three would then be incomprehensible" (p.171). In other words, if the three were only different expressions of love (their common nature) there would be no reason why that love might not take many forms of expression as it, in fact, does in the biblical narratives about God who is known in many "personifications" such as the female Sophia, or even in angels, but who remains indisputably one throughout.

For Moltmann it is ultimately the Father-Son relationship as seen at the cross of Jesus that defines the uniqueness of the three Persons of the Trinity. "What happened on the cross of Christ between Christ and the God whom he called his Father" (1974, p.241) is "the material principle of the doctrine of the Trinity."

> The Father delivers up his Son on the cross in order to be the Father of those who are delivered up. The Son is delivered up to this death in order to become the Lord of both dead and living (1974, p.243).

The Spirit "proceeds from this event between Father and Son" and "justifies the godless, fills the forsaken with love and even brings the dead alive" (1974, p.244). The doctrine of the Trinity "is nothing other than a shorter version of the passion narrative of Christ" (1974, p.246). Unless the first two Persons, at least, are different individuals the whole transaction does not make any sense; and even if the transaction is conceivable between the two different Persons it is a highly contrived interpretation of the event of the cross, especially the idea that God had to deliver up the Son in order to be the Father of god-forsaken people. The idea hinges on believing that Jesus, the Son, was both "utterly godforsaken" by God and "most inwardly one" with God at the same time on the cross, and that God "suffers the death of his Fatherhood" while forsaking the Son because he loves what the Son represents. Such convolutions of interpretation have been typical of trinitarian thinking in all ages. In the social doctrine of the Trinity, in particular,

> The speculative possibilities are endless, once one breaks free of the traditional relationships of origin as the definitive mode of explanation for the connection of the persons with one another within the Trinity. The big question, of course, is whether one can and should take that step (Bracken 1979, p.79).

The really big question is why not stop all the acrobatic speculations about these divine Persons and go back to the biblical idea of one God who can be spoken about in many different metaphors — among which Spirit is possibly the metaphor with the widest ranging applications?[43] The traditional answer to this question was the claim of Jesus' deity, his being "of one substance" with God, but an interpersonal Spirit christology of God's mission in Jesus can account for the oneness or uniqueness of Christ without getting involved in the logic of Aristotelian metaphysics. Moreover it can do so with more integrity to the biblical witness.

---

[43] Berkhof (1976), while seeing some value in ancient trinitarian theology — notably in its affirmation of the divinity of the Holy Spirit, complains that "the confused and confusing phrase 'the three persons of the Trinity' is still used" and states flatly that "it is no use to maintain it any longer, especially since this formula from the very beginning has functioned not as a power of unity but as a source of confusion" (p.115).

There is some triadic language in the New Testament although "binitarian" language far excells it in frequency.[44] The Matthean "Great Commission" (28:19) and the Pauline benediction (II Cor 13:14) are perhaps the two best known and most repeated formulas that mention Father, Son and Holy Spirit. The centrality that these passages have had in the liturgical life of the church raises the question if interpersonal Spirit christology might be compatible with an "economic" view of the Trinity even if it is clearly incompatible with an "ontological" Trinity. The triadic formula is so seldom used in the New Testament, compared, for example, to the Pauline "Grace to you and peace from God the Father and our Lord Jesus Christ" which appears in virtually all his letters, that it should be seen in proper perspective as a possible variation but not an essential theological formula in the New Testament. The triadic formula includes more theological allusions and ideas than the "binitarian" language and for that reason is attractive as a summary of Christian remembrance of New Testament religious tradition. It does not, however, sum up all of the main theological currents in the New Testament. It makes no mention of Sophia, for example, which was a very central factor in New Testament thinking. The triadic formula has the distinct disadvantage in our times of offending feminist sensitivities and should be relinquished in liturgy, for that reason alone. Its continued use also perpetuates the trinitarian paradigm which is not an accurate reflection of biblical faith. It is also not appropriate to suggest a significant distinction between "Father" and "Spirit" as the triadic formula does, unless one keeps in mind that Spirit is in the same class of distinctions as Face, Hand, Arm, Glory, *Shekinah,* Wisdom and Word, all of which equally refer to God's self in both New Testament and the Hebrew scriptures.[45] If this biblical axiom could be kept firmly in mind it would be possible to have a lot of flexibility in the design of liturgical expressions.

The "economic" activity of God in the Bible is not actually triadic. The claim that it is triadic has clearly been influenced much by later trinitarian thinking. Therefore, it would be more biblical and better theology to give up trinitarian thinking altogether, economic as well as ontological.[46]

Interpersonal Spirit christology lets God be God and Jesus be human. The unity and exclusiveness of God is not jeopardized by positing other divine Persons. At the same time, God cannot be claimed to belong exclusively to Christians. The one God of the Universe is known in Christ but not *constituted* by Christ. This is extremely important for

---

[44]Thüsing (in Rahner and Thüsing 1980, p.182): "We are, however, bound to ask here how any doctrine of the Trinity can be maintained and safeguarded, when the New Testament appears to point less to a Trinity and more to a 'Binity'".

[45]Cf. Lampe (1977): Such terms as 'Word', 'Wisdom', and 'Spirit' are quasi-poetical words, expressive of a profoundly mysterious inner awareness of confrontation with transcendent personal grace, love, demand, judgement, forgiveness, and calling. In their original usuage they are not metaphysical terms, analytically descriptive of the structure of deity itself; nor do they denote hypostatically existent mediators between God and the world. ... They indicate one and the same basic reality, the sense of being approached by God (p.37).

[46]Cf. Brunner (1934): "The doctrine of the Trinity ... is a defensive doctrine, which would not have been necessary at all if the two fundamental statements of the Christian creed had been allowed to stand: God alone can save, and Christ alone is the divine salvation" (p.276).

solidarity of human beings from different religious traditions. The one God has all people as children or friends; no single religious tradition can call itself the people of God, implying that others are "lesser breeds" and not people of God. God's initial and basic covenant is with the whole creation and all its peoples and creatures; other particular covenants are instrumental means of serving this most basic covenant. God in Christ is offered to the whole world, but he came "not to condemn the world, but that the world might be saved through him" (Jn 3:17). He is made to condemn the world when he instead of God is made the exclusive saviour of the world. Whoever does not know Jesus is condemned to be excluded from salvation. This is not the case when the Spirit who was in Christ is also known to be at work throughout the whole creation.

The Spirit who related to Jesus of Nazareth is also the living God, moving as mysteriously as wind or fire, pouring like water on a thirsty land, building community with "living stones."[47] God is named as a noun but "We might come closer to what is meant in the Bible by the word 'God' if we understood it as a verb ... implying a process accomplishing itself" (Frye 1982, p.17). To designate God the Holy Spirit as a noun in the category of things and objects, (let alone calling God three independent entities), is, as Frye observes, what Whitehead might have called "a fallacy of misplaced concreteness" (p.17). To think of God appropriately as dynamic and holy (i.e. mysterious) "would be a reversion to the metaphorical language of primitive communities" (Frye 1982, p.17), such as the community that produced the Hebrew scriptures. It would be to think of God as "I will be what I will be" (Ex 3:14), the Holy One who is like the fascinating and awesome realities of wind, breath, fire, light, water and rock.[48] To think metaphorically of God in this way "would also be oddly contemporary with post-Einsteinian physics where atoms and electrons are no longer thought of as things but rather as traces of processes" (Frye 1982, p.17-18).

God does not have to be three Persons in order to suffer with those who suffer and rejoice with those who rejoice. Such scholastic rationalism does not create or sustain faith in the midst of suffering. Jesus can convince us of God's suffering love with a story of a forgiving Father or with an act of mercy for those who are suffering. So could Hosea. God need not die himself on a cross in order to know what human suffering is like.[49] That logic is plainly faulty, despite its sentimental appeal. God, who as Spirit is closer than hands and feet and nearer than breathing, has been suffering with the creation since the first moment of creaturely defection and creaturely suffering. If God does not show this merciful Presence to the suffering ones no amount of rational argument will

---

[47] Cf. Sobrino (1978): "Jesus' view of God, then, is taken from the Old Testament. God does not simply 'exist'. God exists insofar as he 'acts', insofar as he 'reigns' in the world" (p.357).

[48] Cf. Ramsey (1973): "Spirit is a noun whose logical tradition is more reliably a verb: being active, God-active. It tells of a becoming, not a being; it is a vector whose logical character is often misunderstood as a scalar" (p.14).

[49] Hebblethwaite (in Goulder (ed) 1979, p.94) states the traditional logic explicitly: "Only if we can say that God has himself on the cross, 'borne our sorrows' can we find him universally present 'in' the sufferings of others."

convince them that God loves them and is with them.

The God of interpersonal Spirit christology is the God of Jesus' "*Abba*" experience, the God who can be present in the ethos of groups as well as the personalities of individuals. This God does not cause or justify the culture of narcissism but creates, by grace, such attitude-virtues as generosity, trust, prophetic and pastoral concern, friendship and contemplation. Nor is this God an oppressive monarchial destroyer of freedom, for "where the Spirit of the Lord is, there is freedom" (II Cor 3:17).

## 8. *Historical Christ or Cosmic Christ.*

The question that exclusive monotheism raises for Christians is "what are you going to do with the risen Christ?" In trinitarian theology the risen Jesus becomes a cosmic divine figure to whom Christians relate in all the same ways in which they relate to God. They pray to Jesus, have faith in Jesus, hope in Jesus, worship and praise Jesus. "It is conviction of Christ as a living presence, both spiritually and sacramentally, that differentiates specifically Christian awareness of God from all other" (Hebblethwaite in Goulder 1978, p.95).[50] So say the trinitarians. They have difficulty, however, saying what the actual difference is between praying to Jesus and praying to God. Some are uncomfortable about praying to "Jesus" who was an historical character but pray to "Christ" whom they have accepted as a cosmic deity larger in some way than the historical Jesus.

In interpersonal Spirit christology there is only one divine Person in the mythological and real universe. Jesus is not God; Jesus is the Christ; the Christ is not God; the Christ is Jesus. In the biblical traditions of both the Hebrew scriptures and the New Testament the Christ was not God. Christ became God in the development of the Christian tradition after Christianity left its origins in Hebrew religion and appropriated the metaphysics and cosmology of Greek culture. That development away from the religion of Jesus and the Bible need not be irreversible. Modern scholarship is capable of recovering biblical thinking and can discern the accumulations to Christian tradition from the Greek philosophical and religious milieu. It is possible to return to the idea of an historical Christ and to reform the idea of a divine cosmic Christ.

It is increasingly difficult in our times not to think of Jesus as an historical human being. He should and must be so understood or he will become incredible to the majority of human beings. For many contemporary people there is no choice but to think in historical categories about Jesus. To do otherwise is to fly in the face of the knowledge we have about him and about the scriptures.

---

[50]Contrast Lampe (1979): "It is, in fact, impossible to distinguish prayer to Christ from prayer to God. ... It seems clear that Christian devotion does not require the concept of a continuing personal presence of a risen and ascended Jesus.

The same is true of the eucharist. ... Very diverse liturgical and theological traditions have also agreed that this eucharistic presence of Christ is effected or mediated by the Holy Spirit. ...

The eucharist, then, is a sacrament of the life 'in Christ' which is life in Christ's Spirit, life motivated and inspired by God the Spirit who was in Jesus (p.116-167).

For reasons that no doubt have to do with the politics of religious truth, modern theology has been slow to admit openly that when your categories of religious thinking become historical rather then metaphysical you must cease to regard the exalted Christ as a metaphysical object and must instead see him as a symbol of human destiny and as an ideal object of aspiration. It has been even slower to see that the original dynamic of the Gospel required this latter interpretation (Cupitt 1982, p.111).

It is and has been Christian liturgies that, by addressing prayers and confessions *to* Jesus and not only *through* Jesus, make him equivalent to God in religious practice, from whence the theory follows. "[Prayer addressed to Christ] became so regular and deeply rooted a practice that it exerted a strong influence on the development of Christology" (Lampe 1977, p.165). The New Testament, however, and even such third century theologians as Origen did not characteristically pray to Jesus. Origin in fact, thought it was "sin" to pray to Jesus rather than through him (See Lampe, 1977, p.165). Thüsing, who believes in prayer to Jesus, carefully looks at the New Testament evidence and concludes that "the only necessary element here is certainly faith in God through Jesus and praying to God through Jesus at least from the point of view of the New Testament and in the light of New Testament thinking" (Rahner and Thüsing 1980, p.118). Thüsing goes on to say that the love for Jesus, which people who knew him had, "had to be expressed in an address" (p.119). This may still be the case but it need not lead to the claim that Jesus is God.

The New Testament certainly does affirm the living Christ who is with God and also with his followers in some way. Jesus' function or vocation as the Christ of God did not cease when he died. In fact it was through his death and after his death that the messianic secret became an open affirmation by his followers.

There is evidence that the earliest Christian communities had a "*Maranatha*" christology rather than "resurrection" christology and looked to Jesus as "one who is to come rather than one who is above" (Cupitt 1982, p.109). But the church soon came to understand the vital influence of Jesus on their new life in the Spirit in terms of Jesus being "risen" and alive again so that St Paul could say "it is no longer I who live, but Christ who lives in me" (Gal 2:20). This is usually interpreted as the cosmic Christ present in St Paul, but in the very next phrase Paul explains that "the life I now live in the flesh I live by faith in the Son of God, who loved me and gave himself for me." In other words, Christ is primarily, for Paul, an historical Christ rather than cosmic Christ.

Jesus as the historical Christ continues to live in God's eternity, if human beings are raised to life in eternity. This is the Christian hope and it is not necessary for interpersonal Spirit christology to question it. It is only necessary to remember that life after death is a matter of hope, not knowledge, and "hope that is seen is not hope" (Rom 8:24).

The risen and ascended Jesus is no longer himself an active agent in human history except in as much as God as Spirit continues to encounter people in and through their remembrance of Jesus. It was God as Spirit who was in Jesus of Nazareth during his lifetime and realized in him the Reigning of God.[51] Jesus cooperated with God in loving obedience but the revelatory and saving power and meaning of Jesus were his by the grace of God. God continues to work in history through the historical Christ but since Jesus' death the work of God is through the remembrance of Jesus which does not involve Jesus' own agency or his cooperation and obedience. We may say, as the early Church did, that Jesus is "standing at the right hand of God" (Acts 7:56), but this does not imply Jesus continuing to act in history. The action of God in the world is God present as Spirit working in all the ways God works and has worked since the beginning of creation plus working through the living memory of Jesus to create a body of followers of Jesus who love and serve God and the world in the name of Jesus.

Jesus is not the only historical person whose vocation continues after death. God uses many people after their deaths through the remembrance of them to continue the vocations that God as Spirit realized in them while they were alive. The church has acknowledged this in the remembrance of the saints, especially the great saints such as Mary and Joseph and the original disciples. In St. Joseph's Oratory in Montreal, for example, Joseph appears to continue his vocation as protector of families. An endless succession of devout parents pray to God in the name of Joseph to give them or their families the grace sufficient for their needs. Joseph continues to be used by God as Spirit to grace human history even though Joseph is no longer an active agent himself in the world and even though Joseph is certainly not divine or part of the Godhead.

The vocation of the historical Christ was unique in God's economy of salvation. Perhaps in God's view the vocations of other human beings are also unique in their own ways. The Christ might be in the same class as the prophets in some respects but the difference in his vocation is very significant. The vocation of the historical Christ was unique and it continues to be unique as it continues to be operative through the working of God as Spirit. He continues to be the pioneer and perfecter of the way of God's Reigning, the way of the Spirit, the way of the cross, for all who encounter God in remembrance of his life, death and resurrection. He continues to be the one by whom the spirits of all the powers in creation are tested. He continues to be the way and the truth and the life for all who come to know him and care passionately about him.

## 9. Provisionality or Finality.

The uniqueness of Jesus' vocation raises the question of finality. Just how unique was Jesus as the Christ? Does his uniqueness imply

---

[51]Cf. Lampe (1977): "By the 'Christ-Spirit' is meant the indwelling presence of God as Spirit in the freely responding spirit of man as this is concretely exhibited in Christ and reproduced in some measure in Christ's followers" (p.114).

exclusiveness and finality which, in turn, imply that all other religious traditions are inauthentic and should be replaced as soon as possible with Christianity? The traditional christocentric-trinitarian paradigm has certainly claimed such finality and exclusiveness for Christ and applied the implications as vigorously as possible. Kasper states the logic unequivocally: "Only through the historical solidarity of God in the God-man, Jesus Christ, can solidarity be established among men" (1976, p.225).

The claims of finality, absoluteness and exclusivity have not, however, made for solidarity among human beings. "That this final Christ is inevitably totalitarian is shown by the story of the Church's anti-Semitism, with its fluctuations determined by the dogmatic and political security of the Church at any given time" (Soelle 1967, p.109). In an earlier chapter the concurring views of a number of other theologians were cited. The claims for Christ's finality and absoluteness have been a destructive force in history. They have been transferred from Christ to Christians who have wielded the authority of Christ literally as swords to destroy any who refuse to acknowledge their claims of Jesus' deity. Such absolutism is totally inimical to the Reigning of God, to life in the Spirit of Jesus who gave his own life rather than take the lives of others.

Some would say that the very idea of a Christ entails claims of finality and exclusiveness. Some would insist that the so-called "messianic secret" and other New Testament evidence shows that Jesus did not accept the designation of Christ for himself.[52] There were clearly some commonly accepted ideas about the Messiah that Jesus did not accept. However, there is evidence that he did not eschew the title altogether but gave it his own interpretation that the disciples finally understood after his death in his resurrection.[53] Jesus' interpretation of Messiah was crucially affected by his linking it with the Suffering Servant concept and the idea of the eschatological prophet. The former concept makes the very centre of the meaning of Messiah un-imperialist and constitutes the messianic vocation as one of non-violent self-sacrifice in the prophetic service of God. To create this messianic idea and embody it in his own person was a unique vocation that Jesus was called to do and in fact did.

For Christians, the model that Jesus created of the Reigning of God is the definitive one, the "classic instance," the ultimate criterion for their own living. To call it final or exclusive, however, is to miss the main point of it, namely, that it was a pioneering vocation intended for others to follow in the same Spirit of self-sacrificing love. It is not

---

[52]Trudinger (1983) claims that "a very large number of highly competent scholars hold the considered opinion that Jesus not only never really claimed outrightly to be the Christ, but that he went out of his way to reject any such claims about him by others." Pannenberg (1968) is an example: "Today it must be taken as all but certain that the pre-Easter Jesus neither designated himself as Messiah (or Son of God) nor accepted such a confession to him from others" (p.327).

[53]Schillebeeckx (1979) argues that there was an alternative in Jewish tradition to the concept of a 'Davidic' militaristic messiah, namely, the prophetic-sapiential concept of messiah. "The meek and gentle messiah is not a Christian 'topsy-turvy' version of the Jewish idea of the messiah but a reaching out under the pressure of the reality that was Jesus, for a different equally Jewish, messianic conception" (p.506). Dodd (1965) as we saw earlier, credits Jesus with the ingenious reinterpretation of the concept of messiah which links it with the Suffering Servant and Son of Man to create a new conception.

"final" or "exclusive" because the Reigning of God as Spirit goes on all over the universe and will not be "finally" realized until all sin and sorrow are removed from the world.[54]

One of the main elements in Jesus' gospel of the Reigning of God was what we termed prophetic apocalyptic or what some others have called "permanent" or "comic eschatology." Jesus explicitly denied the finality of his own existence and pointed to the future consummation of God's Reigning in a time of which "no one knows the day or the hour." There was an element of unfinishedness and open futurity in the messianic model that Jesus embodied. The idea of finality was renounced by Jesus' acknowledging the freedom of God and disclaiming his own knowledge of the future. If one reflects on the idea of God that Jesus had it is highly incongruous to suggest that Jesus could pose or be posited as the exclusive revelation of God or the final manifestation of God's Reigning.

One of the most important theological aspects of interpersonal Spirit christology is that it does not restrict the work of God to Christ but provides an understanding of Jesus as the Christ that leaves room for God's universal working in Spirit both before and after the time of Jesus. "A pneumatically conceived eschatology makes it possible to conceive ecclesial and secular history as conducive to the cosmological fulfillment of the divine promise which derives its meaning not from the past but from the future" (Rosato 1981, p.167). The promise of the Reigning of God that Jesus proclaimed was a promise of the future work of God as Spirit. The Kingdom of the Spirit was "coming" as well as already present.[55] This means that the "finality" of the messianic vocation and gospel remains in the future and should not be limited to the past. "The Church's hope for salvation — and also the many secular drives for a transformed cosmos — must not be christically restricted, but pneumatically freed" (Rosato 1981, p.172). This, in order to be true to Jesus himself and his gospel of the Reigning of God.

If the finality of the messianically revealed Reigning of God is in the future then Jesus the Christ with his unique vocation has a provisional rather than final or exclusive status in the economy of God's saving work. His uniqueness is provisional in that it provides a model for a process that will only be completed in the future, a process that has to be engaged in by others if it is to have any saving significance beyond the life of Jesus' himself.[56]

---

[54]Cf. Pannenberg (1985): "What is final and definitive is thus present in the relativity and flow of history, not indeed in the mode of finality but in the form of anticipation. ... To speak of the experience as one of anticipation is not to detract in any way from the presence of the eternal. Quite the contrary: the understanding that the experience is one of anticipation alone makes it possible to preserve the conviction that it is a true experience despite the changing interpretations of it as our historical experience expands. The viewpoint of anticipation enables us to understand that later interpretations are simply looking at the same totality of meaning and significance in different ways" (p.516). Again: "To this presence of the true and definitive amid the processes of history ... I give the name 'spirit'" (p.519).

[55]Cf. Perrin (1976): "That the Kingdom of God is a future expectation in the teaching of Jesus is not a matter of dispute in the current discussion. ... this emphasis was a part of the teaching of Jesus; there is still more than sufficient evidence to show this" (p.159-160).

[56]Cf. Soelle (1967): "If Christ provisionally represents us before God, this means that the company of believers must also take responsibility for someone before God. For the Church, this someone can only be the world, which the Church represents before God" (p.112).

Christians believe that Jesus was the true Christ of God, the authentic revelation of the way of God's salvation. We are not looking for another revelation or saving act of God to supercede or displace Christ. We anticipate that the final consummation of God's Reigning will be consistent with the gospel and promises that we have come to know in Jesus. Every human being, in fact, has to act, and live on the assumption that the meaning and values that they espouse are true.[57] Christians are no different from anyone else in this regard. They should be different, however, in acknowledging the provisionality of their criterion of meaning and values, the proleptic character of the Messiah.[58] Christians are ones who can say, with integrity to their Messiah, that the future belongs to God and that the final coming of the Reigning of God has not been absolutely determined yet.

> It would be very serious if Jesus ceased to be the way to God, as he was in his earthly life, and simply became the goal. The fact is that even after the resurrection Jesus is seen in relationship to the Father, not in terms of himself alone (Sobrino 1978, p.271).

Jesus is misrepresented when he is turned into God Incarnate. "Jesus does not think of himself as the 'last word of God' but points beyond himself to 'One who is to come'" (Ruether 1983, p.121).

Our christological statements should honour Jesus' vision of God who is coming in the future. When we affirm the saving significance of Jesus and commit ourselves to be his followers, when we reflect on his vocation as pioneer of the way of the cross and celebrate that vocation as unique to the best of our knowledge, when we give Jesus the title of Christ we should do so with the proviso that the truth will be known absolutely only in the end when God "will be what [God] will be."

> All such statements [christological conclusions] anticipate something that will be shown to be real before the eyes of all only in the eschatological future, even though it has already happened in Jesus. This proleptic structure constitutes the inadequateness, the provisionalness of all Christological statements ( Pannenberg 1968, p.397).

The provisionality of Christ does not exclude the possibility of making a decisive commitment of one's life to following Jesus. "Religious commitment can indeed be combined with critical reflection" (Barbour

---

[57] Newbigin (1969) deals with the issue of Christ's finality as sensitively and unimperialistically as anyone could do. His definition of finality is close to the definition I have given of Christ. "To claim finality for Christ is to claim that this is the true clue to history, the standpoint from which one truly interprets history" (p.86). However, he does not stress the provisionality of our judgment of Christ's significance and continues to use strong language about the "summons to men to forsake other claims to ultimate loyalty and to be converted" (p.87) This hardly seems compatible with the reality of a pluralistic world in which God as Spirit is working in many agencies and people besides Christians and the church. A proleptically recognized Christ is appropriately "lifted up" in word and deed by the church in the hope that God will reveal God's self through Christ to all who have ears to hear and eyes to see. This is somewhat different, at least in ethos, from a "summons ... to forsake other claims ... and to be converted.".

[58] Ruether (1981): "There are two steps in this critique of christology which are necessary. First, Christians must formulate the faith in Jesus as the Christ in terms which are proleptic and anticipatory rather than final and fulfilled. ... Secondly, ... we must accept its relativity to a particular people" (p.42-43).

1974, p.136). The claims for Jesus' absolute deity are a pre-critical way of expressing personal commitment to him. It is no longer possible to avoid the critical questions about Jesus' humanness and about his comparability to other great religious leaders in human history. One can no longer "pull rank", so to speak, and claim deity for Jesus while denying it to Gautama Buddha, for example. This does not mean, however that one cannot find grounds for following Jesus rather than Gautama and for hoping that Christ's way of salvation will eventually prevail in the whole earth. The model or paradigm of God's reigning in peace and justice that we find in Jesus can cause us to "return" and believe while not condemning all other models and those who believe in them. "In place of the absolutism of exclusive claims of finality, an ecumenical spirit would acknowledge a plurality of significant religious models without lapsing into a complete relativism" (Barbour 1974, p.8). Jesus can provisionally and proleptically be called the Christ of God without destroying Christian commitment on the one hand or denying authenticity absolutely to all others on the other hand. This can only be credible if Jesus is seen to be an historic fully human Christ and not an ontological Incarnation of the Second Person of the Trinity.

*10. Titles.*

The names given to Jesus imply the "logic of Christ" of those using them. They are usually metaphorical, which is to say that they invite the hearers to discern certain connotations that are to be transferred from the original symbol or image and applied to Jesus in order to indicate his identity or function. Whether metaphorical titles are appropriate or not depends on whether their particular connotations are logically compatible with the paradigmatic understanding of Jesus. For example, in an interpersonal Spirit christology it would not be appropriate to call Jesus "God the Son" as it would be in intrapersonal christology. Son of God might be appropriate if it meant one sent to do God's work and if it did not have the connotation of exclusive ontological relatedness. Child of God is a better title because it is non-sexist and the scriptures apply it to others besides Jesus to indicate their relatedness to God.

Some titles consistent with interpersonal Spirit christology have been used in the theological reflections up to this point. These include: Christ, in an historical sense, Pioneer and Perfecter of our faith, Servant of God, Agent of God, Representative, Eschatological Prophet, Teacher of gospel, law, wisdom and apocalyptic and Mediator of the way of salvation. I agree with Sobrino (1978) that "we must rehabilitate a neglected New Testament category: The designation of Jesus as the 'firstborn', the elder brother, the first of the believers" (p.106). Saviour is appropriate, providing it is understood as mediator of God's saving work because in the biblical understanding it is only God who saves. The same applies to Redeemer. Lord is problematic because of its sexist and imperious connotations and because the title has been used of God.

The earliest Palestinian Aramaic-speaking Christians used Maran(a) for Lord which was explicitly different from the word used for God.

It was the Greek-speaking Christians who, in using Kyrios, adopted a title that was used for God as well as emperors.[59]

Son of Man and Son of David have obscure cultural connotations that are not readily accessible to people today. So do High Priest and Lamb of God. Some of the vivid images that Jesus was reported to have used in his teachings are more readily understandable: vine, door, shepherd, bread, light, way, truth, life, sower, friend. There is no limit to the number of appropriate metaphors that could be used, providing the main connotations elucidate some aspect of Jesus' role as understood theologically.[60] Recently the title "The Human One" has been used to translate Son of Man. Whether or not it conveys all the obscure connotations of the biblical term, it is valuable in the present time to signify Jesus' real humanness.

The use of titles for Jesus is especially relevant in liturgical practice and in hymns where poetic imagination can endlessly create new metaphors. Liturgical titles and poetic metaphors are part of the extension of christology which is beyond the scope of this book. Here it is important only to point to the fact that interpersonal Spirit christology should have a decisive effect on the kinds of titles and metaphors that are used in connection with Jesus.

---

[59]Cf. Fuller (1969): "The effects of this adoption [by Hellenistic Jewish Christians] of the *kyrios* title for the exalted Jesus are far-reaching. ... Tentative beginnings are made in transferring to Jesus LXX passages referring to YHWH-kyrios, a procedure which would have been impossible in Aramaic speaking Christianity. At this stage all that is involved is a transference of *functions* from God to the exalted Jesus. Or rather, it is precisely through the exalted Jesus that God carries out these *functions*. ... Later ... in the gentile mission ... the transference of the divine name to Jesus is stated quite consciously (Phil.2:10f.) and with ontic implications (p.186).

[60]Cf. Sobrino (1978): "The utilization of those [biblical] titles was simply a way to help people understand the import and relevance of Jesus' person within the context of a specific culture and theology. There is no reason why such titles need be the exclusive prerogative of one particular culture, even that of the New Testament writers. Thus today Jesus could quite rightly be called 'The liberator', so long as we remember that it is through Jesus that we learn what liberation really is and how it is to be achieved" (p.379).

## Chapter Seven
## CONCLUSION: WHAT IS NEW AND WHAT IS OLD

The paradigm which interpersonal Spirit christology represents as an alternative to the christocentric-trinitarian paradigm is not by any means entirely new in Christian tradition. The essence of this Spirit christology is the idea of a relational unity between Jesus and God rather than an ontological, substantial, essential or biological unity.[1] A relational unity precludes Jesus and God being identical or sharing one identity because it takes two different persons or entities to have a relationship. The idea of Jesus and God being united in a personal, "moral" or covenantal relationship has clear biblical support and, in fact, persisted as a common view in the early church until it was replaced by the substantialist view in the fourth century. This fact is gradually emerging with increasing clarity and force as modern biblical and historical studies penetrate more deeply into the ancient situation.

The crucial decision in favour of a substantialist unity between Jesus and God emerged from the controversy between the Arians and the Alexandrians. New studies of Arian theology have shown its consonance with both the New Testament and with much ante-Nicene theology. "The antecedents for the contested Arian formula lie not in Gnostic systems but in biblical language and, more particularly, in eminent church writings belonging to the 'mainstream'" (Gregg and Groh 1981, p.93). We have already cited Thüsing's conclusion that the idea of Jesus being "sent" by God to carry out his mission or vocation is implicit in the synoptic tradition and "provides an adequate safeguard for the special saving significance of Jesus" (Rahner and Thüsing 1980, p.167). Ignatius, Justin Martyr, Hippolytus, Clement and Origen, not to mention Paul of Samosata and others in the Antiochene tradition, spoke, as the Arians did, of Jesus being Son of God by the will and power of God to whom Jesus was obedient and faithful. Frances Young concludes:

---

[1]This idea of relational unity of Jesus and God is gaining acceptance in present theology because it is an unavoidable corollary of taking Jesus' humanness seriously. McFague (1982), for example, argues that theology should be metaphorical and that metaphorical theology "demands that the central model in Christianity for human and divine life — the model of personal, relational existence as found in the story of Jesus — be allowed to guide us both in form and in content" (p.32). Cf. also Sobrino (1978): "[Jesus'] person is essentially relational, not absolute in itself" (p.50). "It is the Father, not the eternal Logos, that is directly correlated with Jesus. It is his relationship to the Father that constitutes the essence of his person. ... Here we propose to reformulate in relational categories what Chalcedon, affirmed in ontic categories" (p.105). Sobrino does not address the fact that Chalcedon, and Nicaea much earlier, explicitly rejected relational christology in favour of ontic or substantialist christology. He also does not appear to realize that a relational christology entails a change in the basic paradigm of Christian theology.

We should never forget that [Arius'] language was so firmly in the mainstream tradition that solid churchmen like Eusebius of Caesarea felt more at home with his ideas than those of the opposition ... . Indeed, Arius could give a thoroughly realistic exposition of those New Testament texts which assume that in temptation Jesus had the same moral experience as we have; ... . The fact that he did not sin was of profound soteriologial significance, for it meant that by following him, other [people] were potentially capable of not sinning. It is unjust to Arius to describe his doctrine as utterly unbiblical, or to accuse him of being exclusively concerned with logic at the expense of soteriology. (Young in Hick (ed) 1977, p.26).

For Arius, as for the New Testament, Jesus was a creature and like all creatures "ultimately and radically dependent on a Creator whose sole method of relating to his creation was by his will (*Boulema*) and pleasure (*Thelema*)" (Gregg and Groh 1981, p.5). The Arian relational view of Jesus' unity with God allowed for Jesus' humanity to be taken seriously. Indeed Jesus' humanity was essential to the Arian logic of salvation. The main hope of salvation was that the same dynamic power of God that made Jesus what he was is also able to make other people like Jesus.

The Alexandrian substantialist view of Jesus' unity with God virtually relinquished any credible claim for the complete humanity of Jesus in favour of his being essentially deity. At the same time, the Alexandrians advanced a view of salvation that included the misconstrued "biblical" idea of juridical forgiveness by substitutionary sacrifice and the unbiblical idea of divinization by means of irresistible grace, rather than by cooperation within a covenantal relationship.

The controversy between the Arians and Alexandrians was basically over the logic of salvation.[2] Both parties' christologies were derived from their views of what constitutes salvation by God. For Athanasius, the champion of Alexandrian orthodoxy, it was absolutely essential that Christ be an eternal deity with no possibility of change or sin.[3] Only such a Christ could effect redemption absolutely and store up "the grace which has reached us" (cited in Gregg and Groh p.144). The deification of humanity was only possible, in his view, if the instability of human nature was replaced in the case of Jesus by the absolute stability of the eternal deity. This Christ of "irreversible grace" dispenses benefits of his perfect life and death through the church to other human beings, giving a firm assurance of salvation which is not possible if grace is conceived to be resistible, allowing the possibility of sin recurring in future. "Because the Word has united himself to our nature, we are

---

[2]Cf. Cobb (1975): "The overwhelming concern in this tradition centering in Alexandria was for God's overcoming corruption and death in Jesus and establishing a new order of incorruptibility" (p.129).

[3]Young (in Hick 1977) challenges the logic of Athanasius on this point: "Athanasius' position is problematical for two reasons: (i) a real son is not needed to produce adopted sons. Since we only receive an adopted sonship and a derivative divinity, the *essential* Godhead and Sonship of the one who passes it on to us is not logically required, (ii) ... If the Logos is inherently perfect and incapable of change, progress or suffering, he is no more able to mediate than the transcendent God himself ... . Where Arius severed the mediator from God, Athanasius severed him from the world" (p.27).

able to remain free from sin, to have permanent power over the demons ... so that now one may look securely to life in Christ rather than to a series of present or future worlds in which sin might occur again" (Gregg and Groh 1981, p.180).

For Arians, salvation was a continuing struggle with inevitable uncertainty because of the continuing possibility that the grace of God's Spirit might be forgotten or relinquished in favour of other attractions. The covenant with God can always be broken by human beings, even if God never forsakes it. From a positive perspective, salvation offers the possibility of advancing in the participation in God's Spirit towards "the fullness of the stature of Christ." Jesus himself, as a human being, advanced or "increased in wisdom and in stature and in favour with God and man" (Lk 2:52).[4]

Jesus' advance in obedience to the will and Spirit of God was so complete, in Arius' view, that God promoted him to be the Christ with a status beyond any other human being. The promotion of Jesus to be the Christ was made by God before the world was created because God foreknew what Jesus' obedience would be like. Hence, for Arius, Christ was the first of all that God created and he becomes a cosmic figure who assisted God in the creation of the world. He was very divine but not in the same class as God, the Father, the only "true" God who was God before Christ was created and became "Father" only after the Son was created.

Arius' christology at this point becomes as problematic for modern people as it was for the Alexandrians, but for different reasons. For us the whole idea of a pre-existent, personal Jesus "before the foundation of the world" in untenable, except possibly in the mind of God as God may foreknow all creatures. Even such an idea of God's foreknowledge has serious logical difficulties because it seems incompatible with real human freedom. For the Alexandrians, Arius' view of Christ was inadequate because it left Christ still basically a changeable creature in spite of all the high praises given to him for his perfection and promotion to the status of firstborn among all the creatures.

The Alexandrians won the controversy and established their view of salvation and christology as the orthodox paradigm of Christian faith that has prevailed up to the present time.[5] As the controversy is more clearly understood, however, it becomes increasingly questionable whether the church chose the best option in favouring the logic of

---

[4]Sobrino (1978) opts for an advancing view of Jesus' sonship without apparently realizing that it was the Arian view. "The category of 'relationship' allows for a dynamic and *evolutionary* (my emphasis) conception of Jesus' sonship which is not apparent at least theoretically, in the category of 'divine nature'" (p.105). Whether or not Sobrino realizes his christology is basically "Arian" in this respect, it demonstrates clearly that christology which takes Jesus' humanness seriously and starts with the historical Jesus can hardly ignore the fact that Jesus "increased in wisdom."

[5]Cf. Pagels (1979): "It is the winners who write history — their way. No wonder, then, that the viewpoint of the successful majority has dominated all traditional accounts of the origin of Christianity" (p.142). Also Cf. Frye (1981): "The one thing that would naturally be resisted by a socially established church by every means in its power would be the suggestion of a transcending of its authority within history. Such teachings as those of Joachim of Floris about a third historical age of the Spirit ... consequently were regarded as heretical" (p.85). The same logic can be applied to the declarations of Arians as heretics.

Athanasius and his supporters.⁶ At the very least, the Arian alternative deserved to exist as part of the diversity of Christian faith so typical of the New Testament itself.⁷ The triumphalist logic of salvation by irreversible grace may give some people "blessed assurance" but it is not as true either to the scriptures or to human experience as is the covenantal logic of salvation proposed by Arius. One also cannot help wondering if the prospect of the church leadership dispensing the "stored grace" of Christ, and thereby ensuring their own power over all who seek salvation, had anything to do with the option chosen in the controversy. The question of *cui bono*?, in whose interests?, certainly points to the fact that the clerical hierarchy in the church has benefitted immensely from its exclusive prerogative of dispensing the merits of Christ's sacrificial death.

The Arian view of salvation as processive rather than absolute or juridical is much more resonant with the contemporary thought world. So is the Arian view of Jesus as a complete human being who was "improvable" with limited knowledge, who had faith in God, who had genuine freedom, and who received the grace of God by participation in God's Spirit, pioneering and perfecting the way of salvation for those who follow him in the way of God's Reigning. This is a *theologia crucis* rather than *theologia gloriae*, a much more realistic and biblical understanding of anthropology, soteriology, christology and theology, and it provides no apparent benefits to the clergy by giving them an essential role in salvation as dispensers of divine grace. Everyone alike depends on God as Spirit for salvation.

It is not my intention to promote or emulate Arian theology for its own sake but only to show that for several centuries in the early history of the church the paradigm of an interpersonal relationship between Jesus and God was widely believed.

It is also possible to claim that the ideas of Jesus as a complete human person and of salvation as following him in the way of the Reigning of God have persisted in the spirituality of countless individual Christians over the centuries, even if the main focus of the official theology and liturgy of the church was on Jesus' deity and on his "finished work" of salvation. In the present century, especially, with new translations and paraphrases of the Bible abounding, it is not surprising that the human Jesus of the New Testament should be more important to many people than the cosmological *Logos* of tradition. Numerous christologies and studies of Jesus have reflected the concern for Jesus' humanness but only a few theologians have explicitly affirmed the relational rather

---

⁶Cf. Young (in Hick 1977): "There are strong reasons then for seeing the patristic development and interpretation of incarnational belief, not as a gradual dawning of the truth inspired by the Holy Spirit, but as a historically determined development which led to the blind alleys of paradox, illogicality and docetism" (p.29). Also Cf. Hick (in Goulder 1979): "The incarnational motif should in fact be understood as a basic metaphor. If this is right, the centuries-long attempt of Christian orthodoxy to turn the metaphor into metaphysics was a cul-de-sac. For the metaphor has always evaded the attempts to convert it into a coherent theory or hypothesis. The history of Christian thought is littered with frustrated attempts (p.48-49).

⁷Cf. Dunn (1977) "Perhaps then the tragedy of early Catholicism was its failure to realize that the biggest heresy of all is the insistence that there is only one ecclesiastical obedience, only one orthodoxy" (p.366).

than substantialist view of Jesus' unity with God and claimed continuity with biblical and anti-Nicene understanding of Jesus[8] The prospect of such christology being summarily dismissed as "adoptionist" appears to have prevented all but a dauntless few from declaring it openly. The question of "adoptionism" needs to be addressed head on.

Bishop John A. T. Robinson (1973) maintained that the New Testament has a "functional conception of sonship" (p.194) that was later labelled "adoptionism" and rejected by the church.[9]

> Nowhere in the New Testament are we closer than in the Fourth Gospel to the functional Hebraic use of sonship to designate not an absolute status or title but a functional relationship marked by character. ... To be a son is to show the character, to reproduce the thought and action, of another whether it be Abraham, or the Devil, or God (p.188).

The "adoptive" sonship of Jesus, in which he images or reflects the character of God present to him as Spirit, was not of a different kind, basically, than the sonship and daughtership of God that the New Testament authors conceive to be the relationship with God of all children of God for human life. "When we cry '*Abba*! Father!' it is the Spirit ... bearing witness ... that we are children of God, and if children, then heirs, heirs of God and fellow heirs with Christ, provided we suffer with him in order that we may also be glorified with him" (Rom 8:15-17). *The First Letter of John* speaks at length of the meaning of being children of God, stressing love for God and for one another, keeping the commandments of God, doing right and destroying the works of the devil. This relationship is realized "by the Spirit which [God] has given us" (3:24) and by believing "in the name of [God's] Son Jesus Christ" (3:23). Matthew describes children of God as "peacemakers" (5:9). According to St Paul the relationship is not yet completely realized: "We ourselves who have the first fruits of the Spirit, groan inwardly as we wait for adoption as sons [and daughters], the redemption of our bodies" (Rom 8:23).

Adoption is a useful and appropriate term to describe the covenantal relationship of the children of God, including Jesus to God.[10] It denotes a real family relationship that depends for its existence on free, loving commitment on the part of both the parent and the children. Anyone who has had adopted children will know that the family relationship depends as much on the children "adopting" the parents as it does on the legal and personal commitments made by the parents. An adoptive family relationship is like a covenantal marriage relationship. It does not exist primarily "on paper" but in the Spirit who joins people together

---

[8] McFague (1982), Robinson (1973), Pittenger (1970), D. Baillie (1948), Sobrino (1978) and Schoonenberg (1971) are some who have taken Jesus' humanity and relational unity with God seriously.

[9] Schoonenberg (1971) makes the following statement: "The New Testament suggests for us a christological pattern which is precisely opposed to the above scholastic concept. It is the already mentioned adoption christology."

[10] Schoonenberg (1971) is one of the few theologians to acknowledge this. He says: "It is necessary to include adoption christology in incarnation christology. Jesus' divine sonship is at the same time with his manhood a reality-in-becoming: the whole fullness of the Godhead takes possession of him more amd more by affirming Jesus in obedience and by making him conquer sin and Satan"(p.146).

in love and trust and all the other attitude-virtues that make a marriage and a family into the real thing. A parental blood-relationship does not guarantee a real family relationship with children any more than sexual relationships or legal documents guarantee a real marriage relationship. There has to be something like an adoptive relationship even between people who have blood-relationships or sexual relationships if a family is to become an actual family. (One wonders, as an aside, if the stress on Jesus' "true" biological sonship of God has helped to create the prevalent opinion in Western civilization that adopted children are not "real" children compared to biological offspring. In fact, whether they are "real" children or not depends on their personal relationship with parents not merely on physical or legal factors).

The church rejected the biblical conception of adoptive sonship for Jesus because it wished to stress his deity for soteriological reasons. It used, or misused, the protological statements in the New Testament to create a mythology about Christ as a pre-existent heavenly being who was with God and was God before descending to earth. It also used the ontological concepts of Aristotle and Plato to insist that Jesus' substance was the substance of God, making him essentially a deity. Robinson comments as follows:

> Both the mythological and the ontological stories use what I have called the supranaturalistic projection. In other words, they locate the most real in another realm above or beyond this world impinging upon it from without. ... This is in contrast to the Jewish prophetic way of thinking which is much nearer the modern functional (1973, p.195).

The "orthodox" theologians of the early church agreed with St Paul that human beings have an adoptive relationship as children of God but insisted that Jesus' relationship with God was not adoptive but biological.

> The orthodox ... will only allow that the Son is "from" or "out of" the Father in the sense that he is "offspring of the paternal essence" (*Tes Patrikes ousias ... gennema*) [quoted from Athanasius]. Biblical passages which suggest the begetting of the Son are understood in a physical sense. ... In conceiving the Son's link with the Father in natural terms, Alexander seeks to distinguish his relationship from that in which creatures stand to the Creator. (Gregg and Groh 1981, p.85).

While it is possible to sympathize with the Alexandrian intention of explaining the uniqueness of Jesus it is difficult now to agree with the way in which Jesus' uniqueness was established. That uniqueness is better established on Jesus' vocational role than on ontological uniqueness.

If Jesus was a complete human being his relationship with God must have been of an adoptive nature like the relationships that other people have with God.[11] Human beings can only have an adoptive relationship with God. If Jesus was human he was no exception. To have a biological, ontological or substantial relationship with God would be to cease being human and become divine, or at least partly divine. The humanness or creatureliness simply cannot coherently be thought to continue in one who is essentially divine. If Jesus was human he could not at the same time be deity. His relationship with God had to be adoptive.

The adoptive relationship is one constituted by God's parental and prevenient grace which is reflected in "return" to God in faith, hope and love. The church has always rejected "adoptionism" as an interpretation of Jesus' relationship with God because adoption is understood as a kind of contingent arrangement in which the choice of the one adopted depends on the merit of the adopted one. According to this logic, whether the adoption took place or not would depend on God finding someone who is already worthy enough to be adopted. The saving work of God in Christ, in this case, would become dependent to some extent on the human Jesus. This seems to reduce God's power to save. "Adoptionism is objectionable because it derogates from the divine initiative"(Robinson 1973, p.198).

The response to this logic is to point out that in fact adoption does not have to be contingent on the merit of the one adopted. In our times, countless parents have adopted children without any conditions attached and without looking for any merit in the ones to be adopted. To say that the relationship between Jesus and God was an adoptive one does not "derogate from the divine initiative" in any inappropriate way; God as the "parent" still takes the decisive initiative to establish the relationship, an initiative that can be said to have begun at the time of Jesus' conception or even before that time, if God does in fact have such foreknowledge that makes prevenient grace and providential initiative possible. If it was true for Jeremiah that God consecrated him before God "formed [him] in the womb"(Jer 1:5) the same might appropriately be said of Jesus. God's initiative for salvation in Jesus as the Christ does not have to be seen as compromised by speaking of their relationship as adoptive.

The contingent element of Jesus making a faithful and loving response

---

[11]Dunn (1973) sees in Rom 1:3f, where Paul uses the term "Son" to refer to both Jesus' life in the flesh and his risen life "a striking parallel with Paul's understanding of the Christian's sonship, for it too falls into the same two stages — the adoption which comes with the Spirit of adoption (Rom.viii.15), and the full adoption in glory which awaits the redemption/resurrection of the body (Rom.viii.23). Sonship *in* both stages is clearly a function of the Spirit. ... The parallel between Rom.i.3f. and viii.15,23 is too close to admit any doubt that the sonship of *Jesus* in the first stage is likewise a function of the Spirit" (p.55-56).

Should it not follow that Jesus' relationship with the Spirit during his earthly life was an adoptive relationship as it is for those who follow him? Only the orthodox prejudice for an ontological unity of Jesus and God prevents the acceptance of the clear biblical teaching on the point. Dunn himself does not accept the conclusion.

Dunn shows, however, that the form of Spirit christology seen in Rom 1:3f. is present in many other places in the New Testament including I Tim 3:16 and I Pet 3:18. "In particular it is related to the so-called 'Messianic secret' in Mark, and it is clearly present in the more fully developed three-stage or programmatic Christology of Luke-Acts. ... The same sort of Christological thinking also underlies the Fourth Gospel's talk of the Spirit as the *allos paracletos*" (p.65-66). Rosato (1983) also speaks of Spirit christology as "the primary model by which the NT authors comprehend Jesus Christ's being and mission" (p.265).

to God is not to be avoided, of course, if Jesus is thought to be a fully human person. This might be taken to mean a reduction in God's power, but any real saving changes in the conditions on Earth necessarily depend partly on human faithfulness. That appears to be the way God has created the world; God has shared power with creatures and works for the salvation of the world under those conditions. To make God's saving work in Jesus an exception to the conditions that exist for God's working with all other human beings does nothing to further actual change in the world. It may give a false sense of security if one is consoled by the thought that God could intervene unconditionally on the single occasion of Jesus' life, but it will not change the fact that God's actual work of salvation, century in and century out, depends on human beings responding freely to God and receiving the reigning presence of God as Spirit, a presence which is not irresistible and which is, therefore, "contingent" to some extent.

The Reigning of God on which Jesus focused his life and teachings was not a different kind of reigning from the way God reigns in others; if it were, there would be no hope in it for the rest of humankind. If all human beings are created for adoption into the family of God, or "life in the Spirit," then precisely because Jesus lived the adoptive relationship in the same way that others can do he can be a true teacher and mediator who has genuine saving significance for the world.

An adoptive relationship presupposes the freedom of both parent and children. This implies that divine grace is not irresistible or irreversible, although it may be persistent and ingenious in its influence, to the extent that it will ultimately prevail in its purpose. If God's grace were absolutely irresistible there would be no way to avoid blaming God for all the evil in the world and no way to maintain a claim for human freedom. Because God has made creatures to be free and called them to enter into the covenant of creation they are capable of sin as well as love and obedience, evil as well as good. The actual result of human freedom is an ambiguous mixture of good and evil in every individual and, in the case of those who have "returned" to God, a process of growth in grace in which they increase in wisdom and in stature and in favour with God and humanity.

In biblical anthropology human beings are characterized by their capacity for an adoptive or covenantal relationship with God. In this capacity people are able to "image" or reflect or echo God's presence as Spirit and Word in a cooperative process of creating and recreating the world.[12] Biblical soteriology is correlated with this anthropology and has to do with overcoming of evil powers that despoil creation. Salvation consists in these powers, and the creatures in subjection to them, returning to the Reigning of God which is "righteousness and peace and joy in the Holy Spirit" (Rom 14:17).

Christology also can and should be correlated with this biblical anthropology and soteriology. That was the case in the New Testament,

---

[12]Cf. Soelle (1984): "I have come to realize that our capacity to praise creation hinges on our capacity to involve ourselves in creation. ... Only through participation in creation can we affirm it, cherish it, praise it" (p.1).

even though Jesus' also contributed to the clarifying and completing of biblical anthropology and soteriology. The revelation of God's purposes and the way of God's Reigning in Jesus are consonant with the understandings of humanity, God, and salvation in the Hebrew scriptures and also bring these understandings to a new stage of development. Jesus and the New Testament authors who bore witness to him were like the "scribe who has been trained for the kingdom of heaven ... who brings out ... what is new and what is old" (Mt 13:52). Jesus as the Christ pioneers and mediates a new understanding of God's (old) covenant with creation.

Anthropology, soteriology and christology are ultimately derivations of theology, the logic of God. Here, too, Christian understanding should render what is old and what is new. What is old in our tradition is exclusive monotheism, the undeniably prevailing view of God in the Bible. A long, protracted struggle took place before this view was relinquished in early Christian history in favour of a trinitarian logic of God. Monotheism died hard as dynamic monarchians and modalist monarchians and Arians and Antiochenes, among others, resisted the trinitarian logic. Moltmann, who acknowledges that "Arianism is monotheistic Christianity in its purest form" (1981, p.133), complains that Western Christianity never did sufficiently lose its monotheistic tendencies. The monarchians, who were declared to be heretics certainly thought that monotheistic tendencies were relinquished by the "orthodox" Christian views. So did the Jews and Moslems and others like Servetus who were put to death for challenging the doctrine of the Trinity.

In the pluralistic world of the present there is an urgent need to recover the monotheism of the Bible that is shared by Jews and Moslems and that extends the family of God to all people on Earth. That "old" idea from the Bible is too good to give up. It should be the premise of Christian anthropology, the axiom on which the unity of the human race is founded. From the logic of one God follows the ethic of equal rights for all human beings, including the rights to health, economic and political justice and all that constitutes the *shalom* of God.

Christian soteriology and christology do not need to relinquish the singleness of God. If Jesus' relationship with God is conceived to be interpersonal rather than intrapersonal and Jesus' complete humanness is affirmed there is no question of confusing the idea of one God with more than one divine person. Jesus' singularity can be seen, true to the scriptures, in terms of his vocation; and salvation can be seen, true to the scriptures, in terms of the Reigning of God that Jesus both preached and practised.

What is "new" in Christian theology, compared to the Hebrew faith out of which it emerged, is the development of an understanding of human vocation.[13] The New Testament writings reveal an understanding

---

[13]Robinson (1962) explains the Pauline development of the biblical theology of Spirit as follows: "As he came to realize that the human personality of Jesus, dominated by the ethics of the Cross, really belonged to the "heavenlies", and was therefore the most essential link in the chain of the Spirit, the doctrine of the Spirit was transformed for him—personalized, ethicized as never before. It claimed the whole of human life, and claimed it for new ends and in new ways of working" (p.20).

of God's presence as Spirit which is not so much different from what the Hebrew scriptures reveal as a development of it with some new emphases that can radically change the way people live.[14] The intimacy of God as Spirit in every dimension and aspect of the creation is highlighted in Jesus' '*Abba*' relationship with God. In the theology of Spirit developed in Chapter Three we spoke of God as Spirit involved in the energy, information, imagination, discernment, attitude-virtues, vocation and ethos of creatures, and especially of people. The manner of God's presence as seen in Jesus is a new emphasis on the loving, forgiving, empowering Spirit who liberates people as God's children rather than forcing them as slaves to do what is right. God calls for return to the family covenant of creation; the purposes of God are seen primarily as gospel and only derivatively in terms of law.

The vocation of the human family of God is shown by Jesus in a new light to be the realizing of the Reigning of God with all the rehabilitative and distributive justice, liberty, truth and peace that this implies. The vocation is to preach and practise return to the Reigning of God by unmasking and overcoming the demonic and profane powers that distort and despoil God's good creation. The vocation is to express, in Spirit and in truth, the ethos of God in the community and communities of humankind.[15] The commandment that issues from the gospel is to love one another. This love is a vocation of self-giving and self-risking for the sake of others, a "way of the cross" like the active, subversive strategy of non-violent, trusting love that Jesus supremely exemplified. His vocation as represented in his life, death and resurrection is the new definitive paradigm for those who follow him.

The "new" emphases on the presence of God as Spirit and the new understanding of vocation, especially the realization that Jesus' "way of the cross" was not futile, that Jesus is "risen," became the catalyst for a new religious movement — the church. The catalytic efficacy of Jesus or, more precisely, the catalytic efficacy of God in and through Jesus, continues to the present day and promises to continue into the future until the whole creation is liberated from bondage to idolatrous powers. This hope, this logic of salvation and logic of Christ does not imply that God is working for the liberation of the world only through the church. The Christ and his followers are not the only servants of God, but the Christ was the Servant chosen and "anointed" to be the definitive paradigm of God's purposes and God's presence with human beings. This is our hope; time and eternity will tell. Meanwhile we affirm it proleptically and proceed to practise the implications as best we can.

---

[14]Cf. McFague (1982): The Jewish paradigm is distinguished by its monotheistic, personalistic character as well as by its profound sense of history. It manifests itself as a story of a people in a covenantal relationship with the one God of the universe. ... an anomaly enters this paradigm in the person and activity of one of them, the man from Nazareth ... Thus a revolution in the paradigm occurred spearheaded by a new root-metaphor. ... Its distinctive note is not a new view of God or a new image of human being; neither divine nor human nature is at its center, but a new quality of relationship, a way of being in the world under the rule of God (p.108-109).

[15]Cf. Lampe (1977) "The supreme manifestation of the Spirit is love, and the effect of the Spirit's inspiration is to build [God's] human creation into a community of which [God's] indwelling persence becomes the corporate as well as the individual life-principle" (p.177).

The difficulties and dangers of doing this credibly put the controversies over the finer points of theo-logic and christo-logic into a proper perspective.[16]

A paradigm change in the Christian tradition from christocentric-trinitarianism to a theocentric Spirit christology might serve the purposes and truth of God that are seen in Jesus of Nazareth. It might better place Jesus of Nazareth and what he preached and did on the map of our contemporary thought-world. Those who encounter God in Jesus' life, death and resurrection might be better enabled to relate that revelation of God to the world as they know it and live in it. The logic of Christ might commend itself to them and facilitate their living what they say they believe. That, after all, is the point of christology. It is finally to be evaluated by its "performative function" not by the measure of psychological comfort it provides.

The paradigm which has prevailed in the Christian church over the centuries has not by any means been unproductive of the purposes of God. In any case it is not our business to conduct the final assessment of it. Above all we have to be thankful for what it has given us. We cannot ignore, however, the ways in which that logic of Christ as deity seemed to produce destructive prejudice and terrible persecutions. We cannot ignore the frightening implications of the fundamentalists in our time who claim to be the most faithful defenders of the traditional logic of Christ and who talk glibly of the destruction of the vast majority of human beings who do not believe in the deity of Jesus Christ. We cannot ignore the new learnings that the explosion of knowledge is bringing to studies of the Bible and Christian history. There is a crisis in christology that we can no longer ignore. We cannot continue killing the traditional paradigm with the death of a thousand qualifications. Better to change the paradigm in the light of our best knowledge of the Bible and the world so that Christ might be lifted up and draw all people to himself. The Christian tradition, like the scientific tradition, can embrace new paradigms. It has done so before. It could do so again.

---

[16]Cf. Boff (1978) "In all theological reflection we must not forget that Christology is not primary, nor does it substitute for faith. Life is more important than reflection" (p.157). Again: "The important thing is not to do Christology, but to follow Christ" (p.231).

# Works Consulted

ADAM, KARL
    1957    *The Christ Of Faith: The Christology of the Church.* New York: Pantheon Books.

ALDWINCKLE, RUSSELL F.
    1976    *More Than Man: A Study In Christology.* Grand Rapids: Eerdmans.
    1982    *Jesus — A Savior or the Savior?: Religious Pluralism in Christian Perspective.* Macon, GA: Mercer.

ALFS, MATTHEW
    1984    *Concepts of Father, Son, and Holy Spirit: A Classification and Description of the Trinitarian and Non-Trinitarian Theologies Existent Within Christendom.* Minneapolis: Old Theology Book House.

ASHBROOK, JAMES B.
    1984    *The Human Mind And The Mind Of God: Theological Promise In Brain Research.* Lanham, MD: University Press Of America.

AULEN, GUSTAF
    1969    *Christus Victor: An Historical Study Of The Three Main Types Of The Idea Of Atonement,* trans. A.G. Herbert. New York: Macmillan.

BAILLIE, D.M.
    1948    *God Was In Christ.* New York: Charles Scribner's Sons.

BARBOUR, IAN G.
    1966    *Issues in Science and Religion.* London: SCM Press.
    1974    *Myths, Models, and Paradigms: A Comparative Study in Science and Religion.* New York: Harper & Row.

BARRETT, C. K.
    1966    *The Holy Spirit And The Gospel Tradition.* London: S.P.C.K.

BARRY, F.R.
    1968    *The Atonement.* London: Hodder And Stoughton.

BARTH, KARL
    1960    *Church Dogmatics.* Edinburgh: T. and T. Clark.

BEKER, CHRISTIAAN J.
    1980    *Paul The Apostle: The Triumph of God in Life and Thought.* Philadelphia: Fortress Press.

BELO, FERNANDO.
    1981    *A Materialist Reading of the Gospel of Mark,* trans. Matthew J. O'Connell. Maryknoll, NY: Orbis Books.

BERKHOF, HENDRIK
    1962    *Christ and the Powers,* trans. John H. Yoder. Kitchener, Ont: Herald Press.
    1976    *The Doctrine Of The Holy Spirit.* Atlanta: John Knox Press.

BOFF, LEONARDO
    1978    *Jesus Christ Liberator: A Critical Christology for Our Time.* Maryknoll, NY: Orbis Books.

BONHOEFFER, DIETRICH
    1971    *Christology,* trans John Bowden, London: Collins.

BRACKEN, JOSEPH A.
    1979    *What Are They Saying About the Trinity?* New York: Paulist Press.

BROWN, ROBERT McAFFEE
    1978    *Theology in a New Key*

BROWNING, ELIZABETH BARRETT
    1900    *The Complete Poetical Works of Elizabeth Barrett Browning.* Boston & New York: Houghton Mifflin Company.

BRUNNER, EMIL
    1934    *The Mediator: A Study of the Central Doctrine of the Christian Faith.* New York: Macmillan.

BUBER, MARTIN
    1970    *I and Thou,* trans. Walter Kaufmann. Edinburgh: T. & T. Clark.

BURBIDGE, JOHN.
    1977    *Being And Will: An Essay In Philosophical Theology.* New York: Paulist Press.

CAIRD, G.B.
    1956    *Principalities and Powers.* Oxford: Oxford University Press.

    1968    "The Development of the Doctrine of Christ in the New Testament" in N. Pittenger (ed.), *Christ for Us Today.* London: SCM Press.

CAMPBELL, JEREMY
    1982    *Grammatical Man.* New York: Simon & Schuster.

CASSIDY, RICHARD J.
    1978    *Jesus, Politics and Society: A Study of Luke's Gospel.* Maryknoll, NY: Orbis Books.

COBB, JOHN B.
    1975    *Christ in a Pluralistic Age.* Philadelphia: The Westminster Press.

COME, ARNOLD B.
    1959    *Human Spirit And Holy Spirit.* Philadelphia: The Westminster Press.

CONGAR, YVES, M.J.
    1983    *I Believe In The Holy Spirit.* (3 Vol.) New York: The Seabury Press.

CROSSAN, JOHN DOMINIC
    1973    *In Parables: The Challenge Of The Historical Jesus.* New York: Harper & Row.

    1975    *The Dark Interval: Towards A Theology Of Story.* Niles, Illinois: Argus.

    1976    *Raid On The Articulate: Comic Eschatology in Jesus and Borges.* New York: Harper & Row.

    1980    *Cliffs Of Fall: Paradox and Polyvalence in the Parables of Jesus.* New York: The Seabury Press.

CUPITT, DON.
    1971    *Christ And The Hiddenness Of God.* Philadelphia: The Westminster Press.

    1976    *The Leap Of Reason.* London: Sheldon Press.

    1979    *Explorations In Theology 6.* London: SCM Press.

    1980    *Taking Leave Of God.* London: SCM Press.

    1982    *The World To Come.* London: SCM Press.

DALY, MARY
    1973    *Beyond God The Father: Towards a Philosophy of Women's Liberation.* Boston: Beacon Press.

DALY, ROBERT J.
    1978    *The Origins Of The Christian Doctrine Of Sacrifice.* Philadelphia: Fortress Press.

DAVIDSON, ROBERT
1983    *The Courage To Doubt: Exploring an Old Testament Theme.* London: SCM Press.

DAVIS, CHARLES
1976    *Body As Spirit.* New York: The Seabury Press.

DILLISTONE, F.W.
1968    *The Christian Understanding Of The Atonement.* Digswell Place: James Nisbet & co.

DODD, C.H.
1965    *According To The Scriptures: The Sub-structure of New Testament Theology.* London: Collins.

DRIVER, TOM F.
1981    *Christ in a Changing World: Toward an Ethical Christology.* New York: Crossroad.

DUNN, JAMES D. G.
1970a   "2 Corinthians III. 17 — 'The Lord Is The Spirit'." *Journal of Theological Studies,* XXI: 309-320.
1970b   "Spirit And Kingdom." *The Expository Times,* 82: 36-40.
1973    "Jesus — Flesh And Spirit: An Exposition Of Romans I. 3-4. *"Journal of Theological Studies,* XXIV: 40-68.
1975    *Jesus And The Spirit: A Study of the Religious and Charismatic Experience of Jesus and the First Christians as Reflected in the New Testament.* London: SCM Press.
1977    *Unity and Diversity in the New Testament: An Inquiry Into the Character of Earliest Christianity.* Philadelphia: The Westminster Press.
1980    *Christology in the Making: A New Testament Inquiry into the Origins of the Doctrine of the Incarnation.* London: SCM Press.

ECHEGARAY, HUGO.
1984    *The Practice of Jesus,* trans. Matthew J. O'Connell. Maryknoll, NY: Orbis Books.

EVANS, DONALD
1979    *Struggle and Fulfillment. The Inner Dynamics of Religion and Morality.* Toronto: Collins.

FERGUSON, MARILYN
1980    *The Aquarian Conspiracy: Personal And Social Transformation In The 1980's.* Los Angeles: J.P. Tarcher, Inc.

FIORENZA, FRANCIS SCHUSSLER
1980    "Christology After Vatican II" in *The Ecumenist,* Vol.18, No.6, pp.81-89.

FRANKL, VIKTOR E.
1975    *The Unconscious God: Psychotherapy and Theology.* New York: Simon And Shuster.

FROMM, ERICH
1961    *Marx's Concept of Man,* with a translation from Marx's *Economic and Philosophical Manuscripts,* trans. T.B. Bottomore. New York: Frederick Ungar Publishing Co.

FRYE, NORTHROP
1971    *Anatomy of Criticism.* Princton, NJ: Princeton University Press.
1981    *The Great Code: The Bible and Literature.* New York and London: Harcourt Brace Jovanovich.

FULLER, REGINALD H.
1969    *The Foundations Of New Testament Christology.* London: Collins.

GOULDER, MICHAEL, (ed.)
1979    *Incarnation and Myth: The Debate Continued.* London: SCM Press.

GREEN, MICHAEL. (ed.)
　1977　*The Truth of God Incarnate.* London: Hodder And Stoughton.

GREGG, ROBERT C. and GROH, DENNIS E.
　1981　*Early Arianism — A View of Salvation.* Philadelphia: Fortress Press.

GUNDRY, ROBERT H.
　1982　*Matthew: A Commentary on His Literary and Theological Art.* Grand Rapids, Michigan: Eerdmans.

GUNKEL, HERMANN
　1979　*The Influence Of The Holy Spirit: The Popular View of the Apostolic Age and the Teaching of the Apostle Paul,* trans. Roy A.Harris and Philip A.Quanbeck II. Philadelphia: Fortress Press.

HANSON, R.P.C.
　1973　*The Attractiveness of God: Essays in Christian Doctrine.* London: SPCK.

HARVEY, A.E. (ed.)
　1981　*God Incarnate: Story And Belief.* London: SPCK.

HENDRY, GEORGE S.
　1957　*The Holy Spirit In Christian Theology.* London: SCM Press.

HERON, ALASDAIR I.C.
　1983　*The Holy Spirit.* Philadelphia: The Westminster Press.

HICK, JOHN. (ed.)
　1977　*The Myth Of God Incarnate.* London: SCM Press.

HODGSON, LEONARD
　1944　*The Doctrine Of The Trinity.* New York: Charles Scribner's Sons.

HODGSON, PETER C.
　1971　*Jesus — Word And Presence: An Essay In Christology.* Philadelphia: Fortress Press.

HOLMES, URBAN T.
　1980　*History Of Christian Spirituality: An Analytical Introduction.* New York: The Seabury Press.

　1981　*Ministry And Imagination.* New York: The Seabury Press.

KAUFMANN, YEHEZKEL
　1980　*The Religion of Israel.* trans. and abridged by M. Greenberg. Chicago: University of Chicago Press.

KASPER, WALTER
　1976　*Jesus The Christ.* New York: Paulist Press.

KEE, H.C.
　1971　"The Gospel According To Matthew" in Charles M. Laymon (ed.) *The Interpreter's One Volume Commentary On The Bible.* Nashville: Abingdon.

KEIFERT, PATRICK R.
　1985　"Interpretive Paradigms: A Proposal Concerning New Testament Christology" in Robert Jewett (ed.) *Christology and Exegesis: New Approaches.* Decatur, GA: Scholars Press.

KELLY, J.N.D.
　1978　*Early Christian Doctrines.* New York: Harper & Row.

KNOX, JOHN
　1967　*The Humanity And Divinity Of Christ: A Study Of Pattern In Christology.* Cambridge: Cambridge University Press.

LAMPE, G.W.H.
　1972　"The Holy Spirit And The Person Of Christ." In *Christ, Faith And History,* ed.G.W. Sykes and J.P. Clayton. Cambridge: Cambridge University Press.

　1977　*God As Spirit.* Oxford: Clarendon Press.

LAYMON, CHARLES M. (ed).
　1971　*The Interpreter's One-Volume Commentary On The Bible.* Nashville:

Abingdon.

LEIVESTAD, RAGNAR
1954    *Christ the Conqueror*. London: SPCK.

LIKOUDIS, JAMES
1982    "Christ Among Us For The Devil" in *The Wanderer*. Minneapolis, Minn.

LOSSKY, VLADIMIR
1976    *The Mystical Theology of The Eastern Church*. Crestwood, N.Y: St Vladimir's Seminary Press.

MACDONALD, A.J.
1927    *The Holy Spirit*. London: SPCK.

MACHOVEC, MILAN
1976    *A Marxist Looks At Jesus*. Philadelphia: Fortress Press.

MACQUARRIE, JOHN
1966    *Principles of Christian Theology*. New York: Scribners.

MARSHALL, HOWARD I.
1976    *The Origins of New Testament Christology*. Downers Grove, IL: Intervarsity Press.

MAY, ROLLO
1972    *Love and Will*. London: Collins.

McFAGUE, SALLIE
1982    *Metaphorical Theology: Models of God in Religious Language*. Philadelphia: Fortress Press.

McINTYRE, JOHN
1966    *The Shape Of Christology*. London: SCM Press.

MELMAN, SEYMOUR
1974    *The Permanent War Economy: American Capitalism in Decline*. New York: Simon & Schuster.

MIRANDA, JOSE PORFIRIO
1974    *Marx And The Bible,* trans. John Eagleson. Maryknoll, NY: Orbis Books.

MOLTMANN, JÜRGEN
1974    *The Crucified God: The Cross of Christ as the Foundation and Criticism of Christian Theology*. New York: Harper & Row.

1981    *The Trinity and the Kingdom of God: The Doctrine Of God*. London: SCM Press.

MONTAGUE, GEORGE T.
1976    *The Holy Spirit: Growth of a Biblical Tradition*. New York: Paulist Press.

NEVE, LLOYD
1972    *The Spirit of God in the Old Testament*. Tokyo: Seibunsha.

NEWBIGIN, LESSLIE
1969    *The Finality Of Christ*. London: SCM Press.

NEWMAN, PAUL W.
1981    "Humanity With Spirit" in *Scottish Journal of Theology* Vol.34, pp.415-426.

1983    *Humanity And Spirit: An Anatomy of Hope*. Toronto: Image.

NIEBUHR, REINHOLD
1960    *Moral Man and Immoral Society*. New York: Charles Scribner's Sons.

O'COLLINS, GERALD
1983    *What Are They Saying About Jesus?* (revised). New York: Paulist Press.

OGDEN, SCHUBERT M.
1982    *The Point of Christology*. San Francisco: Harper & Row.

PAGELS, ELAINE
1979    *The Gnostic Gospels* New York: Random House.

1982    "The Gnostic Jesus and Early Christian Politics" The University Lecture in Religion at Arizona State University. Tempe, Arizona: Arizona State University.

PANNENBERG, WOLFHART
1968    *Jesus — God And Man,* trans. Lewis L. Wilkins and Duane A. Priebe. Philadelphia: The Westminster Press.
1985    *Anthropology in Theological Perspective,* trans. Matthew J. O'Connell. Philadelphia: The Westminster Press.

PAWLIKOWSKI, JOHN T.
1982    *Christ In The Light Of Christian-Jewish Dialogue.* New York: Paulist Press.

PELIKAN, JAROSLAV
1971    *The Christian Tradition: A History of the Development of Doctrine, Vol.1, The Emergence of the Catholic Tradition (100-600).* Chicago and London: The University of Chicago Press.

PERRIN, NORMAN
1974    *A Modern Pilgrimage In New Testament Christology.* Philadelphia: Fortress Press.
1976    *Rediscovering The Teaching Of Jesus.* New York: Harper & Row.

PITTINGER, NORMAN
1970    *Christology Reconsidered.* London: SCM Press.
1974    *The Holy Spirit.* Philadelphia: United Church Press.

PREGEANT, RUSSELL
1978    *Christology Beyond Dogma: Matthew's Christ In Process Hermeneutic.* Philadelphia: Fortress Press

RAHNER, KARL
1968    *Spirit in the World,* trans. W.Dyck. New York: Herder and Herder.
1970    *The Trinity,* trans. Joseph Donceel. New York: Herder and Herder

RAHNER, KARL and THÜSING, WILHELM
1980    *A New Christology.* New York: The Seabury Press.

RAMSEY, IAN T.
1973    *Models for Divine Activity.* London: SCM Press.

RICHARD, LUCIEN
1981    *What Are They Saying About the World Religions?.* New York: Paulist Press.

RICOEUR, PAUL
1967    *The Symbolism Of Evil.* Boston: Beacon Press.

RIFKIN, JEREMY
1980    *Entropy.* New York: The Viking Press.

ROBINSON, H. WHEELER
1962    *The Christian Experience of the Holy Spirit.* London: Collins.

ROBINSON, JAMES M. and KOESTER, HELMUT
1971    *Trajectories through Early Christianity.* Philadelphia: Fortress Press.

ROBINSON, JOHN A.T.
1973    *The Human Face Of God.* London: SCM Press.

ROSATO, PHILIP J.
1977    "Spirit Christology: Ambiguity and Promise." *Theological Studies,* 1977: 423-449.
1983    "Holy Spirit." In *Westminster Dictionary of Theology,* (ed.) Alan Richardson & John Bowden. Philadelphia: The Westminster Press.
1981    *The Spirit As Lord: The Pneumatology of Karl Barth.* Edinburgh: T. & T. Clark.

RUETHER, ROSEMARY RADFORD
1970    *The Radical Kingdom: The Western Experience of Messianic Hope.* New York: Paulist Press.

| | |
|---|---|
| 1972 | *Liberation Theology: Human Hope Confronts Christian History and American Power.* New York: Paulist Press. |
| 1974 | *Religion And Sexism: Images of Woman in the Jewish and Christian Traditions.* New York: Simon & Schuster. |
| 1975 | *New Woman New Earth: Sexist Ideologies & Human Liberation.* New York: The Seabury Press. |
| 1979 | *Faith and Fratricide: The Theological Roots of Anti-Semitism.* New York: The Seabury Press. |
| 1981 | *To Change The World: Christology and Cultural Criticism.* London: SCM Press. |
| 1982 | *Disputed Questions: On Being A Christian.* Nashville: Abingdon. |
| 1983 | *Sexism And God-Talk: Toward a Feminist Theology.* Boston: Beacon Press. |

RUSCH, WILLIAM G.(ed.)
    1980    *The Trinitarian Controversy.* Philadelphia: Fortress Press.

SCHAFF, PHILIP AND WACE, HENRY
    1983    *A Select Library of Nicene And Post-Nicene Fathers of The Christian Church, Volume VIII, St.Basil: Letters And Selected Works.* Grand Rapids, Mich: Eerdmans.

SCHILLEBEECKX, EDWARD
    1979    *Jesus: An Experiment in Christology.* New York: The Seabury Press.
    1980    *Christ: The Experience of Jesus As Lord.* New York: The Seabury Press.
    1981a    *Interim Report on the books Jesus and Christ* New York: Crossroad.
    1981b    *Ministry: Leadership in the Community of Jesus Christ.* New York: Crossroad.

SCHILLNGS, PAUL
    1977    *God And Human Anguish.* Nashville: Abingdon.

SCHLIER, HEINRICH
    1961    *Principalities and Powers in the New Testament,* Edinburgh: Nelson.

SCHOONENBERG, PIET
    1971    *The Christ: A Study of the God-Man Relationship In the Whole of Creation and in Jesus Christ.* New York: The Seabury Press.

SCHWEIZER, EDUARD
    1960    *Spirit of God.* New York: Harper & Row.
    1970    *The Good News According To Mark,* trans. Donald H. Madvig. Atlanta: John Knox Press.
    1975    *The Good News According To Matthew,* trans. David E. Green. Atlanta: John Knox Press
    1980    *The Holy Spirit,* trans. Reginald H. and Ilse Fuller. Philadelphia: The Fortress Press.

SEGUNDO, JUAN LUIS
    1974    *Liberation of Theology,* trans. John Drury. New York: Orbis Books.
    1984    *Faith And Ideologies.* Maryknoll, NY: Orbis Books.

SHULER, PHILIP L.
    1982    *A Genre For The Gospels: The Biographical Character of Matthew.* Philadelphia: The Fortress Press.

SINGER, ISADORE. (ed.)
    1916    *The Jewish Encyclopedia.* New York: Funk & Wagnalls.

SLATER, PETER
    1978    *The Dynamics of Religion: Meaning and Change in Religious Traditions.* New York: Harper & Row.

SLOYAN, GERARD S.
    1983    *Jesus In Focus: A Life In Its Setting.* Mystic, Conn: Twenty-Third Publications.

SOBRINO, JON
    1978    *Christology At The Crossroads: A Latin American Approach.* Maryknoll, NY: Orbis Books.

SOELLE, DOROTHEE
    1967    *Christ The Representative: An Essay in Theology after the 'Death of God'.* London: SCM Press.
    1984    *To Work and To Love: A Theology of Creation,* with Shirley A. Cloyes. Philadelphia: Fortress Press.

SUGGS, M. JACK
    1970    *Wisdom, Christology and Law in Matthew's Gospel.* Cambridge, Mass.: Harvard University Press.

TAYLOR, JOHN V.
    1972    *The Go-Between God: The Holy Spirit and the Christian Mission.* New York: Oxford University Press.

TESELLE, SALLIE McFAGUE
    1975    *Speaking In Parables: A Study in Metaphor and Theology.* Philadelphia: Fortress Press.

THOMPSON, LEONARD L.
    1978    *Introducing Biblical Literature: a more fantastic country.* Englewood Cliffs, NJ: Prentice-Hall Inc.

TILLICH, PAUL
    1951    *Systematic Theology,* Vol. 1. Chicago: University of Chicago Press.
    1957    *Systematic Theology,* Vol. 2. Chicago: University of Chicago Press.
    1957a    *Dynamics of Faith.* New York & Evanston: Harper & Row.
    1963    *Systematic Theology,* Vol. 3. Chicago: University of Chicago Press.

TRACY, DAVID
    1979    *Blessed Rage For Order: The New Pluralism in Theology.* New York: The Seabury Press.
    1981    *The Analogical Imagination: Christian Theology and the Culture of Pluralism.* New York: Crossroad.

TRUDINGER, PAUL
    1983    *Honest To Jesus: On Not Being A Christian.* Winnipeg: Frye Publishing.

TURNER, VICTOR
    1974    *Drama, Fields, And Metaphors.* Ithaca: Cornell University Press.

VAHANIAN, GABRIEL
    1966    *No Other God.* New York: George Braziller.

VAN BEECK, FRANS, JOZEF
    1979    *Christ Proclaimed: Christology as Rhetoric.* New York: Paulist Press.

WILES, MAURICE
    1974    *The Remaking of Christian Doctrine.* London: SCM Press.
    1976    *Working Papers in Doctrine.* London: SCM Press.
    1979    *Explorations in Theology 4.* London: SCM Press.
    1982    *Faith and the Mystery of God.* Philadelphia: Fortress Press.

WINK, WALTER.
    1984    *Naming The Powers: The Language of Power in the New Testament.* Philadelphia: Fortress Press.

YATES, J.E.
    1963    *The Spirit And The Kingdom.* London: SPCK.

YODER, JOHN H.
  1972   *The Politics of Jesus.* Grand Rapids, Mich: Eerdmans.
YOUNG, FRANCES M.
  1975   *Sacrifice And The Death Of Christ.* Philadelphia: The Westminster Press.

# Index of Scripture Passages

**Genesis**
1.26-28—91
1.2—106
1.3—79
9.4—72

**Exodus**
3.14—202
14.30—146
20.5—88
31.1-11—91
34.29-35—173

**Leviticus**
4.6—144
22.19—178
25—115

**Numbers**
5.14,30—96
11.25—109
20.17—73
24.2—80

**Deuteronomy**
5.6,7—146
30.2-3—149
32.4,15,18—73

**Judges**
9.23—96

**I Samuel**
10.1-9—91
11.6—75
15.22—144
16.13—92
16.14—96

**II Samuel**
22.2—73
23.2—80

**I Kings**
17.17-24—119

**II Kings**
4.18-38—119
4.42-44—119

**Job**
33.4—75
38.1—85
38.12,24—72

**Psalms**
27—130
28.1—73
33,6—78
51,6,17—145
104,3—70
104,16—72
104,30—76
119,146—146

**Proverbs**
1.7—84
3.5—85
9.10—84
21.3—144

**Ecclesiastes**
11.9—85

**Isaiah**
1.11—145
1.17—144
6.—53
6.5—49,126
17.10—73
32.1-2—73
32.15—73
40.31—152
42.1-2—92,130,131
42.3—92
43.1-4—144
43.11—146
44.2—130
53.—144
55.7—149
61.1-2—92,115

**Jeremiah**
1.5—217
3.12—149
50.34—144

**Ezekiel**
11.5—80
18.23—149
36.23—93

**Hosea**
4.12—96
5.4—96
6.6—145
9.7—80
13.4—146
14.1-4—149

**Joel**
2.13—149
2.28—93

**Amos**
5.24—144
9.7—100

**Micah**
6.8—47

**Zechariah**
4.6—93
7.12—71,80

**Malachi**
3.7—149

**Matthew**
4.1—108
5.9—215
5.17—117
5.28—117
6.1-7,27—118
6.5-8—129
6.21—118
6.25—118
6.25-27—124
7.1—118
7.12—117
7.13—88
7.20—63
7.24—118
8.5-13—109
8.27—109
9.6—109
9.8—109
9.14—129
9.29—109
9.34—109
10.20—81
11.29—116,117
12.10f—110
12.25—111
12.28—108
12.39—119
12.41-42—119
13.11—81
13.52—219
13.57—119
14.22,23—123
14.23—128
17.5—118

18.4—126
18.12—150
18.21-22—116
20.1-16—117
20.25f.—.114
21.12—125
22.18—111
22.37-40—116
26.25—111
26.39—133
27.46—125
28.19—93,201

**Mark**
1.12—108
1.14-15—112
1.15—17,149
1.18—129
1.22—109
2.41—109
2.8—111
2.10—109
2.12—109
2.23-28—117
3.1f.—110
3.15—109
3.22—109
3.27—108
4.41—109
5.9—96
5.30—109
5.42—109
6.2—108
6.3—128
6.4—119
6.7—109
6.45-52—123
6.46—128
6.51—109
7.6—118
8.34—183
9.2f.—118
9.29—152
9.37—126
10.15—125,126
10.18—121,126,165
10.21—111
10.38—133
10.42f.—114
10.43,44—126
10.46f.—110
11.11—162
11.15—125
12.17—157
12.29-31—116
12.30—152
12.33—145
13.32—120
13.52—113
14.24—114,123
14.36—133

15.34—125
15.39—123

**Luke**
1.35—106
2.41-52—128
2.52—177,213
4.1—39,108,173
4.3-9—132
4.14—108
4.18-19—108,115
4.24—119
4.25-27—119
5.17—108
5.24—109
5.26—109
5.33—129
6.5-10—117
6.6f.—110
6.8—111
6.12—129
6.15—133
6.19—109
7.1-10—109
7.10—187
7.11-17—119
7.16—119
7.36-50—150
8.3—134
8.17—126
8.25—109
9.28f.—118,129
9.48—126
9.51—125,162
10.1—109
10.29—116
11.20—108
12.11-12—81
13.10-17—109,117
13.17—109
13.33—119
15.32—166
17.20-21—120
18.1—129
18.27—125
19.5—111
19.10—144
19.41—125
19.45—125
22.3—109
22.25—114
22.31—110
22.34—111
22.42—133
22.44—159

**John**
1.1—173,182
1.14—174,192
1.17—118
1.18—186

1.42—111
1.47—111
2.2—167
2.25—111
3.8—74,121
3.17—94,202
3.34—81
4.24—79,129
5.2-18—117
6.14-15—132,133
8.1-11—124
8.11—166
8.50—187
11.1-44—127,182
12.32—187
12.44—126
14.9f.—194
14.12—179
14.17—81
14.26—49,81
14.28—182
15.13—163
16.13—49,81
18.11—133
18.14—162
20.20-23—92
20.22—135
20.28—193
21.15-17—135

**Acts**
2.1-13—135
2.3—72
2.22—109
2.36—135
7.56—205
13.1-4—93,157
15.28—93,158
16.67—93,158
17.25—100
17.28—100

**Romans**
1.3f.—217
6.3-11—53,145
7.6—151
7.12—157
8.2—116,145,147
8.11—75
8.15-17—215
8.15—217
8.16—114
8.23—215,217
8.24—204
8.27—81
8.28—163
8.29-30—193
8.29—29,87
8.39—89
12.2—152
12.6-8—81,91

13.1—157
13.14—169
14.17—218
15.2f.—169
16.25,26—178

**1 Corinthians**
1.24—135
1.24,30—192
2.10—81
2.13—81
3.16—93
4.17—169
8.6—192
10.4—73
11.1—169
12.3—81
12.10—108
12.11—91
12.13—72,93
12.31—153
15.44—73
15.45—177

**2 Corinthians**
3.3—81
3.17—173,203
3.7-18—173
3.18—29,87,165,176
4.4—29,87
4.6-7—85
4.7—47,121
5.17—145
8.8f.—169
13.14—201

**Galatians**
1.10—169
2.20-21—204
5.5—89
5.17—142
5.22—87
6.15—145

**Ephesians**
1.14—116
1.17—81
2.21-22—93
4.13—30
4.20,32-5.2—169
4.24—169
6.17—81

**Philippians**
2.5-8—169
2.6f.—192
2.5-11—47
2.7—128
2.8—195
2.10f.—210

**Colossians**
1.15—29,177
1.15f.—87

1.15-17—192,193
1.16-17—77
2.6—169
2.15—166
3.9-10—29,87

**1 Thessalonians**
1.6—169

**1 Timothy**
3.16—217

**Hebrews**
1.1-3—176,193
1.3—29,88
2.10,14-15—163
3.7—81
4.15—126,178
9.8—81
9.14—134
10.15—81
12.29—150

**James**
2.23—195
3.9—30

**1 Peter**
2.5—93
3.18—217
12.21—169

**1 John**
2.36—168
4.1-6—58
4.2—185
3.23—215
3.24—215
5.20—193,194

**Revelation**
2.7,11,17,29—81
3.6,13,22—81
3.19—150
8.11—72
21.1—145
21.3—63
21.5—63,152

# Index of Authors

Adam, K., 199
Aldwinckle, R., 15, 25
Alfs, M., 196
Anselm, 17
Arius, xii, 211, 212, 213
Ashbrook, J.B., 19, 20, 37
Athanasius, xii, 212, 214
Aquinas, T., 172
Augustine, 12, 197
Aulen, G., 17, 165
Baillie, D. M., 182, 215
Barbour, I. G., 4, 25, 36, 46, 60, 63, 64, 65, 67, 208
Barrett, C. K., 106, 107, 108, 109, 112, 113, 130, 131
Barry, F. R., 17
Barth, K., 40, 41, 42, 82, 89, 197, 198
Basil, 18
Becker, E., 97
Beker, C. J., 96, 163, 186
Belo, F., 161
Berkhof, H., 77, 151, 157, 163, 200
Bethune-Baker, J. F., 11
Boff, L., 1, 40, 94, 111, 114, 122, 123, 124, 132, 148, 150, 159, 169, 195, 221
Boys, M., 6
Bracken, J. A., 200
Brown, R. M., 38
Browning, E. B., 90
Brunner, E., 178, 201
Buber, M., 83, 84, 151, 154
Bultmann, R., 121
Burbidge, J., 24

Caird, G. B., 157, 192
Calvin, J., 41
Campbell, J., 76
Cassidy, R. J., 114, 115
Clement, 211
Cobb, J. B., 1, 212
Come, A. B., 172
Congar, Y. M. J., 27, 28, 130, 171

Crossan, J. D., 8, 9, 61, 120, 121, 122
Cupitt, D., 6, 9, 16, 27, 33, 34, 41, 56, 57, 58, 66, 204
Cyprian, 184
Cyril, 18, 185

Daly, M., 16
Daly, R. J., 17, 166, 167
Dillistone, F. W., 17, 167
Dodd, C. H., 119, 121, 131, 206
Dostoevoski, F., 12
Driver, T. F., 13, 14, 15, 21, 31, 32, 38, 43, 44, 45, 48, 54, 56, 57, 63, 113, 189, 197
Dunn, J. D. G., 7, 65, 87, 109, 112, 117, 118, 127, 131, 169, 173, 179, 180, 192, 193, 214, 217
Echegaray, H., 148
Edwards, D. M., 12
Einstein, A., 23
Evans, D., 33, 66, 87, 88, 89, 90, 123, 124, 129

Ferguson, M., 21, 33
Fiorenza, F. S., 35
Forsythe, P. T., 128
Fouyas, M., 196
Frankl, V. E., 45, 84, 87
Freud, S., 22, 33, 99
Fromm, E., 155
Frye, N., 70, 72, 73, 76, 85, 86, 87, 96, 115, 155, 157, 162, 175, 195, 202, 213
Fuller, R. H., 29, 210

Gadamer, H. G., 38, 63
Goulder, M., 23, 185
Green, M., 56
Gregg, R. C., 181, 211, 212, 213, 216
Gregory of Nazianzus, 198
Groh, D. E., 181, 211, 212, 213, 216
Gundry, R. H., 118
Gunkel, H., 107

Habermas, J., 38
Hanson, R. P. C., 197
Hebblethwaite, P., 189, 197, 202, 203
Hegel, G. W. F., 22, 74, 199
Hendry, G. S., 30
Heron, A. I. C., 73, 87, 113
Heschel, A., 194
Hick, J., 2, 14, 47, 171, 214
Hippolytus, 211
Hodgson, L., 188
Hodgson, P. C., 43, 59
Holmes, U. T., 52, 86, 94
Huizinga, J., 122
Ignatius, 211
Irenaeus, 33

Joachim of Floris, 213
Justin Martyr, 211

Kaufmann, W., 17, 18
Kaufmann, Y., 80
Kasper, W., xi, 7, 27, 29, 35, 36, 40, 41, 44, 53, 64, 119, 171, 181, 193, 196, 197, 205
Kee, H. C., 117
Keifert, P. R., 105
Kelly, J. N. D., 18, 167, 174
Knox, J., 190
Kuhn, T., 3, 4
Küng, H., 1, 4, 56

Lampe, G. W. H., 10, 28, 93, 134, 158, 173, 176, 179, 180, 187, 189, 193, 197, 201, 203, 205, 220
Lash, N., 23
Lawrence, D. H., 175
Laymon, C. M., 133
Leivestad, R., 157
Likoudis, J., 111
Lossky, V., 196
Luther, M., 90, 150

Macdonald, A. J., 50
Machovec, M., 126, 162
Macquarrie, J., 128
Marx, K., 22, 99, 154
May, R., 141

McFague, S., 9, 14, 16, 30, 32, 36, 39, 40, 41, 60, 61, 65, 69, 211, 215, 220
McIntyre, J., 63, 64
Miranda, J., 147
Moltmann, J., 11, 12, 190, 194, 195, 197, 198, 199, 200, 219
Montague, G. T., 81, 148, 162
Moule, C. F. D., 128
Nestorius, 185
Newbigin, L., 148, 208
Newman, P.W., 30, 98, 177
Niles, D. T., 48
Novatian, 50

O'Collins, G., 15, 168
Ogden, S. M., 35, 41
Origen, 191, 204, 211
Otto, R., 51

Pagels, E., 213
Pannenberg, W., 2, 29, 35, 44, 75, 128, 174, 175, 206, 207
Paul of Tarsus, xiv, 50, 58, 86, 87, 91, 217
Paul of Samosata, 211
Pawlikowski, J. T., 114
Perrin, N., 112, 114, 116, 207
Pittenger, N., 181, 215
Pregeant, R., 164
Rahner, K., 40, 83, 162, 186, 196
Ramsey, I. T., 60, 202
Ricoeur, P., 51, 53, 60, 69
Rifkin, J., 140
Robinson, H. W., 30, 70, 71, 74, 82, 96, 158, 171, 189, 219
Robinson, J. A. T., 2, 25, 36, 128, 182, 186, 192, 193, 215, 216, 217
Robinson, J. M., 117
Rosato, P. J., 5, 27, 82, 181, 189, 198, 199, 207, 217
Roszak, W., 141
Ruether, R. R., 13, 14, 16, 31, 34, 56, 57, 59, 63, 141, 142, 164, 181, 208

Sartre, J. P., 63
Schillebeeckx E., 1, 7, 15, 29, 36, 37, 42, 55, 56, 104, 113, 114, 119, 134, 136, 151, 152, 169, 187, 188, 206
Schilling,, P., 94
Schlier, H., 157

Schoonenberg, P., xi, 26, 111, 124, 165, 172, 175, 181, 190, 191, 215
Schweizer, E., 73, 96, 118, 120, 123
Segundo, J. L., 24, 83
Servetus, M., 219
Shuler, P. L., 127
Slater, P., 34
Sloyan, G. S., 117, 123
Sobrino, J., 1, 34, 57, 111, 112, 124, 125, 132, 133, 154, 158, 160, 163, 169, 202, 208, 210, 211, 213, 215
Soelle, D., 35, 206, 207, 218,
Suggs, M. J., 117

Taylor, J. V., 18, 29, 74, 75, 76, 79, 83, 113, 175
Taylor, V., 194
Teilhard de Chardin, 35
Tertullian, 167
Thompson. L. L., 85, 86
Thüsing, E., 6, 8, 164, 165, 167, 185, 186, 192, 193, 194, 201, 204, 211
Tillich, P., 1, 17, 24, 27, 40, 41, 43, 46, 47, 59, 60, 74, 75, 76, 82, 84, 90, 93, 98, 99, 100, 177, 183, 189
Tracy, D., 29, 33, 36, 37, 39, 43, 44, 45, 46, 49, 50, 51, 53, 55, 59, 62, 63, 66, 86, 103
Trudinger, P., 206

Vahanian, G., 33
Van Beeck, F. J., 38, 39, 48, 49, 63

Wiederkehr, D., 41
Wesley, J., 178
Whale, J. S., 10
Whitehead, A. N., 202
Wiles, M., 9, 10, 11, 12, 16, 54, 183
Wink, W., 77, 78, 157, 163

Yoder, J. H., 115, 132, 169
Young, F. M., 7, 11, 14, 17, 65, 171, 184, 185, 194, 211, 212, 214

# Index of Subjects

abba, 113, 120, 121, 151, 152, 219, 220
absolutist, 9, 206
adoption, 215f.
Alexandrian, 174f., 177, 196, 211f.
anhypostatic, 15
aniconic, 9, 31, 122
Antiochene, 175f., 196
anti-Semitism, 12, 206
apocalyptic, 9, 84, 86, 96, 120f., 141f.
Apollonian, 19
apophatic, 52, 196
attitude-virtues, 87f., 123f., 142, 153

baptism, 107f., 130f., 148
becoming Trinity, 191
Binity, 200, 201
*Boulema*, 212

catalytic, 164f
Chalcedon, 7, 15, 104, 211
christocentric, 5, 6, 186f.
*Christus Victor*, 135, 165
*circumincession*, 188, 199
classical, 8f., 19
*communicatio idiomatum*, 188, 196
comparative religions, 23
Constantine, 5
consubstantial, 1
contextuality, 62
conversion, 148f.
Copernicus, 21
correlation, 59
cosmic Christ, 203f.
crisis, 24
criteria, 62f.
cross, 47, 53, 158f., 179
crucifixion, 47, 179

Death of God theology, 2
death of Jesus, 47, 129f., 160f., 163
degree, 182f.
deity of Jesus, 176f., 179f., 184, 185, 193f.
demonic, 94f., 107, 114, 155
diabolic, 94
dialogue, 59
Dionysian, 19
discernment, 82f., 85, 98, 112f., 141f., 153
divine nature, 15
divinity of Jesus, 7, 179f., 193f.
docetism, 15

Easter, 135, 171
economic Trinity, 11, 201

energy, 74, 75f., 94, 98, 106f., 110, 139, 152
enthusiasm, 42, 89
entire sanctification, 178, 179
entropy, 140
eschatological, 9, 120f.
eschatological prophet, 118f., 132, 206, 209
ethos, 93f., 98, 134f., 142
ethnocentrism, 13, 14, 18, 49, 92, 126
exclusive, 99f., 187f.
exclusive monotheism, 99f., 187f.
exorcism, 108f.
experience, 39, 43f., 51f., 103, 110
expiation, 17, 167f.
explosion of knowledge, 21
extensibility, 64
evil, 2, 41, 94f., 139f.

faith of Jesus, 123f., 133, 160,
fall, 126
feminist theology, 2
field theory, 23
*filioque*, 188, 197
finality, 205f.
forgiveness, 18
freedom, 176, 195
from below, from above, 36f.
functional presence, 181f., 215
fundamentalist, 14, 221

Galileo, 21
*genus majestaticum*, 196
gospel of Jesus, 112f., 182
Greek Orthodox, 196

healings, 108, 109
*heilsgeschichte*, 6, 35
Hellenistic, 17
hermeneutics of suspicion, 33, 66, 85
hierarchical, 16, 184, 196
historical Jesus, 56f., 203f.
historical retrieval, 47, 57, 104f., 180
*homoousia*, 185
*homopraxis*, 185
hope, 125
humanness of Jesus, 30, 124, 126, 175f., 188, 203, 214, 216f.
humility, 89, 125f.
hypostases, 12
hypostatic union, 3
iconoclast, 9

ideology, 2, 20, 22
image of God, 29f., 126
imagination, 82f., 98, 111f., 141, 153
*imitatio Christi,* 169
incarnation, 5, 7f., 10, 183f.
incoherence, 15, 16
individualism, 18
inerrancy, 24
information, 76f., 79f., 94, 98, 106f., 110, 140, 152
interpersonal model, 171f., 186, 196, 198, 201, 203, 207
intrapersonal model, 173f., 209
irony, 9

Jewish, 6, 8, 9, 131, 194, 219
judge metaphor, 144
juridical, 18, 184, 212
justice, 147, 150, 156
justification by grace, 150

kataphatic, 52
kenotic, 47, 66
Kingdom of God, 5, 8, 93, 107, 112f., 116, 132, 163, 207
knowledge explosion, xi, 21
*Kyrios,* 209

Latin doctrine of atonement, 17f., 149, 164f.
law, 9, 84f., 116f., 141, 156f.
left brain bias, 19, 37f., 83
liberation theology, 2, 19
*lingua franca,* 33
linguistic, 8f.
literary criticism, 2, 54f., 105
logical coherence, 66
*Logos,* 7, 175

manifestation, 38, 51, 83
*Mara(n),* 209
messiah, 5, 103, 106, 113, 131, 136, 143, 172, 183, 185, 206, 208
*metanoia,* 17, 114, 149f.
metaphor, 4, 9, 30f., 38f., 61f., 143f.
miracles of Jesus, 108, 110, 180
modalism, 12, 198
model, 4, 30, 60f.
monarchian, 190
monophysite, 174
monotheism, 6, 96, 99f.
*mysterium fascinans,* 48, 51, 73
*mysterium tremendum,* 48, 51, 73
mystical, 20, 52

naive realism, 20
new life metaphor, 145
*nexus amoris,* 197
Nicaea, 1, 7, 11
nonviolence, 162
numinous, 52, 95

ontological presence, 181f
orthodox, 1, 2, 5, 6, 8, 184

orthopraxy, 38, 148

pacifism, 162
Pantocrator, 16
parable, 8f.
paradigm, 1-5, 11, 20, 184, 211, 219, 221
passion, 109, 110
patriarchal, 16, 190
patristic, 18
*perechoresis,* 188, 199
performative function, 38, 220
pioneer, 171, 209
Platonism, 184, 191
pluralism, 2, 20, 22
polytheism, 95, 96, 182, 198
praxis, 38, 54
prayer of Jesus, 128f., 152
pre-existence, 7, 170, 191f., 213, 219
preunderstanding, 40f., 100, 171
principalities and powers, 77f., 93, 96, 98, 107, 139, 142, 156, 165f.
proclamation, 38, 51, 83
Proleptic, 208, 220
prophecy, 9, 84f., 118f., 141, 154f.
protestant, 1, 7, 92
protestant principle, 47
protological, 170, 193

provisional, 205f.
radical, 24, 154
recollection, 40, 43, 54f., 103f., 136
redeemer metaphor, 144, 209
redemption, 10
regeneration, 151f.
Reigning of God, 9, 107, 114, 120, 127, 132, 135, 148, 158f., 174, 218
reflection, 40, 59f.
Reformed theology, 43
relational thinking, 21
relational unity, 65, 211f., 215
relativity, 2, 23
repent, 17, 88
representative, 185f., 209
resurrection, 49f., 53, 134f., 160f.
return, 17, 86, 114, 119, 148f., 217
revelation, 6
revisionary, 35, 54
rhetorical, 48
Roman Catholic, 1, 6, 7, 92, 111
*Ruach,* 70f., 79, 86, 96, 121, 122

sacrifice, 17f., 144f., 166f., 168, 178
salvation, 2, 6, 139f., 143, 145, 157, 164f.
salvation as process, 10, 147f., 164f., 168, 213
Satan, 96, 109f., 179, 215
satisfaction, 17f., 167
*scientia infusa,* 111
Second Adam, 126
Second Council of Constantinople, 15
secular theology, 2
Servetus, 219

Second Council of Constantinople, 15
secular theology, 2
Servetus, 219
shepherd metaphor, 143
sin, 18, 139f., 166
sinlessness of Jesus, 126f., 177f.
social doctrine of
   Trinity, 190f., 196, 197, 198, 199, 200
soteriology, 2, , 17, 139f.
structuralism, 21
subordination, 182
substitution, 17, 167f., 183
subversive, 161
symbols, 60f., 69f.
syncretism, 42
systems, 22f., 76f., 92, 94, 96, 155
systems theory, 22f., 76f.

temptations of Jesus, 132f., 159
*thelema,* 212
theocentric, 5, 6, 186f.
*theologia crucis,* 31, 187, 214
*theologia gloriae,* 114, 187, 214
Thomas, Gospel of 104
*theosis,* 165
titles, 209f.
tradition, 1-7, 24, 211-221
trinitarian monotheism, 100, 187ff.
Trinity, xi, 2, 5, 11, 12, 187f.
tritheism, 12, 196
trust, 88f., 123f., 162, 163
*Tsuvah,* 17, 86, 119, 148f.
two-nature model, 15, 65, 173

unitarian, 188, 189

virgin birth, 106f.
vocation, 5, 91f., 129f., 136, 142, 153,
         183, 186, 205
void, 34, 66, 86

wholistic, 20, 32f.
wisdom, 9, 11, 85, 117f., 157f.
Word, 5, 78f.

## About the Author

Paul W. Newman is Professor of Systematic Theology in St. Andrew's College, Saskatoon, Saskatchewan. He is an ordained minister in The United Church of Canada who served as a pastor in Ontario and as a missionary theologian in Chung Chi College, The Chinese University of Hong Kong. Dr. Newman graduated with a B.A. (Honours Philosophy and English) and a B.D. from the University of Toronto and earned his Ph.D. from the University of St. Andrews, Scotland. He is author of *Humanity and Spirit: An Anatomy of Hope* (Toronto: Image Publishing Inc., 1983)